CLINICAL PSYCHOLOGY AND PERSONALITY

George A. Kelly, 1905–1967   *Ralph Norman*

CLINICAL PSYCHOLOGY AND PERSONALITY

The Selected Papers of George Kelly

EDITED BY

BRENDAN MAHER

Riklis Professor of Behavioral Science
Brandeis University

John Wiley & Sons, Inc.

NEW YORK · LONDON · SYDNEY · TORONTO

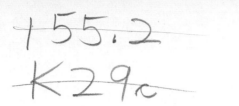

Preface

GEORGE KELLY's MAJOR work, *The Psychology of Personal Constructs,* was published in 1955. In the eleven years that followed he wrote a number of papers elaborating this theoretical position and applying it to specific problems of psychological interest. During the same period other psychologists adopted his concepts and techniques for their own purposes, producing a sizable body of empirical research and a correspondingly large literature. The progress and findings of this latter work have been reported in several other sources.

At the time of his death, Kelly was working on plans for a new book intended to present the developments in his thinking that had occurred in the past decade. Unfortunately this plan could not come to completion. In this present volume I have selected a group of papers from the decade beginning 1957, a selection that includes all papers of a theoretical nature together with most of Kelly's contributions to problems of applied psychology. The major part of this selection consists of works previously unpublished but delivered to audiences in various parts of the academic world. Also included are some contributions that have already been published in journals but which for one reason or another may not have been widely available to the general psychological public.

Addresses that are delivered orally do not always transcribe directly into the printed form. Consequently I have exercised the customary prerogative of removing those minor marks and references of purely local interest to a particular audience, in the expectation that this will make matters run more smoothly for the reader. An additional problem is that of the arrangement of the separate papers into some order within the book. Chronological sequence has been eschewed in favor of a division into *theory*, *psychotherapy*, and *specific problems*. Inevitably, as Kelly so often emphasized, such systems of classification are reflections of the classifier rather than immanent features of the papers themselves. Perhaps more than most psychologists, Kelly wrote in such a fashion that issues of theory, epistemology, methodology, and practice are always intimately connected. Consequently, the placement of papers in order in this selection has been influenced by the apparent emphasis of each paper rather than by the operation of any reliable system of categories.

As many of these papers were intended for, and delivered to, specific audiences there is, inevitably, some reiteration of the central ideas of the psychology of personal constructs. Many of these reiterations have been preserved, mainly where they have been elaborated severally through different metaphors or illustrations and thus serve to clarify or extend the implications of the ideas. In some cases parts of papers have been omitted where the reiteration runs the risk of appearing as mere repetition to a reader with the entire selection of papers here at hand.

This book is a selection of papers and not a collection. For the convenience of readers there is appended a complete bibliography of the published works of George Kelly including those previously published items that appear in this present volume.

Publication of this volume is materially due to the efforts and encouragement of Gladys Kelly. Mrs. Kelly was significantly responsible for the location of original manuscripts and together with my wife, Barbara Maher, bore the burdens of checking and proofreading the manuscript. Many ambiguities in the editing were eliminated as a result of their observations. Dr. Jack Adams-Webber, Professors Ricardo Morant and John Darley provided valuable help in preparing and providing suggestions in the editing of this volume. Special gratitude is due to Mrs. Alice Duffy, former secretary to Professor Kelly, who typed the entire manuscript and assisted its progress in many other ways. From colleagues and fellow-students of George Kelly were received many expressions of support and assistance in this enterprise. It is my hope that the finished work will justify their faith and will properly represent the work of one of the important personality theorists of mid-century.

Brendan Maher

Waltham, Massachusetts
May 1968.

Contents

* Previously published elsewhere

* Previously published elsewhere

CLINICAL PSYCHOLOGY AND PERSONALITY

Introduction

GEORGE KELLY: A BRIEF BIOGRAPHY

GEORGE ALEXANDER KELLY was born in 1905 in Kansas. He pursued undergraduate study for three years at Friends University followed by one year at Park College. Here he graduated with the Bachelor's degree in physics and mathematics, but his interests had already begun to shift to social problems—perhaps in part because of experiences that he had gained in intercollegiate debates. In line with this newly developing interest, he pursued graduate study in educational sociology at the University of Kansas. His master's thesis was a study of the leisure time activities of workers in Kansas City, and he completed minor studies in labor relations and sociology.

At this point, George Kelly's activities expanded to include a wide range of teaching in different situations. He was a part-time instructor in a labor college in Minneapolis; he taught classes in speech for the American Bankers Association, and he taught an Americanization class for future citizens. An additional brief spell as an aeronautical engineer in Wichita followed teaching experience in Iowa and at the University of Minnesota. In 1929, he moved to the University of Edinburgh as an exchange scholar. Here he worked under the direction of Sir Godfrey Thomson, completing the Bachelor of Education degree in 1930 with a thesis dealing with the prediction of teaching success. He then returned to the United States and became a graduate student in psychology at the State University of Iowa. In 1931, he received the Doctor of Philosophy degree with a dissertation dealing with common factors in speech and reading disabilities.

He remained for a summer to teach at Iowa and then moved to the Fort Hays Kansas State College, where he remained until World War II. During the decade at Fort Hays, George Kelly's major interest was focused on the practical problem of providing clinical psychological services for the schools of the state. He was able to develop a program of traveling clinics, serving the entire state and providing training experiences for his students there. In the period 1935–1940, he published a series of papers, six in all, mainly concerned with practical

1

questions of clinical diagnosis, the operation of clinical psychology in
school settings, the use of diagnostic testing, etc. Although, his later
and major work was to be in the area of personality theory, George
Kelly never abondoned his interest in the applied problems of clinical psychologists and in their training.

With the coming of World War II, Kelly entered the Navy as
an aviation psychologist and was placed in charge of the program
of training for local civilian pilots. Later he went to the Bureau of
Medicine and Surgery of the Navy in Washington and remained in
the Aviation Psychology Branch until 1945. In that year he was appointed Associate Professor at the University of Maryland and in
the following year a Professor and Director of Clinical Psychology
at the Ohio State University. In the twenty years that George Kelly
was to spend at Ohio State, he developed his major contributions to
psychology. For the first few years of this period, his energies were
mainly devoted to the organizing and administration of the graduate
program in clinical psychology. In a few short years he succeeded
in leading this program into the front rank of graduate training programs in the United States. He managed to achieve an atmosphere
in which clinical interest and perceptiveness were combined with
firm commitment to the methods and standards of science in a blend
that was, unfortunately, rarely found in other similar programs.

In the meantime, he was working on the book that was to make
his major contribution to the psychology of personality, and was to
make him known to psychologists in all parts of the world. In 1955,
the two-volume work, *The Psychology of Personal Constructs*, was
published and gained immediate recognition as a unique and major
development in the study of personality. Hard on the heels of its appearance came invitations to teach and lecture at universities in many
corners of the globe. He held visiting appointments at the University
of Chicago, University of Nebraska, University of Southern California,
Northwestern University, Brigham Young University, Stanford University, University of New Hampshire; he lectured at many other
institutions in the United States, as well as a wide range of universities
in Europe, the Soviet Union, South America and the Caribbean, and
in Asia.

During this same period there developed an increasing volume of
research into the implications and the applications of his theoretical
viewpoint. He was elected President of the Clinical Division and also
of the Consulting Division of the American Psychological Association.
In addition to his teaching, writing, and administrative responsibilities,
George Kelly was widely known and sought after as a consultant and

counsellor on many matters pertaining to professional clinical psychology. He had served as President of the American Board of Examiners in Professional Psychology and his experience was valued as a wise guide in many problems of training and of ethics.

In 1965 he moved to Brandeis University where he was appointed to the Riklis Chair of Behavioral Science. It was as occupant of this chair that he died in March 1966, leaving incomplete his work on a new book in which he had planned to assemble and edit the many papers that he had delivered in the previous decade. More than most psychologists, perhaps, George Kelly's papers are themselves an autobiography of the man. In them, the reader will find the warmth, humor, and tolerance that characterized him so well to those who knew him best.

Part I

THEORY

1

Ontological Acceleration

MODERN PSYCHOLOGY is concerned with the scientific study of human behavior. Unfortunately this is usually taken to mean that the psychologist wants only to find out how he can predict human actions, or, at most, how to control them. But human behavior can be regarded as an expression of anticipation, as well as something to be anticipated. Moreover, it can be regarded as man's means of controlling himself and his surroundings, as well as something to be controlled. This makes it not only an object of human inquiry, scientific or otherwise, but a vital instrument of human investigation. Behavior, therefore, commands the interest of the psychologist, not merely as a set of events he would like to forecast and manage, but as something he can scarcely hope to understand until its own forecasting and managing capabilities are envisioned.

As I see it, what I have just proposed is not an abandonment of the principle of sequential explanation, of which ordinary notions of prediction and control are limited examples, but rather a proper extension of that principle. To be sure, to predict what will happen can be an exciting psychological experience, particularly if it is something the like of which has never occurred before. But human anticipation—the stuff that life is made of—unfolds its full meaning only when one is keenly appreciative of what might actually happen instead, and when he comes to forecast the events of his future in the rich context of all else that may be possible.

Applied to human behavior, then, the principle of sequential explanation challenges us not only to predict correctly what a man will do under given conditions—or to master him momentarily by creating circumstances with which the poor fellow has not yet devised any

alternative means of coping—but also to join him in testing the limits
of his unsuspected talents, including especially those that would enable
him to surmount the circumstances by which we have hitherto sought
to control him.

A full-fledged psychological inquiry into the behavior of a baby,
for example, is not confined to calculating what he will pop into his
mouth next, nor to training him to do what we want by frustrating
all his ingenious efforts to escape the strictures we have imposed, but
invites us to look at him and wonder what vast and unforeseen alternatives might lie ahead. More than that, no psychologist, I think, is all
that he might be until he has undertaken to join the child's most
audacious venture beyond the frontiers of social conventions and to
share its most unexpected outcomes.

The psychological question is not merely what will this child be,
given the worldy conditions we have allowed ourselves to take for
granted, nor what we can make of him, assuming our own unfulfilled
aspirations are to be hung around his neck, but what might he become.
Of course we should not be so unreasonable as to expect him to actualize all his potentials; he can live only one life at a time. But even
when it is clear that he has not become all that is possible, the significance of what he has actually achieved comes into focus only when
it is outlined against a background of what might have been.

To ask a question is to invite the unexpected. If any man seriously
asks the question of what his possibilities are—as indeed men are now
doing at an accelerating pace—something shocking is likely to come
of it, as indeed it has. The very process of posing questions about
himself with deeds rather than words transforms the questioner, even
before he is aware of any rewarding answers. As long as most men
were so overawed by nature that they treated events as stimuli to
which their behavior must be attuned, man appeared as an object
so vestigial that psychologists could explain him as a tail wagged by
the dog of antecedent events. But no modern man, no race, no people—
its fears and its scholars notwithstanding—accepts this post-Darwinian
premise indefinitely. Instead, behavior that probes his possibilities
transforms a man beyond the scholar's recognition—as it is known
to transform a child. The bolder the questions the more remarkable
the transformation. And what is psychology to say about that!

PSYCHOLOGICAL EXPLANATION
IMPLIES CONTRAST

What I have said in these initial paragraphs is no more than a
sketchy introduction to a theme I would now like to develop in some

psychological detail. Rather than pursuing the exposition in the usual structural manner, piling point upon point, I shall try to expound components of the theme recurrently through varying passages, bringing the reader back again and again to the same idea at a new level. In attempting this I shall be seeking to conform to an aspect of one of the things I shall be talking about—sequential explanation.

Let us start with what at first will appear to be some strange brand of logic rather than psychology. Yet I hope it will become clear that it stems as much from the psychological observation of inarticulate human experience as from the conventions of logic or of linguistic systems. Particularly I hope no one will think I am talking about "cognition," as contrasted with "affect." As a matter of fact, I can associate nothing with either of those terms that would justify treating it as a category rather than a dimension of appraisal—and one of doubtful utility, at that.

The classical notion of a concept as a property attributable to two or more objects which are otherwise distinguished from each other ignores an important psychological fact. That fact is that, while a concept may be defined academically in this way, it serves no human purpose unless the user is immediately concerned with at least one other object in which he intends to negate the property. If he were not immediately concerned with such a negation his current reference to a common property would be indiscriminate and psychologically footless. Thus a concept as defined in the dictionary is of little concern to a psychologist. But a concept on the occasion of its use is quite another matter.

It is not enough to say that when a man employs a concept he has simply embraced a set of objects and ignored all others, the way a dictionary does. To be sure, not all the excluded objects could possibly have had relevance to him at the moment the concept was invoked. Some, therefore, could properly be ignored. But other excluded objects surely did have relevance, else he would have had nothing to say. If the realm of a concept embraces all objects relevant to the occasion, then it must embrace some that were implicitly chosen for exclusion as well as those ostensibly included in the abstraction. Sometimes what is implicitly denied is more focal to the person's intent than what was affirmed, as when the disgruntled first mate entered in the ship's log that "the captain was sober tonight."

All this is to remind us of what is generally well enough understood in everyday discourse between persons. Construction, when it arises as a human act and thereby becomes a subject of psychological inquiry, serves, whether it is verbal or preverbal, symbolized or portrayed, to differentiate objects as well as to associate them. Indeed, it must do

both at once, for association implies that objects are thereby differentiated from others of immediate relevance, and differentiation implies
that objects are thereby selectively identified with others in contrasting
classes. Otherwise, human conceptualization is psychologically point-
less—that is to say, who would bother to bring the matter up!

But instead of using the term *concept*, and thus offer ever more
reluctant hostages to a language which already threatens our thoughts
with excommunication, let us at least employ a more modern term—
construct. It will be easier for us to envision *construct* as something
devised by man for his own lively purposes. And that is precisely
what we want to conjure up. As for *concept*, that is too likely to
be presumed a latent category of nature—something for man's dili-
gence to discover rather than for his ingenuity to contrive. Moreover,
a *construct* is more easily perceived as a structural member of a system
erected by man, and, therefore, as having dimensionality or two-
endedness.

DIMENSIONALITY PROVIDES GROUNDS
FOR RELEVANCE

Dimensionality is important. It has universal utility in the life
of man, even though I propose we regard it as dichotomous rather
than continuous. This is to say that a construct is at heart a black
and white affair, rather than a scale of grays. Indeed, it is precisely
because constructs do comprise pairs of sharply drawn contradistinc-
tions that they enable man to make his choices and get on with the
human enterprise.

But it must be noted that I have not said that objects fall naturally
into black and white categories. It is the constructs that are dichotomous, not the objects. If we had assumed that constructs were properties
of objects or something distilled out of them, as is often intended when
concepts are mentioned, we would be in hot water the instant we
called them categorically black or white.

It must always be clear that the construct is a reference axis devised
by a man for establishing a personal orientation toward the various
events he encounters. It is not itself a category of events or even
the focus of a class—as we usually imagine a concept to be. Man
can, in turn, use this portable device for ordering symbols along scales,
for placing events into categories, or for defining classes in the various
familiar ways that suit his needs. Being a reference axis, rather than

representation of something, the construct is much more clearly a psychological guideline against which objects may be referred, than it is either a limited collection of things or a common essence distilled out of them.

The use of the construct rather than the concept as a unit opens for the scientist a door to quite a different line of thinking. It enables him to regard science, along with other modes of endeavor, as a system of ventures open to psychological study, quite apart from their material referrents and outcomes. More than this, it turns our attention to the matter of relevance, a matter that has aroused the special concerns both of the Vienna Circle and of the critics of the atom bomb.

Where a construct is used in the dimensional sense we have proposed, the important distinction drawn between elements is not simply between what is included within the realm of the construct and what is excluded, but is in the way selected elements are projected onto the contrasting poles of the construct. To be sure, there are elements that fall outside the realm of personal concern—or, better, beyond the construct's range of convenience. Those elements, I have already conceded, are irrelevent to it. But relevance, in the manner of thinking I have proposed, is not limited either to one pole of construction or to events that have already occurred. What is most important in the life of man is what may yet occur, and the part he will choose to play in its realization.

Whatever one says about any event gathers its meaning from what contrasting things could otherwise have been said about it, as much as from the other events of which the same might have been said or those occurrences of which a contrasting statement might have been made. Since every perception we have, as well as ever statement we make, is no less a denial than it is an assertion, it becomes important to note what is perceptually negated as well as what is verbally affirmed. For example, what one does in life can be subjected to moral judgment only in the context of what he might have done—and didn't. It is in such a manner that construct theory embraces both relevance and responsibility. There is little elsewhere in science that goes as far as that.

APPRAISING HUMAN BEHAVIOR
IN A CONTEXT OF RELEVANCE

Construct theory, or better, *personal construct theory*—a term which implies that a construct is as much a personal undertaking as it is a disembodied scheme for putting nature in its place—suggests that human behavior is to be understood in a context of relevance. That is to say that the mere prediction of what a person will do, even if it is subsequently confirmed, does not demonstrate a full understanding of his behavior, any more than it defines his responsibility for his acts. A fuller explanation requires us to be aware of what he might have done. The construct dimension that lends structure to the behavioral event does so by providing contrasting poles, and unless we take the trouble to explicate both of them the directional trend of the behavior we have observed cannot be plotted.

Note that we have not claimed that a person's act is set off by all that it is not. To say that would invoke a host of irrelevancies. But it is brought into a relevant perspective by our structured awareness of what it might have been. That awareness is sharpened by the bipolar constructs we have erected for surveying such acts.

To be sure, this makes it very difficult to ever claim that we finally understand a human act, for the behavioral possibilities it must have displaced could not be displayed. But we can sometimes infer them from other experiences. Constructs help us do that.

Likewise, it is a tricky matter to pass moral judgment on something that has not been undertaken or before its consequences have played themselves out. But the fact that we cannot foresee outcomes does not prevent them from occurring, nor does it permit us to disavow our own contribution to the state of affairs that later materializes. Sin is not a self-evident property of any act and therefore to be avoided by the inhibitions of self-conscious innocence. Sin is a risk that every well-intentioned man must take and innocence is subject to harsh judgment for what it does not venture to try. Constructs help us anticipate what the risk and judgment might be.

But perhaps we are in too much of a hurry to come to conclusions about human behavior anyway, and thereafter to stop wondering what undisclosed potentialities it has. Indeed, I suspect that historically the questions men have asked have turned out to be more important than the conclusions they reached. Questions breed actions that lead to further questions, and these, in turn, to the boldness of further inquiring acts. Conclusions, however, perpetuate themselves and often serve to limit, if not stultify, both action and thought. Thus the living history of man is the story of the questions he has enacted, rather than the conclusions he has anchored in science or dogma.

Besides, it is for "the last judgment," whenever that may come about, to write all human epitaphs. Perhaps this is the reason that awesome event is identified with the end of the world. Such a definitive pronouncement of truth would scarcely dare leave questions remaining to be asked, and certainly none that man might reopen by his latter deeds. The questioning endeavor we know as the human enterprise would simply have to come to an abrupt halt. In reaching terminal conclusions, moral or psychological, man commits the ultimate suicide of his race.

So I am not greatly disturbed by the fact that I have proposed a criterion for understanding human behavior that makes stable conclusions about it virtually impossible. As a matter of fact, I hope the criterion of relevant contrast will serve to keep us from deciding once and for all that our confirmed predictions of any man's acts encapsulate all that may ever be expected of him. A science that respects relevance simply cannot rest upon conclusions, save as tentative grounds for further questions. And I think there is no place where this is more true or more pertinent than in the science of human behavior. So I hope my criterion will keep all conclusions quivering on their empirical foundations and will confront us with such disturbing questions about the potentialities of man that all sorts of imaginative inquiries will be provoked.

What has just been said about the tentative outcomes of successful prediction can be said also—and perhaps with even greater emphasis—about control. The claim that a man can, on demand, be compelled to live the life of a slave, or a soldier, or a doctor, or a criminal, or an intellectual—even if true—does not mean that his behavior is thus comprehensively defined. Nor does it mean that a life so successfully shackled to circumstances must have been psychologically understood—not even when its every act has been precisely regulated, right down to the batting of an eyelash. There is always the relevant and morally responsible issue of what would have enabled the slave to explore the reaches of freedom, what the soldier might have disciplined himself to do besides march and shoot, or what the intellectual might have understood if he had allowed his thoughts to be shaped by compassion.

BEHAVIOR IS MAN'S WAY OF POSING A QUESTION

What I have managed to say up to this point still falls far short of what I have hoped to convey. It is not enough to argue that an enlightened psychology projects the behavior of man against a background of his unrealized potentialities. It must do more than that. And it does. It incorporates behavior as the instrument of its own exploration. In this respect a good psychologist is like a man, for behavior, I have observed, happens also to be man's favorite way of posing a question.

It is perhaps best, in developing this point of view, to start out by noting just how the psychologist uses his own behavior to pose questions. Generally he tries to follow the canons of science, and particularly those of experimental science. This means that he does not content himself with armchair speculation, nor does he regard his logical inferences as anything but tentative. He makes predictions which are expressions of hypotheses. What he hypothesizes then becomes a basic for his ventures in action. These ventures he calls experiments. In performing them he takes a certain personal risk and, if he survives, he reassesses his position in the light of the outcomes. Being a scientist he never wholly trusts either his arguments or his forecasts; he is much too aware of the fallibility of uncommitted thought. So he must try things out for himself. Thus experimental science, at its best, turns out to be a humble blending of piercing ingenuity and wide-eyed ingenuousness.

It is easy enough to see that a psychologist who believes in active experimentation uses his own behavior as his instrument of inquiry. However, those psychologists who are not so obviously scientific in their approach to man also invest themselves in action. They go out of their way to talk about what they believe is so. They make claims. They publish. And what makes it clear that they really are asking questions all the while is the way they prick up their ears when what they have done appears to provoke a reaction.

Thus psychologists who are less self-consciously scientific can be seen to initiate their actions in order to present themselves with outcomes they think they can assess. They launch inquires by means of their behavior, even when they seem to be demanding against odds that all results confirm their anticipations. In fact I have noted that the more dogmatic they are the more they betray their distress and covertly express the hope that vigorous declarations and actions will dispel the lurking doubts that trouble their minds—replacing uncertainties with convictions they need not continually defend. For them, I think, no less than for their more disciplined cousins, behavior is the expression of a question. More often than we suppose it may be a question of frantic proportions.

To be sure, the issues unctuous men raise may center more around the public credibility of their claims than the essential truth expressed.

They want to know, I suppose, what they can sell. As with salesmen, truth may appear to be a consensus of customers. But then we should not be too impatient with such colleagues, for science itself leans more heavily on credibility than on revelation. At least the behavior of would-be prophets offers a challenge to more circumspect men.

But if there is a fallacy in the outlook of most psychologists, it is not that they sometimes put their questions in the form of overeager assertions—for an assertion, once one is bold or imaginative enough to make it, tends to set in motion the processes that will ultimately test its validity—but that they deny to other men the penchant for behaviorally implemented inquiry they find so crucial to their own endeavors.

What is so special about a psychologist? He experiments? Who doesn't? He enacts his questions? Don't we all? His inquiries produce more questions than answers: Who has ever found it to be otherwise? Not Adam! Not Eve! Not Pandora! Not John Alden! Not Robert Oppenheimer!

Now that we think of it, does the psychologist do anything that other men do not do, except, possibly, that he does it less spontaneously? And if he did do what other men do not, would he be much of a psychologist? Is he a scientist—a creature apart—whose own behavior is explained by his undertakings, while the behavior of other men is to be explained only in terms of stimuli, motives, physiology, and the momentum of their biographies? Or is he not as often the pompous and unwitting subject in the experiments less pretentious intellects perform—perhaps his perceptive wife, his wide-eyed children, his whispering students, and even those whom he has employed to enact the parts he prescribes for "subjects." As I see it, being a psychologist is doing what man does, though perhaps more systematically than most men, and concentrating all the while on behavior for its own sake rather than on physics, government, art, commerce, recreation, or any of the particular enterprises in which human efforts are channeled.

If a psychologist's own life is taken up in behaviorally expressed modes of inquiry, is it not appropriate to examine the lives other men lead to see how they may similarly be up to their ears in asking questions? And if behavior is the way other men ask questions too, what does that mean to the perceptive student of human behavior? Is the scientific formula of "predict and control" still to be applied to human behavior in the same way it is applied to electricity or the weather? I think not, though, as I have already said, I see no need for psychologists to abandon the broad principle of sequential explanation.

THE PSYCHOLOGIST'S SHIFTING TASK

What I think this view of man as the paradigm of the scientist—and vice versa—does mean is that the ultimate explanation of human behavior lies in examining man's undertakings, the questions he asks, the lines of inquiry he initiates, and the strategies he employs, rather than in analyzing the logical pattern and impact of the events with which he collides. Until one has grasped the nature of a man's undertakings, he can scarcely hope to make sense out of the muscular movements he observes or the words he hears spoken. In dealing with human behavior we inevitably find ourselves confronted with the human ingenuity it expresses. And that is the point of confrontation at which most psychology breaks down.

While human ingenuity is something that is continually challenged by circumstances, it is never dictated by them. History confirms that. Besides, it would hardly make sense for one to claim ingenuity in producing what had been dictated by his circumstances. As I tried to say in my introductory paragraphs, behavior cannot be fully understood except in the context of all that is humanly possible, and mere circumstances are stone silent as to what that may be. Still, the constructs against which human behavior is to be reflected to give it meaning must, as I have noted, take some account of what is relevantly excluded.

Furthermore, our best constructs notwithstanding, we cannot know for sure what is possible until we try. This goes for all of us. The behavior of Twentieth Century Man will be much better understood when the Twenty-First Century has rolled around and we see what has come of man's present undertakings. While we may continue in that century to make progress in understanding the psychology of man, the end will still not be in sight. New ventures will be under way, and the appraisal of the behaviors channelized by them will await their still later outcomes. Thus human behavior will prove to be a changing phenomenon, caught up in the constantly expanding human enterprise, and its explanation will be a continually reopened question. Since man persists in being creative it will probably be no easier to predict his most significant acts in the coming generations than it will be to forecast the research imaginative psychologists will contrive and what will come of it.

In the perspective of this viewpoint the task of the psychologist is not simply to tabulate the categorial ways in which men presently behave, and the circumstances in which each occurs, but to engage himself with fellow men in exploring the uncharted realms into which the human quest may be expanded. And in this mutual enterprise one may well wonder what outcomes will ensue and to what unexpected vantage points their joint experience will lead. So now, in order to survive, psychology must invent as well as discover. That will make it a discipline disconcertingly alien to the one in which most of us were once trained.

WHAT A TEACHER HAS YET TO LEARN

So where does this put us? Perhaps I had better start by putting the question to myself. I am a teacher. I have been a teacher for about thirty-five years, not counting some time spent doing other things. During the graying years I have picked up a few tricks of the trade—how to enable students to buckle down and learn what I think they should know, some persuasive arguments for their learning by teaching each other instead of asking me to explain everything to them myself, a little about how to build morale in a class or in an educational program, some ways of disengaging myself from footless dialogues with students who would rather be clever than explore the breathless wonderment of a world reserved for self-acknowledged idiots, devices for managing a large class without too much investment of time and effort, phrases that teach a few and entertain the rest, and, in my rarer moments of genius, how to get students to forget what I once told them. Early in my career I developed some talent for predicting which students would go far; at least I bet on some pretty unlikely candidates and—often to the consternation of my colleagues and my own egotistical delight—have won.

I recall that ten of the ninety or so seniors of the Class of 1938 at the Fort Hays Kansas State College continued elsewhere to earn the Ph.D. in psychology, and, regardless of what the facts may be, I am reluctant to let anyone convince me that I did not have something to do with that. If I remember correctly, when I went to western Kansas to teach in the fall of 1931, only four graduates in the history of the college had ever completed doctoral degrees in any field. So much for one teacher's experience with prediction and control.

But what eludes me still is an understanding of human behavior, and particularly that of my students. I have only the faintest idea of what they might have achieved if they had made the most of their opportunities, or what failures otherwise awaited them in that depression-ridden, drought-stricken dustbowl of the 1930's. Only in the context of what was possible can I make a proper assessment of their behavior, or of mine.

Now and then, over the years, I have caught passing glimpses of students exploring life by acting out their questions. On occasion I have accepted an invitation to join one of them in his efforts. But mostly I have remained on the sidelines, a psychologist living in the world he has known, and content to predict and control behavior without participating in its venture.

Now I wonder how much more of a psychologist I would have been if I had seen behavior, not as something merely to be forecast and managed, but as an investment in questions, as man's projection of himself into the enterprise of inquiry. If I had I might by now have formed some clearer notion of human nature from observing how it is variously engaged and what can come of it.

So, what do I find myself saying? I must be confessing that I can understand even my own behavior only in a context of what it might have been, and I can measure it only in alignment with the construct dimensions in which its diminishing future potentialities may be seen to lie.

PSYCHOTHERAPY IS PRACTICED BY WHOM?

Besides being a teacher, I am a psychotherapist. I have engaged in psychotherapy almost as long as I have taught. During a good deal of that time I have supervised psychotherapists, as well as offered more formal instruction in psychotherapeutic procedures. So what kind of a psychologist does this make me? Does it mean that I have some experience in the control of human behavior? And, if so, does it also mean that I understand it?

I regret to say that it took me a long time and the persistent efforts of a number of able and determined patients to make it clear to me that psychotherapy is not simply a form of treatment by which they could be managed. At last they were somehow able to demonstrate that what I did to them did not make them well or compel them to conduct themselves with propriety. It was their behavior that eventually made them well, just as their original distress had been an ill-fated undertaking of their own contrivance. They were not patients who submitted to my treatment—at least the ones who got well weren't—but clients who made some use of me. This proved to be no less true of hospitalized psychotics than of those who came to my office.

What I did, I think, was pose issues for them, sometimes by what I attempted on my own initiative, sometimes by my rejoinders to their initiatives, and sometimes only by my presence at an opportune moment when they were ready to reach for some human resource. They sought to cope with me—sometimes, I suppose, because they could see no alternative—and often they resented their dependent commitment to me. The transference neurosis, long before noted by Freud, proved to be one from which the patient must extricate himself. So always the inquiring venture turned out to be my clients' own. What I offered may have been something worth their effort—either to seek or escape—and a facility they could use to explicate their questions in terms they could enact and comprehend.

Gradually my clients taught me that a symptom was an issue one expresses through the act of being his present self, not a malignancy that fastens itself upon a man. What they experienced as symptoms were urgent questions, behaviorally expressed, which had somehow lost the threads that lead either to answers or to better questions. The symptom was even a fragment of a proper human experiment—one designed in childhood, perhaps, and repeated again and again in later years. Yet the experiment could never be carried through to its conclusion because the generating hypotheses had lost their contexts or because the current outcomes had slipped out of focus. It was for the psychotherapist to help his client pick up the elusive theme and follow it to its psychological conclusion—that is to say, to some point where its consequences would be reflected back upon its anticipations and its implications expressed in the enactment of more fruitful questions.

But if I managed to help my clients overcome symptoms, as I am sure I sometimes did, does this provide an adequate measure of my psychological understanding of man? Only partly so, I think, for the "normal" behavior that replaced the "abnormal" symptoms may have been only the acceptable neurosis of the times. Ask, rather, what was possible.

Now if I only knew the answer to that question—or even had some better approximation to an answer—I might be able to appraise my understanding of those who seek psychotherapeutic help. The significance of any successful clinical prediction we make, or any therapeutic cure we effect, is not disclosed by the degree of success in reaching a goal, but looms up only in the context of what might have happened. So we, together with those who do not claim to be the psychologists we are, continue to test those missing potentialities through the curiosity of our own deeds.

BEHAVIOR IS WHAT BEHAVIOR ASKS

What I said earlier about understanding behavior as a questioning act engaged in exploring its own contextual possibilities raised the urgent question of where psychology must now find itself. The actuarial relations between antecedents and consequents, in terms of which stimulus response psychology has heretofore been attempting to explain behavior, is being changed by the very thing it seeks to explain. Is psychology then scrambling head over heels in the ever more swiftly moving transitions that human behavior itself produces? I think it is.

Acturial explanations take no account of projected future developments. They concern themselves instead with the regularity with which human actions are associated with antecedent events. What they measure, then, is not man's imagination, but his lack of it. Yet the pace of man's imaginative ventures is accelerating. He is asking ingenious questions—a great many of them—and the behavior in terms of which he asks them is as free of antecedent events as imagination is free of tradition.

A quick look at what man has been doing with himself in the last three decades should be enough to make one suspect what is going' on. Behavior is man's way of changing his circumstances, not proof that he has submitted to them. What on earth, then, can present-day psychology be thinking about when it says that it intends only to predict and control behavior scientifically? Does it intend to halt the human enterprise in its tracks?

Since I am a psychologist—or have been representing myself as one long enough to establish considerable seniority over most of my colleagues—it seemed that I had better ask myself if I too have been practicing a psychology of the unimaginative man. Do I understand behavior's achievements, or only its repetitive failures? That is a fair question.

In the preceding paragraphs I reminded myself that, in some degree, I have been able to predict and control the behavior I observed. But now it strikes me that is not enough. With man's efforts actualizing unheard-of possibilities on every hand, my predictive and managerial accomplishments of the past begin to look rather puny. It is small consolation to note that the successes of so many of my "behavioristic" colleagues seem even more petty.

So let us be bold enough to pursue our venture further. In suggesting new criteria for a genuine understanding of human behavior, and in seeing psychology as a science that must try to make predictions about behavior in an exploding universe of human accomplishments, I may have a bear by the tail. If I want to continue posing as a psychologist, I may get carried along a good deal further than I ever intended to go. Yet, for the moment at least, I am willing to be drawn into the wake of my own behavior. As a youngster riding a horse through flood waters I learned that the safest thing to do is to swim downstream.

ANTICIPATION

None of what I have been saying should be taken to suggest that prediction and control are footless undertakings when they are assigned their proper place in sequential explanation. As I said at the outset, the principle of sequential explanation, of which prediction and control are only cases in point, also challenges us to join man in testing the limits of his unsuspected talents. What must be kept in mind throughout is that behavior is our questioning act.

Behavior puts itself into perspective by exploring its own possibilities, as well as by allowing itself to be the object of our psychological inquiries. For psychologists to continue to assign it a passive role puts them, and all who take them seriously, out of touch with the accelerating pace of human adventure. Behavior is not *the answer* to the psychologist's question; it *is* the question. And, just as all questions are anticipatory, behavior is anticipatory too. Let us see what this may mean.

To ask a question is to invite a reply. If the question is relevant to anything of human account then presumably the reply will change one's perception of himself and his world. Sometimes one anticipates a reply which will confirm a position he has already taken, that is to say, one from which he has been accustomed to launch his inquiries. But the confirmation, if it occurs, will nonetheless alter his experience—if only because it puts his position in a more presumptuous light. He must know that.

Sometimes one anticipates a reply which will disconfirm his present outlook. In that case he may assert his position with particular vigor on the occasions when it is most likely to be challenged. A person who seems to go out of his way to fail does that. Again, sometimes, one appears to ask for no particular reply, only for something he can grasp. In this case the relevance of the question may give us a clue to a construct dimension we might envision within his system. That, in turn, should give us some hint as to the kind of reply he is prepared to accept.

The tricky part of all this, both for him and for us, is that replies seldom end up being acceptable conclusions. At best they are grounds for further inquiries. The best answer to a question is two better ones. Any of us may, of course, think he has had a conclusion revealed to him, and therefore discontinue making adventuresome inquiries. But if he stops asking questions altogether someone will probably have to take him out and bury him. At least we can be reasonably sure his wife will start looking for another man who is not so sure the answers he knew twenty years ago still hold.

Questions are restless bedfellows. When they are behaviorally activated they disturb all sleep nestled in foregone conclusions and elicit dreams of unprecedented replies. Ask the most foolish question you can imagine and, sure enough, someone will offer an answer. Even a stunned silence in the midst of an animated conversation is an outcome not to be ignored. And before the questioner's ears have told him what is happening in the room he will begin to sense his own internal response to the venture. One so often remembers his foolish questions longer than he does his sensible ones, and he wonders over and over why on earth he asked them. Behavior is like that; it puts itself into perspective by exploring its own outlandish possibilities.

If man's behavior poses important questions, something of one sort or another is bound to come of it, even the stunned silence that follows a bomb. It will not do to say that what comes of it will always be conclusive. History, the long-term behavioral record of man, gives us precious few conclusions. The few it does appear to offer keep turning themselves unexpectedly into the most urgent questions of the day. The longer they are held as conclusions, it seems, the bigger questions they turn out to be.

And whoever heard of a child who took a pat answer and let it go at that? Or, if he did acquiesce to a pat answer, how much more overwhelming a question it proved to be in his adult moments of extremity! All of this explosive emergence in the enterprises of man sets a particularly exasperating task for the psychologist who is out to account for behavior in terms of its antecedent events—as if the ventures of man were a phenomenon already fixed in space and time, and curiosity a lawless state that befalls the unwary mind.

HUMAN BEHAVIOR IS ITSELF AN EVOLUTIONARY PROCESS

Psychology, emerging in the late Nineteenth and Twentieth Centuries, sought to identify itself with a science it had no part in creating. It seemed enough that the science of the day was wonderful and good. In the world that scientists envisioned nature was a relatively stable entity. Evolution had run its course. At last the outcome of the long slow process could be studied to see what nature's assembled menagerie had turned out to be.

But it is increasingly clear that human behavior has not settled into orbit. It is, indeed, the one part of nature that now is most in transition—perhaps transforming itself at a pace no other aspect of nature has ever matched. Man, inquisitive chap, is irrepressibly engaging in new enterprises, just as psychologists themselves seek to do, and the formulas we derive for binding events to his subsequent actions keep losing touch with the novel human engagements of our day. Man is not content to cope with his circumstances forever in the same way. At an ever-increasing tempo he casts his anticipation in fresh varieties of searching questions and, to pose them, the behavior that psychologists want so much to explain is redeployed in an ever-varying encounter with circumstances.

For example, the psychological interpretations that brilliantly illuminated the plight of Viennese women in Freud's time have become less and less appropriate to the troubles in which women now involve themselves. The mind-body dualism of the mid-Victorian era provided a woman with a ready-made protective barrier she could place between herself and humiliation—both public and private. She had only to invoke the mechanism of conversion, safely portraying in what she supposed to be medical terms the sweetly petulant and vulgar questions she had caught herself experiencing in mental terms. Nowadays, with the bulkheads of mind-body dualism gradually giving way, and the terms of feminine humiliation and vulgarity almost reversed, women are puzzled about stranger matters, and when they behave they articulate the wordless queries of our times.

ABANDONMENT OF SUBSTANTIAL EXPLANATION

There are those who argue that since we know reality only in the dubious terms of our own construction of it, there is no point in assuming that it exists at all, except as a figment of our imagination. Our own contrived constructions—sometimes called "experience"—are all we shall ever have, they say, and we had better make up our minds to be content with them. This is not to deny there is heavy thinking to be done, for our subjective perceptions often turn out to be at odds with each other. But if something upsetting occurs, such as a death in the family, the problem is not in what has happened, but in how to reconcile our grief-stricken thoughts of today with our compound evasions of years past.

This phenomenological view keeps all the turmoil within the man and offers him neither the challenge of external threats nor the comfort of resources beyond himself. In its light no circumstances lying beyond the outermost layer of his skin can be seen to constrain his impulses or to offer any hint of the enticing mysteries of anticipations. There is nothing, absolutely nothing save the image he himself conjures up, to dictate his acts, to disclose their consequences, or to suggest that anything other than chaos awaits him. There is no venture, and hence no ominous risk and no hairbreadth escape. All the story will ever tell is what he will set down for himself to read.

Life provides this man with no scientific footholds on reality, suggests to him no narrative plots, offers no rhythmic metaphor to confirm the moving resonance of a human theme. If he chooses to write tragedy, then tragedy it will be; if comedy, then that is what will come of it; and if burlesque, he, the sole reader, must learn to laugh at its misanthropic caricatures of the only person he knows—himself.

Most of all, phenomenological man cannot share his subjective plight, for even his most beloved companion is a manakin fabricated out of his own moods. A blind poet, imprisoned alone in a cell whose walls he cannot touch, the only sound man hears is a ringing in his ears. With no voices to haunt him, no future to dread, no consequences to stir remorse, he experiences the absolute freedom that only utter emptiness can guarantee the human soul.

This rather dismal phenomenological picture I have sketched should be enough to warn the reader that I have something else in mind to suggest. If he has not sensed it, let me remind him of what I have said about understanding man, not so much in the context of his present circumstances, but in the context of all his behavioral possibilities, both manifest and potential. As long as man can enact his questions the world of which he is a moving part can scarcely stand still—and neither can he. One is not finally engulfed by circumstances he can still manipulate.

Besides, I am neither phenomenologist enough to advocate the kind of encapsulated redundancy I have described, nor realist enough to believe it is forced upon me. The fact that my only approach to reality is through offering some responsible construction of it does not discourage me from postulating that it is there. The open question for man is not whether reality exists or not, but what he can make of it. If he does make something of it he can stop worrying about whether it exists or not. If he doesn't make something of it he might better worry about whether he exists or not.

Moreover, I see no reason why I cannot approach some objective which men such as I may hope to achieve only at some infinitely remote point in time. Like Sisyphus, one may commit himself to a continuing endeavor as well as to more limited projects. Perhaps if I were a Euclidian psychologist, sharply dividing events into those which do happen before my eyes and those which can never happen, I would be overwhelmed by a growing awareness of man's failure to reach any ultimate conclusions about nature. I might then be tempted to throw in the sponge and concede that the lines of human construction and outer reality can never, never touch.

But I prefer the more cosmic view which supposes these two progressions may ultimately join hands, though that auspicious moment may prove to be an infinity of years away. Now that seems to me to be a proposition of quite a different order. It is, I suspect, only a once naive realist, now too suddenly disillusioned to cope with his own transition, who ends up with no remaining alternative save the extreme existentialism I have described. He steps into a trap. It is one into which men, who have grown up expecting science or religion to offer conclusions rather than ways of asking further questions, are prone to fall. To be sure, I am such a man, but, my biography notwithstanding, I do not choose to stumble into this particular manhole.

EXPLANATION BY MANIPULATION

Phenomenology's abandonment of all hope of finding substantial explanations of the behavior of man need not be man's own final answer. He can assume a reality without having to believe that his life is run by it. He can assume that he, with other men, is a part of that reality, and may act accordingly. And he can assume that when he ventures to act nature is refreshed. The response to the question his behavior poses confronts him with new and mystifying natural occurrences about which he may dare ask even more meddlesome questions.

Even the questioning act of man is a disturbance of nature, as well as a provocation to it. The more interrogations he presses upon his world, and the more vigorously he plies his resources, the more altered his world of resources becomes. His act of questioning even changes himself, to the consternation of psychologists who want to understand him as the stabilized product of antecedent events—evolutionary, biographical, and official. Thus a man comes to understand for himself what is happening—within and without—not as an academic dilettante whose ethereal propositions impinge on nothing, but as the impact of his own actions demonstrates what is possible.

This brings us to the point where we can selectively agree and disagree with phenomenology. We can agree that we cannot find the explanation of human behavior neatly wrapped up in antecedent events. Events do not prophesy. Besides, we know as little intrinsically, and perhaps even less, about those events as we might know simply from asking a man to account for himself. The properties one may attribute to occurrences in nature seem limitless and our perceptions of what they are shift again and again as time affords us with different perspectives. It is not hard to agree that it is the personal experience of the observer that makes one event appear different from another and one account of it turn out to be at odds with another.

But we can disagree with phenomenology by declining to accept its implicit assumption that perception is passive. Let us say, rather, that we know an event through our own act of approach to it. We ask questions about it, not academically merely, but experimentally. We intervene and there are outcomes. We invent and new accomplishments materialize. We traverse space and strange objects heave into view. Academic impossibilities yield to demonstrated achievements. The scholar has only to look outside his study window to see less educated men doing what he once said could not occur. The psychologist has only to participate in the human enterprise to find that man does what "intelligence" tests have said he can't.

PERSONAL CONSTRUCT THEORY

None of what we have been talking about need be taken to prove that human behavior is unpredictable. To be sure, it cannot be predicted solely from circumstances; we have already noted that man is too recalcitrant to allow that to happen. Furthermore, as time goes on, he seems less and less disposed to accept the dictatorship of circumstances.

Even God, the most powerful circumstance of them all, is nowadays said to be dead. Such a statement is obviously not atheistic, or even agnostic. In a general way it concedes the creation of circumstances and does not deny their historical importance, yet in a peculiar theological way it is a sweeping declaration of independence on the part of men who are ready to accept responsibility for their acts and are ceasing to acknowledge the guiding power of any circumstances, even the greatest of them—God. As theologians sometimes do—to the amazement of scientists who rather think of themselves as being more precise with words—these men state the new humanistic proposition most succinctly. They say simply, "God is dead." When this sort of thing begins to happen it becomes very difficult indeed for psychologists to predict human behavior from any circumstances at all, regardless of what prior "learning processes" have been observed.

But does all this mean that the psychologist must from now on disregard God or any other set of circumstances altogether and pin everything on some unanalyzable and inaccessible experience of the individual man? I think not. There ought to be some way for psychology to outgrow circumstantial explanation without having to choose between dissection and metaphor.

Events can be construed. There is a particular way to do this. One may chart his psychological space in many dimensions—certainly many more than the three we ascribe to physical space, or four, if we enlarge our notion of space and include time, or five, if we enlarge it still more and include Michelsonian observation. The dimensions we ascribe are expressed in terms of reference axes, and the events we experience can be located in our personal hyperspace by projecting them onto these axes. The more independent axes upon which we project an event the greater the psychological depth in which we see it, and the more meaningful it becomes to us.

In personal construct theory these dimensions of one's psychological space, in terms of which meaning emerges for him, are the constructs about which we spoke earlier. They are not, as I tried to make clear, intrinsic properties of the events—either real or imagined. One asks of an event only that it can be plotted with reference to an axis, not that it somehow produce the axis out of itself or that it confess to him the full depth of its meaning—as if all well-bred events spoke Shakespearian English.

It is to be noted that no disruptive analysis is performed on the event by construing it. This becomes an important point when man or a bit of human behavior is construed. In this respect personal construct theory is a form of mathematics, not a natural science. On the other hand, it is a scientific theory to the extent that it postulates that each man devises his own construction system, a statement that offers numerous experimental derivatives.

To suggest that each man contrives his own system and plots events within it is not to say that each of us is bottled up forever in his own private world. Different men can construe the same events, though each starts out by doing it in his own way. Two people, say a mother and a newborn child, may not have a full intellectual meeting of minds the first time they try to enter into a discourse with each other in the maternity ward. But by sharing their encounter with events—including the events produced by their own behavior—some mothers and daughters do develop a fair understanding, each of what the other is talking about. Each may rely upon her own system, but the constructs of one system can be devised to plot the approximate positions of those of the other.

Children and men, therefore, cease to be altogether alone when they try to see events through the spectacles others use, even while reserving the privilege of using their own. And when they couch this interrogatory effort in behavioral terms they make roles for themselves—in the special sense in which "role" is regarded in personal construct theory. A society thrives on the roles its members play. It can emerge and remain viable as long as men see each other as construing beings rather than merely reactive objects, as long as questions are asked through deeds, and as long as the reconstruing of outcomes continues apace.

Events, then, are of supreme psychological significance, even though we do not see man's behavior dictated by them. The circumstances that encompass a man are his always resources, and his shackles only on those occasions when his behavior does not alter them. Events play their crucial part, not only because two men may encounter the same event, but also because each may ask a question of the other by putting it into the form of an event for the other to construe. Similarly, man can even ask an important question of himself—or of inanimate nature—through his behavior. This is sometimes called psychotherapy, sometimes commitment. To be sure, he sometimes confronts himself with more than he is prepared to manage. But then, no one has yet gone so far as to say that experimentation is a safe undertaking. All I have said so far is that in a universe on the move it is the only undertaking that counts.

CAN PSYCHOLOGY EVER BE PART OF THE
ON-GOING HUMAN ENTERPRISE?

What I have said so far represents a far-reaching effort to show how enormous the problems confronting modern psychology are. I picked up the thread of what I wanted to say by pointing out how hard it is to say one understands the behavior of a man until he has some idea of what other behavioral possibilities were open to him. Let us look closely. If a man is observed doing one of two things only, can we say we understand his behavior if we develop a formula for predicting which of the two he will do tomorrow? If it should be that there are these two possibilities and these two only, then I suppose it would be good enough to be able to predict accurately which of the two it would turn out to be. It might even be good enough if there were a third possibility—if we could be sure he would not think of it. But it certainly would not be good enough if he did think of the third possibility—not even if he refrained from attempting it. He just might change his mind and try it one of these days. And even if he doesn't, one can scarcely say he understands the man's behavior until he knows why that dangling third possibility is allowed to remain dangling.

But men can do more than two things—more than three. That makes the problem a little more complex. But what begins to make it seem so vastly difficult for today's psychology is the fact that men can do things that once were considered utterly impossible—at least to psychologists. That ought to be enough to make us suspect they can do in the future what now seems incredible. Furthermore, we see men doing things that men of a century ago did not even think to try. Does this not suggest that men will be accomplishing feats a hundred years hence so strange that psychologists do not now have even enough foresight to declare them impossible?

Now, if we take all these vaguely suspected possibilities into account, what happens to our sense of understanding human behavior? Can we say we understand what it is until we have some idea of what it might be instead? I think not.

Psychology has pretty much gone about its business under the "Darwinian" assumption—though I am not sure Darwin himself would have made it—that mankind has finally stopped evolving and all psychologists have to do now is see how the individual man grows up. But it is becoming increasingly hard to ignore the fact that the cultural and behavioral patterns of man are changing explosively. In the midst of such rapid transitions I don't think modern "experimental" psychology—as we know it anyway—can accomplish anything except identify itself more and more with cultural and behavioral obsolescence. I fear that it may end up being no more than a nuisance to the human enterprise. Men would rather find out what they can do by actually attempting it, than to be told what they can't do by a psychologist who assumes the future of all men but himself must be a repetition of the past.

The point is that the men the psychologist seeks to understand are resorting to experimentation as much as he is. When a man does that he does not behave as he did last year, or in the fall of 1929, nor does he treat his circumstances in the familiar ways that have been repeatedly "reinforced." He tries something different, just as a reasonably inventive psychologist does. He even ventures to do it without a Ph.D. or a state license to innovate. Psychologists, having observed only his past behavior, may undertake to tell him what he can or cannot do. But he, recalcitrant chap that he is, will go ahead and try something anyway. When he succeeds he will turn to the psychologist and tell him what he can do—or what both of them can do!

PROBABILITY AND INNOVATION

Now it is time to point this discussion more directly to the problems involved in trying to explain behavior in terms of sequences of events. I have made several glancing references to a principle of sequential explanation, enough to suggest that I am not for an abandonment of that idea. I have indeed argued as effectively as I know how that in today's plunging stream of human innovations the acts which implement those innovations cannot be adequately understood as a mere product of antecedent stimuli. Yet I have continued to insist also that life is essentially anticipatory, if for no other reason, by virtue of the fact that his most significant behavior is man's expectant way of posing an honest and courageous question. Such anticipation must imply that, in spite of what I have said about stimulus response psychology, there is indeed some kind of antecedent-consequent relationship between my present and my future. What that relationship may be is of prime concern to any psychologist who cares to participate in the quickening human enterprise. Let us deal with it so.

Admittedly, most of what I do today is easily enough construed as similar to what I did yesterday. Friends who have known me during the past few years have little difficulty recognizing my walk, my posture, my facial expression, my voice, and even some of the ideas I express. Probabilistically, then, it would be a poor bet for anyone to wager that my personality tomorrow would be unrecognizably different from what I have exhibited in the past.

But statistical probability is not the same as psychological significance. The most important things in a man's life are mostly those which have never happened to him before—his birth, his marriage, his first child, the departure of grown children from his home, the loss of a loved one, his retirement, his feeble years alone, his death. To be sure, we can sometimes predict—in a very superficial way—these very personal experiences from what we have seen others go through. But none of us, when he approaches them in his own life, finds much in his past that tells him what it will be like when his turn comes.

Yet forecasts are made, and most of us come up with some versions, variously intellectualized, of what we think is going to happen to us. When some of these important events do occur for the first time in our own lives the similarities and contrasts between anticipation and realization stand out with shocking clarity. Few would say in such a poignant moment that what was occurring was so unusual there was no point in taking it seriously.

There are first-time occurrences in the history of mankind too. Again, as in the lifetime of the individual, it is these, rather than the repetitions of history, to which thoughtful appraisal must, in retrospect, attach greater significance. Yet human history records no event so novel it was utterly unexpected. The posture of anticipation, which is the identifying psychological feature of life itself, silently forms questions, and earnest questions erupt in actions. Unprecedented consequences ensue. But when the novel contingencies occur, who, knowing how it was they came about, can say they fell wholly outside the realm of human anticipation? Moreover, it is the historical events precipitated in this manner, rather than those having greater actuarial probability, which tell us most about man in his hastening transitions.

A psychology that pins its anticipations on the repetitions of events it calls "stimuli," or on the concatenations of events it calls "reinforcements," can scarcely hope to survive as man's audacities multiply. More and more it will find its accurate predictions confined to the trivialities of man's least imaginative moments and to the automatisms of persons given in to despair. It seems to me that most of what we know as "modern psychology" is a monotonous tale told of men left behind by the quickening tempo of human undertakings. It is such men, and such men only I suspect, who enact nothing save what has been reinforced, who are carried on by the momentum of their biographies rather than compose their diaries afresh each day, and who become transfixed by their identities. And yet I doubt that there are ever men who are altogether like this. Perhaps it only seems that way from listening to psychologists.

PREDICTION WITHIN A SYSTEM OF CONSTRUCTS

Earlier in this discussion I pointed out how man begins to cope with events by devising reference axes called *constructs*. A system of such referrents permits him to put the events he encounters in some kind of perspective. What he devises is not dictated by the events, nor is it a property extracted from them. Nevertheless its utility in enabling him to make accurate predictions is constantly subject to check. Although what a man anticipates is not necessarily a reenactment of what has gone on before, its referrents, in terms of which he pinpoints his forecast, may have been subject to prior tests of their utility.

Whether the phenomenon that occurs can ever be said to be the one that was anticipated is a question not easily answered. One's anticipation of a future incident is scarcely more than a plotted position within a system of personal constructs. If subsequent observations made within the same system seem to coincide with the forecasted plot, one may say, within the referrents of his system, that his anticipation has been confirmed. Later, of course, he may devise other reference axes against which the occurrence may take on new meaning. Then he may wonder if what happened is what he would have anticipated if he had been using the new reference axes at the time he made his original forecast. But this is a question he can scarcely hope to answer. The best he can do is make another forecast, this time in terms of his augmented dimensional system.

Does a succession of accurate predictions serve to demonstrate that one has hit upon the truth at last? Perhaps it might if all the possible reference axes were taken into account in plotting the prediction. But such omniscience is next to impossible. From the point of view I have been expounding this cannot even be considered a good question. One may well keep in mind that it is improbable that any fragment of truth can be nailed down in such a finite manner.

But, more than this, what needs to be noted in the second place is that a construct is not a facsimile of any set of events; only one of an ad hoc system of guidelines for apprehending events. It is hardly appropriate, then, to argue about whether or not a construct is true to reality. A more appropriate question is whether or not it provides a perspective in which anticipations can be checked against realizations. But even if it does serve this purpose, there always remains the likelihood that further constructions will be devised to do the job better.

There is a third, and even more important, consideration. Does a construct, or system of constructs, open up the vastness of a man's psychological space and permit him to dream in new dimensions? And does it provide such definition within its realm that he can implement what he imagines? In short, is it fertile?

Accurate prediction, then, can scarcely be taken as evidence that one has pinned down a fragment of ultimate truth, though this is generally how it is regarded in psychological research. The accuracy confirms only the interim utility of today's limited set of constructs. Tomorrow's genius will erect new dimensions, open up unsuspected degrees of freedom, and invite new experimental controls.

And yet, however useful prediction may be in testing the transient utility of one's construction system, the superior test of what he has devised is its capacity to implement imaginative action. It is by his actions that man learns what his capabilities are, and what he achieves is the most tangible psychological measure of his behavior. It is a mistake to always assume that behavior must be the psychologist's dependent variable. For man, it is the independent variable.

THE STULTIFYING EFFECT
OF ACTUARIAL PREDICTION

Back in the 1920's the Soviet Union shifted its educational policy in a way that puzzled many Western educators. It removed chapters on individual differences from its psychology textbooks and it took a stand against all psychological testing. It is interesting to note that a similar movement is afoot in this country today, though I am inclined to believe it is not the communists who are behind it. It does appear, however, to be led by persons with an uncanny ability to identify communism's faults and virtues, for what is good they consistently oppose and what is evil, they imitate.

Moscow planned to industrialize. The choice had proved urgent. Having alienated itself from the economic and humanistic obligations honored by industrialized nations, and being therefore no longer in a relationship of mutual trust with the rest of the world, it could scarcely hope to attain economic viability unless it could produce by itself the goods upon which modern civilization in part depends. But Soviet scholars, including psychologists, could find little in the behavioral record and measured aptitudes of the people to support the hope they could ever operate machines and man factories, much less supply the vast needs of an industrialized society for advanced engineering and technical skills. What was the USSR to do? The choice was to listen to the experts or throw away the book. They threw away the book.

What happened is becoming history. Through two generations human behavior has been used as an instrument to explore its own potentials. While it seems clear that communism still has much to learn about the potential of the individual—perhaps as much as corporate Western Society seems bent on forgetting—no one can now say, as actuarialists would once have said, that the USSR cannot reach the moon.

Similar predictions were voiced when Egypt took over the Suez Canal. Egyptians could not develop the skills required of the Canal's pilots. Yet with Soviet help and encouragement, now grounded on experience doing what behavior experts once said was impossible, the Egyptians took on the job. Soon they were operating the Canal more efficiently than their predecessors. These were instances in which human actions came to be understood better in the context of their own potentialities. Actuarial prediction, however it may have previously been confirmed in both cases, proved to be grossly misleading. When human behavior was taken as an independent rather than a dependent variable, its functional relationship with other variables was radically changed. This is something for psychology to note if it intends to survive the Twentieth Century.

BEHAVIOR AS THE PSYCHOLOGIST'S INDEPENDENT VARIABLE

It has been customary for psychologists to attempt to explain behavior as dependent variable. They point out its antecedents, as if in saying what brought it about, they could demonstrate their understanding of it. Yet there is much more to psychological explanation than that. As I have been insisting, behavior can scarcely be understood until one has caught a glimpse of what it might be as well as of what it is. What one does comes into perspective as a contrast to what he might have done. This is to say that human behavior takes on additional meaning when one sees it as a contrast, a denial, an abandonment of alternatives, or as a choice which has left other possibilities unexplored.

To see behavior in this kind of perspective one needs reference axes within which he can plot what he actually does in a structured context of what he might possibly do. Without such a framework there are no grounds for assessing relevance and one's understanding of human behavior is limited to the lowest order of mechanistic description. The reference axes are the constructs devised by man, and each person erects a system of his own, though it is not necessarily a verbalized one. Within the realm of relevance his personal construct system defines for him, each man initiates what he says and does. Thus his words and his acts are not mere events consequent upon previous occurrences, but are expressions of what is relevantly affirmed and denied within his system.

A man curses. What he says is scarcely understood by looking up the purple phrases in a dictionary. One must understand the relevance of his verbal expression—what his curse emphatically deny, and what it would mean to him if he could not disavow what is so important to him to negate. Any word, whether an oath or a benediction, has a meaning in the context of its usage and within the construct system of the speaker that no dictionary can make clear. This is because dictionaries cannot provide the framework of relevance that makes language come alive.

Or a man makes love. One does not understand such an act from a description of its motor and physiological properties. There are the circumstances to be taken into account. But even a description of these—the moon and the girl—does not tell us all the act means. There is the structure of relevance, a highly personal matter that is often so difficult for others to understand, and, perhaps on a later occasion, even difficult for the man himself to understand. What did his affection assert? What did it deny? What are the boldly outlined dimensions that channelized his enactment so spontaneously it seemed to run its course without intent? It is within these parameters that his love-making begins to make sense, rather than following simply as the next link in a primordially forged chain of natural events.

But the context of relevance, as dimensioned by a man's personal construct system, is still not all that is needed to understand his behavior. Accomplishments must be noted too, for it is through his behavior and through his behavioral investment only, that man makes his entrance into the world of reality. When he acts he poses a question, and what ensues gives the question its import, the act its potency, and his life its meaning.

Behavior is man's independent variable in the experiment of creating his own existence. But to the extent that he loses sight of this fact and, thinking that he is being "psychological," regards his actions as a dependent variable, he denies himself a role in the human enterprise. And that, I think, amounts to abdicating his existence, except as an after-the-fact occurrence. A psychology that presumes to make a man an echo of once meaningful events must ultimately destroy him altogether, and, doing so, engrave its own final epitaph as well.

Behavior must be the independent variable for the psychologist too, just as it is for all children and for most men who have managed to stay clear of modern psychology. Rather than drawing from their actuarial studies the inference that human initiative is only what it has heretofore been, psychology's greater task is to join mankind in the exploration of what human behavior might be, and what would happen if it were. This is not merely a speculative or an artistic undertaking; it can be just as rigorously scientific as the psychology that treats behavior as its dependent variable—indeed, more so.

GUIDELINES

For psychology to launch into such a venturesome participation in the human enterprise it must concern itself with the guidelines that give behavior its directionality. The temptation is to say, in the tradition of Nineteenth Century determinism, that the guidelines are no more than reverberations of what has gone on before, and the best man can do is resonate to them. But if the psychologist does say that, humanity's present entry to the on-going human experiment we call existence is negated. And if he should go so far as to believe it of himself, his own experiment will collapse too. Psychology would then have no basis in ontology.

A psychology that participates in the human enterprise must perceive that the guidelines channelizing a person's processes are drawn by the person himself—that they are therefore personal constructs, and may be redrawn and revalidated by the user to structure anew his thought and his behavior. They are not the residue of biographical incidents, nor are they projected facsimiles of reality. They are, instead, the axes of reference man contrives to put his psychological space in order and to plot his varying courses of action.

With such personal constructs a man can make his entrance into the world of reality by acting with initiative and ingenuity. Failing to erect them he can only repeat concretely what has been "reinforced," in the circular manner that psychological journals—themselves deliberately acting, I fear, as products of their own concrete satisfactions—describe. It is difficult to see how a psychology so addicted to its reinforcements can ever participate imaginatively in the mounting behavioral ventures of the coming generation.

PREDICTION

What has been said so far about understanding human behavior might be catalogued under three headings. First, one must recognize behavioral alternatives—what man might do as well as what he does. In this generation men are exploring their behavioral alternatives at a pace never before equaled in the history of man. A psychology preoccupied with human behavior as a system of events primordially linked to prior occurrences can look forward to no substantial part for itself in this expanding human enterprise.

Second, neither science nor psychology can continue to ignore the relevance of what man does. Human behavior makes the world a different kind of place—though not always a very good one to live in. Man tampers with the scheme of things. But what do we know about what is happening to that scheme while it is being meddled with, except as we have some awareness of the dimensions of the psychological space within which the intrusive ventures are initiated? Yet the only dimensions we know are those erected by man himself—by *each* man himself. We call them constructs. Without them novel human acts can only appear as disruptive, disjunctive, chaotic, and somehow precipitated by hidden antecedents. But with them one can begin to see behavior probing for new avenues for man to extricate himself from prior circumstances and seeking them in a context of relevance to the current transition in human affairs.

Third, the meaning of human behavior cannot be assessed until its accomplishments are noted. It is through his behavioral initiative that man makes his entry into the real world of human events. He seizes life by starting something, and he becomes aware of his existence by noting what happens as a consequence. This is to say that life is anticipatory, not in a mere passive sense, but in an active, participative one.

Most scientists would agree with me, I am sure, if I said that the advancement of knowledge depends on the confirmation of predictions. Indeed, I do want to say just that. But I want to say more too. Before I do say more, however, let me make a few comments about the confirmation of predictions.

If we can agree that there is a reality beyond what pure phenomenology is willing to concede we can concern ourselves with the procedures by which man makes contact with it. We might say, of course, that if we keep our eyes and our ears open, sooner or later nature will reveal herself to us. But I think she is more coy than that. Instead of taking the initiative in disclosing herself to a passive man, or responding directly to a cross-examination logically phrased in plan English, I think that she, being every bit as feminine as they say she is, more likely lowers her lashes and murmurs, "Try me and see."

If this seems a much too anthropomorphic explanation for mechanistic stomachs, let me simply turn it around and suggest that feminine women know how to behave naturally. Is that better? But it's really all the same. It is just that when metaphors are turned around they don't sound so prejudicial. In any case, this view of the matter passes the initiative along to man—where it probably belongs if he is ever going to amount to anything—and generally makes him responsible for nature's reputation, called "science," as well as for his own existence.

If man is to comprehend natural events at any level—even at preverbal levels—he must anticipate them. This means predicting in some manner when and how they will occur. If what turns up resembles what he expected he can say his prediction was confirmed, at least in part. If it does not, he had better do something about it or reconcile himself to being left out of the goings-on.

The apparent failure of a prediction calls for reassessment. That may mean reidentifying the events from which inferences were drawn, reconsidering the inferences themselves, or questioning the constructs one has employed in structuring his psychological space. On the other hand, the apparent success of a prediction also leaves much in doubt. The confirming occurrence may not have depended on what the adventurer thought it did; it may look like what he expected only as long as he does not examine it too closely, or both his prediction and the outcome may have been so loosely defined that they could not possibly have turned out to be at odds with each other.

There is also the matter of just what it is a successful prediction confirms. Does it confirm only the specific prediction itself? Does it confirm the general hypothesis from which the prediction was derived? Or does it confirm something else—as when a person who thinks his neighbors are prejudiced against him finds his prediction well enough confirmed when he keeps complaining about it?

As a matter of fact, no confirmed prediction can be taken as evidence that one has struck bedrock truth. If one thinks science is a simple digging operation by which solid bits of truth are uncovered, he is likely to be in for some disappointments, especially if he relies upon the confirmation of his predictions as firm evidence that he has struck something conclusive.

At best, the confirmation of a prediction is no more than tentative evidence that one may be on the track of something. The psychology of living in a world that is largely unknown—and in rapid transition, besides—leads us to hope for little more than ad interim support for our beliefs. The confirmation of our local predictions, equivocal as that may be, is about the most we can expect. No, there is one thing more, vastly important—our ability, while alive, to pose further questions by our invested behavior, and thus to enter the stream of nature's fluid enterprise as an entity in our own right.

One thing more about confirmation of predictions: the basis upon which a prediction is formulated is more generalized and more tenuous than the observation which confirms or disconfirms it. A man predicts he can reach the moon. He can ordinarily be less sure about the accuracy of his advance calculations than he can about his observation of whether he reached it or not. There are a number of grounds for this—consensus of observers, previous validation of criteria, exhaustiveness of the construct axes of reference, multidimensional fix of the observed event, etc.—none of them absolute, of course. But, at least for the moment, it appears he can tie his unsure predictions to outcomes that seem sufficiently obvious. While this usually turns out to be short-lived scholarship, as it was in the case of Columbus who hurried home to tell Isabella that he had been right all along about reaching India— and had "Indians" to prove it—it probably serves to account well enough for so many scientific practitioners believing their task is only a matter of accumulating information about such linkages with "the obvious," bit by bit, and holding off replications of their experiments long enough to publish their results. However, this is not the place to discuss that particular fallacy at greater length than we already have.

CONTROL

If one can control events, as well as predict them, can he then allow himself to believe he understands them? Or, to make the question applicable to psychology, if one can control another's behavior does it means he understands that person's actions? Or, to bring the question within the realm of personal experience, does it mean that I understand my own behavior if I succeed in making it conform to a chosen pattern?

When the question is thus pinpointed it is easier to see how the answer has to be "no." At the very least the answer has to be "no" in the light of what has been said about understanding behavior in the context of its alternatives. A man who commits suicide probably knows very little about his own behavior, simply because its alternatives are so chaotically perceived by him. Yet there can be no doubt about his controlling it definitively.

Still it must be taken for granted that there have been some cases—Socrates and Jesus, for example—when the act leading to death was understood in the light of a careful examination of its alternatives. Even if we apply our third criterion for understanding human behavior—awareness of its consequents—one would still have to concede that some suicidal attempts may be fairly well understood by those who make them, though certainly most of such acts are pretty short-sighted. In any case, the point is that even this most definitive control of one's subsequent behavior cannot be taken as evidence it is understood. And as for what it means to be able to control the behavior of others, I am most reluctant to agree that all tyrants are proven psychologists.

It appears that I have set up an impossible standard for judging human behavior psychologically. That is true; I have. But it is a good one, nonetheless. I am less concerned, anyway, about definitive criteria than I am about usable ones which enable us to get on with the human enterprise. The task of the psychologist is to enable human behavior to make something out itself, not nail it dead to rights! This is a moving universe, especially those aspects of it with which the psychologist ought to be concerned, and the psychologist who thinks he cannot understand it until it settles down to a routine is the one who has really set an impossible standard for himself.

Yet to control behavior, as to predict it successfully, is to put it into a sequence; in the case of control, to make it follow upon intent, and, in the case of prediction, to envision outcomes before they happen. Both imply reaching a threshold of understanding, though the success of either has often been taken by psychologists as grounds for stopping short of understanding, and has thereafter led to grief. Both are anticipatory, and therefore express, in some degree, the spirit of human life. Both are useful to the human quest, particularly if they are taken to mean only that one may be on the track of something. Both represent, in part, the methodology of sequential explanation, by which psychologists can participate intelligently in the expanding human enterprise without asking it to stand still or spin around in orbital facsimiles of itself.

SEQUENTIAL EXPLANATION OF BEHAVIOR

The principle of sequential explanation comprehends a number of things. There is the notion that human behavior falls into a progressively moving sequence, an orbit of infinite proportions, and is not restricted to the little stimulus response circuit some psychologists examine so minutely in their laboratories. The exciting thing about the psychology of man is that he, for one, tries what he has never tried before and thus transforms himself before the psychologist's eyes, not that so much of his life at the same time continues to be routinely repetitive. And what makes it all the more exciting is that the pace of sequential transformation is accelerating, causing the task of the "Darwinian" psychologist, who assumes the evolution of human behavior has leveled off, to get so far out of hand he is threatened with extinction.

Not only must the principle of sequential explanation take into account the possibilities of behavioral orbits having infinite elements, but it must concern itself with successions pursuant upon entries undertaken at various points in the sequence of human events. In spite of some disparaging remarks I have made about stimulus response psychology, I am in no position to deny that a psychologist may intervene at the point of a "stimulus" and profitably observe what ensues as a behavioral "response." But he can also, and more often with profit I think, intervene in the cycle at the point marked, "response," and observe what stimulating events follow in the sequence. This is what I meant when I urged psychology to treat behavior as the independent variable in the ongoing experiment we call human existence.

The sequence of events that follows from a behavioral innovation contributes quite as much—even more—to our understanding of the action as do the action's antecedents. What it is important for man to know about the psychology of his behavior is what its alternatives are and what each might lead to, not how monotonously repetitive it is. The principle of sequential explanation must never be regarded as limited to an account of the succession of things that have already happened. To be sure, a prediction confirmed in the past is a case of sequential explanation, and it most certainly means something, but if it is taken as ground for a terminal conclusion, supposedly rendering inevitable what man may do tomorrow, the principle itself is violated.

Where human behavior is concerned, one must always take into account the sequential implications of unprecedented behavioral undertakings. As those implications begin to be suspected it is pretty likely that someone will venture the unprecedented undertakings, regardless of what stimulus response psychology predicts he will do. He may not get a research grant from the National Science Foundation for his venture, but that will not necessarily stop him.

The notion of relevance fits in here too. Increasingly men have projects up their sleeves. Without a hint as to what those projects might be some of their behavior may look very strange, and psychologists who can explain behavior only by looking to the stimulus events that have impinged upon these persons are likely to have a hard time of it. They may have to break with psychological tradition and ask the persons outright what they are up to.

But even asking a man what his objectives are may not throw much light on his behavior. Objectives have to be plotted in psychological space, and if one does not know the coordinate axes being used he may not be able to locate the objective. In that case his respondent's plotted courses of action will remain as obscure as his objective. One can scarcely trace a sequence wandering around through uncharted space, much less rely upon it to make something clear.

The reference axes—personal constructs—used by man must be inferred if one is to understand how a sequence goes and what bearing human objectives have upon the direction of human behavior. Thus the principle of sequential explanation, the wide-angled view of what follows what or what might follow what in this volatile world, demands that antecedents and consequents be plotted within the same construction system, or at least within construction systems that are cognate to each other. All of this is a rather philosophical way of saying that behavior is not understood until its relevance is straightened out.

So psychology needs to make use of sequential explanation when it deals with a subject so much in transition as human behavior. This means more than reliance upon confirmed predictions of human acts and the successful control of men. The events falling in sequence upon behavioral innovations must be considered. Behavioral alternatives must be envisioned if explanations of manifest behavior are to be entertained. Relevance must come to light, and not be dismissed as a "value" beyond the concern of scientific psychology. It can come to light if the dimensional structure of psychological space is explored, and the course of events, behavioral and otherwise, is plotted within personal construct systems that hopefully are cognate to each other.

LIVING WITH SEQUENTIAL EXPLANATION

What constitutes an adequate explanation in science or elsewhere is a matter of some perplexity to man, just as it is to a child who is asked to explain his behavior to his teacher or his parent. For some it seems to require a sort of proof that an event could not have occurred otherwise than the way it did. This usually backs up the explanation to antecedent events which are expected to take the rap for what has happened, and this, in turn, involves us in an assumption of a primordial linkage of natural occurrences in some sort of inevitable succession. For others explanation means the removal of all contradictions between what happened and all other things known to exist. For still others it means that an event is explained by its essential membership in a complex which, as a whole, can be taken for granted, or that the event can be designated precisely by terms derived from axioms. Then there are those who consider it enough to point out that the event was premeditated.

Before you get very far in this kind of discussion the question gets itself mixed up with the issue of freedom versus determinism, an issue I prefer to discuss elsewhere. But to a psychologist, explanation, in my opinion, turns out to be pretty much a matter of convenience. We want to get on with what we are doing and the kind of explanation that helps us in the undertaking, or suggests more attractive undertakings, is the one we are likely to accept.

Finding the ultimate explanation of something is about the same kind of quest as trying to capture certainty in a formula or truth in a dogma. For the time being, we are going to have to accept explanations that fall short of such conclusive pronouncements. Besides, I am not sure most of us would care to be dragged, kicking and screaming, through life by its certainties, or to have our burning curiosities extinguished by being doused with a bucketful of truth.

But we seem to be safe enough for the time being. No one seems to have pinned down the primordial explanatory event from which all others must ensue, nor has anyone come up with a terminal explanation which blockades all alternative routes. Since we cannot see either the beginning or the end very clearly, we shall just have to work our way out from the middle—which is where we find ourselves.

As I see it, the way to do that is to have a look at what follows what, and in what order. We can, for example, look at what has already followed what. But that is not enough, unless we are content to walk through life facing backwards. We had better have a look also at what is going to follow what, since the world, especially the world of human behavior seems to be turning up a lot of novelties. It is even more challenging to look at what else could be undertaken and consider what might follow in sequence from that.

Explanation in a humanistic or psychological sense seems to me to be a matter of seeing where something fits into a sequence. We can explain events by looking at their antecedents, as the stimulus response psychologists do, or we can explain them by lining them up with their consequents, or we can look at alternative successions to see what would have ensued—or would ensue—if they had been initiated. Such an explanation might not be of much comfort to a philosopher who generally dislikes having to live with his ignorance— or with ours. But as psychologists, we have to get along with our human handicaps, and the limited knowledge we can glean about what follows what is enough to enable us to get along gratefully with whatever it is we are trying to do.

In any case, whether it is satisfying or not, this is what the principle of sequential explanation means, and this is why the psychology of human behavior can live with it. Mostly the point I want to make about it is that ordinary notions of prediction and control, while they are limited examples of sequential explanation, are insufficient for a psychology that must not only remain out of touch with primordial beginnings and ultimate endings but must also find itself swept along in a mounting tide of behavioral innovations and their consequences as well.

BEHAVIOR IS BOTH THE PROBLEM AND MAN'S KEY TO SOLVING IT

Most of all, psychology, if it is to provide us with an understanding of human behavior, must help us see that man's behavior is his admission ticket to human existence. It is through behavior that questions are posed, and without it there is little that is new or worth anticipating in the realm of human events. What man does, whether in the outer world of international affairs or in the inner world of his mind, is what makes things turn out differently for him.

It will not be easy for a psychology modeled on Nineteenth Century science—and a science that believed that evolution had leveled off, at that—to participate in the accelerated behavioral innovations that promise to change the shape of the human affairs that confront it. Did I say, "not be easy?" I should have said, "be incredible!" Yet I think it should be possible for psychologists, who are less self-conscious about being scientists, to participate in the quickening human enterprise, once they appreciate the creative role of behavior in the affairs of man.

2

The Autobiography of a Theory

THIS IS THE autobiography of a certain theory is psychology known as the *psychology of personal constructs*. I feel myself uniquely qualified to write this account because I wrote the theory also, though I realize that writing a theory does not necessarily mean you know how you came by it. Undoubtedly what I wrote is hopelessly entangled in the ideas of my predecessors. However that may be, I can at least write about what I now recall.

Rather than starting with the basic premises of *personal construct theory*, the usual strategy for making a theory appear respectable, I would like to mention certain events and tentative conclusions reached and abandoned along the way to its formulation. This is not to say that the events shaped the theory—not that at all—but what I have to describe are the happenings out of which, in some accountable way, the theory has sought to make sense.

In the first course in psychology that I took I sat in the back row of a very large class, tilted my chair against the wall, made myself as comfortable as possible, and kept one ear cocked for anything interesting that might turn up. One day the professor, a very nice person who seemed to be trying hard to convince himself that psychology was something to be taken seriously, turned to the blackboard and wrote an "S," an arrow, and an "R." Thereupon I straightened up my chair and listened, thinking to myself that now, after two or three weeks of preliminaries, we might be getting to the meat of the matter.

Although I listened intently for several sessions after that the most I could make of it was that the "S" was what you had to have in order to account for the "R" and the "R" was put there so the "S" would have something to account for. I never did find out what that arrow stood for—not to this day—and I have pretty well given up trying to figure it out. I can see, of course, that once you step into this solipsism you can go round and round without feeling obligated to come out with anything useful.

Some of my friends have tried to explain to me that the world is filled with "S's" and "R's" and it is unrealistic of me to refuse to recognize them. But before they have talked themselves out they become pretty vague about which is which. Others, who are not so concretistic, argue that the formula represents only a relationship between events, not the events themselves. This makes a little more sense, and might continue to make sense if they didn't persist in talking about the matter, rubbing their forefingers across that arrow in the formula. That gets me all confused again, for they seem to be contradicting themselves and saying that it is the *arrow* that expresses the relationship between the events, not the "S" and the "R."

Out of all this I have gradually developed the notion that psychology is pretty much confined to the paradigms it employs and, while you can take off in a great many directions and travel a considerable distance in any of them—as indeed we have with stimulus-response psychology—there is no harm in consorting with a strange paradigm now and then. Indeed the notion has occured to me that psychology may best be regarded as a collection of paradigms wooed by ex-physicists, ex-physiologists, and ex-preachers, as well as a lot of other intellectual renegades. Even more recently it has struck me that this is the nature of man; he is an inveterate collector of paradigms. But now I am getting ahead of myself again.

About three years later, after I had abandoned engineering as a career and had entered graduate school in an effort to learn something about sociology and labor relations, I decided it was high time I had a look at Freud. I can remember the occasion rather well. I was in the northeast corner of the reading room of the library at the University of Kansas. I don't remember which one of Freud's books I was trying to read, but I do remember the mounting feeling of incredulity that anyone could write such nonsense, much less publish it. It was not the pan-sexualism that makes Freud objectionable to some new readers, but the elastic meanings and arbitrary syntax that disturbed me. If I had any misgivings about having abandoned psychology so readily after my first encounters, I had very few regrets after reading Freud that day.

But this is not the end of the story. It might have been the end of the story if what psychologists say about learning and sociologists say about subcultures were true. What happened was that about four years later Dean Seashore, in person, conferred on me the Ph.D. in psychology, prefacing his part of the ceremonies with a little speech about the Doctor of Philosophy Degree being the highest that any university could bestow. The events that filled this transitional period are not particularly relevant to this discussion, except, possibly, the fact that during the interval I had taught soap-box oratory in a labor college for labor organizers, government in an Americanization institute for prospective citizens, public speaking for the American Bankers Association, and dramatics in a junior college, that I had taken a Master's degree with a study of workers' use of leisure time, and an advanced professional degree in education at the University of Edinburgh, and that I had dabbled academically in education, sociology, economics, labor relations, biometrics, speech pathology, and cultural anthropology, and had majored in psychology for a grand total of nine months. This, I might say in case any of you are wondering, is not what I recommend for my own students.

COPING WITH CIRCUMSTANCES

Now, with a doctoral degree and the depression of 1931 on my hands, and with recently acquired aspirations in physiological psychology, I set out with my bride for what was soon to become the notorious dust bowl. During the following twelve years at a small college in western Kansas I had, shall we say, several more priceless opportunities to revise my outlook. I might add that during this time I had a minimum of intellectual interference from my colleagues in psychology, although I did, from time to time, find myself confronted with less formidable obstacles to intellectual progress, the nature of which I shall not inflict upon you.

It did not take many weeks in those depression times to reach the decision to pursue something more humanitarian than physiological psychology. Too many young people were wondering what, if anything, to do with their lives. The schools, only recently established at a secondary level in that part of the state, were only barely functioning as educational institutions, and there were many who thought public education should be abandoned altogether. It was a time for a teacher to talk of courage and adventure in the midst of despair. It was not a time for the "S," the arrow, and the "R"!

Again, let me state my conviction that it was not the circumstances that dictated the conclusions I reached. I could have used the same circumstances to confirm stimulus response psychology. It is to say, rather, that the premises with which I entered the situation no longer were useful to me. Or perhaps it would be more correct to say that it was the actions that derived from my premises that did not seem appropriate. Of course I would still have liked to pursue some exciting hunches I had about physiological psychology, and particularly something which had turned up and I had called "transient aphasia." As a matter of fact, it would have been even more fun to have stayed with my original love of engineering, for I have always found the drafting board an instrument of relaxation.

So why did I at this point turn from the things I spontaneously enjoyed to the heart-breaking tasks of the psychotherapist? Was it the circumstances? I think not. It was I! Was it a sense of inner duty to fellow man? If you mean by that that there was something called "duty" that intruded itself into my life and beckoned me to follow it, then the answer is definitely no. Nothing like that ever happened to me. As a matter of fact, when someone tries to tell me what my duty is I am not likely to take him very seriously, for it seems to me he is probably a busybody who, having failed to make something out of his own circumstances, wants someone else to fulfill his neglected aspirations.

In other words, I do not regard my career in psychology as a "calling." Everything around us "calls," if we choose to heed. Moreover, I have never been completely satisfied that becoming a psychologist was even a very good idea in the first place—a doubt that I am sure some of my colleagues share. The only thing that seems clear about my career in psychology is that it was I who got myself into it and I who have pursued it. But, again, I am ahead of myself, for this is part of the theory whose autobiography I am reciting.

A PSYCHOLOGY OF MAN HIMSELF

It was somewhere around this point in my experience that it occurred to me that what seemed true of myself was probably no less true of others. If I initiated my actions, so did they. I suppose you might say that this position commits me to a psychology of man rather than of his circumstances. It is a psychology concerned with what we do and why we do it, rather than one that attempts to pinpoint the events that compel others to do what they do not choose to do. There is, I suspect, a lot of difference between these two psychologies. But so far, it must be said, there was nothing in my thinking that could be called a full-blown theory of personality—only a kind of convenient posture I assumed toward what confronted me.

But to believe that man is the author of his destiny is not to deny that he may be tragically limited by his circumstances. I saw too many unfortunate youngsters, some of them literally starving in that depression-ridden dust bowl, for me not to be aware of their tragic limitations. Clearly there were many things they might have liked to do that circumstances would not permit. But, nevertheless, this is not to say that they were victims of circumstances. However much there was denied them, there was still an infinity of possibilities open to them. The task was to generate the imagination needed to envision those possibilities. And this is a point of departure for a psychology of man, the canons of Nineteenth Century scientific determinism notwithstanding.

MAN IN TROUBLE

So I listened to people in trouble and I tried to help them figure out what they could do about it. None of the things I had studied or pursued in the years before seemed to have any very specific bearing on what confronted us, though at one time or another through this period I probably attempted to make some use of everything I knew.

Certainly there was not much point in pinning pathological diagnoses on the persons who came to me. That is one of the moves in *the referral game* that some clinical psychologists like to play. But it has to be played in metropolitan areas where there is a suitable proliferation of agencies and specialists on whom you can unload your less profitable clients. In western Kansas when a person came to me we were pretty much stuck with each other. Our job was to figure out what the two of us could do ourselves. Now that I look back on it this was an open invitation to approach psychology from an unconventional angle. And that is what I am afraid I did.

The strangest thing about this period is that I went back to Freud for a second look. My recollections of Rasmussen's *Principal Nervous Pathways* and of Thorndike's electrical condenser theory of learning applied at the synapses had not proved very helpful to people troubled about what was to become of them. But now that I had listened to the language of distress, Freud's writings made a new kind of sense.

That fellow Freud, he was indeed a clinician! He too must have listened to these same cries echoing from deep down where there are no sentences, no words, and no syntax.

So it was that I became a "Freudian," if not by training, at least by persuasion. The Freudian language of explanation provided me with a way of understanding the difficulties of those who came to me for aid, of anticipating their thoughts, and of helping them regain the initiative in their lives. In short, I began to have what I thought was "insight." Through my Freudian interpretations, judiciously offered at those moments when clients seemed ready for them, a good many unfortunate persons seemed to be profoundly helped.

I suppose it is clear that none of this was under psychiatric supervision, nor under any kind of supervision, for that matter. My clients and I were on our own and, while I think I have come a long way since this period in my psychological career, we—my client and I—are still pretty much on our own whenever we buckle down to a difficult problem. It is important that this be understood in order to visualize what happened next.

BEWARE OF THE OBVIOUS

There is something about the obvious things in this world that repeatedly rises to plague me. I know that many persons complain that they are tormented by the uncertainties of life, by its ambiguities, or by the fact that there seem to be no final answers. I think I know how they feel, and to some extent, I am troubled by such things too, though thus far I have no very serious complaints about my uncertainties. But those things I once thought I knew for sure, those are what get me into hot water, time after time. They are a lot more troublesome than those things I have known all along that I didn't understand. Moreover, a world jam-packed with lead pipe certainties, dictionary definitives, and doomsday finalities strikes me as a pretty gloomy place. How can there be any room in a world like that for such a nascent thing as life?

I suppose it would have to be conceded that life in the opposite kind of world—a world of chaos—might seem pretty hopeless after a while. But, as between the two—a world without hopes or a world without doubts—I think, for myself, I would prefer the world without hopes. Of course, I would prefer some of both, hopes and doubts. But, still, if I had to end my life on some final note I think I would like it to be a question, preferably a basic one, well posed and challenging, and beckoning me on to where only others after me may go, rather than a terminal conclusion—no matter how well-documented. There is something exciting about a question, even one you have no reasonable expectation of answering. But a final conclusion, why that is like the stroke of doom; after it—nothing, just nothing at all!

It was with some such thoughts as these in the back of my noggin that I began to be uncomfortable with my Freudian "insights." It was not that they were failing me so much as it was that I felt myself beginning to take them for granted. And ideas, like women, when too long taken for granted are likely to turn fickle.

So I began fabricating "insights." I deliberately offered "preposterous interpretations" to my clients. Some of them were about as un-Freudian as I could make them—first proposed somewhat cautiously, of course, and then, as I began to see what was happening, more boldly. My only criteria were that the explanation account for the crucial facts as the client saw them and that it carry implications for approaching the future in a different way. Now you can see what it meant to me not to be under supervision during this period.

What happened? Well, many of my preposterous explanations worked, some of them surprisingly well. To be sure, the wilder ones fell flat, but a reexamination of the interviews often suggested where the client's difficulty with them lay. Now I would not want to say that as a general rule, my fabricated "insights" worked as well as my Freudian ones. But I can say that some of them out-performed normal expectations.

Perhaps I should add that I have some doubts that this experiment could easily be repeated. Even my friends in western Kansas have picked up some Freudianisms in the past thirty years and if I tried this sort of thing again I might insult their sense of orthodoxy. Certainly many of them would get the impression that I was not much of a psychologist. But in those days psychology was regarded locally as a pretty far-out kind of th'ng anyway, and if I said that a nervous stomach was rebelling against nourishment of all kinds—parental, educational, and nutritional—most of my clients were willing to try to make something of it.

Nowadays, of course, clients have a lot of preconceived sophistries about what has to happen in psychotherapy—notions about authority relationships, sexual potency, mother fixations, etc.—and besides they expect a detailed accounting for all the frustrations of childhood they can remember, as well as all the daily household episodes they can cram into their therapeutic hour. They want their autobiographies thoroughly psychologized—preferably Freudianized, if they can afford a little higher fee—and kept right up to date.

PSYCHOTHERAPY: THE COOPERATIVE VENTURE

Before I go too far with this account I would like it made clear that I do not think a psychologist has the right to exploit his clients. There is a difference between exploitation and doing something unconventional in psychotherapy. Two considerations underlie this difference: first, the client has to be a participant in the experimental venture. He should himself be looking for new solutions emerging out of the experience and just as ready as the therapist to accept disconfirming evidence. What is proposed to him as an interpretation should always be in the form of a hypothesis, not in the form of a natural truth exempt from any human appraisal. In other words it should be clear that the psychologist is his fellow experimenter, not an unctuous priest. Second, both of them should keep themselves, moment by moment, as sensitive as possible to what emerges from the undertaking; no waiting for fifty cases to accumulate before concluding that your method has brought half of them to the brink of suicide.

There is something else, too. The therapist should do his best to prepare himself for the kind of responsibility he carries. This, as you can now readily see, means training himself as a scientist, not merely as a practitioner. It seems to me that the extensive training of therapists in theory and technique only, and failing to demonstrate scientific methodology as an actual interview-room procedure, is itself unethical. Only as the therapist approaches his client's problem as a scientist, and invites his client to do the same to the limit of his ability, can he avoid the tyranny of dogmatism and the professional exploitation of his clients.

It is much more feasible to get this kind of training now than it was thirty years ago, although a lot of the most prestigious preparation today seems to me to unfit the therapist for joining his client in a truly sensitive and humble exploration of the world. Too often the training substitutes doctrine for inquiry; it makes the therapist feel respectable rather than responsible—and there is a lot of difference between the two.

SOMETHING TO GO ON

As a result of this exploration of preposterous explanations, I developed the notion that what many clients needed was something they could use to give them a fresh approach to life, some explanation they could employ to cover a rather large number of future contingencies. While it might be helpful if the new constructions of events covered the original complaints, I was not at all sure this was essential. And when I say that what is needed is something to facilitate the composed anticipation of contingent events, I would like it to be clear that I refer to internal events such as those we commonly call "feelings," as well as to external events.

About this possibility of ignoring the original complaints; I reached this hypothesis more or less by accident. It came about in this way. After a time the requests for psychological help exceeded my spare hours. This was not particularly surprising. So it was that often, after listening to a person describe his difficulties, I had to explain to him that it would be months before I could see him.

It occurred to me that I had some responsibility to suggest some things he might do while waiting his turn. Sometimes this took the form of reminding him that there were others in distress too, and there were certain kinds of things that anyone might do to be helpful. This was not intended to "cure" him, but was merely something that needed to be done and he might as well make himself useful while waiting to see me. Besides, his contribution would be a measure of how much he wanted help for himself. I might add at this point that I charged no fees. In fact, after more than thirty years, I have still to collect my first fee for psychotherapeutic services.

To my surprise, a considerable number of these persons, when they were finally told their turn had come, reported either that they no longer felt the need for help, or that they had come to realize that other persons they knew needed it more than they, and that therefore they were willing to wait a few weeks longer. Most of them said that what they had done in the meantime had put their problem in a new perspective.

It was not so much that they had been "cured" by the experience, but that their troubles, though still with them, no longer seemed unmanagable. By this time I knew what most therapists have observed—that this kind of statement is often about what you get from so-called successfully treated clients, and that it actually suggests a better prognosis than the euphoric claims that some clients make in their fervent "flights into health."

Whether this means that my clients, whose treatment had been postponed and who made themselves useful in the meantime, were actually "therapized" by their altruistic efforts is a question I am not prepared to answer. It may not even be a very good question. What the experience does suggest is that the new structure that emerges from psychotherapy may not need to cover the old complaints at all. Indeed psychotherapy may not even need to deal with that elusive entity called "the self," regarded by so many of our colleagues as the focal point of their efforts.

THE ROLE OF DISPROOF

There was something else that began to dawn on me at this time, though I did not attempt to put it into words until years later. It is the notion that one does not have to disprove one proposition before entertaining one of its alternatives. A lost of footless controversy between scientists could be avoided if this possibility were explored. Each could go about his business without distraction long enough to see what he could turn up on his own, without becoming embroiled in controversy with his colleagues.

The same is probably true of all of us. One way of life need not be invalidated before the outcomes of another are examined. If a person in psychotherapy can free himself from the indicative moods of our language system long enough to entertain some novel hypotheses about other ways of living, he can save himself and his therapist a lot of trouble overcoming the "resistances" and "false premises" of his previous outlook. Therapy could then become concerned with alternatives instead of involving the participants in long, intricate, and reductionistic analyses designed to disabuse the client of his "neurotic" notions.

WORDS AND DEEDS

It is a short step from this psychological vantage point to which my psychotherapeutic efforts had thus far led me and the next idea in the sequence. But it took a long time to take that step—it took *me* a long time, that is.

Moreno's writings, when they began to come out in the 1930's, seemed intriguing to me as well as to others, particularly what he had to say about psychodrama. But whereas psychodrama for him led back into the classical personality theories implied in Greek drama, just as Freud's clinical experiences reminded him of classical themes, I was led no further back than to the development of the extemporaneous theater out of "method acting" in Europe after World War I. I suppose, too, in some way I may have been thinking about the James-Lange Theory of Emotion.

In any case I began to pursue the notion that one's current acts and undertakings might have as much to do with the development of his personality as did the imprint of the events with which he came in contact or the insights he was able to conjure up with the help of his therapist. To put it very simply, man was shaped by his commitments and what he did to fulfill them. Even a momentary commitment, experienced for no more than a fleeting instant during a psychotherapeutic interview or in a split second in some fast-breaking emergency on the highway might make a lifetime of difference.

There is much in man's social history that confirms this idea. It is said that the United States Presidency may make a statesman out of a politician, provided he commits himself to it. Professional controls may also make the man who dedicates himself to professional objectives. More than one of us has assumed the ways of scholarship by first undertaking the responsibilities of teaching.

But closely allied to these concepts of role commitment was something else that came to my attention in the late 1930's. Korzybski's newly published *Science and Sanity* raised questions about the ways in which language and thought are interrelated. His ideas about general semantics seemed to me to fit not only my own experiences in psychotherapy, but also what I thought I saw in psychodrama.

Not only did it seem that the words man uses give and hold the structure of his thought, but, more particularly, the names by which he calls himself give and hold the structure of his personality. Each of us invests his name with a particular kind of meaning. It has been so for thousands of years. The man who knew himself as "Saul" became the man who martyred himself as "Paul," perhaps in a way that would have been impossible if he had persisted in identifying himself as "Saul." Women, whose marriages confronted them with particular difficulties in complementing their husbands' lives, were greatly aided in the transition by the change in their names. I had seen this happen in cases where I had some intimate knowledge of what the woman had to overcome. Moreover, those professions which supposedly required the greatest sublimation of personal impulses often made the task easier for their members by attaching some title such as "Reverend" or "Doctor" to the man's name. This bit of disidentification with the rest of humanity does not, of course, work in all cases.

It is not, I am sure, that there is any special magic in names—only the magic that we invest in them. Behind the name is the identity that we put there. To the extent that we remain faithful to that identity we remain faithful to the name, and vice versa. If the identity is to be changed it does, of course, require more than a mere change in name. But the change in name, along with all the other terms of one's identity can have profound psychological implications.

SOMETHING MORE

But now where are we? We have seen persons change as a result of carrying out new commitments and we have seen them change as a consequence of their redefinitions of themselves. But enlightening as these glimpses of what a viable psychology of man might be, it still seems as if the objective eludes our grasp. How often the client in psychotherapy says, in effect, "I see what I want to do; I see now how to do it and where; and I see how someone like me could step out into an entirely new way of life; but I cannot picture myself— *me*—ever becoming anything other than what I am."

It hardly seems enough to say that such a person lacks "emotional insight," or even to say that there is something wrong with "the boundaries of his ego." Nor is it adequate to argue that his thoughts are straightened out, but not his behavior. There must be something more than emotion, thought, and behavior that goes to make the man. To find this "something" is the challenge of psychology, though I doubt that very many psychologists see it this way. And so this particular venture that started with the "S," the arrow, and the "R" on the classroom blackboard continued to blunder on its way, without, I am afraid, any very respectable identification with the mainstream of American psychology.

But howsoever thoughts may fail to progress, one's circumstances move ahead without waiting for him. So it was with me. With the unsolicited help of some legislators in western Kansas and the gratuitous opposition of the State's most prominent psychiatrist we were given a thousand dollars a year to conduct traveling psychological clinics. Mostly these clinics were sponsored by schools, though occasion-ally other agencies took the initiative, including, I am happy to say, some county medical societies which, while they characteristically found it difficult to cooperate on an equalitarian basis in any community enterprise, did have a certain intimate appreciation of the personal distress of the families on whom they made house calls.

MOTIVES AND COMPLAINTS

One of the salient features of this state-wide experience was the opportunity to examine the language of complaint used by teachers, parents, children, and others. Each person seeks to communicate his distress in the terms that make sense to him, but not necessarily in terms that make sense to others or to the person complained about. The result is a great deal of misunderstanding in psychological matters. Teachers do not understand how their pupils feel, pupils are unable to sympathize with their teachers' frustrations, and neither is able to put himself into the shoes of parents.

After a time it became abundantly clear that a complaint, as for example a teacher's complaint about a child, reflected primarily the disruption in her own life and did not necessarily state the issue or provide adequate grounds for approaching the person complained about. A teacher might complain that a child was "lazy," but when asked to observe him for several days to see how he went about being "lazy," come up with a description of some very active and purposeful behavior. "Laziness," then, although attributed to the child, had as its principal referrent, as far as the psychologist was concerned, the frustration the teacher experienced in trying to get the child to join her in something she thought they ought to be doing.

There was something more that came out of this experience—one of many more things, in fact. An analysis of the context of the language of complaint suggested that all of us are inclined to use motivational terms, such as "laziness," when others do not do what we think they should, and sometimes even when we do not do what we think we should. Yet it is neither accurate nor descriptive to say that someone does nothing at all. So with all motivational terms—they lose their descriptive value when one becomes intimate with what is going on in the world of another person.

Thus our state-wide travels brought us face-to-face with a strange paradox: the more we understood what was actually happening the less useful was our lexicon of psychodynamic terms. Already we had come a long way from Freud, even further than we then suspected. But nonetheless our next step was to be bolder than any we had yet taken.

AN EXPERIMENT IN LIVING

What if a person thinks he is neurotic—or even is neurotic—does he have to act that way, or continue to live that way? This may not be a well-posed question, but it was with some such proposition as this in our minds that my students and I undertook a radical approach to psychotherapy. Radical, but perhaps not altogether new!

Having observed that man often makes something of himself by undertaking a commitment—even a commitment undertaken without full conviction—and having observed that many of us refuse to budget from our neurotic positions without first stretching out a safety net of rationalizations—and hence never succeed in making anything of ourselves at all—it occurred to us that the key to therapy might be in getting the client to get on with a new way of life without waiting to acquire "insight." After all, is not that the way man has been treating himself for thousands of years? Rarely does one know where he is going when he launches out into a new way of life, and even less often does he know what is wrong with the pathway he abandons. It is only in a semantically rationalized and elaborately psychologized society that one insists on knowing all the *whys* before seeking to experience the *whats*.

So we set about asking each client to write a self-characterization and to Q-sort the Maller Inventory cards containing self-descrptive statements. This was before the days of the Minnesota Multi-Phasic Inventory and before this kind of task was called Q-sorting. Then a group of three or four of us would take this information and write another sketch, as it might have been written by another person. Embodied in this sketch of ours would be a different outlook and some illustrations of how such an outlook led to characteristic social behavior. The therapist would then take this sketch back to the client, ask him to pretend that he was the other person, for perhaps two weeks, rehearse the part with him every day or two, and invite the client to pay particular attention to the results of the experiment.

There was, of course, a good deal more to it than play acting. We soon realized that there were tricks to writing the new role, ways of setting up real-life situations, and, particularly, a framework for presenting the undertaking to a skeptical and usually reluctant client who would ordinarily prefer to talk about himself. This is not the place to go into detail as to how this fixed-role therapy, as we have come to call it, was carried out. Let me say only that it produced some exciting results. A little later on in this account I shall come back to it and attempt to say what I think the experience contributed to the devlopment of the theory whose autobiography I am pretending to write.

AN AFTERNOON WITH THE OBVIOUS

It is commonly said that the clinician at his best is an artist and not a scientist, and that the scientist at his best is a man of cold intellect without passion or empathy. Sometimes it is conceded that the clinician might be regarded as an applied scientist, that is to say, a technician who takes what the true scientist has discovered and exploits it for the benefit of fellow man. But most psychologists believe that the scientist and the clinician are really two quite different kinds of persons.

Perhaps I have described enough of my experiences to make it clear that this distinction between the clinician and the scientist runs counter to what I have seen. Whatever progress I may have made in shaking loose from the old notions and in developing novel hypotheses out of intimate experience with man in distress was progress in science, and, as I soon hope to make clear, what I did as a clinician emerged out of my thinking more or less in the manner of a scientist. Indeed I suspect that the best scientist is one who approaches his subject intimately as a clinician may be expected to approach it, and the best clinician is one who invites his client to join him in a controlled investigation of life. Nowhere, it seems to me, is this intrinsic relationship more basic than in psychology, and no discipline stands to lose more by failing to recognize it.

One of my tasks in the 1930's was to direct graduate studies leading to the Master's degree. A typical afternoon might find me talking to a graduate student at one o'clock, doing all those familiar things that thesis directors have to do—encouraging the student to pinpoint the issues, to observe, to become intimate with the problem, to form hypotheses either inductively or deductively, to make some preliminary test runs, to relate his data to his predictions, to control his experiments so that he will know what led to what, to generalize cautiously, and to revise his thinking in the light of experience.

At two o'clock I might have an appointment with a client. During this interview I would not be taking the role of the scientist, but rather helping the distressed person work out some solutions to his life's problems. So what would I do? Why, I would try to get him to pinpoint the issues, to observe, to become intimate with the problem, to form hypotheses, to make test runs, to relate outcomes to anticipations, to control his ventures so that he will know what led to what, to generalize cautiously, and to revise his dogma in the light of experience.

At three o'clock I would see a student again. Likely as not he was either dragging his feet, hoping to design some world-shaking experiment before looking at his first subject to see first-hand what he was dealing with, or plunging into some massive ill-considered data-chasing expedition. So I would again try to get him to pinpoint the issues, to observe open-mindedly, to become intimate with the problem, to form hypotheses—all the things that I had had to do at one o'clock.

At four o'clock another client! Guess what! He would be dragging his feet, hoping to design a completely new personality before venturing his first change in behavior, or plunging into some ill-considered acting-out escapade, etc., etc. But this, of course, was not my hour for science; it was my hour for psychotherapy. And what I had done with that student back in the hour before, that was obviously not psychotherapy; it was science!

I must say that this sort of thing went on for a long time before it ever occurred to me that I was really doing the same sort of thing all afternoon long. It seems incredible now that it took me so long to realize this, but at the time it seemed so perfectly obvious that science and psychotherapy were different, even contrasting kinds of experience. Science was objective and cold; psychotherapy was subjective and warm. Science dealt with truth but psychotherapy dealt with humanity. But, as I have said before, all my life it has been the obvious things that have gotten me into trouble! I have even speculated that man's greatest challenge and noblest undertaking may be to transcend the obvious. And that is something I wish I knew how to do.

RIGHT-HAND AND LEFT-HAND THEORIES
OF PERSONALITY

There was something else that was slow in dawning on me. I must tell you about that before attempting to distill something out of blunt fixed-role therapy and my afternoons with the obvious.

Almost any textbook written before 1940, and, indeed, most of the textbooks in elementary psychology turned out in the decades since, made quite an issue out of psychology's being a science. Generally psychologists have emphasized the point that science is characterized more by its method than by its accumulated body of knowledge. This being so, they argue, psychology is really pretty scientific stuff, even though it does not have many solid facts to point to. In fact, psychologists, being self-conscious about their methodology, may have a wee bit better claim to being scientists than a lot of physicists who spend their time making engineering hay out of a few classic experiments.

In order to clarify what they meant the authors of these psychology texts would describe the essentials of scientific method, which is, as we all know, the inside story of how the scientist behaves. This fellow called the scientist pinpoints the issues, they said, he observes, he becomes intimate with the problem, he forms hypothesis inductively and deductively, he makes test runs, he relates his data to predictions, he controls his experiments so that he knows what leads to what, he generalizes cautiously, and he revises his thinking in the light of experimental outcomes. These are the operations that explain the behavior of a person who has achieved the status of a scientist. All of this is very interesting, particularly because it represents a particularly coherent theory of personality, albeit one that is reserved for scientists only.

But now, as the author of our textbook turns from his credentials to his contributions, he abandons this perceptive theory of personality and starts to tell us how ordinary human beings, which he usually prefers to call "organisms" rather than "scientists," function. In doing so he spins an altogether different kind of personality theory, or perhaps two or three such theories. Man, the organism, he says, responds to stimuli, learns what he is taught, is propelled by his motives, is helplessly suspended in his culture, and is swept along with the tides of social change.

Now that I look back on it I cannot understand how one could have failed to be struck immediately by the contrast in personality theories espoused by the same psychologist; on the one hand, the one he universally uses to explain himself and, on the other, the various concoctions he uses to explain ordinary mortals. Yet few of my colleagues find this paradox amusing. They say, "But of course the scientist is different!" But I must admit also that it was a long time before I myself became aware of this inconsistency, and perhaps if I had been more of a psychologist it would have been even longer.

Now it seems that it might prove interesting to do one of two things: either apply to psychologists themselves the psychologies they designed to explain the behavior of ordinary mortals, or to apply to man the psychology they designed to explain themselves. Since there are a lot more mortals in this world than there are psychologists, for the time being at least, we might run into more possibilities if we tried the latter. If we do so, then it may be said that our model of man is that of man-the-scientist and our questions will revolve about the issue of whether man can be understood in this manner, both in the floodlight of history and in the dark of his closet.

It has been only recently in my professional life that I have been willing to regard myself as either a philosopher or a theoretician in any measure whatsoever. A long time ago, however, I fell to fancying myself as a scientist of sorts. Now I am quite prepared to concede that I may not be very much of any of these, but at least nowadays if someone describes me as a personality theorist I do not protest as vigorously as I might have twenty years ago.

From time to time I wrote chapters and prepared condensed drafts of a handbook of clinical techniques for my students. But the serious writing always bogged down because it seemed as if I should say why something should be done as well as how to do it. Moreover I was confronted with the growing realization that I had got out of step with a good deal of the psychological thinking of my times and therefore my reasons for doing things in certain ways would not make much sense to my colleagues, even in cases where our techniques might happen to be identical.

How far out of the mainstream of psychology had I drifted and what was there about this outlook I had developed that was essentially unique? It seemed as if I were overdue for some extensive self-examination, and perhaps an overhaul. Could I state my position in a coherent fashion and, if I could, would it be something that would open any new vistas and stand up to the demands of rigorous testing?

I suppose the issue I faced was: could I put into words what I meant and, if I could, would I still mean it? As I describe these meanderings in the maze of human distress, as I now remember them, it may appear to my reader or listener that there are some converging lines of thought. Take the last two things I have mentioned—the afternoon of interviews alternating between psychotherapy and advice to researchers, and the two kinds of personality theory each textbook writer espoused. Both suggest that, in practice, the struggles of man the mortal and man the scientist were against the same obstacles and that those obstacles were to be surmounted in what has proved over the centuries to be the human way. And as we look back on our iconoclastic ventures with fixed-role therapy we can see these also as fitting into a personality theory that says, in effect, that the means by which man has, over the centuries, coped most successfully with his historical obstacles are in some general way the basic devices he can extend and improve in coping with his personal distress.

Fixed-role therapy is, according to this model, not a panacea but an experiment. In fact, we have learned that if it is presented as a panacea it fails its purpose and the client does not get on with the life process of finding out for himself. So do all panaceas tend to immobilize man at those moments when he ought to be exploring his alternatives creatively. The important thing about the fixed-role enactment is not that it gives the person an authentic way to live, but that it invites him to try a new way, calculated and venturesome, and to appraise its outcomes. Certainly the role as written may not turn out well at all. But that is true of the attempts of any life that is approached wholeheartedly. Not all the new things men try prove to be good, but, if nothing is ever tried, then even the old ways, which once might have been regarded as good, will become oppressively stagnant. The only valid way to live one's life is to get on with it.

Man lives best when he commits himself to getting on with his life. Since I see the concept of learning as nothing less than this, the term seems redundant when applied to a living creature. And so, too, with the objectives of therapy, for therapy is a way of helping man get on with it, to live wholeheartedly. However, if you prefer to call the whole thing "learning" then I have no objection to this use of the term—as long as its meaning is now narrowed down to something less than life's basic enterprise by the textbook writers.

THE OUTCOME

This account is intended to describe the course of certain psychological experiences, as I now remember them, which led to the formulation of a particular position in psychology I have called *personal construct theory*. I should say also that as a result of trying to cope with these experiences I seem to have brought myself to a philosophical position for which I can think of no better term than *constructive alternativism*. When it appeared that clients in therapy could often make good use of my preposterous explanations and when it occurred to me that it was not necessary, or even desirable, to refute one proposition before investigating its alternatives—as one does not refute the old self in fixed-role therapy before inviting participation in the experiment—I was groping toward such a philosophical position.

To be sure, personal construct theory can be expounded in the conventionally logical manner. It has a basic postulate and a set of corollaries. And it has some constructs that arise from the pursuit of its implications. All this, if it were expounded, would make it seem more or less rational, I suppose. I know this is what a theorist is expected to do. But I am convinced that this is not the way theories happen. Certainly it is not the way personal construct theory came into being.

What I have done, therefore, is tell you how this theory happened. Or perhaps it would be more accurate to say that this is how, in retrospect, I think it happened. If I had kept a diary I might be surprised at what I would actually now find written there—perhaps something quite different from what I remember.

3

Man's Construction of his Alternatives

THIS PAPER, throughout, deals with half-truths only. Nothing that it contains is, or is intended to be, wholly true. The theoretical statements propounded are no more than partially accurate constructions of events which, in turn, are no more than partially perceived. Moreover, what we propose, even in its truer aspects, will eventually be overthrown and displaced by something with more truth in it. Indeed, our theory is frankly designed to contribute effectively to its own eventual overthrow and displacement.

We think this is a good way for psychologists to theorize. When a scientist propounds a theory he has two choices: he can claim that what he says has been dictated to him by the real nature of things, or he can take sole responsibility for what he says and claim only that he has offered one man's hopeful construction of the realities of nature. In the first instance he makes a claim to objectivity in behalf of his theory, the scientist's equivalent of a claim to infallibility. In the second instance he offers only the hope that he may have hit upon some partial truth that may serve as a clue to inventing something better and he invites others to follow this clue to see what they can make of it. In this latter instance he does not hold up his theoretical proposal to be judged so much in terms of whether it is the truth

SOURCE. This paper appeared first in Lindzey, G. (Ed.), *The Assessment of Human Motives*. New York: Holt, Rinehart, Winston, 1958. Acknowledgment is made of the kind permission of the Editor and Publisher to include this paper.

at last or not—for he assumes from the outset that ultimate truth is not so readily at hand—but to be judged in terms of whether his proposition seems to lead toward and give way to fresh propositions; propositions which, in turn, may be more true than anything else has been thus far.

One of the troubles with what are, otherwise, good theories in the various fields of science is the claim to infallibility that is so often built into their structure. Even those theories which are built upon objective observation or upon first-hand experience make this claim by their failure to admit that what is observed is not revealed but only construed. In fact, the more objectively supported the theory at the time of its inception, the more likely it is to cause trouble after it has served its purpose. A conclusion supported by the facts is likely to be a good one at the time it is drawn. But, because facts themselves are open to reconstruction, such a theory soon becomes a dogmatism that may serve only to blind us to new perceptions of the facts.

Take, for example, the body of theoretical assumptions that Freud propounded out of his experience with psychoanalysis. There was so much truth in what he said—so much new truth. But like most theories of our times, psychoanalysis, as a theory, was conceived as an absolute truth, and, moreover, it was designed in such a manner that it tended to defy both logical examination and experimental validation. As the years go by, Freudianism, which deserves to be remembered as a brave outpost on the early frontier of psychological thought, is condemned to end its days as a crumbling stockade of proprietary dogmatism. Thus, as with other farseeing claims to absolute truth, history will have a difficult time deciding if Freudianism did more to accelerate psychological progress during the first half of the Twentieth Century than it did to impede progress during the last half.

This business of absolutism in modern science and the havoc it creates is a matter that has been given a good deal of thought in recent decades. It has been attacked on several fronts. First of all, modern science has itself attacked dogmatism through its widespread use of the method of experimentation. But experimentation, if assumed to be a way of receiving direct revelations from nature, can often be found living quite happily side by side with dogmatisms of the lowest order.

There is nothing especially revelational about events that happen in a laboratory—other events that happen elsewhere are just as real and are just as worth taking account of. Even the fact that an event took place in a manner predicted by the experimenter gives it no particular claim to being a special revelation from nature. If an experimenter's predictions come true, it means only that he has hit upon one of many possible systems for making predictions that come true. He may be no more than a wee bit closer to a genuine understanding of things as they really are. Indeed, the fact that he has hit upon one such way of predicting outcomes may even blind him to alternatives which might have proved far more productive in the long run.

Absolutism is coming under other forms of attack. It has been pointed out, for example, that the subject-predicate form of our Indo-European languages has led us to confound objects with what is said about them. Thus every time we open our mouths to say something, we break forth with a dogmatism. Each sentence, instead of sounding like a proposal of an idea to be examined in the light of personal experience, echoes through the room like the disembodied rumblings of an oracle. Even as we try to describe a theory of personal constructions of events, one that stands in contrast to theories that claim to spring from events directly, we are caught up in the assumptions and structure of the very language upon which we depend for communication. In view of this fact, we can think of no better way of disclaiming the assumptions of our language than by introducing this paper with the paradoxical statement that we are proposing half-truths only.

A second feature of this paper is its outright repudiation of the notion of motivation. Since the topic of the conference stories, in which we have been so graciously invited to participate, is "The Assessment of Human Motives," such a repudiation may appear to be in bad taste. It seems a little like being honored with an invitation to preach a sermon in church, and then taking advantage of the solemn occasion in order to present the case for atheism. Yet the forthcoming volume on the assessment of human motives may not lose flavor from this kind of seasoning. Perhaps one chapter of heresy may even strengthen the reader's convictions about human motives, just as an occasional rousing speech on atheism might do more than a monotony of sermons to bring a church congregation face-to-face with its own convictions—or lack of them.

Certainly the repudiation of "motives" as a construct is a major undertaking, not to be ventured into without giving some thought to its consequences. For a period roughly corresponding to the Christian era, metaphysics, including psychology, has conceptualized its spiritual realm in terms of a trichotomy just as Christianty has envisioned itself in terms of a trinity. The classic trichotomy is variously called by such terms as cognition, conation, and affection; or intellect, will, and emotion; or even, in somewhat more modern terms, thought, action and feeling. Psychologists keep coming back to this trichotomous division, perhaps because they have never been able to venture beyond it. For us to say now that we propose to abandon motives will seem to many listeners to be a kind of unforgivable sin, something like the unforgivable sin of rejecting the Holy Ghost.

In the classic psychological trichotomy, cognition, on the one hand, has been viewed as a realm governed by verbalized rationality, while affection, on the other, has been viewed as a very chaotic, though often pleasant place, where inarticulate irrationality is in command. Conation, the middle category which deals with behavior or determination to act, has been caught between the other two, sometimes believed to be swayed by the rationality of the cognitive mind, but at other times, suspected of having a secret allegiance to the whimsical irrationality of feeling and emotion.

Because the topic of motivation falls into this disputed area where modern man has had such a difficult time reconciling rationality with irrationality, we propose to start our serious discussion at this particular point. We would like to deal with those matters which are called rational—and, therefore, by quirk of our language structure assumed actually to be rational—together with those matters which are called irrational—for the same reason—both in the very same psychological terms. In doing so we shall, if our previous experiences repeat themselves, be perceived by some as capitulating to the classic rationalism of Thomas Aquinas, and by others as giving hostages to the supposed intuitive irrationality of Freud, Rogers, or Sullivan. Not that we really mind being bracketed with any of these great names; but rather the burden of our comments, it seems to us, rests on other grounds.

This is the risk we take. Why? Why will some see this as conforming to classical rationality and others see it as lapsing into irrationality? We have already mentioned the tendency to confound objects with what is said about them. Some philosophers, Bertrand Russell being possibly the first and foremost, have seen this tendency to confound words and facts as being embedded in the subject-predicate structure of our language. But it involves also the highly questionable *law of the excluded middle*, a law accepted as a basic principle of logic for the past twenty-four hundred years, though now under sporadic attack.

What this law proposes is that for any proposition there is only one alternative. I call an object a spade. There is only one alternative to calling it a spade—to call it not a spade! I can't say, "to heck with it," or "who cares," or "who brought that up," or that the object cannot be sensibly called either a spade or not a spade; I have to

stick with one or the other. Once the object is accused of being a
spade it has to plead innocent or guilty, or I have to plead its innocence
or guilt in its behalf.

Now if we combine this dictum with the subject-predicate mode
of thought we put ourselves in a stringent position with respect to
our world. We call an object a spade. Not only do we, therefore, imply
that it is a spade because we cannot say that it is not a spade, but
we put the onus of choosing between the two alternatives on the object
itself. We disclaim responsibility for our propositions and try to make
the objects we talk about hang themselves on the horns of the dilemmas
we invent for dealing with them. If a woman is accused of being
a witch, she has to be either a witch or not a witch—it is up to her.
The speaker disclaims all responsibility for the dilemma he has imposed
upon her.

For centuries Western Man has roamed his world impaling every
object he has met on the horns of the dilemmas he chose to fashion
out of his language. In fact, an individual, if he was very bright and
had a vocabulary well stocked with psychological terms, could do a
pretty substantial job of impaling himself. Recently so many people
have learned to do it in so many ingenious ways that it appears that
half the world will have to be trained in psychotherapy in order to
keep the other half off its own hooks. Yet, even at that, it may be
what most of the psychotherapists are doing is lifting people off one
set of hooks and hanging them on other more comfortable, more socially
acceptable, hooks.

Let us see if we can make this point a little clearer. For example,
on occasion I may say of myself—in fact, on occasion I *do* say of
myself—"I am an introvert." "I," the subject, "am an introvert," the
predicate. The language form of the statement clearly places the onus
of being an introvert on the subject—me. What I actually am, the
words say, is an introvert.

The listener, being the more or less credulous person to whom
I make the statement, says to himself, "So George Kelly is an introvert—I always suspected he was." Or he may say, "Him an introvert?
He's no introvert," a response which implies scarcely less credulity
on the part of my listener. Yet the proper interpretation of my statement is that *I construe* myself to be an introvert, or, if I am merely
being coy or devious, I am inveigling *my listener into construing me*
in terms of introversion. The point that gets lost in the shuffle of
words is the psychological fact that I have identified myself in terms
of a personal construct—"introversion." If my listener is uncritical
enough to be taken in by this quirk of language, he may waste a

lot of time either in believing that he must construe me as an introvert or in disputing the point.

In clinical interviewing, and particularly in psychotherapeutic interviewing, when the clinician is unable to deal with such a statement as a personal construction rather than as fact or fallacy, the hour is likely to come to a close with both parties annoyed with each other and both dreading their next appointment. But more than this, if I say of myself that I am an introvert, I am likely to be caught in my own subject-predicate trap. Even the inner self—my self—becomes burdened with the onus of actually being an introvert or of finding some way to be rid of the introversion that has climbed on my back. What has happened is that I named myself with a name and, having done so, too quickly forgot who invented the name and what he had on his mind at the time. From now on I try frantically to cope with what I have called myself. Moreover, my family and friends are often quite willing to join in the struggle.

Now back specifically to the law of the excluded middle. Here, too, we find a failure to take into account a psychological fact, the fact that human thought is essentially constructive in nature and that even the thinking of logicians and mathematicians is no exception. I say that I am an introvert, whatever that is. If I now go ahead and apply the law of the excluded middle, I come up with the dilemma that I must continue to claim either to be an introvert or not an introvert—one or the other. But is this necessarily so: may not introversion turn out to be a construct which is altogether irrelevant? If it is not relevant is it any more meaningful to say that I am not an introvert than to say that I am? Yet classical logic fails to make any distinction between its negatives and its irrelevancies; while modern psychology ought to make it increasingly clear to each of us that no proposition has more than a limited range of relevance, beyond which it makes no sense either to affirm or deny. So we now ought to visualize propositions which are not universal in their range of application but useful only within a restricted range of convenience. For each proposition, then, we see three alternatives, not two: it can be affirmed, it can be denied, or it can be declared irrelevant in the context to which it is applied. Thus, we argue, not for the inclusion of the long excluded middle—something between the yes and the no—but for a third possibility that is beyond the meaningful range of yes and no.

Apply this more psychological way of thinking to the proposition, "I am an introvert." Instead of lying awake trying to decide whether I am or am not an introvert, or taking frantic steps, as so many do, to prove that I am not, I simply go off to sleep with the thought that, until the construct of introversion is demonstrated to be of some practical usefulness in my case, there is no point of trying to decide whether I am or not or what to do about it if I am. Thus we treat the subject-predicate problem and the excluded middle problem in pretty much the same way—we insist on demonstrating relevance before we lose any sleep over a proposition.

Let us try to summarize our criticisms of the two features of Western thought which have gone unchallenged for more than two thousand years. First of all, there is the dogmatism of subject-predicate language structure that is often presented under the guise of objectivity. According to this dogmatism, when I say that Professor Lindzey's left shoe is an "introvert," everyone looks at his shoe as if this were something his shoe was responsible for. Or if I say that Professor Cattell's head is "discursive," everyone looks over at him, as if the proposition had popped out of his head instead of out of mine. Don't look at his head! Don't look at that shoe! Look at me; I'm the one who is responsible for the statement. After you figure out what I mean you can look over there to see if you make any sense out of shoes and heads by construing them the way I do. It will not be easy to do this, for it means abandoning one of the most ancient way of thinking and talking to ourselves.

As far as the law of the excluded middle in this particular context is concerned, it does not matter whether a person has ever heard of this law or not, or whether he has ever sat down to puzzle out a similar notion on his own. The law is an everyday feature of nearly every educated man's more intellectualized thought processes. The law says, assuming that the term "introvert" ever has meaning, that that shoe, at which we looked a moment ago, has to be construed either as an introvert or as not an introvert; it has simply got to be seen as one or the other. There is no middle ground.

Some people argue against the law of the excluded middle by claiming that the shoe could be a little introvertish, but not completely introvert, or that it could be a little nonintrovertish, though not wholly nonintrovert. This is the notion of shades of gray that can be perceived between black and white. But this notion of reifying the excluded middle by talking about grays is not what we are proposing. In fact, we see this gray thinking as a form of concretism that merely equivocates and fails to get off the ground into the atmosphere of abstraction.

What we are saying, instead, is that "introversion" may well enough be a term that has meaning in some contexts, but that it does not go well with shoes. Since it does not apply to shoes, it makes no more sense to say that Professor Lindzey's left shoe is not an intro-

vert than to say that it is. Thus we see three possibilities, not two
as the law would insist: the shoe is an introvert; the shoe is not an
introvert; and the shoes do not fall within the context of the construct
of introversion versus nonintroversion. The third possibility is not a
middle proposition in any intermediate sense, but rather a kind of
outside, beyond the pale, kind of proposition.

So much for a summary of this section of our discourse. In spite
of our criticsms let us not say that the inadequacies we have pointed
out prevented our language and thought from leading us along a path
of progress. Remember that we believe that half-truths serve to pave
the way toward better truths. Time spent with a half-truth is not
necessarily wasted; it may have been exceedingly profitable. In order
to appreciate a half-truth one has to examine two things: what it replaced, and what it led up to. Let us see what the kind of thing we
have been criticizing actually replaced. Let us compare it with more
primitive modes of language and thought.

Western thinking, which has pretty much overrun the world recently, takes the very practical view that a word is beholden to the
object it is used to describe. The object determines it. This is a moderate
improvement over the so-called magical way of thinking which has
it that the object is beholden to the word. The improvement has been
the basis of scientific thinking, particularly the experimentalism that
has psychologists and others bubbling with so much excitement these
days.

Let us see how the improvement works. Say the word and the
object will jump out at you—that is magical thinking; very bad! Prod
the object and the word will jump out at you—that is objective thinking; very good! Worth publishing! Say "Genie, come genie" and hope
that a genie will pop out of the bottle—that is magical; no good! Kick
the bottle until either a genie pops out or does not pop out—now
that is *science!*

But there is something one can do besides shouting, "Genie, come
genie," or kicking the bottle through a series of statistically controlled
experiments. He can ask himself, and the other people who have
worked themselves up over the genie business, just what they are trying
to get at. This is what the skilled psychotherapist does in dealing with
the thoughts of man. It is based on the notion that "genie" is a construct
that someone erected in order to find his way through a maze of events.
The approach is not a substitute for experimentation but a useful pre-
lude to it. It is a proper substitute, however, for random measurement
of verbalizations.

This is the way we see the matter: magical thinking has it that the object is beholden to the word—when the word is spoken the object must produce itself. So-called objective thinking, under which it has been possible to make great scientific progress, says that the word is beholden to the object—kick the bottle to validate the word. If, however, we build our sciences on a recognition of the psychological nature of thought we take a third position—the word is beholden to the person who utters it, or, more properly speaking, to the *construction* system, that complex of personal constructs of which it is a part.

This concern with personal meaning should prove no less valuable to the scientist than it has to the psychotherapist. It stems from the notion that when a person uses a word he is expressing, in part, his own construction of events. One comes to understand the communication, therefore, not by assuming the magical existence of the word's counterpart in reality and then invoking that counterpart by incantation; nor does he understand it by scrounging through a pile of accumulated facts to see if one of them will own up to the word, but rather he understands the communication by examining the personal construction system within which the word arose and came to have intimate meaning for the individual who attempted to communicate.

How does this apply to motives? We have already said that we do not even use the term as a part of our own construction system, yet it enters our system, perforce, as a matter to be construed. If one catches his friends in the act of using such a term as "motives," how does he act? Does he put his fingers in his ears? Does he start kicking the bottle of reality to see if it produces the phenomenon? If it fails shall he accuse his friends of irrationality? We think not.

Again, if we so much as start to inquire into motivation as a construct, do we not thereby reify it? Or if we deal with a realm which so many believe is essentially irrational in nature, are we not capitulating ourselves to irrationality? And if we attempt to think rationally about the behavior of an individual who is acting irrationally, are we not closing our eyes to an irrationality that actually exists? Are we not hiding behind a safe intellectualism? All of these are questions that rise out of the long-accepted assumptions of a subject-predicate mode of thought that tries to make reality responsible for the words that are used to construe it. Because of the currency of this kind of interpretation we run the risk we mentioned a few moments ago—the risk of being bracketed with either the classic rationalists or the modern intuitionists.

Actually we are neither. Our position is that of a psychology of personal constructs, a psychologist's system for construing persons who themselves construe in all kinds of other ways. Thus I, Person A,

Construct A', a component construct within my own construction system, to understand Construct B', a component construct within Person B's construction system. His B' is not a truth revealed to him by nature. Nor is my A' revealed to me by his human nature. Construct A' is my responsibility, just as B' is his. In each case the validity of the construct rests, among other things, upon its prophetic effectiveness, not upon any claim to external origin, either divine or natural.

Now let us hope we are in a safe position to deal with the assessment of human motives without appearing either to reify them or to talk nonsense. Our discussion might as well start where our thinking started.

Some twenty years or more ago a group of us were attempting to provide a traveling psychological clinic service to the schools in the state of Kansas. One of the principal sources of referals was, of course, teachers. A teacher complained about a pupil. This word-bound complaint was taken as prima facie grounds for kicking the bottle—I mean examining the pupil. If we kicked the pupil around long enough and hard enough we could usually find some grounds to justify any teacher's complaint. This procedure was called in those days, just as it is still called, "diagnosis." It was in this manner that we conformed to the widely accepted requirements of the scientific method—we matched hypothesis with evidence and thus arrived at objective truth. In due course of time we became quite proficient in making something out of teachers' complaints and we got so we could adduce some mighty subtle evidence. In short, we began to fancy ourselves as pretty sensitive clinicians.

Now as every scientist and every clinician knows and is fond of repeating, treatment depends upon diagnosis. First you find out what is wrong—really wrong. Then you treat it. In treatment you have several alternatives; you can cut it out of the person, or you can remove the child from the object, or you can alter the mechansim he employs to deal with the object, or you can compensate for the child's behavior by taking up a hobby in the basement, or teach the child to compensate for it, or if nothing better turns up, you can sympathize with everybody who has to put up with the youngster. But first, always first, you must kick the bottle to make it either confirm or reject your diagnostic hunches. So in Kansas we diagnosed pupils and, having impaled ourselves and our clients within our diagnoses, we cast about more or less frantically for ways of escape.

After persevering in this classical stupidity—the treatment-depends-on-objective-diagnosis stupidity—for more years than we like to count, we began to suspect that we were being trapped in some

pretty fallacious reasoning. We would have liked to blame the teachers
for getting us off on the wrong track. But we had verified their complaints, hadn't we? We had even made "differential diagnoses," a way
of choosing up sides in the name-calling games commonly played in
clinical staff meetings.

Two things became apparent. The first was that the teacher's complaint was not necessarily something to be verified or disproved by
the facts in the case, but was, rather a construction of events in a
way that, within the limits and assumptions of her personal construction sytem, made the most sense to her at the moment. The second
was the realization that, in assuming diagnosis to be the independent
variable and treatment the dependent variable, we had placed the cart
before the horse. It would have been better if we had made our diagnoses in the light of changes that do occur in children or that can
be made to occur, rather than trying to shape those changes to independent but irrelevant psychometric measurements or biographical
descriptions.

What we would like to make clear is that both these difficulties
have the same root—the traditional rationale of science that leads us
to look for the locus of meaning of words in their objects of reference
rather than in their subjects of origin. We hear a word and look to
what is talked about rather than listen to the person who utters it.
A teacher often complained that a child was "lazy." We turned to
the child to determine whether she was right or not. If we found
clear evidence that would support a hypothesis of laziness, then laziness
was what it was—nothing else—and diagnosis was complete. Diagnosis
having been accomplished, treatment was supposed to ensue. What
does one do to cure laziness? While, of course, it was not quite as
simple as this, the paradigm is essentially the one we followed.

Later we began to put "laziness" in quotes. We found that a careful
appraisal of the teacher's construction system gave us a much better
understanding of the meaning of the complaint. This, together with
some further inquiry into the child's outlook, often enabled us to arrive
at a vantage point from which one could deal with the problem in
various ways. It occurred to us that we might, for example, help the
teacher reconstrue the child in terms other than "laziness"—terms
which gave her more latitude for exercising her own particular creative
talents in dealing with him. Again, we might help the child deal with
the teacher so as to alleviate her discomfort. And, of course, there
was sometimes the possibility that a broader reorientation of the child
toward himself and school matters in general would prove helpful.

We have chosen the complaint of "laziness" as our example for a more special reason. "Laziness" happens to be a popular motivational concept that has widespread currency among adults who try to get others to make something out of themselves. Moreover, our disillusionment with motivational conceptualization in general started with this particular term and arose out of the specific context of school psychological services.

Our present position regarding human motives was approached by stages. First we realized that even when a hypothesis of laziness was confirmed, there was little that could be said or done in consequence of such a finding. While this originally appeared to be less true of other motivational constructs, such as appetite or affection, in each instance the key to treatment, or even to differential prediction of outcomes, appeared to reside within the framework of other types of constructs.

Another observation along the way was that the teachers who used the construct of "laziness" were usually those who had widespread difficulties in their classrooms. Soon we reached the point in our practice where we routinely used the complaint of "laziness" as a point of departure for reorienting the teacher. It usually happened that there was more to be done with her than with the child. So it was, also, with other complaints cast in motivational terms. In general, then, we found that the most practical approach to so-called motivational problems was to try to reorient the people who thought in such terms. Complaints about motivation told us much more about the complainants than it did about their pupils.

This is a generalization that seems to get more and more support from our clinical experience. When we find a person who is more interested in manipulating people for his own purposes, we usually find him making complaints about their motives. When we find a person who is concerned about motives, he usually turns out to be one who is threatened by his fellowmen and wants to put them in their place. There is no doubt but that the construct of motives is one which is widely used but it usually turns out to be a part of the language of complaint about the behavior of other people. When it appears in the language of the client himself, as it does occasionally, it always—literally always—appears in the context of a kind of rationalization apparently designed to appease the therapist, not in the spontaneous utterances of the client who is in good rapport with his therapist.

One technique we came to use was to ask the teacher what the child would do if she did not try to motivate him. Often the teacher would insist that the child would do nothing—absolutely nothing—just sit! Then we would suggest that she try a nonmotivational approach and let him "just sit." We would ask her to observe how he went about "just sitting." Invariably the teacher would be able to report some extremely interesting goings-on. An analysis of what the "lazy" child did while he was being lazy often furnished her with her first glimpse into the child's world and provided her with her first solid grounds for communication with him. Some teachers found that their laziest pupils were those who could produce the most novel ideas; others that the term "laziness" had been applied to activities that they had simply been unable to understand or appreciate.

It was some time later that we sat down and tried to formulate the general principles that undergirded our clinical experiences with teachers and their pupils. The more we thought about it, the more it seemed that our problems had always resolved themselves into questions of what the child would do if left to his own devices rather than questions about the amount of his motivation. These questions of what the child would do seemed to hinge primarily on what alternatives his personal construction of the situation allowed him to sense. While his construed alternatives were not necessarily couched in language symbols, nor could the child always clearly represent his alternatives, even to himself, they nonetheless set the outside limits on his day-to-day behavior. In brief, whenever we get embroiled in questions of motivation we bogged down, the teachers bogged down, and the children continued to aggravate everybody within earshot. When we forgot about motives and set about understanding the practical alternatives which children felt they were confronted by, the aggravations began to resolve themselves.

What we have said about our experiences with children also turned up in our psychotherapeutic experiences with adults. After months or, in some cases, years of psychotherapy with the same client, it did often prove to be possible to predict his behavior in terms of motives. This, of course, was gratifying, but predictive efficiency is not the only criterion of a good construction, for one's understanding of a client should also point the way to resolving his difficulties. It was precisely at this point that motivational constructs failed to be of practical service, just as they had failed to be of service in helping children and teachers get along with each other. Always the psychotherapeutic solution turned out to be a reconstruing process, not a mere labeling of the client's motives. To be sure, there were clients who never reduced their reconstructions to precise verbal terms, yet still were able to extricate themselves from vexing circumstances. And there were clients who get along best under conditions of support and reassurance with a minimum of verbal structuring on the part of the therapist. But even in these cases, the solutions were not worked out in terms of anything that could properly be called motives, and the evidence always pointed to some kind of reconstruing process that enabled the client to make his choice between new sets of alternatives not previously open to him in a psychological sense.

Now, perhaps, it is time to launch into the third phase of our discussion. We started by making some remarks of a philosophical nature and from there we dropped back to recall some of the practical experience that first led us to question the construct of motivation. Let us turn now to the formulation of psychological theory and to the part that motivation plays in it.

A half century ago William McDougall published his little volume, *Physiological Psychology*. In the opening pages he called his contemporary psychologists' attention to the fact that the concept of *energy* had been invented by physicists in order to account for movement of objects, and that some psychologists had blandly assumed that they too would have to find a place for it in their systems. While McDougall was to go on in his lifetime to formulate a theoretical system based on instinctual drives and thus, it seems to us, failed to heed his own warning, what he said about the construct of energy still provides us with a springboard for expounding a quite different theoretical position.

The physical world presented itself to preclassical man as a world of solid objects. He saw matter as an essentially inert substance, rather than as a complex of related motion. His axes of reference were spatial dimensions—length, breadth, depth—rather than temporal dimensions. The flow of time was something he could do very little about and he was inclined to take a passive attitude toward it. Even mass, a dimension which lent itself to more dynamic interpretations, was likely to be construed in terms of size equivalents.

Classical man, as he emerged upon the scene, gradually became aware of motion as something that had eluded his predecessors. But, for him, motion was still superimposed upon nature's rocks and hills. Inert matter was still the phenomenon, motion was only the epiphenomenon. Action, vitality, and energy were the breath of life that had to be breathed into the inertness of nature's realities. In Classical Greece this thought was magnificently expressed in new forms of architecture and sculpture that made the marble quarried from the Greek islands reach for the open sky, or ripple like a soft garment in the warm Aegean breeze. But motion, though an intrinsic feature of the Greek idiom, was always something superimposed, something added.

It belonged to the world of the ideal and not to the hard world of reality.

Today our modern psychology approaches its study of man from the same vantage point. He is viewed as something static in his natural state, hence, something upon which motion, life, and action have to be superimposed. In substance he is still perceived as like the marble out of which the Greeks carved their statues of flowing motion and ethereal grace. He comes alive, according to most of the psychology of our day, only through the application of special enlivening forces. We call these forces by such names as "motives," "incentives," "needs," and "drives." Thus, just as the physicists had to erect the construct of energy to fill the gap left by their premature assumption of a basically static universe, so psychology has had to burden itself with a construct made necessary by its inadequate assumption about the basic nature of man.

We now arrive at the same point in our theoretical reasoning at which we arrived some years earlier in appraising our clinical experience. In each case we find that efforts to assess human motives run into practical difficulty because they assume inherently static properties in human nature. It seems appropriate, therefore, at this juncture to reexamine our implied assumptions about human nature. If we then decide to base our thinking upon new assumptions, we can next turn to the array of new constructs that may be erected for the proper elaboration of the fresh theoretical position.

There are several ways in which we can approach our problem. We could, for example, suggest to ourselves, as we once suggested to certain unperceptive classroom teachers, that we examine what a person does when he is not being motivated. Does he turn into some kind of inert substance? If not—and he won't—should we not follow up our observation with a basic assumption that any person is motivated, motivated for no other reason than that he is alive? Life itself could be defined as a form of process or movement. Thus, in designating man as our object of psychological inquiry, we would be taking it for granted that movement was an essential property of his being, not something that had to be accounted for separately. We would be talking about a form of movement—man—not something that had to be motivated.

Pursuant to this line of reasoning, motivation ceases to be a special topic of psychology. Nor, on the other hand, can it be said that motivation constitutes the whole of psychological substance; although from the standpoint of another theoretical system, it might be proper to characterize our position so. *Within our system*, however, the term, "motivation," can only appear as a redundancy.

How else can we characterize this stand with respect to motivation? Perhaps this will help: motivational theories can be divided into two types, push theories and pull theories. Under push theories we find such terms as drive, motive, or even stimulus. Pull theories use such constructs as purpose, value, or need. In terms of a well-known metaphor, these are the pitch fork theories on the one hand and the carrot theories on the other. But our theory is neither of these. Since we prefer to look to the nature of the animal himself, ours is probably best called a jackass theory.

Thus far our reasoning has led us to a point of view from which the construct of "human motives" appears redundant—redundant, that is, as far as accounting for human action is concerned. But traditional motivational theory is not quite so easily dismissed. There is another issue that now comes to the fore. It is the question of what directions human actions can be expected to take.

We must recognize that the construct of "motive" has been traditionally used for two purposes: to account for the fact that the person is active rather than inert, and also for the fact that he chooses to move in some directions rather than in others. It is not surprising that, in the past, a single construct has been used to cover both issues; for if we take the view that the human organism is set in motion only by the impact of special forces, it is reasonable to assume also that those forces must give it direction as well as impetus. But now, if we accept the view that the organism is already in motion simply by virtue of its being alive, then we have to ask ourselves if we do not still require the services of "motives" to explain the directionality of the movement. Our answer to this question is, no. Let us see why.

Here, as before, we turn first to our experiences as a clinician to find the earliest inklings of a new theoretical position. Specifically, we turn to experiences in psychotherapy.

When a psychologist undertakes psychotherapy with a client he can approach his task from any one of a number of viewpoints. He can, as many do, devote most of his attention to a kind of running criticism of the mistakes the client makes, his fallacies, his irrationalities, his misperceptions, his resistances, his primtive mechanisms. Or, as others do, he can keep measuring his client; so much progress today, so much loss yesterday, gains in this respect, relapses in that. If he prefers, he can keep his attention upon his own role, or the relationship between himself and his client, with the thought that it is not actually given to him ever to know how the client's mind works, nor is it his responsibility to make sure that it works correctly, but only that he should provide the kind of warm and responsive human setting in which the client can best solve his own problems.

Any one of these approaches may prove helpful to the client. But there is still another approach that, from our personal experience, can prove most helpful both to the client and to the psychotherapist. Instead of assuming, on the one hand, that the therapist is obliged to bring the client's thinking into line, or, on the other, that the client will mysteriously bring his own thinking into line once he has been given the proper setting, we can take the stand that client and therapist are conjoining in an exploratory venture. The therapist assumes neither the position of judge nor that of the sympathetic bystander. He is sincere about this; he is willing to learn along with his client. He is the client's fellow researcher who seeks first to understand, then to examine, and finally to assist the client in subjecting alternatives to experimental test and revision.

The psychologist who goes at psychotherapy this way says to himself, "I am about to have the rare opportunity of examining the inner workings of that most intricate creation of all of nature, a human personality. While many scholars have written about the complexity of this human personality, I am now about to see for myself how one particular personality functions. Moreover, I am about to have an experienced colleague join me in this venture, the very person whose personality is to be examined. He will help me as best he can, but there will be times when he cannot help, when he will be as puzzled and confused as I am."

When psychotherapy is carried out in this vein the therapist, instead of asking himself continually whether his client is right or not, or whether he himself is behaving properly, peers intently into the intimate psychological processes the unusual relationship permits him to see. He inquires rather than condemns; he explores rather than rejects or approves. How does this creature, man, actually think? How does he make choices that seem to be outside the conventionalized modes of thought? What is the nature of his logic—quite apart from how logicians define logic? How does he solve his problems? What ideas does he express for which he has no words?

Out of this kind of experience with psychotherapy we found ourselves becoming increasingly impatient with certain standard psychotherapeutic concepts. "Insight" was one of the first to have a hollow sound. It soon became apparent that, in any single case, there was any number of different possible insights that could be used to structure the same facts, all of them more or less true. As one acquires a variety of psychotherapeutic experience he begins to be amazed by how sick or deviant some clients can be and still surmount their difficulties, and how well or insightful others can be and yet fall apart at every turn. Certainly the therapist who approaches his task primarily as a scientist is soon compelled to concede that unconventional insights often work as well or better than the standardized insights prescribed by some current psychological theory.

Another popular psychotherapeutic concept that made less and less sense was "resistance." To most therapists resistance is a kind of perverse stubbornness in the client. Most therapists are annoyed by it. Some accuse the client of resisting whenever their therapeutic efforts begin to bog down. But our own experiences with resistance were a good deal like our experiences with laziness—they bespoke more of the therapist's perplexity than of the client's rebellion. If we had been dependent entirely on psychotherapeutic experiences with our own clients we might have missed this point; it would have been too easy for us, like the others, to blame our difficulties on the motives of the client. But we were fortunate enough to also have opportunities for supervising therapists and here, because we were not ourselves quite so intimately involved, it was possible to see resistance in terms of the therapist's naivete.

When the so-called resistance was finally broken through—to use a psychotherapist's idiom—it seemed proper, instead of congratulating ourselves on our victory over a stubborn client, to ask ourselves and our client just what had happened. There were, of course, the usual kinds of reply, "I just couldn't say that to you then," or "I knew I was being evasive, but I just didn't know what to do about it," etc.

But was this stubbornness? Some clients went further and expressed it this way, "To have said then what I have said today would not have meant the same thing." This may seem like a peculiar remark, but from the standpoint of personal construct theory it makes perfectly good sense. A client can express himself only within the framework of his construct system. Words alone do not convey meaning. What this client appears to be saying is this! When he has the constructs for expressing himself the words that he uses ally themselves with those constructs and they make sense when he utters them. To force him to utter words which do not parallel his constructs, or to mention events which are precariously construed, is to plunge him into a chaos of personal nonsense, however it may clarify matters for the therapist. In short, our experience with psychotherapy led us to believe that it was not orneriness that made the client hold out so-called important therapeutic material, but a genuine inability to express himself in terms that would not appear, from his point of view, to be utterly misconstrued.

Perhaps these brief recollections of therapeutic experience will suffice to show how we began to be as skeptical of motives as direction-finding devices as we were skeptical of them as action-producing forces. Over and over again, it appeared that our clients were making their choices, not in terms of the alternatives we saw open to them, but in terms of the alternatives they saw open to them. It was their network of constructions that made up the daily mazes that they ran, not the pure realities that appeared to us to surround them. To try to explain a temper tantrum or an acute schizophrenic episode in terms of motives only was to miss the whole point of the client's system of personal dilemmas. The child's temper tantrum is, for him, one of the few remaining choices left to him. So for the psychotic; with his pathways structured the way they are in his mind, he has simply chosen from a particular limited set of alternatives. How else can he behave? His other alternatives are even less acceptable.

We have still not quite answered the question of explaining directionality. We have described only the extent to which our therapeutic experiences led us to question the value of motives. But, after all, we have not yet found, from our experience, that clients do what they do because there is nothing else they can do. We have observed only that they do what they do because their choice systems are definitely limited. But, even by this line of reasoning, they do have choices, often bad ones, to be sure, but still choices. So our question of directionality of behavior is narrowed down by the realization that a person's behavior must take place within the limited dimensions of his personal construct system. Yet as long as his system does have dimensions it must provide him with some sets of alternatives. And so long as he has some alternatives of his own making we must seek to explain why he chooses some of them in preference to others.

Before we leave off talking about clinical experience and take up the next and most difficult phase of our discussion, it will do no harm to digress for a few moments and talk about the so-called neurotic paradox. O. H. Mowrer has described this as "the paradox of behavior which is at one and the same time self-perpetuating and self-defeating." We can state the paradox in the form of a question. "Why does a person sometimes persist in unrewarding behavior?" Reinforcement theory finds this an embarrassing question, while contiguity theory, to which some psychologists have turned in their embarrassment, finds the converse question equally embarrassing. "Why does a person sometimes *not* persist in unrewarding behavior?"

From the standpoint of the psychology of personal constructs, however, there is no neurotic paradox. Or, to be more correct, the paradox is the jam certain learning theorists get themselves into rather than the jam their clients get themselves into. Not that clients stay out of jams, but they have their own ingenious ways of getting into them and they need no assistance from us psychologists. To say it another way, the behavior of a so-called neurotic client does not seem paradoxical to him until he tries to rationalize it in terms his therapist can understand. It is when he tries to use his therapist's construction system that the paradox appears. Within the client's own limited construction system he may be faced with a dilemma but not with a paradox.

Perhaps this little digression into the neurotic paradox will help prepare the ground for the next phase of our discussion. Certainly it will help if it makes clear that the criteria by which a person chooses between the alternatives, in terms of which he has structured his world, are themselves cast in terms of constructions. Men not only construe their alternatives, but they construe also criteria for choosing between them. For us psychologists who try to understand what is going on in the minds of our clients it is not as simple as saying that the client will persist in rewarding behavior, or even that he will vacillate between immediate and remote rewards. We have to know what this person construes to be a reward, or, better still, we can bypass such motivational terms as "reward," which ought to be redefined for each new client and on each new occasion, and abstract from human behavior some psychological principle that will transcend the tedious varieties of personalized motives.

If we succeed in this achievement we may be able to escape that common pitfall of so-called objective thinking, the tendency to reify our constructs and treat them as if they were not constructs at all, but actually all the things that they were originally only intended to construe. Such a formulation may even make it safer for us to write operational definitions for purposes of research, without becoming lost in the subject-predicate fallacy. In clinical language it may enable us to avoid concretistic thinking—the so-called brain-injured type of thinking—which is what we call operationalism when we happen to find it in a client who is frantically holding on to his mental faculties.

Now we have been procrastinating long enough. Let us get on to the most difficult part of our discussion. We have talked about experiences with clients who, because they hoped we might be of help to them, honored us with invitations to the rare intimacies of their personal lives and ventured to show us the shadowy processes by which their lives were ordered. We turned aside briefly in our discussion to talk about the neurotic paradox, hoping that what we could point to there would help the listener anticipate what needed to come next. Now we turn again to a more theoretical form of discourse.

If man, as the psychologist is to see him, exists primarily in the dimensions of time, and only secondarily in the dimensions of space, then the terms which we erect for understanding him ought to take primary account of this view. If we want to know why man does what he does, then the terms of our whys should extend themselves in time rather than in space; they should be events rather than things; they should be mileposts rather than destinations. Clearly, man lives in the present. He stands firmly astride the chasm that separates the past from the future. He is the only connecting link between these two universes. He, and only he, can bring them into harmony with each other. To be sure, there are other forms of existence that have belonged to the past and, presumably, will also belong to the future. A rock that has rested firm for ages may well exist in the future also, but it does not link the past with the future. In its mute way it links only past with past. It does not anticipate; it does not reach out both ways to snatch handfuls from each of the two worlds in order to bring them together and subject them to the same stern laws. Only man does that.

If this is the picture of man, as the psychologist envisions him— man, a form of movement; man, always quick enough, as long as he is alive, to stay astride the darting present—then we cannot expect to explain him either entirely in terms of the past or entirely in terms of the future. We can only explain him, psychologically, as a link between the two. Let us, therefore, formulate our basic postulate for psychological theory in the light of this conjunctive vision of man. We can say it this way: *a person's processes are psychologically channelized by the ways in which he anticipates events.*

Taking this proposition as point of departure we can quickly begin to sketch a theoretical structure for psychology that will, undoubtedly, turn out to be novel in many unexpected ways. We can say next that man develops his ways of anticipating events by construing—by scratching out his channels of thought. Thus he builds his own maze. His runways are the constructs he forms, each a two-way street, each essentially a pair of alternatives between which he can choose.

Another person, attempting to enter this labyrinth, soon gets lost. Even a therapist has to be led patiently back and forth through the system, sometimes for months on end, before he can find his way without the client's help, or tell to what overt behavior each passageway will lead. Many of the runways are conveniently posted with word signs, but most of them are dark, cryptically labeled, or without any word signs at all. Some are rarely traveled. Some the client is reluctant to disclose to his guest. Often therapists lose patience and prematurely start trying to blast shortcuts in which both they and their clients soon become trapped. But worst of all, there are those therapists who refuse to believe that they are in the strangely structured world of man, insisting only that the meanderings in which they are led are merely the play of whimsical motives upon their blind and helpless client.

Our figure of speech should not be taken too literally. The labyrinth is conceived as a network of constructs, each of which is essentially an abstraction and, as such, can be picked up and laid down over many, many different events in order to bring them into focus and clothe them with personal meaning. Moreover, the constructs are subject to continual revision, although the complex interdependent relationship between constructs in the system often makes it precarious for the person to revise one construct without taking into account the disruptive effect upon major segments of the system.

In our efforts to communicate the notion of a personal construct system we repeatedly ran into difficulty because listeners identify personal constructs with the classic view of a concept. Concepts have long been known as units of logic and are treated as if they existed independently of any particular person's psychological processes. But when we use the notion of "construct" we have nothing of this sort in mind; we are talking about a psychological process in a living person. Such construct has, for us, no existence independent of the person whose thinking it characterizes. The question of whether it is logical or not has no bearing on its existence, for it is wholly a psychological rather than a logical affair. Furthermore, since it is a psychological affair, it has no necessary allegiance to the verbal forms in which classical concepts have been traditionally cast. The personal construct we talk about bears no essential relation to grammatical structure, syntax, words, language, or even communication; nor does it imply consciousness. It is simply a psychologically construed unit for understanding human processes.

We must confess that we often run into another kind of difficulty. In an effort to understand what we are talking about a listener often asks if the personal construct is an intellectual affair. We find that, willy-nilly, we invite this kind of question because of our use of such terms as thought and thinking. Moreover, we are speaking in the terms of a language system whose words stand for traditional divisions of mental life, such as "intellectual."

Let us answer this way. A construct owes no special allegiance to the intellect, as against the will or the emotions. In fact, we do not find it either necessary or desirable to make that classic trichotomous division of mental life. After all. there is so much that is "emotional" in those behaviors commonly called "intellectual" and there is so much "intellectualized" contamination in typical "emotional" upheavals that the distinction merely becomes a burdensome nuisance. For some time now we have been quite happy to chuck all these notions of intellect, will, and emotion, and, so far. we cannot say we have experienced any serious loss.

Now we are at the point in our discourse where we hope our listeners are ready to assume, either from conviction or for the sake of argument, that man, from a psychological viewpoint, makes of himself a bridge between past and future in a manner that is unique among creatures, that. again from a psychological viewpoint, his processes are channelized by the personal constructs he erects in order to perform this function, and finally, that he organizes his constructs into a personal system that is no more conscious than it is unconscious and no more intellectual than it is emotional. This personal construct system provides him both with freedom of decision and limitation of action—freedom. because it permits him to deal with the meanings of events rather than being helplessly pushed about by them, and limitation, because he can never make choices outside the world of alternatives he has erected for himself.

We have left to the last the question of what determines man's behavioral choices between his self-construed alternatives. Each choice that he makes has implications for his future. Each turn of the road he chooses to travel brings him to a fresh vantage point from which he can judge the validity of his past choices and elaborate his present pattern of alternatives for choices yet to be made. Always the future beckons him and always he reaches out in tremulous anticipation to touch it. He lives in anticipation; we mean this literally; *he lives in anticipation!* His behavior is governed, not simply by *what* he anticipates—whether good or bad, pleasant or unpleasant. self-vindicating or self-confounding—but by *where* he believes his choices will place him in respect to the remaining turns in the road. If he chooses this fork in the road will it lead to a better vantage point from which to see the road beyond or will it be the one that abruptly brings him face-to-face with a blank wall?

What we are saying about the criteria of man's choices is not a second theoretical assumption, added to our basic postulate to take the place of the traditional beliefs in separate motives, but is a natural outgrowth of that postulate—a corollary to it. Let us state it so. *A person chooses for himself that alternative in a dichotomized construct through which he anticipates the greater possibility for extension and definition of his system.*

Such a corollary appears to us to be implicit in our postulate that a person's processes are psychologically channelized by the ways in which he anticipates events. For the sake of simplification we have skipped over the formal statement of some of the intervening corollaries of personal construct theory: the corollary that deals with construing, the corollary that deals with construct system, and the corollary that deals with the dichotomous nature of constructs. But we have probably covered these intervening ideas well enough in the course of our exposition.

What we are saying is this crucial *Choice Corollary* gives us the final ground for dismissing motivation as a necessary psychological construct. It is that if a person's processes are channelized by the ways in which he anticipates events, he will make his choices in such a way as to define or extend his system of channels, for this must necessarily be his comprehensive way of anticipating events.

At the risk of being tedious, let us recapitulate again. We shall be brief. Perhaps we can condense it into three sentences. First we saw no need for a closet full of motives to explain the fact that man was active rather than inert; there was no sense in assuming that he was inert in the first place. And now we see no need to invoke a concept of motives to explain the directions that his actions take; the fact that he lives in anticipation automatically takes care of that. Result: no catalogue of motives to clutter up our system and, we hope, a much more coherent psychological theory about living man.

At this point our discourse substantially concludes itself. What we have left to offer are essentially footnotes that are intended to be either defensive or provocative, perhaps both! Questions naturally arise the moment one begins to pursue the implications of this kind of theorizing. One can scarcely take more than a few steps before he begins to stumble over a lot of ancient landmarks that remain to serve no purpose except to get in the way. Perhaps it is only fair that we spotlight some of these relics in the hope of sparing our listeners some barked intellectual shins.

Is this a dynamic theory? This is the kind of question our clinical colleagues are likely to ask. We are tempted to give a flat no to that question. No, this is not what is ordinarily called a dynamic theory: it intentionally parts company with psychoanalysis, for example—respectfully but nonetheless intentionally. However, if what is meant by a "dynamic theory" is a theory that envisions man as active rather than inert, then this is an all-out dynamic theory. It is so dynamic that it does not need any special system of dynamics to keep it running! What must be made clear, else our whole discourse falls flat on its face, is that we do not envision the behavior of man in terms of the external forces bearing upon him; that is a view we are quite ready to leave to the dialectic materialists and to some of their unwitting allies who keep chattering about scientific determinism and other subject-predicate forms of nonsense.

Is this rationalism revisited? We anticipated this question at the beginning of our discussion. We are tempted to answer now by claiming that it is one of the few genuine departures from rationalism, perhaps the first in the field of psychology. But here is a tricky question, because it is not often clear whether one is referring to extra-psychological rationalism or to an essential-psychological rationalism that is often imperfect when judged by classical standards and often branded as "irrationality," or whether the question refers simply to any verbalized structure applied to the behavior of man in an effort to understand him.

Certainly ours is not an extra-psychological rationalism. Instead it frankly attempts to deal with the essential rationalism that is actually demonstrated in the thinking of man. In doing so it deals with what is sometimes called the world of the irrational and nonrational.

But in another sense our interpretation, in its own right and quite apart from its subject matter, is a psychologist's rationale designed to help him understand how man comes to believe and act the way he does. Such a rationale approaches its task the way it does, not because it believes that logic has to be as it is because there is no other way for it to be, not because it believes that man behaves the way he does because there is no other way for him to react to external determining forces, nor even because the rationale's own construction of man provides him with no alternatives, but rather, because we have the hunch that the way to understand all things, even the ramblings of a regressed schizophrenic client, is to construe them so as to make them predictable. To some this spells rationalism, pure and simple, probably because they are firmly convinced that the nether world of man's motives is so hopelessly irrational that anyone who tries to understand that world sensibly must surely be avoiding contact with man as he really is.

Finally, there is the most important question of all: how does the system work? That is a topic to be postponed to another time and occasion. Of course, we think it does work. We use it in psychotherapy and in psychodiagnostic planning for psychotherapy. We also find a place for it in dealing with many of the affairs of everyday life. But there is no place here for the recitation of such details. We hope only that, so far as we have gone, we have been reasonably clear, and a mite provocative, for only by being both clear and provocative can we give our listeners something they can set their teeth into.

ADDENDUM

The invitation to prepare this paper was accompanied by a list of nine issues upon which, it was presumed, would hinge the major differences to be found among any group of motivational theorists. On the face of it such a list seems altogether fair. But one can scarcely pose even one such question, much less nine of them, without exacting hostages to his own theoretical loyalties. And if a correspondent answers in the terminology of the questions posed, he, in turn, immediately bases his discourse on the assumptions of an alien theory. Once he has done that he will, sooner or later, have to talk as if the differences he seeks to emphasize are merely semantical.

Yet the nine questions need to be met, if not head on, at least candidly enough to be disposed of.

1. Is it essential in assessing motives to provide some appraisal of the ego processes, directive mechanisms, or cognitive controls that intervene between the motive and its expression?

"Ego" is a psychoanalytic term; we still don't know what it means. "Cognitive" is a classical term that implies a natural cleavage between psychological processes, a cleavage that confuses everything and clarifies nothing; let's forget it. The notion of a "motive" on the one hand and "its expression" on the other commits one to the view that what is expressed is not the person but the motivational gremlins that have possessed him. Finally, if the term "directive mechanisms" is taken in a generic sense, then we can say that we see these as in the form of constructs formulated by the person himself and in terms of which he casts his alternatives. What needs to be assessed are these personal constructs if one wishes to understand what a person is up to.

2. How important are conscious as opposed to unconscious motives in understanding human behavior? Are there conditions under which one type of motivation is likely to be of particular importance?

We do not use the conscious-unconscious dichotomy, but we do recognize that some of the personal constructs a person seeks to subsume within his system prove to be fleeting or elusive. Sometimes this is because they are loose rather than tight, as in the first phase of the creative cycle. Sometimes it is because they are not bound by the symbolisms of words or other acts. But of this we are sure, if they are important in a person's life it is a mistake to say they are unconscious or that he is unaware of them. Every day he experiences them, often all too poignantly, except he cannot put his finger on them nor tell for sure whether they are at the spot the therapist has probed for them.

When does a person fall back upon such loosened thinking? Or when does he depend upon constructs that are not easily subsumed? Ordinarily when one is confronted with confusion (anxiety) the first tendency is to tighten up, but beyond some breaking point there is a tendency to discard tight constructions and fall back upon constructs that are loose or which have no convenient symbolizations. It is in the human crises that it becomes most important to understand the nature of a person's secondary lines of defense.

3. What is the relative importance of direct as opposed to indirect techniques for assessing human motives? Under what circumstances is the contribution of each type of technique likely to be greatest?

Let us change the word "motives" to "constructs." They are not equivalent, of course, but "motives" play no part in our system while "constructs" do. If we ask a person to express his constructs in words, and we take his words literally, then we may say, perhaps, that we are assessing his constructs "directly." If we assume that his words and acts have less patent meanings and that we must construe him in terms of a background understanding of his construct system, shall we say that we have used a more "indirect" technique? But is anything more direct than this? Perhaps the method that takes literal meanings for granted is actually the more indirect, for it lets the dictionary intervene between the client and the psychologist. If time permits we vote for seeking to understand the person in the light of his personal construct system.

4. In assessing human motives how important is it to specify the situational context within which the motives operate?

Each of a client's constructs has a limited range of convenience in helping him deal with his circumstances. Beyond that range the construct is irrelevant as far as he is concerned. This is the point that was so long obscured by the Law of the Excluded Middle. Knowledge, therefore, of the range of convenience of any personal construct formulated by a client is essential to an understanding of the behavior he structures by that construct.

5. How necessary is knowledge of the past in the assessment of the contemporary motivation?

It is not absolutely necessary but it is often convenient. Events of the past may disclose the kind of constructions that the client has used; presumably he may use them again. Events of the past, taken in conjunction with the anticipations they confirmed at the time, may indicate what has been proved to his satisfaction. Again, events of the past may indicate what a client has had to make sense out of, and thus enable us to surmise what constructions he may have had to erect in order to cope with his circumstances. Finally, since some clients insist on playing the part of martyrs to their biographical destinies, therapy cannot be concluded successfully until their therapists have conducted them on a grand tour of childhood recollections.

6. At this time is the area of motivation more in need of developing precise and highly objective measures of known motives or identifying significant new motivational variables?

Neither.

7. Is there a unique and important contribution to the understanding of human motive that can be made to present through the medium of comparative or lower animal studies that cannot be duplicated by means of investigations utilizing human subjects?

No.

8. In attempting to understand human motivation is it advisable at present to focus upon one or a small number of motivational variables or should an effort be made to appraise a wide array of variables?

Human impetus should be assumed as a principle rather than treated as a variable or group of variables.

9. What is the relative importance of detailed studies of individual cases as compared to carefully controlled experimental research and large-scale investigation?

All three have their place in the course of developing psychological understanding. The detailed case studies provide excellent grounds for generating constructs. Experimental research, in turn, permits us to test out constructs in artificial isolation. Large-scale investigations help us put constructs into a demographic framework.

4

A Mathematical Approach
to Psychology

MANY DIFFERENT APPROACHES to psychology are possible, but most of them have not been invented yet. The purpose of this paper is to describe an approach that is now in the process of being invented. Like all the others which have preceded it, as well as those to come later, it is a construction and not a discovery. I must make this clear at the outset; I did not find this theory lurking among the data of an experiment nor was it disclosed to me on a mountain top or in a laboratory. I have, in my own clumsy way, been making it up.

INVENTION AND DISCOVERY IN SCIENCE

A scientist's inventions assist him in two ways: they tell him what to expect and they help him see it when it happens. Those that tell him what to expect are theoretical inventions and those that enable him to observe outcomes are instrumental inventions. The two types are never wholly independent of each other, and they usually stem from the same assumptions. This is unavoidable. Moreover, without his inventions, both theoretical and instrumental, man would be both disoriented and blind. He would not know where to look or how to see.

While invention is the key to progress in science, as well as in

SOURCE. Prepared at the invitation of the Moscow Psychological Society (U.S.S.R.) and read at Moscow, April 10, 1961.

other forms of human inquiry, discovery is important also. But when we speak of discovery we must be explicit about what we mean, else we shall find ourselves enmeshed in the same difficulties as those who think that the natural events of the world go around introducing themselves by name and whispering theoretical revelations into the ears of deserving scientists.

First of all, theoretical inventions are used to make predictions. Then, still using inventions, but of a more instrumental type, we examine the outcomes to see if there is any correspondence between what we have predicted and what our instrumentalized perceptions tell us has occurred. If we find such a correspondence, we call it a discovery. We do not discover our theory; we do not discover our prediction; we do not even discover the ensuing event. What is discovered is a correspondence—a practical correspondence—between what our theoretical invention leads us to anticipate and what, subsequently, our instrumental invention leads us to observe.

When a scientist repeatedly fails to find any correspondence between what appears to happen and what his theoretical invention has led him to expect, he is likely to conclude, sooner or later, that his theory is worthless. Thus, if the invention I am about to describe to you fails to produce expectations that materialize. I, too, am likely to conclude, sooner or later, that my invention is worthless. Others may reach this conclusion sooner than I, for, having gone to the trouble of inventing the theory and writing papers about it, I shall want to explore its possibilities extensively before abandoning it. Some of you may be happy to abandon the theory at the very outset, while others may wish to pursue it, along with me, for some distance, if only out of sheer curiosity to see where it leads.

This paper, then, begins with a personal invitation to you to join me aboard my theoretical vessel and set out on a voyage of discovery, and, sharing with me such instruments as I have on board, to observe the islands we pass. If, at any time, you despair of discovering any correspondence between what we seek and what looms up on the horizon, you are free to turn back. I, too, may turn back at some point, if I become discouraged with the outcomes of our venture, while some of you, who are not so easily discouraged, may press the voyage further.

CONSTRUCTIVE ALTERNATIVISM

These statements I have been making so far are more epistemological than psychological. But let me continue further with them, for they have a bearing on the psychological statements I shall want to make later.

For a long time scientists have assumed that before they could advance a new theory they must first prove something wrong with the old ones. I do not consider this a necessary assumption. It is true that our disappointments with one kind of explanation do often serve to set us off in search of a better one. There is nothing wrong with that. But does one always have to wait until he is frustrated and embittered before he dares start looking for new horizons? I think not.

The adventure in which I have invited you to join me for a little while does not, therefore, require you to deny anything you now believe or to destroy anything you now find useful. That is why I have said that you are free to return whenever you find the voyage discouragingly unproductive. You need not scuttle your present ships in order to embark on this one. Nor need you wait until you are discouraged before you quit my vessel for another.

The question of whether a theory is true or false, good or bad, useful or futile is not identical with the question of whether or not to explore its implications. These two types of questions arise properly at different times, and therefore are not to be answered concurrently. This is a point of view which is a convenience in dealing with what I have to offer; but it is more than that—it is an essential feature of the theory itself, as I hope to show during the course of this paper.

The underlying philosophical position which I have sketched briefly in the preceding paragraphs may be called "constructive alternativism." This is to say that reality is subject to many alternative constructions, some of which may prove to be more fruitful than others. The discovery of an ultimate correspondence between the constructions we are able to devise and the flow of actual events is an infinitely long way off. In the meantime, we shall have to be content to make a little progress at a time, to invent new alternative constructions— even before we have become dissatisfied with the old ones, and hope that, in general, we are moving in the right direction.

CONVERGING LINES OF INFERENCE:
I. GENERALIZATION OF THE PSYCHOLOGY OF SCIENTIFIC BEHAVIOR

Now, having said something philosophical, we are prepared to go on to say something more psychological. Since, as I am sure Professor

Luria will agree, it is helpful to have a verbal response for something if we are to control all our other reactions to it. let me say that the theory I am about to describe may be called "the psychology of personal constructs."

The theory may be said to represent the convergence of several lines of inference. Naturally, I shall not attempt to describe all of them, but it is appropriate to mention one or two.

One thing that has struck me is that nearly every psychologist of our time inadvertently uses two quite different systems for explaining human behavior. While I see nothing particularly wrong in this, as you already know from my discussion of constructive alternativism, it does raise the fascinating question of whether one or the other of the two systems might not suffice to explain the whole spectrum of human behavior.

Let me try to explain what I mean. Most psychologists consider themselves scientists. This is true in my country as well as in yours. They see *science* as progressing according to certain principles and by means of certain methodologies. But when these same psychologists turn their attention to *man*, they speak in another language. In the first chapter of their books they say that *science* progresses by inducing or deducing theoretical statements, by formulation of hypotheses, by specifying predictions. by experimentation. by observing outcomes and comparing them with expectations, and by constant revision of one's line of reasoning. But in the ensuing chapters they forget all about this and they attempt to describe *man's* behavior in quite different terms, the particular terms depending somewhat upon their theoretical orientation at the moment.

But science is itself a form of human behavior, and a pretty important one, at that. Why, then, should we feel compelled to use one set of parameters when we describe *man-the-scientist* and another set when we describe *man-the-laboratory-subject?* I pose this question, not as one to be answered immediately by logical inference, or to be dismissed with the supposition that scientific behavior must require a unique psychology because it constitutes so small a part of human behavior, but as a question to be explored. I pose it, not as a philosophical question, but as a psychological one—and hence one to be answered or reformulated by scientific inquiry.

Answering a question of this sort, as I am sure you will agree, involves a good deal more than one simple laboratory experiment. One way of exploring this question is to take our notions of scientific progress, philosophical notions of what science is and how it proceeds, remove them from the context of a speculative philosophy and logic, and elaborate them as a system of psychological theory of man's behavior. Thus we would prepare our question for scientific investigation. We could then deduct hypotheses, raise issues, develop methodologies, devise instruments, generate data, perform experiments, induce further hypotheses, and revise our theoretical formulations. The psychology of personal constructs is an attempt to prepare our question in just such a way.

CONVERGING LINES OF INFERENCE: II. THE DOUBLE ENTITY CHOICE

Let me mention another of the converging lines of inference, merely one of many, which points to the psychology of personal constructs. From the time of Aristotle we have understood propositional speech as a way of denoting entities. We may say, "A is B." This statement is a way of asserting a conclusion, the antithesis of which would have been to say, "A is not B." This is a familiar logical form and its intrinsic validity is generally taken for granted.

But we can look at this matter as psychologists and pose a scientific question about it. When one says that "A is B," is he, in fact, merely abandoning the alternative proposition that "A is not B"? Or is he, in fact, denying some other alternative? This is a question about human behavior, not a question of classical logic. Since it is a question about human behavior, it should be open to psychological examination.

Experience with clients undergoing psychotherapy, as well as with persons in the process of changing their lives under other conditions, leads one to suspect that a person never makes his choice merely between an entity and a nonentity. When he says that "A is B" it seems that he is also asserting that "A is not C." The choice he makes is not, therefore, between "B" and "not-B," but between "B" and "C"— between two entities. Let us call this "the double entity choice," to distinguish it from "the single entity choice" envisioned by classical logic.

If you prefer, we can state this observation in behavioral terms. We may then say that a person never chooses between behaving in a certain way and not behaving at all. Rather, he chooses between one behavior and another. He does not choose between activity and inactivity; instead, he chooses between alternative kinds of activity. At least, for the moment, this is the way it seems.

It must be clear that what I am offering here is an incident observation only. But it is an observation that can be pursued psychologically to see whether, as a generalization, it can be supported in a scientific manner. In order to examine it psychologically it is best that we first elaborate it in some theoretical form, preferably in one that is simple, coherent, communicable, productive of reasonably explicit hypotheses, and amenable to the operational definition of experimental terms.

And so, this time by a different route, we come again to the psychology of personal constructs, a theory which, among other things, attempts to do just this. It takes our incidental observation of the double entity choice in human behavior and incorporates it in a theoretical structure. The constructed theory, because of all its predictive implications, then becomes a basis upon which a series of scientific inquiries can be undertaken. Eventually, this series of inquiries should reveal to us whether or not we have invented anything useful.

THEORETICAL COMPOSITION OF THE PSYCHOLOGY OF PERSONAL CONSTRUCTS

Thus far in this paper we have mentioned only three main ideas. The first is *constructive alternativism*, a philosophical position which simultaneously sustains a vast variety of competing theoretical formulations, and the research that stems from them, even though some of those formulations appear as alternatives to what is currently acceptable. The other two ideas are the two incidental observations that give rise to converging lines of inference. The first of these suggests the possibility of *generalizing the psychology of scientific behavior* to all human behavior, and the second suggests the possibility of incorporating the *double entity choice* into a psychological theory. There are, of course, many other initial ideas and observations that might have been mentioned as leading to this theory, but these three are sufficient for this paper. Actually most of our further discussion will center around the third idea, the idea of the double entity choice, since this is the one that leads us most directly to an unusual kind of mathematical approach to psychology.

Suppose a child distinguishes between two objects, say, a ball and a cube. On the following day let us say he distinguishes between another ball and another cube. Why are his two performances similar? One thing we can say is that because the pairs of objects were physically similar on the successive days the child's responses were similar.

This explanation is based on the assumption that the child is under the control of the objects and therefore similar pairs of objects must always elicit similar responses. This is one type of explanation, and it is satisfactory, as far as it goes.

But suppose we make use of the principle of constructive alternativism and seek other kinds of explanation. Suppose we turn our attention to the child, rather than to the objects, and ask how it is that he was able to do with them what he did. Suppose we say it is not enough that the objects be similar; what more is required is that the child have some capability that enables him to respond as if they were similar. The psychological point I want to emphasize is that he construed the objects similarly, in spite of the fact that the occasions were different and the particular concrete objects were different.

One way of throwing light on the child's behavior is to examine the history of his performances. Such an examination has the advantage of enabling us to apply theories of conditioning or other historical types of explanation directly to particular acts. But, without burdening myself with the task of finding fault with such explanations—or others with the task of defending them—let me simply continue to take advantage of constructive alternativism and ask how the child, conditioned or not, copes with balls and cubes when they are presented to him.

One thing is obvious; the psychological feature we are seeking is itself neither a ball, a cube, a day, or a set of circumstances—we are not looking for stimuli. The feature must be, instead, the child's own way of dealing with balls and cubes, his own way of channelizing his response to them, regardless of changing circumstances, and, therefore, one that he need not abandon at the end of the day when he goes to bed. Moreover, it is based on his personal construction of balls and cubes, a construction which he did not discover but which, as a kind of scientist, he invented. Since he is a "scientist" who is alive and active we may presume he is experimenting with his invention and is in the process of discovering its predictive utility.

It is at this point in the elaboration of the theory that I must pause to make a special stipulation. Nothing that I have said implies that the child's way of managing balls and cubes is necessarily based upon language or upon so-called conscious thinking. Nor do I mean to suggest that there are classical ideas or concepts floating around in his head. I have done no more than to invite your attention first to what the child actually does, and now I am asking you to go one step further with me and pay particular attention to his ways of doing it. Thus, from now on, I shall be referring to the *forms* his life processes take, rather than to concrete processes themselves. The question of whether or not the processes are naturally physiological, mental, cognitive, spiritual, verbal, or unconscious is not relevant to what I have to say. We shall be talking about the ways these processes operate, not about their essences.

ASSESSING THE PERSONAL CONSTRUCT

Now that we have left behind the particulars of human behavior and are dealing with the abstractions of human behavior which we hope will provide the grounds for systematic scientific inquiry, we can start to delineate the forms into which we may cast those abstractions. We shall take our cue, as I have already indicated, from the observation that persons appear to make a double entity choice, rather than a single entity choice. Thus a child, in identifying a ball, appears to distinguish it from some other type of object—perhaps a cube—rather than merely picking it out, all at once, from all the things in the world which are not balls. If it appears to us that he picks it out all at once we may suppose that this is only because he has applied a sequential series of distinctions, and the types of objects he has eliminated along the way are not easily recognizable in his final identification of the ball.

If we give the child a ball, a cube, and a disc, and then ask him to put together the two that are alike, he can respond in at least three ways. (1) He can put the disc and the ball together, in which case we suspect that he has erected some construction that distinguishes a curvilinearity he ascribes to those two objects from an angularity. (2) He can put the cube and the disc together, in which case we suspect that the underlying distinction is between flatness and convexity. (3) Or he can put the cube and the ball together, in which case we might guess that he is distinguishing between thickness and thinness.

But how can we be sure? Suppose he actually puts the cube and the disc together, thus distinguishing them from the ball. Can we be sure that this means he has construed in the form, "convex versus flat?" Unless we are confident we can rely upon an exchange of language symbols with him, we must resort to the further explication of his construct by other means.

Suppose we next give him a lozenge and a feather. Suppose, instead of placing the convex lozenge beside the ball and the flat feather beside the cube and the disc, he does the reverse. Now he has the feather and the ball together, and on the other side he has the lozenge, the cube, and the disc.

Now that his construct has been explicated through five objects we may have a somewhat better understanding of the pattern his behavior follows. But we may still find it hard to predict accurately how he will arrange additional objects. We may hypothesize, at this point, that we can predict his further arrangements by using ourselves a construct of stable objects, such as the cube, the disc, and the lozenge, versus mobile objects which are easily dislodged, such as the ball and the feather. But this is only our hypothesis. Still, if by using it we do accurately predict his sorting of the next twenty objects given him, we may begin to feel some confidence that we have devised a useful notion of how his construct enables him to function in this simple laboratory situation.

THE PERSONAL CONSTRUCT AS AN ABSTRACTION OF HUMAN BEHAVIOR

When a person identifies an object we may say he has applied a construct to it. This is to say he has abstracted his behavior into a form we call the personal construct, and that he can now move consistently from situation to situation by the generalized application of this form. Indeed, when a person behaves discriminatingly it is quite likely that he has made use of several personal constructs. His employment of several constructs enables him to fix both objects and behaviors multidimensionally, as one fixes points geometrically in hyperspace.

The application of a construct to an object has certain implications. Let me put two of these implications systematically, so they may become an explicit part of the theory we are developing. The first implication is that there is at least one other imaginable object which stands in contrast to the one immediately construed. The second implication is that there is at least a third object which is similar to one of the other two.

You will recognize the first of these two systematic statements as a theoretical formulation based on the incidental observation I mentioned earlier—that persons make double entity choices. The second statement is required if we are to deal with the abstraction of behavior, rather than isolated incidents of behavior. We may go on to say, then, that the minimum context in which a construct can be said to exist is three objects, or, to be more precise, three incidents. No less than three is required. As a matter of fact, of course, personal constructs are usually employed in much larger contexts.

It must also be understood that the personal construct abstracts similarity and difference simultaneously. One cannot be abstracted without implying the other. For a person to treat two incidents as different is to imply that one of them appears to be like another he knows. Conversely, for a person to treat two incidents as similar is to imply that he contrasts both of them with at least one other incident he knows. We intend this to be considered as an essential feature of the personal construct by means of which we hope to understand the psychology of human behavior.

THE PERSONAL CONSTRUCT AS A MATHEMATICAL FUNCTION

We come now to a more difficult point. I must confess that I find this point hard to explain to my students and colleagues. The discussion usually starts with the innocent question, "Do you envision the personal construct as a dichotomy or as a continuum?" My answer is, "I envision it as a dichotomy." But when I give this answer trouble starts. It appears to my listeners that I have said that human behavior must conform only to stereotypes and that everything in the world is judged as either black or white—never in shades of gray. This, of course, is not true.

I think I am beginning to understand what the root of the difficulty is. Most of us think about psychological matters concretely rather than abstractly. When we think of the form of human behavior we think of reflexes, of material learned, of decisions made, much as the child who, when he thinks of the mathematical value "four," thinks of "four apples," "four pieces of candy," "four pencils," or "four wheels."

Perhaps if we step outside the field of psychology for a moment we can make sure we have recovered our ability to think abstractly. Let us step into the field of geography. Consider the geographical construct of "north versus south." This is a dichotomous construct, and it is abstract. As far as the construct itself is concerned, there are no "partial norths" or "partial souths" crammed in between "north" and "south." And there certainly are no objects which are, of themselves, "north" or "south."

However, it is a simple matter to use this dichotomous construct to create an array of objects ranged from north to south. All we have to do is take advantage of the fact that the construct is abstract, and therefore readily available for use in a wide variety of circumstances. We may then apply it sequentially to the different objects we want to place in the array. But the array of objects we have thus set in order is not the construct; it is only one kind of concrete explication of the construct.

We can go further. We can use our abstract construct to build a scale, as for example, a scale of degrees along a meridian. This is simply a matter of creating an array of symbols which have been differentiated by our construct. Such a device has the advantage of being somewhat portable—and it is undoubtedly convenient. But never should it be confounded with the abstract construct of "north versus south," which is the basis for the device, and without which such a scale could never have been imagined.

Let us turn back, now, to psychology and visualize this same kind of dichotomous abstraction taking place. Let us visualize it taking place, not only with respect to geography, but with respect to all matters with which men, consciously or unconsciously, must cope. The particular behavioral content may vary from subject to subject and from person to person, but we propose the term, "personal construct" for the general form in which construing takes place.

As for the question of whether men deal with their world in terms of categories or continua, that is a heuristic matter. The fact is they do both, as we all well know. But the baseline, from which we may proceed to erect either categories or continua, and upon which we are free to project any behavior in our effort to understand it, may be regarded as essentially a dichotomous differentiating and integrating unit—the personal construct. It is in this sense, and in this sense only, that it properly becomes a mathematical function.

THE GEOMETRY OF PSYCHOLOGICAL SPACE

Now that we have our basic unit, the personal construct, partially defined, we can turn our attention to the question of how the world appears when structured in such terms. Perhaps it is already clear that our psychological geometry is a geometry of dichotomies rather than the geometry of areas envisioned by the classical logic of concepts, or the geometry of lines envisioned by classical mathematical geometries. Each of our dichotomies has both a differentiating and an integrating function. That is to say it is the generalized form of the differentiating and integrating act by which man intervenes in his world. By such an act he interposes a difference between incidents—incidents that would otherwise be imperceptible to him because they are infinitely homogeneous. But also, by such an intervening act, he ascribes integrity to incidents that are otherwise imperceptible because they are infinitesimally fragmented.

For the present we do not need to ask how man performs this intervening act—whether with his brain, his stomach, or his glands. Nor do we need to concern ourselves just yet with the essence of the act—whether it is cognitive, conative, or affective. Finally we need not agree on what kind of substance fills the psychological space we have structured—whether the space is stuffed with physiological things, social things, or mental things. All these matters are, at most, no more than subsequent issues, and indeed, as I personally suspect, may prove to be no issues at all, after we have put our mathematics to work.

In this kind of geometrically structured world there are no distances. Each axis of reference represents not a line or a continuum, as in analytic geometry, but one, and only one, distinction. However, there are angles. These are represented by contingencies or overlapping frequencies of incidents. Moreover, these angles of relationship between personal constructs change with the context of incidents to which the constructs are applied. Thus our psychological space is a space without distance, and, as in the case of non-Euclidian geometries, the relationships between directions change with the context.

If we turn from the geometry of the psychology of personal constructs to its arithmetic, we find that the computation is essentially digital rather than analogical, nonparametric rather than parametric. Quantification takes on a different meaning in psychology. But these further implications of our line of theoretical reasoning. exciting as they are, should not be discussed further until after we have talked about more practical matters.

DATA IN TERMS OF PERSONAL CONSTRUCTS

Let us now look at some of the instrumental inventions produced by the psychology of personal constructs, some of the questions the theory poses for psychologists, some of the methodology for answering these questions. and some of the answers that are beginning to appear.

Probably all of you are familiar with the methods used by Vigotsky to investigate concept formation. One of his methods was to have his subject make a systematic arrangement of small wooden blocks of different sizes, shapes, and colors. The purpose was to see what categories or concepts the subject spontaneously employed, how coherent he was, and whether he could effectively alter his system of categories to meet varying requirements imposed by the experimenter.

Now suppose we consider only the first of these objectives—the observation of what categories the subject spontaneously employs. We shall disregard, for the present, the question of how competent he is or how diligently he complies with the experimenter's whims. Suppose, also, that we are more concerned with the question of how he deals with people than with the question of how he deals with blocks or other inanimate objects. Finally—and this is most important of all—let us look behind the separate categories themselves and focus our attention on the differentiation and integration processes that underlie these categories. In doing all this we shall have digressed widely from what Vigotsky had in mind. though we shall be nonetheless indebted to him for establishing a useful methodological point of departure.

Now, where does this put us? Instead of sorting blocks we shall ask our subject to sort persons he knows. Instead of pointing to the categories into which he places them we shall examine the various ways in which he sees them as different and similar to each other. In other words, instead of cataloging classical concepts, we shall be eliciting psychological data in terms of our basic mathematical unit, the personal construct.

Suppose I give one of you a card and ask you to write on it the name of your mother. Then suppose I give you another and ask for the name of your father. On a third you may write the name of your wife, on a fourth the name of the girl you might have married but did not, on a fifth the name of the professor who influenced you most, and so on until you have a pack of cards containing the names of the most important persons in your life.

Next. suppose I take this pack of cards and select three of them for your particular attention. Perhaps they are the ones on which are written the names of your father, your former professor, and your present supervisor. I give them to you and ask you to think of some important way in which you regard two of them as similar to each other but in contrast to the third. You look at the cards and then put at one side the two containing the names of your professor and your supervisor, saying, "These two persons have always seemed to know the answers to the questions I asked, but this one here—my father—usually urged me to seek the answers elsewhere."

Now I may give you the card with the name of your brother and ask you where you will place it—with your professor and your supervisor, on the one side, or with your father, on the other. Perhaps you will place him with the father, saying that he, too, was inclined to advise people to find their own answers. Then may come the card with your wife's name on it. How do you apply this differentiation and integration to her? Perhaps, with respect to this particular personal construct of yours, she seems to be more like your professor and your supervisor; that is to say, she thinks she knows the answers to all questions. And so we may go through all the cards in your pack.

The data you have produced may be placed in a simple array with the names of persons arranged in a horizontal row and below them a corresponding row of symbols—pluses and minuses—indicating in each instance whether you regarded each person as more like your professor and supervisor, or more like your father. The personal construct, insofar as it has been explicated by the data you have produced, is now represented in two ways: (1) verbally, by the words you have used to symbolize it, and (2) incidentally, by the row of pluses and minuses. The context in which you have explicated the construct is represented by the particular group of human figures whose names appear on the cards.

What we have done so far may be repeated, starting with another combination of cards. If I give you the names of your wife, your mother, and the girl you nearly married, what outstanding similarity and difference will you see? Perhaps you will say that your wife and mother are sympathetic, but the girl you once thought you loved turned out to be cruel. And what will you say about each of the other persons in this respect? Again, as before, your arrangement of the cards may be recorded as a row of pluses and minuses.

THE FUNCTIONAL IDENTITY THEOREM

We can now examine the two rows of symbols you have produced to see how similar they are. Consider, first, the rather unlikely possibility that the rows are exactly alike, that each person you identified as willing to answer your questions you also judged as sympathetic, and that each person who urged you to find your own answers was also judged as cruel. Consider, further, the limiting case in which these two constructs might be explicated through an infinity of persons and events, but, throughout, would display exactly the same pattern of pluses and minuses. What may we conclude?

If we assume that the rows of pluses and minuses constitute the complete operational definitions of the two constructs involved, we may now conclude that the two constructs are functionally identical, even though you have used different words to describe them. There is an important theorem here to the effect that two constructs which produce an infinite series of identical operations are themselves identical. Of course, in this particular instance, one may raise the objection that since you have used different words in describing the two constructs the operations are not quite infinitely identical. But this is an issue that would force us to turn aside and deal with the whole question of symbols and their peculiar psychological status as events. This is not the occasion for such a digression.

THE CONSTRUCTION MATRIX

We may now pick up our pack of cards again. Starting from various combinations of three cards each, you may produce row after row of comparable data. When we stop we will have displayed before us a rectangular matrix containing a finite number of rows and a finite number of columns of nonparametric entries. At this point we may, if we wish, discard the words you have used to symbolize your constructs and consider only the configuration of incidents in the matrix. We may also discard the names of persons, too, but let us not do that just yet.

It is possible to do many things with this matrix. For example, we may factor-analyze it to see if there are clusters of similar rows or if it may be reduced to two or three row patterns without losing an undue amount of its discriminating power. We can also look at the columns and ask similar questions. What types of people inhabit your world? Are there many types or only a few? And whom do you identify with whom? Is your wife construed as more like your mother than like any other person you know? Are your father and your supervisor similar in all the respects you have displayed? Do you identify yourself with your father?

Now a host of fresh questions begins to arise, and new issues, both theoretical and practical, emerge. There are questions about the matrix itself. How many of the persons in your life and what sampling of persons is necessary for stable replication of a set of constructs? The indications, so far, suggest that not much is added if more than thirty or forty persons are represented in the matrix. How many constructs should be elicited in order to make the matrix representative of the person's ultimate matrix? This number appears to be smaller; twenty-five or thirty will suffice. The necessary and sufficient matrix is therefore likely to be one that is longer in its horizontal dimension than in its vertical dimension, but we have reason to suspect that these proportions, as well as the required size of the matrix, change as one becomes more mature.

What about changes that take place in the matrix? Do persons undergoing intensive psychotherapy, and who therefore are presumed to be changing radically, see their therapists as more and more like their fathers, as psychoanalytic theory suggests? No; they see them more and more like doctors or like persons who exercise arbitrary authority. Do persons undergoing therapy develop more generalized constructs? To answer this question we must change the subject's sorting task slightly, permitting him to discard those names of persons to whom he cannot apply a given construct. Then we get the interesting answer that in the early stages of psychotherapy the person becomes more restricted in his ways of construing the people he knows. But there is a paradox here. Another study showed that the less restricted he is at the beginning of hospital treatment, the more likely he is to make therapeutic progress—but still that this progress is itself accompanied by constriction!

But is this what happens in education? No; students during their first year away from home in college seem to change in the opposite way. Their personal constructs become more generalized, particularly constructs which emerge from their new social contacts and experiences.

Genetic Changes in the Matrix

There are questions that may be asked about human development, or the changes that commonly occur as one grows from childhood through adolescence and into adulthood. Not much has been done to answer these questions yet, but there are indications that children in general, as well as certain adults who have failed to adapt themselves to the responsibilities of mature life, tend to rely more upon figures and less upon constructs of the type we have been using for illustration. This is to say the persons they already know are used as direct measures of the persons they meet. For example, when they meet a person for the first time the principal judgment they make is whether that person is totally like or totally unlike their mother. Thus the figure of the mother serves as a kind of concretized personal construct. But as one becomes more mature it appears that his more abstract personal constructs, such as the construct, "sympathetic versus cruel," become the more important reference axes in his psychological space.

There are further changes that seem to come with maturity. In early adolescence one expects to find more use of constructs having an immediate personal reference, such as the "sympathetic versus cruel" construct I have been using as an illustration. But, while such constructs are likely to continue in use through early adulthood, there are others of a more outgoing type that are likely to emerge and assume prior importance. The construct, "willing to answer questions versus tending to refer questioners elsewhere," is an example of this somewhat more mature construction.

But these changes may happen gradually. In my earlier illustration of the relationship between two constructs I suggested that this latter construct might prove to be operationally similar to the other construct—that sympathetic people were ones who answered one's questions, and cruel people were ones who send you away to find your answers elsewhere. To suggest that you might construe such a relationship was, of course, rather unfair, as I am sure you sensed at the time I mentioned it. It is, instead, the sort of relationship one would most likely find in middle adolescence. Nevertheless, the fact that a person is able to distinguish two such constructs at all suggests that one of them is beginning to separate itself from the other—that these two axes of reference are beginning to rotate away from each other in the person's psychological space. Later on we may even find the relationship somewhat reversed, with a kind of cruelty perceived in those who suppress our curiosity with too facile answers and a kind of basic sympathy recognized in those who respect the questioner's need to become self-reliant. But it should also be said that by the time this happens both constructs will have been operationally changed, and, indeed, the whole matrix may have been altered considerably.

THE GENERALIZATION OF EXPERIENCE

But now let us turn to another class of questions. If we think of man as we think of a scientist—though we need not always think of him as a "good" scientist—what shall we say happens to his matrix, his theoretical system, when he gets negative results from his experiments. There are several possibilities. He may simply change his particular prediction of what his friends will do, without making other changes in the operations of his personal constructs. Or he may change the grounds for his prediction from one construct to another already present in his repertory. He may also change the operational patterns of the constructs he uses in making his prediction. He may invent new constructs. He may refuse to accept the verdicts given by his data and ignore them, distort his perception of them, or manipulate them in such a way that they will appear to confirm his hypothesis. (Incidentally, this latter manipulative reaction provides the basis for a fresh theoretical understanding of hostility—but that is a matter outside the scope of this paper.) Finally, he may change other constructs in his system which, while not used directly in the prediction that has failed, are nonetheless functionally related to those constructs he did use. All these, and others too, are types of changes that can and do occur, but under different conditions.

The limits of this occasion do not allow discussion of all these types of change, but it may be of interest to look more closely into one of them, perhaps the last one I mentioned—changes in constructs not directly used in making the predictions that have failed. For example, if you fail repeatedly when you make predictions of human behavior based on your construct of "sympathetic versus cruel," what happens to that other construct you use—the one that contrasted those who were ready to answer questions with those who send their questioners elsewhere?

While we are at it, we might as well mention the cognate question; what happens, for example, to your construction of your mother when your wife, whom you have construed to be much like her, turns out to be unpredictable? The first question has to do with rows in the matrix, and the second with columns. But you will also recognize in the first question the classic issue of response generalization and in the second the classic issue of stimulus generalization, although the matrix provides a different set of parameters for dealing with these problems.

According to the usual notion of a generalization gradient, we would be led to suppose that responses that are physiologically much like the one which is changed will be changed also, and that stimuli which are physically much like the one which was misjudged are likely to be reappraised also. Moreover, the more the gradient falls away from the critical response or stimulus, the more unlike it the other responses or stimuli are.

But our matrix enables us to deal with this problem in other terms.

Instead of looking to see how physiologically similar to the critical response other responses are, we can look at the matrix and ask how psychologically similar they are. And the same is true in the case of stimuli; instead of taking account only of their physical similarity, we can examine their functional similarity. Thus we do not ask how much physiological similarity there is between one's responding to persons who appear sympathetic and responding to those who answer questions; we ask, instead, if the conditions for eliciting the responses are the same. And on the stimulus side, we do not ask if your mother and your wife are actually alike; we ask, instead, if your responses to them are usually the same.

Now, with the problem of generalization set up in the psychomathematical terms of the matrix instead of the physiological and physical terms we have customarily used, what do we find? The results, so far, are not conclusive but they strongly suggest that the popular notion of the generalization gradient does not hold when reduced to these terms. If your construct of "sympathetic versus cruel" fails you and you change it, and if your construct of "answering versus sending you after your own answers" is functionally similar—though not too similar—you may, instead of making a moderate change in your use of the latter construct, become quite rigid. Similarly, if your wife and your mother are construed in much the same fashion, your disillusionment with your wife is likely to be accompanied by an idealization of your mother. Your wife, so important to you, must be reconstrued in many ways, but you are unwilling to reappraise your mother, also important to you, in any way whatsoever.

Suppose we look at the reverse situation. What happens when one's predictions are consistently confirmed? Still dealing in the same parameters and with the same tentativeness about conclusions, we find our gradients inverted. It seems, then, that at those points where one is certain of his outcomes he holds fast to his constructions but becomes freer to explore variations in adjacent areas. If you are sure of your wife you can take chances with your mother, or if you are confident of your mother you can be flexibly responsive to changes in your wife—though this is predicated on your original construction of them as similar to each other. Conversely, if you are sure about the meaning of sympathy and cruelty, you can take a second and more mature look at what it means to give glib answers to questions—though this, too, is predicated on an initially close functional relationship between these two constructs.

Tentative as they are, these still are conclusions which gain support from incidental sources. Clinical experience suggests that the child who has a reliable understanding of what is happening at home is the first to venture into the next street where he suspects strange things are going on. And we have seen that children who have found their homes chaotic may develop irrational and inflexible attitudes toward those who function as parents. Or in psychotherapy: there it often proves helpful for the therapist to establish himself as a reliable father-like figure before that timid fellow-scientist of his—the patient—dares reexamine and experiment with his parental relations.

There are other parameters, derivable from the matrix, which bear on this problem of generalization, but perhaps I have said enough to indicate that the matrix is a fertile ground for exploration and that the mathematical operations it supports can be put to good use.

THE CONSTRUCTION MATRIX AS A GENERAL MATHEMATICAL FORM

Now I would like to correct a false impression I may have allowed to occur. I have talked about the matrix as if it were a particular psychological instrument, with persons ranged along one axis and constructs ranged along the other. But this is only a particular case. We could have substituted occupations or job assignments instead of persons and, as one investigator has done, examine the resulting matrix to see how workers construe their tasks and why they do some of the things they do. Or, if we are dealing with children, we could use the matrix to explicate the relationship between toys and games. Or, if we are dealing with rats, we could set up conditioning series to different triads of signals, and then examine the matrix to see what relationships emerge, and the effects of extinction on the patterns of relationship.

Finally, as I think of the uses to which the matrix might be put, I find myself a little depressed. Suppose someone would surreptitiously put "stimuli" instead of persons along one margin of the matrix, and "responses" instead of constructs along the other. If that should ever happen I am sure I would feel that I had been brought back, full circle to where I started. But perhaps no one will be so unkind as to do this; perhaps the most that will happen is that someone will put Leningrad "signals" along one axis and Tbilisi "sets" along the other. In any case, let us say broadly that the matrix is a general mathematical operation for relating events and behavior, and that the concurrence of these two psychological values can be expressed in terms of the psycho-mathematical function I have described—the personal construct.

5

The Strategy of Psychological Research

MAN DOES NOT always think logically. Some take this as a serious misfortune. But I doubt that it is. If there is a misfortune I think it more likely resides in the fact that, so far, the canons of logic have failed to capture all the ingenuities of man, and, perhaps, also in the fact that so many men have abandoned their ingenuities in order to think "logically" and irresponsibly. For each of us the exercise of ingenuity leads him directly to a confrontation with his personal responsibility for what happens. But, of course, he can avoid that distressing confrontation if, through his conformity to rules, he can make it appear that he has displaced the responsibility to the natural order of the universe.

It is, of course, possible to restate many of the achievements of man in terms of the logic we have so far formalized. But this does not tell us much about how the achievements came about. Nor does it help at all in finding how to disengage ourselves from the logic by which those achievements are presently sustained so we can go on to greater ones. For example, most of our formalized logic has to do with the establishment of certainties. But human progress depends

SOURCE. Presented at Brunel College, London, on November 18, 1964 in a seminar series on personal construct theory conducted by Neil Warren, and later published in the *Bulletin of the British Psychological Society*, 1965, **18**, 1–15. Acknowledgment is made of the kind permission of the British Psychological Society to include this paper.

also upon the selective creation of uncertainties; that is to say, the pinpointing of preposterous doubts and the formulation of new questions and issues.

ANSWERS WITHOUT QUESTIONS

We have a logic of answers; now what about a logic of questions? To be sure, the logical positivists urged that we focus our attention upon questions that invite empirical answers. And that helped. At least it helped the research technicians who always like to have something to show for their efforts. But in ruling out all the questions for which no empirical answers could be foreseen the logical positivists aborted the embryonic questions out of which viable issues develop. Fortunately, as they grew older, most of these men sensed the sterility of the system they had been on the point of creating. For all their concern about the validity of questions they appeared to have had little awareness of the psychological processes by which doubts are systematically created and new issues take shape.

Yet doubts and issues are important and answers make no sense without them. Whatever one knows, or thinks he knows, he once approached with vague apprehension and he now experiences within a network of subjectively paired alternatives. If, then, we are to comprehend what he knows, or what he wants to know, or what he thinks, or feels, or dreads, or does, we must understand the system of contradictions within which his possibilities hold their shape and his choices—deliberate or impulsive—are made. These contrasts are, moreover, his own contrivances—his own constructions placed upon reality—and the network, with its restrictive channels of thought, feeling and action, is what we may call his "personal construct system."

But while an answer makes no sense when there is no issue, it is too often assumed that once an answer has been found that is the end of the matter and there is no further point in raising issues. This is to say simply that a pat answer is the enemy of a fresh question. As long as we regard an answer as an objective conclusion we are inclined to make external nature take full responsibility for it. The possibility that it is acceptable as a conclusion, only because it resolves the question we have chosen to ask, does not readily occur to us.

In a naturalistic science, in contrast to a constructive science, the only ground for raising new questions is clear evidence that the old answers are incorrect. If, then, progress is to be made in such an epistemological climate, all alternative constructions must be discredited before a single new one can be seriously entertained. While this makes for lively debate it tends to block any new thinking before it has much of a chance to find out what it can accomplish.

But this kind of epistemological totalitarianism need not occur if human thought is envisioned in psychological rather than prescriptive terms merely. Nature can be regarded as open to an infinite variety of alternative constructions—some of them better than others, to be sure—and with most of the best ones yet to be concocted. In such a system the function of an answer is not to make further questioning unnecessary but to hold things together until a round of better questions has been thought up.

POSING QUESTIONS

This brings us to an important feature of effective strategy in psychological research. It should be constructive. I mean this in both senses of the term—in the sense that it approaches matters by placing a construction upon them and also in the sense that it produces something new rather than preoccupies itself with discrediting prior constructions. Now I want to be careful how I say this, for one of the criteria of a good experiment is that it opens the door to precise disconfirmation. But to attempt to disconfirm an old answer explicitly is implicitly to confirm the old question, while important research, I think, generally starts with fresh questions.

For example, it seems to me to be a waste of time to undertake some massive disproof of Hullian learning theory for that theory, like most elaborated theories can, with a little letting out and taking in here and there, be made to account for most all of what the stimulus-response psychologists like to call "learning." Indeed I have begun to suspect, like psychoanalysis, it can be stretched to account for almost anything human, as well as a lot of things that aren't. But what might be more exciting would be to disengage ourselves from the very notion of "learning"—not because it is wrong but because any human notion is prejudicial—then to recast the issues of intellectual endeavor and see what possibilities emerge for mankind. Good research, in this manner, starts by concerning itself with the kind of questions to be asked, not with answers to questions thoughtlessly posed or taken for granted.

So any statement we make can well be regarded as the answer to a question we ask—a biased question—and emerges as an indicated choice between alternatives previously posed. Furthermore any act, or experience, can be regarded as having such dimensional properties. We go rather than stay. We feel happy not just because we are in a state of mind, but we feel happy rather than sad or bored. We experience daytime in the dimension of night and day. Any act, or feeling, or statement bears equally upon its subjective antithesis without which it has no psychological significance to the person involved. The strategy of research concerns itself with knowing what the antithesis, for the person, is—what the question was, what the dimension of his appraisal may be or, to put it in terms I prefer, what kind of personal construct provides the relevant axis of reference.

THE ANALYSIS OF UNIQUENESS

A perennial problem among Darwinians is the question of uniqueness among organisms. It strikes me as a rather tautological issue, one that would never have arisen if biologists had not so bound themselves to a limited matrix of appraisal. Among psychologists, however, where the axes of reference have not been so parsimoniously devised, the issue scarcely arises at all. Anyone who has tried very hard to understand the human personality has not spent much of his time wondering if people were really different from each other. For him the problem has been, rather, how to transcend the uniqueness of man in order to see him in terms of a comprehensive system simple enough to be understood.

In recent years, in order to cope with the problem of too much uniqueness, psychological research has placed increasing emphasis on multivariant methods. This means designing matrices of input and measurement in which a number of variables are plotted simultaneously. Such a matrix of inquiry provides a model of a psychological hyperspace within which one may understand man in depth rather than continue plotting him one dimension at a time, as, for example, we try to do when we look for the correlates of intelligence. And some psychologists have gone beyond this and have advocated a multivariant multimethod approach to research. This is to suggest that not only should we see man in more than one dimension at a time but also that we should vary the devices by which we manipulate and measure along each of those dimensions.

One way to envision the multivariant approach in research is to see it in terms of an interweave of events and constructs—or, if you prefer, an interweave of observations and issues. Each fixes the other in psychological space. Imagine an array of events, or objects, which are to be understood in a complex manner. We can arrange those events according to some issue—or construct—placing those to which one pole of the issue is more appropriately applied on the one side and those to which the other pole is more applicable on the other. Having done that, we can scramble the events and rearrange them in terms of another construct. As this rearranging proceeds, each event becomes locked into psychological space in greater depth. That is to say, an event seen only in terms of its placement on one dimension is scarcely more than a mere datum. And about all you can do with a datum is just let it sit on its own continuum. But as the event finds its place in terms of many dimensions of consideration it develops psychological character and uniqueness.

Now suppose we want to understand women. This is not an unprecedented undertaking. A good many persons have already tried their hand at this kind of research. So we start out by getting ourselves some women, perhaps all we can lay our hands on. This, too, is not an unprecedented research strategy and one that has been employed by those who find women particularly puzzling or have never figured out just what to do with them.

Now that we have our women, what is to be our question? Which ones are feminine and which masculine? Yes, if we wish, we can sort them out that way. But when we get through we will probably not yet know much about them. So we sort them in other ways, according to other constructs: busy-busy-busy women and oh-so-languid women, provocative women and bland women, passionate women and impacted women, women who look better dressed in expensive clothes and women who look better not dressed in expensive clothes. Now if we are able to keep all these constructs in mind—and not everyone can or wants to—each woman in our sample will begin to look different from all the others. She will appear unique.

But we need to extend our matrix both by adding constructs and by adding events. We should include men too. In understanding women it is as important to understand how they resemble and distinguish themselves from men as it is to assume simply that women are not men. And we need to extend our matrix in other ways. We need to understand how one woman changes her moods, how she responds differently to different men and, ultimately, how she builds her own matrix of appraisal. Only as we undertake this last assessment do we place ourselves in a position to play a role in relation to her.

THE MINIMAX PROBLEM
IN PSYCHOLOGY AND IN SCIENCE

One of the popular prescriptions for science is Occam's Razor or the so-called law of parsimony. It is the rather unimaginative notion that the simpler of two explanations is always the better as long as it covers the facts at hand. I suppose if every conclusion we reach is to be regarded as a terminal point of human inquiry this might not be such a bad rule to follow. But simple explanations are not necessarily the most fertile ones and, since I have a feeling that has been encouraged by the recent American elections[1]—a feeling that the world is going to go on for a while—I think it is more important to come up with explanations that lead somewhere rather than those whose only merit is that they can be punched into IBM cards.

But the law of parsimony can be regarded as a crude attempt to state a psychological principle and that principle is important to the strategy of psychological research. One of man's most pressing psychological problems is to understand his circumstances in variety as well as in depth—most of all to understand himself and his fellow man in variety and in depth. Of course variety and depth are related, but we need not go into that now.

One way to be aware of greater variety is to conjure up more constructs. But the number of constructs needed does not increase in direct ratio to the number of events to be distinguished. So what we have is a minimax problem; how to discriminate meaningfully the greatest variety of events with the least number of constructs. Since constructs are not only hard to come by but are difficult to keep in mind after you get them, it becomes psychologically strategic to devise a system which will do the most with the least.

Now this is not the law of parsimony, but I think it is clear how the law of parsimony must have been formulated by some poor striving student who found himself as much overwhelmed by the multiplicity of his ideas as by the multiplicity of his circumstances. He must have faced his personal minimax problem: how to probe the maximum complexity of events with the minimum complexity of construction. And this, as I see it, is strictly a psychological compromise.

Moreover, the minimax solution must vary within certain human limits from person to person. So its practical variability needs to be

[1] The lecture was delivered shortly after the election of Lyndon B. Johnson over his opponent, Barry Goldwater. (Ed.)

respected by the researcher. He must have some idea of what his own limits of construction complexity are, or what the limits are of the colleagues with whom he must test out his hunches. This, and not some legalistic principle for getting at the essence of nature, is the issue. Of course there is more to it than this, but perhaps I have said enough to suggest the relevance of the minimax principle to the strategy of research and to the model of the rectangular repertory grid with its interweave of events and constructs in unequal proportions.

COLLECTIVIZATION AND INDIVIDUALIZATION

I know that psychological research is frequently regarded as a way of extricating the scientist from the clutter of personal individuality in order to cope with mankind collectively. This leads to a science of categories and pigeonholes rather than to a science of dimensions and units. In one case the generalizations are concrete; in the other, abstract. In one case objects are arranged; in the other, differentiated. But this psychology of categorization, with which we are all too familiar, is quite different from the psychology of differentiation.

I hope I have said enough thus far to tempt you to conjure up in your minds a notion of research headed in the opposite direction—a research that has the effect of making each individual stand out in clearer perspective as a unique person yet accomplishing this new perspective without resorting to the kind of holism that repeats the cliché, "the individual as a whole," and which rejects all precise distinctions. It is, instead, a psychology that is neither fragmental nor holistic. It is constructive; that is to say it uses abstractions and generalizations not to collectivize man, nor to protect him from analysis, but to differentiate him. And by that I mean not merely to differentiate him from other men but to differentiate among his acts and to differentiate between what he once was, what he now is, and what he may choose to become.

So there are, indeed, general things that can well be said about the psychology of man, but they are not the sort of things that most psychologists have been saying. They have to do, instead, with such matters as the methodology of man and the methodology of man's attempts—our attempts—to understand man. They have to do also with the units of psychological science—such as the abstracted "construct" I have proposed—and with the structure of the matrices within which the individual man can see himself and others in greater depth and within which he can be seen in greater depth and perspective. In short, I am proposing the same psychology for the researcher as for the man he studies. Each can profit from employing the psychology of the other; but perhaps of the two the researcher can profit more. Let me now see if I can make this point clear.

INDIVIDUAL DIFFERENCES
AND "THE VARIABLES"

When I glance through a research prospectus before settling down to read it in detail there are a number of special things I look for. For example, I usually turn to the appendix if the writer has been kind enough to include it in the preliminary draft. Even before I know what his problem is I want to see if he knows what it is. One way to tell is to look at his instrumentation, the part of the study that is usually relegated to the appendix. I want to see if it appears to reflect any particular sensitization to the experience of his subjects. If he is merely applying an instrument he did not devise or derive from an intimate study of persons, I wonder if he has any first-hand familiarity with the problem he proposes to investigate and if he is not interposing the instrument between himself and the persons he would rather not know too well. Is he merely playing games with data? If so, it is what I call "slot machine psychology" or "Las Vegas humanism." I shall have more to say about this later.

Then I look to see if the writer has posed his questions well enough to work out his statistical analysis before he has set out to collect his final round of data. While I am not utterly opposed to some post hoc statistical analysis, after misfortune has struck and the student's children are growing pale and hungry, I believe that one should have tried to set up his statistics and his tables before starting the final round of data collection. Only the numerical entries and arithmetic computations should come after. And later I shall have more to say about this too.

But what I want to mention now is that very suspicious little clue to bad research— the "control group." Of course I realize that control groups in psychological research, like apologies for giving low marks in a classroom, are occasionally unavoidable. But when they appear in an experimental design I immediately wonder if the writer wants to understand persons or distribute them.

Now to understand my aversion to control groups let me talk about psychological variables. I don't much like the term "variables" either, for it appears to refer to the things that vary. It shouldn't. It should designate the selected reference axes with respect to which objects can be understood to vary. But then the reference axes should stand still. So it is the objects that vary with respect to the invariant reference axes. But no respectable scientist would say that the objects are the variables he talks about, even though he might concede that they are the only things that vary. It's all very confusing.

Well, anyway, when I mention "variables" you will all know that I am referring to reference axes with respect to which objects can be perceived as variable, and that, although I have not come right out and said so, I really mean *constructs* having dimensional properties—*personal* constructs that is. Sometimes I hear a colleague say something about "taking into account all the relevant variables." That always strikes me as a little expansive—something like taking an inventory of all the lines in hyperspace or going on an expedition to "find" the North Pole.

"SCIENTISTS" OUT LOOKING FOR THOSE PESKY MISLAID "VARIABLES"

I have no objection to the notion that persons might vary; of course not. What seems to me to be considerably less than scientific is the notion that they have variables in their insides and that we should go looking for them. Individuals do vary, both within themselves and among themselves. The problem of the psychologist is to come up with some notions that will enable him to impose structure upon that variation. It is his responsibility to devise some dimensions, if he is capable of such abstractions, in terms of which the variation will make sense.

There are several ways of doing this. The most common way is to collect some subjects, already distributed into obvious categories—like women and men, or sane people and people we lock up for their own good. Then we try to figure out what is the difference. We have had moderate success in the one case, but in the other the distinction is still pretty hazy. In the case of the people we lock up we usually examine them—not the people who lock them up—or subject them to experimental conditions to determine what there is about them that makes them so obviously different. It might be more appropriate to find out what there is about us that makes us judge them as different.

But even that does not quite get to the point. To be sure, the fact that some are locked up suggests that the deterministic choice point resides in the person who made the decision and that probably he himself has not been locked up—at least not yet. But the explanation of the categorization he employed does lie in the constructs accepted by himself and all those who make such decisions. If we want to understand why some people are locked up and some not we should examine the construction system in terms of which the decisions are made. Then we can go further and see if that construction system is truly predictive of what it claims to be. And we can go still further to see if the system is *necessarily* predictive of what the outcome of their lives *might* be.

But the variables—you now know what I mean by "variables"—that explain the differences between persons are not to be confounded with the ones that explain what happens to people or what can happen to them. So when we look for variables by which persons can be distinguished from each other we should not expect to find "the variables" of psychology by which personal lives have variety and accomplish change.

THE PARADOX OF VARIABLES REVEALED

Now about those control groups. They suggest to me that what the person is mainly interested in controlling is interindividual differences. Of course this is all right if he is an administrator and this is really the level of his psychological ingenuity. But usually he is smarter than this—most psychologists are nowadays—and it has occurred to him that psychology might be concerned with variables that could mean something in one's personal life. In that case he has something I think is worth pursuing. But his bland use of control groups suggests that he thinks he can control such intraindividual variables by specifying interindividual variables that have the same names.

Now sometimes they do turn out to be comparable variables or axes of reference. I must concede that. But the glib incorporation of control groups in an experimental design implies that the researcher has assumed that a variable is a variable, and once you have found it there it is, and you will have to control it from now on out.

Well, I don't mean to say I won't go ahead and read the prospectus. There are times when it is pretty hard to control the variation that needs to be specified and you have to settle for a substitute. Still, most of the research I have seen could have been wrapped up into a much tighter design with all the controls defined in intraindividual terms. And this seems to me to be a much better research strategy. Besides, haven't you noticed how much more lenient the formula for the *t*-test is in such cases and how much more powerfully—to use the statisticians' improbable term—an analysis of variance square takes care of things when you subject each person to all experimental conditions?

BAITING THE PSYCHOLOGICAL TRAP

Now I have the feeling that I have left something dangling here. Let's see! Women—we were talking about women. This is a problem that seems to preoccupy so many psychologists: are there *really* sex differences and, if so, what on earth might they be? Well, I wouldn't want to ignore the ladies and, even in my serious role as a "psychologist," I have no intention of doing so. Moreover I have been convinced in my own mind for some time now that there are indeed interesting differences between women and men. The constructs—excuse me, "variables"—that isolate women from men are exciting, no doubt, though the ones that psychologists keep coming up with are not the ones I use in identifying women or relating to them. My colleagues come up with variables like "being able to get better marks in literature courses than in mathematics" or "having more mechanical skill in handling soft objects made of cloth than hard objects such as plumbers' tools." So in these ways women do differ from men.

But what happens to your own life when you attempt to vary it along such an axis? What happens indeed! What happens when you use it to structure intraindividual change? Well, you can become more feminine or you can become more masculine. A lot of people fuss and fuss over that decision. You can take up plumbing or you can take up dressmaking; you can do the things that women do or the things that men do. And that, I am sorry to say, is about the only channel of freedom that many persons have. It is not surprising, therefore, that so many of those who structure their lives, or attempt to alter their predicament, in terms of this dimension complain to their therapists that they "never seem to get anywhere." Certainly the sense of futility in a person whose role as a man or a woman is cast only in terms of sex differences is well known clinically. His problem is not that he doesn't know the difference between women and men. His problem is, rather, that his own life must go on. And since he has no other clear reference axes he can do no better than to vacillate psychologically between gross masculinity and femininity. Not even the idea of taking up plumbing and marrying a dressmaker is likely to occur to him.

But this was not intended to be a discussion of sex roles. It was meant, rather, to do with the strategy of psychological research and I have tried to illustrate, in this particular case, the paradox posed by a psychology of individual differences that presumes to offer structure for the processes by which human lives are lived. Now it is time to go on to something else.

THE PROBLEM OF DISENGAGEMENT

Let me try to distinguish between two views of the scientific enterprise. There is the view that science makes its progress step by step. This is usually taken to mean that we discover nature a fragment at a time, that as each fragment is verified it is fitted into place—much like a piece in a jigsaw puzzle. Some day we'll get it all put together.

The other view is a constructive one. We understand our world by placing constructions on it. And that is the way we alter it too. There is no finite end to the alternative constructions we may employ; only our imagination sets the limits. Still, some constructions serve better than others, and the task of science is to come up with better and better ones. Moreover we have some handy criteria for selecting better ones; at least we think we have, and they, too, are subject to reconstruction.

Now the first view we can call *accumulative fragmentalism*—a term pretentious enough to encourage most readers to leave the definition up to the author—and the second *constructive alternativism*—also a fairly good sized mouthful. They make a difference. In the first case science seeks to verify a hypothesis—determine whether it is really true. In the second case science seeks to confirm predictions—that is to say, observes how well its hypothesis has worked.

All right, so far so good, but the difference still seems to be a matter of semantics. The effective difference comes in what happens next. The man who has verified his hypothesis has, he supposes, a little chunk of 24-carat truth to add to his inventory. The man who has confirmed his prediction has, in the form of the hypothesis he has devised, only another pearl-handled extrapolator for approximating the future. For him there may remain many other ways and, likely as not, some of them will turn out to be better than what he has.

The first man thinks he has captured an essence; the second knows only that he has devised a method.

Now what happens? This, by the way, is a question that is always appropriate, whether we are talking about science or the client who has resolved his transference neurosis and bids a healthy farewell to his psychotherapist. To the accumulative fragmentalist the next step is to find another nugget of truth or another paying client. To the constructive alternativist the next step is to see if he can improve his hypothesis, perhaps by formulating his questions in new ways or by pursuing the implications of some fresh assumption that occurred to him when he was writing up the conclusions to his last experiment. But for the accumulative fragmentalist the only grounds for entertaining further questions about the matter is evidence that he was wrong. Since this kind of nuisance may pop up at any time he is careful to replicate his experiments and make sure the answer to his question is absolutely, positively, and irrevocably right!

Once a man has "verified" his hypotheses he guards his findings jealously. If alternatives to such "proven conclusions" are proposed he immediately suspects someone is trying to snatch his nuggets away from him and his howls of protest will echo from one end of Academia to the other. They will have to prove he is dead wrong before he will release his clutch on what he has acquired in the name of Science, Ltd.—an outfit in which he believes he has become a major stockholder. But to the constructive alternativist it is a matter of no more than momentary interest whether his colleague's findings are disconfirmed or not. To propose a new question does not require the denial of an old answer. Indeed every neat answer makes him wonder what would have happened if the question had been posed differently.

Here, then, is the difference between the two points of view. It has to do with what ensues from the outcome of a successful experiment. It has to do with gracious and respectful disengagement from old and valuable ways of looking at things. In the one case disengagement can come only after brutal disconfirmation; in the other, disengagement is expected from the outset and may be undertaken deliberately and precariously as a step toward a better science. In the case where disconfirmation must precede the posing of new questions, disengagement can take place only in the state of chaos produced by disconfirmation. In the other case one does not wait for chaos to overtake him; he uses those previous conclusions to provide whatever security he may need to order his life while he is out looking for alternatives to them.

While I have been talking about scientists everything I have been saying applies equally to persons who do not claim to be scientists. A psychotherapy patient who accumulates things in pieces such as "good habits," "clever solutions," "sound knowledge," and tokens of "meritorious achievements" is likely to let his life get into pretty bad shape before he starts letting go of what he has acquired. And when he does start to let go everything seems to crumble at once. He had assumed that once his conclusions were verified there would be no point in exploring further what had already been demonstrated to be true. To make matters worse, every proposition his therapist offers or encourages becomes a threat, for it implies a sweeping invalidation of his way of life and a further spread of the chaos that has already engulfed him. The therapist will find himself called upon to exercise great skill in helping such a person collect his wits enough to venture anything new.

So one's epistemology does make a difference, whether in science or in one's personal life. And what I may not have emphasized enough is the depth of the construction that can become involved in this problem of disengagement. I am not talking about formal verbal propositions only; I have in mind all levels of discrimination, including those levels which are frequently catalogued as "somatic."

STEPS IN CREATIVE THINKING

But disengagement is only one small aspect of the process of creative endeavor. Nor should psychological research be regarded merely as the counter-punctate composition of observations and newly formalized propositions; that is to say, a play between experience at two levels only—levels such as "cognition" and "perception." Research involves all the levels of experience that man is capable of having. This is especially true of psychological research. It is an orchestration of all the talents of man, just as psychotherapy is such an orchestration, not the implementation of some talents and the denial of others. And there is a way to put them all together—many, many ways I'm sure.

Let us turn now to what may be called the *creativity cycle*. This is a cycle that starts with a phase of loosened construction and terminates with a phase of tightened construction. These phases are not to be regarded as alternative states but as transitional stages in a continuity in which the vague, unexpected and dreamlike constructions that emerge during the loose phase are not altogether abandoned in favor of tight and neatly defined constructions in the later phase but are, instead, gently lifted from the miasma of incoherence and sensitively shaped to definition without being subjected to prematurely harsh tests of consistency—either tests of consistency with themselves or consistency with other constructions more tightly held. As these constructions take shape they are more tightly formulated and are prepared for an eventual rigorous test and for the confirmation or disconfirmation of all the human anticipations they invoke.

The trick, of course, is to deliver these nascent constructions alive without losing track of what they are or becoming frightened by their monstrous implications. It also requires considerable overall integrity to reach far into the preverbal constructions of our lives without becoming so involved that we want to stay there, or to reserve such self-gratifying indulgences apart for those special occasions when we want to escape responsibilities and "regress in service of our egos." It also requires integrity at the other end of the cycle and so to test reality for whatever it is, or, having tested it, not to hold too fast to its certainties for whatever security they seem to provide against personal chaos.

Without going into further detail let me suggest that the utmost employment of this kind of cyclical continuity is involved in the strategy of psychological research. But I should say also that for any one person there are limits in the extent to which he can go in either direction and still retrieve himself. I once tried to state this consideration as a "modulation corollary" to personal construct theory's basic postulate like this: "The variation in a person's construction system is limited by the permeability of the constructs within whose ranges of convenience the variants lie." Not everyone has set out to erect constructs for himself that are permeable enough to encompass and modulate the extremes of loose and tight thinking. And not many teachers have ever thought to suggest that he should.

THE ROLE OF PERSONAL INVOLVEMENT

Research does not start with the ranging of objective evidence against formal propositions. There is much that goes on before. Indeed this is only the terminal incident in the tightening phase of the creativity cycle. Behind it lies the disengagement from previous conclusions, the loosening, the emerging of new constructions and the posing of fresh questions—all of which I have mentioned.

But what I have not dealt with adequately up to this point are the devices for enlisting the ingenuities of man. Those ingenuities can be tapped only if he takes certain courageous steps to involve himself wholly in what he has undertaken. Otherwise he will think logically about his problem and let it go at that. He may use only those constructions he can put into words and can identify coherently within his favorite rational system.

But every man has other constructs held far back in reserve upon which he will likely rely if he gets into a jam. Some of them are verbally available to him; some are not. If he is to tap such resources he needs to get himself into a predicament, or at least put himself in a position where it will not suffice to act like an academician. There are ways of doing this.

One of the first measures for involving all the ingenuities of man is to go to where the problem is acute, to have him place himself, as best he can, in the midst of the circumstances upon which psychological structure is to be imposed. Not only does this involve the senses, the social "pressures" and the feeling of personal responsibility, but it provides one with an abundance of minor cues which he may weave into the fabric of his new construction. For example, I never conceptualized some of the psychological dimensions of poverty until I smelled the country market in Port-au-Prince, Haiti. Not even the wretchedness of certain parts of India placed the plight of poverty-stricken man in as deep perspective as that sensuous experience did.

Then there is involvement. This, if I understand them correctly, is what the existentialists mean when they talk about being "in the world." It is what we hope will happen when a researcher places himself in the circumstances he wishes to construe psychologically. But it may not happen, even in those circumstances, for one must see *himself as one of those circumstances*, and there are some who are so alien to the world that it is impossible for them to experience themselves as part of it. Still the fact that he himself is there, he himself is there going about being the kind of person he is and doing the things he does; that, too, is one of the circumstances he must cope with. And he may realize, further, that his presence there serves to make matters worse all around. To be involved is to realize that whatever happens, happens to oneself too, that whatever is done, he, too, has had a part in doing it. That is involvement.

Once involved the researcher is confronted with the chilling fact that the constructions, verbal and preverbal, by which his own life is ordered, have had a part in structuring events for which it would never otherwise have occurred to him he had any responsibility. I think it is only when one involves himself in psychotherapy with a disturbed person, for example, that he comes to realize that his own impulses and aversions, or ones like them in others, have had a part in making the person what he is, and that inevitably they will have a part in making him what he is to become. And this kind of realization will also put his research prospectus in quite a new light and will make it clear that man, the researcher, can no more be a stranger to mankind than man, the psychotherapist.

COMMITMENT

But involvement is not enough to generate effective strategy in psychological research. There is commitment. The human venture is not an exercise in passive receptivity, nor is understanding developed out of sensory experience alone. As for the child who must manipulate the world in his mouth or with his ever-moving hands, so for the psychologist, too, who comes to know man only by doing something with men. So he commits himself to a human course of action. Without doing so he can never know what relevance his own construction of life has to the lives that others live.

Commitment, I fully realize, means aggression—personal aggression—and if the outcome brings a sense of having violated his role, the psychologist will experience guilt. Thus commitment can never be undertaken without risking one's virtue and sometimes losing it, nor without the possibility of emerging as a villain and sometimes actually doing just that. So in undertaking commitment the strategy of psychological research requires one to take deep personal risks. No wonder so many of us would like to become scientists and be content to win prizes without having to take an awful responsibility for people.

APPRAISAL

But even commitment is not enough; and here we part company with the existentialists. There must be appraisal and reconstruction. A commitment is not a blind undertaking—at least it should not be. Whatever one does under commitment he must continue throughout to face the possibility that he was wrong and as his experience brings him to new vantage points he must stand ready to reconstrue his whole undertaking. Thus he will stand as his own accuser, and the most penetrating judgments of his failures will be handed down by himself. That hurts, but it is necessary if the human enterprise is to progress. Only with this step is the experiential process complete, and it is complete only to the extent that it sets the stage for the next round. Nor is psychological research, merely because it purports to be scientific, exempt from this step in the human process through which mankind seeks his objectives.

PRACTICAL STEPS

Translated into the more familiar terms of the psychological laboratory, what I have been saying suggests that the researcher is more likely to mobilize his ingenuities in devising important hypotheses if he goes to where the psychological problems are. In my own case I interpret this to mean going to where persons are disturbed enough to try to make something new out of their lives as, for example, where children are, for they are continually trying to make something new out of themselves—counting each year as they grow up and making plans for what they will do when they escape the restraints of size, age, vocabulary, and parental control. Or it may mean going to where adults have taken a critical look at themselves as, for example, to the clinic or the psychotherapy room. Wherever man is struggling mightily to make something of himself there is a fertile place for the researcher to be.

But, in a practical sense, research strategy means commitment too. That is to say the psychologist who wants to find out something about mankind had better join in the human enterprise else he will never know what it is all about. In my own case this has meant nearly thirty-five years of part-time service as a psychotherapist—not because feeling useful was the primary reward I sought but because I knew of no better way to bring all my resources to bear on the problems of scientific psychology with which I had undertaken to cope.

And, of course, there is, for the research strategist, reappraisal. When I look back on those years there are many regrets and many pangs of guilt. But that was the risk I took. Moreover, I am always perplexed at how long it took me to reach certain "obvious conclusions," as, for example, the *naivete* of stimulus-response psychology, or the utter irresponsibility of such a notion as "motivation."

But how does one who has had the full round of generalized experience get his research project under way? I think, first of all, he takes his particular problem through the same cycle of experience. He should go to where his newly posed problem is most acute. He should plunge into some reasonable involvement. And he should appraise what then happens to man—to others and, particularly, to himself.

I urge students, for example, who want to investigate "schizoid" thought to have a round of experience with it themselves. They should talk to their teammates, trying out their hunches about what it is to be a "schizoid" thinker. And they should ask their teammates to do the same thing and report what they observe and what they experience. Then they should see how others react to "schizoid" thought. And, lest the possibility should escape them, they should check their portrayals with experts, that is with "genuine schizophrenics" and the professors who study them.

They should also take advantage of the creativity cycle—lifting from their own loosened thinking tender hypotheses to be developed and, when clearly enough defined, to be rigorously tested in precast experimental designs in which all the statistical logic has been specified before the collection of the final round of data begins.

And, finally, they should not overlook what their subjects have to contribute, for psychological research, as I see it, is a cooperative enterprise in which the subject joins the psychologist in making an inquiry. I am very skeptical of any piece of human research in which the subjects' questions and contributions have not been elicited or have been ignored in the final analysis of results.

SUMMARY

The strategy of psychological research has its philosophical roots and its everyday techniques. It employs man's intellectualisms, but it makes full use also of what many still regard as his irrational stupidities. It concerns itself with constructions that successively approximate the truth, not with the mere accumulation of fragments of truth. It disengages from old scholastic conclusions and reengages with man. It experiences. It tests. It reappraises. But, most of all, it seeks to mobilize all the resources of man—experimenter and subject—and not those of formalized logic alone.

6

Humanistic Methodology in Psychological Research

HUMANISM IS usually regarded as the guiding motif in the intellectual transitions that took place in western Europe during "The Humanistic Century" of 1450 to 1550, A.D. During those years the cultures of classic Greece and Rome were examined in a new light. Whereas the medieval scholastics had rationalized the classics, the humanists put themselves in the place of the men who wrote them. When they did they caught glimpses of the freedom, innovation, and variety that had made the great classical achievements possible.

To the extent that humanism grasped an outlook rather than recapitulated an era it could combine with other forces to write an exhilarating chapter in the story of man. In its course the new study of the classics mobilized aspirations and utilized instruments it did not always intend. Ironically it was the very breath and wit of his humanism that made the classicist Erasmus the unwilling ally of the activist Luther. But the alliance shaped the conscience of man. And without gunpowder, which challenged the impregnability of baronical castles sitting astride the world's highways, and the printing press, which invited every man to become a scholar or a priest in his own right, humanism might have amounted to little more than return to classicism.

THE HUMANISTIC INTENT

Classicism reveres the past; humanism is inspired by it. The classicist engrosses himself in the thought of other times; the humanist uses history as a fulcrum to pry himself loose from the prejudices of his own. Yet humanism's emancipation of the mind accomplishes little except as it molds man's conscience to new subleties and marshals his technology to create fresh and challenging circumstances. A conscience so preoccupied with the evils of other times that it is insensitive to the wretchedness of its own, or a technology that serves only as an instrument of subjugation, renders bootless whatever freedom of thought the disadvantaged are allowed to retain. Soon enough empty-handed men abandon their intellectual freedoms to the prophesies of ideologies and the claims of the most vocal leaders.

One does not need to derive humanism from classicism. Indeed, to the extent that humanism produces novelty it distinguishes itself from classism. As I see it, classism was historically incidental humanism—no more. It seems to me, therefore, that the humanist's research in particular should not restrict itself either to classical topics or to classical methodologies. If a researcher does recapture the outlook of some prescient moment of the past—perhaps one when men were less subservient to deterministic doctrine than they are now—he may do so simply to start his inquiries afresh, rather than to retreat to the precedents of earlier beliefs.

Yet it must be said that much that passes for humanism today is more backward-wishing than forward-seeking, more antitechnological than instrumental. If looking backward will serve to disengage us from the strictures of today's intellectualisms, well and good. But if it renders us insensitive to living man, his immobilizing circumstances and his untried potentialities it will turn us down the path of scholasticism rather than of renaissance.

HUMANISTIC PSYCHOLOGY
AND INSTRUMENTALISM

It would, in my opinion, be a serious mistake for psychologists who hope to raise man from the position of an unwitting subject in an experiment to a posture of greater dignity, to abandon technology. The spirit of man is not enlarged by withholding his tools. Just, as I have recalled, it took the technology of gunpowder and the printing press to turn humanism into something more than classicism, so now it requires an appropriate technology for humanistic psychology to realize its objectives. A man without instruments may look dignified enough to those who do not stand in his shoes, but he most certainly will be incapable of making the most of his potentialities.

Besides, like B. F. Skinner, there are moments when I have doubts about what is meant by "the dignity of man." I can remember my father saying when I was a youngster that as far as he could see dignity often turned out to be stupidity in disguise, and moreover, the disguise was often an honorary degree such as Doctor of Divinity— which he, an erstwhile clergyman, humorously paraphrased as "Doctor of Dignity." I can't say that I altogether agree with him, but of this I am sure: a genuine respect for the dignity of man includes placing the instruments of effective action in his service and it cannot be expressed adequately by making claims for his noble nature or by erecting a statue of him sitting on a stone horse in the park.

Now American psychology has contributed enormously to the literature of behavior modification and instrumental conditioning. Psychologists who see themselves as humanistically inclined are likely to disparage this contribution and, often as not, are alarmed by it. They see it as a giant technological effort to make mankind jump through hoops. They fear the instruments will govern the intentions of those who wield them, as indeed for some men they do.

If this were all there was to it I would be alarmed too. But I must remember that the psychologist who makes it possible for me to accomplish a difficult leap has done me no disservice unless I am endangered by my own impulses. He has shown me how to realize one of my hidden potentialities. That is humanism. What I am still convinced I cannot do I am scarcely free to attempt, but what I have been shown can be done adds a new dimension to my freedom and makes it all the more real. Of course, I must admit that if I am continually prodded by the applied psychologists to make jumps I would prefer to avoid I am likely to become irritable.

If Skinner, the currently popular whipping boy for humanistic psychologists, can make it possible for men to actualize their intentions I would not want to accuse him of being antihumanistic. Or even if he went no further than to show what an imaginative psychologist can do to his subjects I would scarcely bring myself to say he has offered no humanistic inspiration to me, his fellow psychologist. In that event he would at least have demonstrated to me what is possible, rather than left me to the doubtful mercies of the inevitable. That is precisely one of the things I think a good humanist should do. Yet, by comparison, some of my literary colleagues leave me with the impression that "the nature of man" puts more out of my reach than within my grasp. I expect better of them.

This is crucial: humanistic psychology needs a technology through which to express its humane intentions. Humanity needs to be implemented, not merely characterized and eulogized. It is only when the subject, rather than the experimenter, becomes the model of the psychologist's man, or psychology's technology is mistaken for its theory, or theory encapsulates the reality it seeks to envision that humanistic ends are necessarily frustrated. It is not that man is what Skinner makes of him, but rather that what Skinner can do man can do—and more. Skinner's subjects are not the model of man; Skinner is.

THE ROLE OF THE SUBJECT IN
HUMANISTIC RESEARCH

Since the model of man in humanistic research is the experimenter rather than the subject, it follows that the humanistic psychologist will make the most of what those whom he has enlisted to help him have to say (Kelly, 1965a).[1] Too often it turns out that the experiment the psychologist thinks he is performing is not the one in which his subject is engaged. If the two experimenters are to collaborate each needs some idea of what the other is doing. What is frequently regarded merely as the subject's "behavior" may be for him no less of a venture, and have no less extensive implications, than the "experimenter's" efforts. This can be particularly true when students from elementary classes in psychology are required to serve as subjects in dissertation research in order to get satisfactory marks. For many students this provides an intriguing opportunity for some venturesome experimentation with psychologists. In any case, what is confirmed or disconfirmed by a student's experience, even when imperfectly articulated or reluctantly confided, is likely to be vastly more relevant to the outcomes—or the interpretations that should be placed upon the outcomes—than the hypotheses the "experimenter" has secretly perpetrated.

At the very least humanistic research means that each person who participates should at some point be apprised of what the "experimenter" thinks he is doing, and what he considers evidence of what. It is of equal importance to ask what the "subject" thinks is being done, and what he considers evidence of what. Since this can change during the course of the experiment it is appropriate to ask "subjects" what their perception of the experimental design was at each important juncture in the procedure.[2]

[1] Chapter 5 in this volume.
[2] I recall the insistence of one of my teachers, Christian Ruckmick—a Titchenerian—that the subjects in my dissertation research be called "Observers." It has taken me a long time to realize how perceptive he was.

This is not merely a concession to scientific ethics; it can make a great deal of difference in what conclusions are drawn. It is therefore an essential step for any researcher who is intellectually curious enough to want to know what is going on in his own laboratory. To look only at "behaviors" is to lose sight of man, and to dismiss as "too unreliable" what men have to say about what they believed was at stake is to remain willfully ignorant of the experimentation that was actually performed.

But this candor in the exchange between experimenter and subject is only a minimum requisite of humanistically oriented research. An all-out pursuit of humanistic objectives draws much more into its orbit. Even the design of the experiment, including both the intended intervention and the control of other suspected interventions, can take shape from collaboration among those who participate. Moreover, the subject's convictions and doubts about what must govern his efforts to cope with the experimental circumstances are themselves implicit hypotheses in the existential undertaking, regardless of what the experimenter hypothesizes. They ought therefore to be built systematically into the assumptive structure the research is designed to test. The null hypothesis may not be the most ubiquitous alternative in competition with an experimenter's hunch; it often turns out that his subjects' hypotheses are.

It seems to me to be important in advance of setting up the final fixed design of an experiment—after which it is usually too late to do anything very imaginative—or examine anything very perceptively—for the experimenter to collaborate with a number of subjects, setting up hypotheses in the light of their experience with the kind of procedure he has started to develop. For example, Jennings (1963), in generating empirical evidence in support of a "creativity cycle" as propounded by personal construct theory, spent several years trying to set up operations that met the criteria of the theory. At first he treated subjects as subjects. But when, at last, he took them into his confidence and collaborated intimately with them to devise a procedure that produced and separated their experiences of "tightening" and "loosening" as postulated by the theory (Kelly, 1955), he was able to set up a very simple fixed design that could test the notion of a productive creativity cycle in subsequent subjects. When he took this humanistic step a long and discouraging experimental voyage got off the rocks. It stands particularly to his credit that the urgency of completing a dissertation did not frighten him into making a conventional study of "the differences between creative and noncreative individuals," which I am sure he could have completed and published

within a few months using the "good guys versus the bad guys" criterion that has proved so popular with psychological journal editors.

THE ROLE OF THE EXPERIMENTER
IN HUMANISTIC RESEARCH

Much of what has been said about the role of the subject in humanistic research had as much to do with the role of the experimenter
as with the role of the subject. That was because I regard subjects
as experimenters—or, more generally, man as an experimenting creature, of which a scientist is an example. What can be added now
is the humanistic perception that every scientist is, in an important
sense, a subject in his own research. What he comes to think or what
happens to him as a result of the experiment he performs is an important empirical outcome, perhaps even more important than the changes
that are observed in his subjects. Just how far-reaching the implications
of this notion are, and what their immediate bearing on research
methodology is, require a little explaining.

Perhaps more was said at the outset of this discussion than was
necessary to make it clear that the humanism I have in mind when
I talk about research methodology is not classicism. But the point
seemed worth emphasizing because I suspect some of my colleagues
who defend humanism will want to disagree with me. If they do I
hope that between us and the reader it will be clear what the points
of disagreement are. The humanism I have in mind is as free of traditionalism as the adventuresome Greeks appear to have been. For it
seems they were not classicists in their own time, at least not classicists
as some tradition-bound men who now espouse classicism are.

Yet I must still agree that it is important for the psychological
researcher to see the efforts of man in the perspective of the centuries.
To me the striking thing that is revealed in this perspective is the
way yesterday's alarming impulse becomes today's enlivening insight,
tomorrow's repressive doctrine, and after that subsides into a petty
superstition. But I am not cynical enough to believe therefore that
these epochal transitions are futile, or that the quest for truth is il-
lusory. I remind myself that a voyage upon which no man has ever
embarked produces no landfalls, but one which men have pursued
to its mysterious destination may then be abandoned to launch a wiser
venture. Ships are built to be sailed. Ideas are meant to be enacted

rather than preserved. I doubt that they can be both. The fact that their immediate function is to govern transition renders them no less valuable to the ultimate enterprise. The truths we seek may be everlasting, but the ones that must pattern our search are as transient as they are vital to the success of the human venture. This is no less than a humanistic notion, if I read history correctly. It is also a sort of empiric notion, though not in the usual epistemological sense.

All of this may sound more philosophical than methodological, but it has a lot to do with the way the experimenter structures his role. If he is one who imagines himself accumulating nuggets of ultimate truth he will place his primary research emphasis on the unassailability of his fragmentary findings. If he supports something at the .05 level of confidence he is encouraged; if he pushes it to the .01 level he is gratified; if it turns out at the .001 level he is ecstatic; and if it reaches the .0001 level he wonders how one writes an application for the Nobel prize. The research objective of such a man is to nail something down, once and for all. His eternity is in his data. If he is a psychologist he will regard mankind as an accomplished fact, not as a current enterprise.

But if the experimenter sees himself exploring only one of many alternative constructions of man, with the best ones yet to be devised, he will be on a continual lookout for fresh perspectives emerging out of his research experience. What values he places upon his hypotheses will lie in the fertility of the experience in which they engage him, rather than in the certainty and parsimony of the explanations they offer. He will design his experiments to make his experience an optimal one. Thus he can not lose sight of the fact that he is himself the principal subject of his own experimental intervention. His psychology will not then be so much a study of what inescapable state impales man at this immature moment in history as it will be an exploration of what man may next become. He will approach his task with the horizon-scanning vision of a constructive alternativist rather than with the squint of an accumulative fragmentalist.

This is not to say that the humanistic psychologist need be unconcerned with precision in his research, though the scope of his outlook may often make him appear that way. If precise measurement will reveal faint cues to what is going on it should not be befogged by the global phraseologies of existentialism and phenomenology. The object of precision is to provide greater sensitivity to psychological processes not easily perceived, not to build impregnability into one's findings by adding decimal places.

RESEARCH AS EXPERIENCE

There are several ways in which the humanistic psychologist can maximize his confrontation with the phenomena he studies. The intimate collaboration with his subjects, mentioned in a preceding section, is one of them. Subjecting himself to the same experimental procedures he proposes for his subjects is another. To the full extent that he is capable he should experience what his subjects experience. Sights and sounds emanating from outside himself are not the only available clues to what is taking place. From internally manifested experience one may be alerted to crucial external events that otherwise would escape his notice. This is no less true when experimenting with children than when experimenting with adults; indeed, I suspect it is even more true. Close observation of everything that happens, rather than confining one's attention to those events for which the experimental design has preconceived categories, is not only humanistically appropriate; it is good basic scientific method.

I think it is safe to say that when any experimental conclusion, regardless of the statistical level at which it appears to be supported, violates one's sense of experiential reality it should be regarded with more than usual skepticism. This is not the same as saying that subjective judgment is better than objective judgment, but rather, in the best humanistic tradition, they will confirm each other. What man knows best is established by what he fully experiences, not exclusively by what he is compelled to concede.

The reader may have noted that in talking about experience I have been careful not to use either of the terms, "emotional" or "affective." I have been equally careful not to invoke the notion of "cognition." The classic distinction that separates these two constructs has, in the manner of most classic distinctions that once were useful, become a barrier to sensitive psychological inquiry. When one so divides the experience of man it becomes difficult to make the most of the holistic aspirations that may infuse the science of psychology with new life, and may replace the classicism now implicit even in the most "behavioristic" research. This too, as I see it, is a part of "the challenge of humanistic psychology."

Preliminary Stages of Research

Perhaps the role of the experimenter in humanistic psychology is most dramatically affected in the stages of research that precede the statement of a formal experimental design. Most of psychology's discourses on research, and certainly almost all of its published research reports, start with an assumed hypothesis, and tell us in obsessive detail what happens from there on. But the most exciting stages of research occur before this and are seldom mentioned—often not even recognized.

Humanistic psychology's research starts with man and initially leads the researcher to the most intimate understanding of the human experience he is capable of gaining. This may take a long time. It frightens some researchers and they protest that it endangers their "scientific objectivity." Unfortunately some of them never have any sense of confrontation with the phenomena they pretend to investigate. Yet they will argue that their research is definitive.

There is much to be said for a research strategy that insists on the psychologist having a first-hand clinical understanding of what he proposes to investigate before he sits down to write formal hypotheses about it. Certainly much time and expense could be saved if investigators would take the trouble to make the objects of their inquiries palpable before they start talking about intervening variables and mediational processes. Once the psychologist has seen "hostility," for example, with his own eyes, heard its sounds from both victim and obsessed, felt its pangs, restrained its impulses, lifted its myriad masks, struggled with its lingering consequences, and sensed its infinite variations he is in a far better position to undertake the disciplined task of formalizing the test of its properties.

Once during World War II, I was asked to consult with the officer in charge of an experimental research project dealing with a suspected psychological factor in some unexplained crashes experienced by naval aviators while flying in formation at night. A distinguished psychologist had published a paper in which he had dropped the remark that the autokinetic phenomenon might be involved in some way. The remark caught the eye of an ambitious reader and the entire project had been set up to test the hypothesis. The writer of the article, by then a naval officer himself and stationed a few minutes away, had not been consulted.

When I arrived it was immediately apparent that the flight surgeon in charge of the research, a personable chap with three stripes and obviously with a distinguished career ahead of him in the Navy, had probably never identified autokinetic movement in his own experience. He was blandly using a light source about fifty diameters too big. Within a few minutes, with the aid of a pin, a piece of cardboard and a small flashlight, it was possible to demonstrate what it was he was supposed to be investigating. "Well, whaddya know!" he exclaimed in amazement. Yet he had already spent upwards of $75,000 on a special research installation, tied up a number of highly trained enlisted aviation technicians badly needed elsewhere, and collected reams of yard-wide multiple polygraph tracings. He wanted me to detail "a psychologist or two to come over and analyze the data" since he admittedly did not "know anything about statistics." Needless to say, I used all the bureaucratic tricks at my command to get out from under that one. The last I heard of him he had an important role in the national space program.

It is easy enough for psychologists to poke fun at this fellow, since he was not a psychologist as we are, and particularly because he was a physician and a military man. Such stories about the military establishment are always making the rounds, as well as stories of medical efforts to assert proprietary control of all psychological research. Yet I have seen clinically inexperienced "experimental" psychologists set out to measure and manipulate "personality variables" which they would not think of observing in the flesh, and attempt to do so with scarcely a glance at the subjects who arrived at fifteen-minute intervals to sit behind a laboratory screen and push buttons in response to red and green lights. This kind of disengagement with man and the phenomena supposedly under investigation stands, as did the flight surgeon's project, in sharp contrast to the humanistic approach to psychological research.

EXPERIMENTAL PSYCHOLOGY AND HUMANISTIC PSYCHOLOGY

It is incredible that humanistic psychology should allow itself to stand opposed to the study of behavior, as suggested by some of our colleagues. Quite to the contrary, exploration by means of man's behavior is what once set humanism apart from scholasticism. But what now separates humanism from the behaviorism that arose in the early decades of this century—and lingered beyond its time—is that behavior is more to be used than explained. Indeed what best explains behavior is what it does, just as what best explains man is what he does. So the humanist asks what behavior can do.

The behaviorst worries about what made human acts inevitable in the scheme of material things. But I cannot imagine a lively humanist so preoccupied with a guilt-laden inquisition into why behavior had to happen in the otherwise rational life of man. But he may well inquire into the unfortunate undertakings that have brought man so close to the brink of disaster, both in his personal life and in his societal life. He might do so, not so much seeking what to blame them on—for the responsibility must ultimately be borne by man rather than by his circumstances—as seeking the constructions men have erected to channel their efforts so.

So the humanist studies behavior intently, but with an exciting difference. A psychological study of intelligence, for example, turns itself to the realization of various forms of unrecognized intelligent behavior rather than to the limits imposed by one's IQ. A psychological study of delinquency, for example, becomes a study of man's behavioral struggle to cope with his circumstances rather than a search for what can be done to make him obey the law. A psychological study of the psychotherapeutic process, for example, becomes an imaginative inquiry into how an immobilized person can utilize his own capacity for experimental behavior to answer important questions that seem now only to confront him with inexorable conclusions (Kelly, 1966). Behavior is the humanist's way of groping in the dark that engulfs us all not his bête noire. Wherein one can act he need not forever fear.

It should be added at this point that the use of the language of hypothesis is also of particular instrumental value to the humanistic psychologist, for it invites active inquiry rather than logic-tight answers, and it enables the researcher to entertain propositions "obviously untrue" long enough to find out whether they are as untrue as he and everyone else had supposed. But since the use of hypothesis is not an issue between humanistic psychologists and others, as the respective views of behavior are, there is no need to deal at length with the topic here (Kelly, 1964).[3] The only issue here is what kind of hypotheses are worth investigating, and we have already had something to say about that.

Because of the present uncertainty of its stand on experimental research I fear there is a real danger of the recent humanistic psychology movement fizzling out. In their outright opposition to so much that is considered synonymous with "scientific research" and "experimental psychology," humanists may convince themselves and others that they oppose research in general and experimentation in particular. Nothing could be more incongruous than for humanistic psychology to become frozen in this posture. What could be more vital to psychology than

---

[3] Chapter 7 in this volume.

to recognize that experimentation is even more characteristically human than it is scientific?

More than any of the other themes which guide psychologists, humanism invites their audacity and encourages their willingness to attempt what others believe to be preposterous. It would rather be absurd than subservient. In this respect it is allied to existentialism. The humanistic researcher looks for what man can do that he has never done before, rather than for conclusive explanations for what man has been doing all the time—and which, unfortunately, he may continue to do indefinitely should he allow himself to believe that he is what circumstances have made of him, or that he is destined to "be himself" and himself only.

Man's actions are best understood in an expanding context of all that is seen to be possible for him, rather than within the boundaries of his presumed nature, his reflexes, his brain, his complexes, his chronological age, his intelligence, or his culture. This, of course, means that, as unsuspected potentialities materialize, we shall probably have to keep changing the coordinates in terms of which we plot his life processes. But it does suggest, at the same time, that psychology can become a vital part of the on-going human enterprise. It is scarcely that now.

THE EXTENT OF HUMANISTIC
RESEARCH METHODOLOGY

What has been emphasized in this discussion is the broad methodology of humanistic research and a view of mankind that suggests to the scientist what he might be looking for. Little has been said about techniques, except to remind the reader that it expresses the genius of humanism for the psychologist to devise them and to place them within grasp of all men. Humanism, as I see it, must dispute the aristocratic claims of a self-appointed intellectual class, not identify with them. To the humanist every man is a scientist by disposition as well as by right, every subject is an incipient experimenter, and every person is by daily necessity a fellow psychologist.

While we have dwelt largely in the area of personality research, humanism has implications in less obvious arenas. Just as Freud listened patiently and emphasized before he interpreted, so Darwin before him had observed and experienced in every way he was humanly capable. And before that Linnaeus had conceptualized what he had taken infinite pains to examine. Yet none was a passive observer. Each projected himself into his undertaking and thus marked it with his own character. Freud employed his originally eclectic technique, Darwin set sail in the *Beagle*, and Linnaeus collected his plants afield.

Nor is the research of the humanistic scientist an experience of himself alone. Galileo undertook to project his notion of a heliocentric universe into the everyday experience of man. It was for that he was condemned, not for proposing it as an academician's hypothesis, as Copernicus before him had done. Humanistic science is science in the grasp of men, not men in the grasp of science. It orchestrates all the talents of man. In pursuing its course it makes the most of man's range of experiential capacities, even those that are inarticulate. And as it progresses its outcomes are incorporated into the intentions of all men.

Behavior plays a crucial role, and behavior is best explained by what man finds he can do with it. More and more his ventures tell him what that may be. Thus, to the ever-alert humanist, the frame of reference within which the explanation of behavior takes shape is continually changing, and, in doing so, throws man's acts into new psychological and sociological perspectives.

To provide an enabling structure for the progressively shifting referents of behavior is to realize the psychological freedom of man. Such a structure is more substantial to human freedom than tearing down the ghettos in which men without hope congregate or insulating timid souls from the manipulative efforts of applied psychologists. I hope it is clear that this humanistic version of freedom is far removed from that which, too often, men have been able to envision for themselves only in civil chaos, in undisciplined liberty, in hallucinatory indulgence, or in a polite disengagement of man from man (Kelly, 1966).

The antecedents of behavior do not determine what it must be, but, like humanism's antecedent classicism, offer us a breath-catching glimpse of what man's capacity for behavior exploration might accomplish beyond those trackless seas that are too much accepted as the outer boundaries of our psychological world. Yet there is danger that humanistic psychology, in looking back over its shoulder, may, as behaviorism did, lose track of where it is going.

REFERENCES

Jennings, C. L. Personal construct theory and the creativity cycle. Unpublished doctoral dissertation, Ohio State Univ., 1963.

Kelly, G. A. *The psychology of personal constructs*, 2 vols. New York: Norton, 1955.

Kelly, G. A. The language of hypothesis *J. Indiv. Psychol.*, 1964, **20**, 137–152.

Kelly, G. A. The strategy of psychological research. *Bull. Brit. Psychol. Soc.*, April, 1965a, 1–15.

Kelly, G. A. The threat of aggression. *J. Humanist. Psychol.*, 1965b, **5**, 195–201.

Kelly, G. A. A psychology of the optimal man. In (A. Mahrer, Ed.), *Goals of psychotherapy*. New York: Appleton-Century-Crofts, 1966.

7

The Language of Hypothesis:
Man's Psychological Instrument

For ABOUT three centuries now Anglo-Saxon man has labored under the somewhat misleading assumption that knowledge is transmitted through the senses. This was John Locke's great notion in 1690. In expressing it, he provided the essential spadework for both modern experimental psychology and the courageous empiricism of Sigmund Freud. But great ideas, like great men, sometimes have a way of eventually blocking the very progress they once so courageously initiated.

Thus it is, even after continued experience in psychotherapy, most of us still hold doggedly to the belief that one man's understanding of the universe can be somehow encoded within a signal system and then transmitted intact to another man via the senses. The signal system is often called "language." Indeed, Pavlov's psychological term for "language" was simply "the second signal system." And it is interesting to note in this connection that today much of Soviet education, psychotherapy, and prisoner rehabilitation—as well as the dreaded "brainwashing" routine—is supposedly directed at the installation of an accurately tuned signal system for the undistorted reception of messages.

Source. Address at the American Society of Adlerian Psychology and the Alfred Adler Institute graduation exercises, New York, May 16th, 1964, and also published in the *Journal of Individual Psychology*, 1964, **20**, pp. 137–152. Acknowledgment is made of the kind permission of the Editor, *Journal of Individual Psychology* to include this paper.

But, senses notwithstanding, we are coming at last to realize that language occupies a puzzling and paradoxical position between man and his circumstances. On the one hand, it is a device he uses to represent his circumstances, and, on the other, it may interpose itself as a compromise between tender phantasies and harsh realities. It enables man to understand what is going on around him, but it is equally useful in helping him put out of mind what he fears to understand. It provides both the sensitivity for following subtle events and the rigidity for standing against the tides of human affairs. It is a vehicle for communicating with other men, but it often serves us effectively when we want to distort the communications others seek to have with us.

Nowhere are these contradictory usages of language more apparent than in the realm of psychology. A parent, for example, may use language to gain some insight into the mind of his child. But he may also use diagnostic labels and verbal rationalizations to avoid being enmeshed in the magic of childlike perceptions. The experimental psychologist often betrays his ambivalence about having an intimate understanding of other persons by erecting a complex system of categories between himself and his subjects. Even a psychotherapist may employ verbal interpretations of his client's remarks to keep from being taken in by them.

This evening I would like to talk about language in a very special sense. I would like to talk about it as a human device for anticipating the events that are about to happen to us. This is to say I shall not be talking about it so much as a means of representing reality, or of shielding us from it, nor so much as a means of communication between persons, but more as an instrument for probing the future and, at the same time, maintaining our composure in the face of onrushing events.

If I say "The floor is hard," I employ a language system in which the subject-predicate relationship inheres in the subject itself. It is the floor which is hard, and that is its nature, regardless of who says so. The statement stands, not because the speaker said it, but because the floor happened to be what it is. The sentence's validity stems from the floor and not from the speaker.

Contrast with this the phenomenological use of language in which it is presumed that such a statement portrays a state of mind of the speaker and does not necessarily represent anything more than that. While our common language forms are not constructed so as to designate this kind of interpretation specifically, phenomenology has begun to enter the thinking of psychologists at least, and this kind of meaning is much less difficult to understand and live with than it was twenty or thirty years ago. Moreover, this use of language has proved to have some utility in the psychotherapeutic exchange, though many psychologists are skeptical of its ultimate value and find themselves quite uncomfortable when they try to use it.

But suppose we consider the possibility of using language in a third way—neither objectively nor phenomenologically. Suppose our verbs could be cast in the *invitational mood*. This is to say that instead of being used in the popular *indicative mood* of objective speech, or in one of the other moods recognized by our language—*conditional, subjunctive,* or *imperative*—a verb could be cast in a form which would suggest to the listener that a certain novel interpretation of an object might be entertained. For example, I might say, "Suppose we regard the floor as if it were hard."

If I make such a statement I immediately find myself in an interesting position. The statement leaves both the speaker and the listener, not with a conclusion on their hands, but in a posture of expectancy— suppose we do regard the floor as if it were hard, what then? A verb employed in the invitational mood, assuming our language had such a mood, would have the effect of orienting one to the future, not merely to the present or to the past. It would set the stage for prediction of what is to ensue. It suggests that the floor is open to a variety of interpretations or constructions. It invites the listener to cope with his circumstances—in this case, the floor—in new ways. But more than this, it suggests that the view of the floor as something hard is one that is not imposed upon us from without, nor is it isolated from external evidence, as a phenomenological proposition would be, but is one that can be pursued, tested, abandoned, or reconsidered at a later time. "Suppose we regard the floor as if it were hard; what follows and what do we do about it?"

Toward the end of the last century a German philosopher, Hans Vaihinger began to develop a system of philosophy he called the "philosophy of 'as if.' "[1] In it he offered a system of thought in which God and reality might best be represented as paradigms. This was not to say that either God or reality was any less certain than anything else in the realm of man's awareness, but only that all matters confronting man might best be regarded in hypothetical ways. In some measure, I suppose, I am suggesting that Vaihinger's position has particular value for psychology.[2] At least, let us pursue the topic—

[1] Vaihinger, H. *The philosophy of 'as if': a system of the theoretical, practical and religious fictions of mankind.* Translated by C. K. Ogden. London: Routledge & Kegan Paul, 1924.

[2] The writer is indebted to Dr. H. L. Ansbacher for calling attention to the important fact that Alfred Adler, who had studied Vaihinger and had grasped the

which is probably just the way Vaihinger would have proposed that we go at it.

MAKE-BELIEVE AS AN ESSENTIAL FEATURE OF SCIENCE

Science is often understood by students as a way of avoiding subjective judgments and getting down to the hard facts of reality. But I am suggesting that the avoidance of subjectivity is not the way to get down to hard realities. Subjective thinking is, rather, an essential step in the process the scientist must follow in grasping the nature of the universe. Let me see if I can make this point clear.

When we know something, or think we do, we make up sentences about it, using verbs cast in the indicative mood. We talk about it in a way that appears to be objective. But science tends to make its progress by entertaining propositions which appear initially to be preposterous. Quite often this is done secretly, the scientist being careful not to let people know what he is imagining until after he has accumulated some evidence to support his position. After he has a foothold in evidence he can, of course, claim that he was simply a careful observer and that, being a careful observer, he "discovered" something. But unless he had been willing, at some point in the sequence, to open his mind to possibilities contrary to what was regarded as perfectly obvious, he would have been unable to come up with anything new.

The novelist starts his exploration of the world in much the same way. But there are two differences between him and the scientist; he is more willing to confide his make-believe—even publish it—and he is willing to postpone the accumulation of factual evidence to support the generality of characters and themes he has narrated.

---

psychological significance of "as if" philosophy, regarded such notions as "unconscious" and "inferiority complex" as inventions, rather than discoveries.

In 1937 Adler wrote, "I, myself, as the inventor of the 'inferiority complex' have never thought of it as of a spirit, knowing that it has never been in the consciousness or unconsciousness of the patient but only in my own conciousness, and have used it rather for illumination so that the patient could see his attitude in the right coherence" (Psychiatric aspects regarding individual and social disorganization. *Amer. J. Sociol.*, 1937, **42**, 773–780).

Thus Adler's philosophy of science differed sharply from that of Freud, who, in the now-fading Nineteenth Century tradition, regarded the scientific enterprise as an effort to discover bits of truth or to uncover things in the mind heretofore concealed.

But neither of these differences between the novelist and the scientist is very fundamental. Both men employ nonetheless typically human tactics. The fact that the scientist is ashamed to admit his phantasy probably accomplishes little more than to make it appear that he fits a popular notion of the way scientists think. And the fact that a novelist does not continue his project to the point of collecting data in support of his portrayals and generalizations suggests only that he hopes that the experiences of man will, in the end, prove him right without anyone's resorting to formal proof.

But the brilliant scientist and the brilliant writer are pretty likely to end up saying the same thing—given, of course, a lot of time to converge upon each other. The poor scientist and the poor writer, moreover, fail in much the same way—neither of them is able to transcend the obvious. Both fail in their make-believe.

MAKE-BELIEVE AS A WAY OF COPING WITH THREAT

There are few experiences in the biography of a man more distressing than that of feeling himself utterly confused. How disturbing the person finds this confusion in his life depends somewhat on the area in which he experiences it. For example, it does not disturb me greatly when a student says things I cannot understand—I am rather used to that. But when my wife starts saying things I cannot understand I get the feeling that my world is beginning to wobble on its axis. And when I myself start saying things I cannot understand I am likely to become downright upset. Actually, however, all of these add up to about the same thing; the more deeply the confusion enters into my life the more alarmed I become.

Yet almost everything new starts in some moment of confusion. In fact, I cannot imagine just now how it could be otherwise. But this is not to say that confusion always serves to produce something new. It can just as well have the opposite effect, especially if the person finds the confusion so intolerable that he reverts to some older interpretation of what is going on. Here then is the element of risk for the person who ventures confusion in order to create something; he may end up regressing in order to control his panic.

But there is another stage in the creative process that stands midway between the confusion that we try to dispel by seeking either something new or regressing to something old, and the structured view of our surroundings that makes it appear that we know what's what. It is that transitional moment when the confusion has partly cleared and we catch a glimpse of what is emerging, but with it are confronted with the stark realization that we are to be profoundly affected if we continue on course. This is the moment of threat. It is the threshold between confusion and certainty, between anxiety and boredom. It is precisely at this moment when we are most tempted to turn back.

Let us concentrate on this moment of threat—or these moments of threat—in the life of man. Let me suggest that if we can find some way of helping man pass this kind of crisis we will have helped him in one of the most important ways imaginable. It is here that we can employ that part of the language of hypothesis that I have called "the invitational mood." Instead of insisting that old truths are about to give way to new, that we are shifting from one indicative to another, we can take the view that it is not the truth that is changing, but rather that we are tentatively exploring the possibilities of a new approach to the truth. "Suppose we regard the floor as if it were hard." We approach the truth through the door of make-believe.

Probably nothing has contributed so much to the adventuresome development of scientific thinking as the understanding of hypothetical reasoning. A hypothesis is not to be asserted as a fact, for if it is it immediately ceases to serve its purpose. It does not even need to be regarded as an inference, although some scientists, still easily embarrassed at being caught in their unrealistic moments, prefer to limit themselves to what they call the hypothetico-deductive method. At least that makes them appear rational, if not realistic.

The point that needs emphasis, it seems to me, is that the hypothesis serves to make an unrealistic conclusion tenable, or tenable for a sufficient period of time for the person to pursue its implications *as if* it were true. The fact that it is regarded as a hypothesis, and as a hypothesis only, has great psychological importance in man, for it enables him to break through his moment of threat. It is, after all, only make-believe.

HYPOTHESES FOR THE PSYCHOLOGIST, CLIENT, AND GRADUATE STUDENT

Let me turn our discussion from abstractions to certain problems in psychology. It is supposed to be good for psychologists to act like scientists and many of us, I fear, spend more time acting like scientists than we do trying to understand persons. Suppose, instead of trying to apply scientific methods, as we know them, to psychological problems, we embark on an altogether different undertaking. Suppose we attempt to understand the psychology of scientific endeavor.

I have hinted at what such an inquiry might cover—the dread of confusion, the obstacle the scientist confronts at the moment of threat, the psychological role of the hypothesis, and the possible use of verbs in an invitational mood. I have also suggested that people who fancy themselves as scientists are very much afraid of being caught doing anything that is not recognized as scientific, and especially so, if what they are doing has anything to do with their professional field. I suppose it would be very upsetting to a good many of our colleagues if it were seriously suggested to them that they might stop trying to be scientific and get on with the job of understanding man. Yet I am confident that such an abandonment of what we now know as "science" would, in the end, be a good thing both for psychology and for science. In fact I suspect that as the results began to be known the Sigma Xi cult might be only too happy to claim psychology as a "basic science."

For a good many years I have been impressed with the similarities between psychotherapeutic and research activities. The difficulties the client seems to confront in his psychotherapeutic experience seem much like those the graduate student finds most frustrating. Let me illustrate.

Both have difficulty formulating testable hypotheses, and, even when they do, they hesitate to lay them on the line experimentally. Sometimes it appears that they dread to test them lest they be disconfirmed, though often I suspect it is because they fear the evidence *will* confirm the hypotheses and they will be threatened with a new set of verbs, all cast, of course, in the indicative mood. A person, whether in his scientist role or in his patient role, can be threatened by finding himself on the brink of a changed outlook, even though it may be regarded as a rewarding one.

Moreover, both in the client and in the graduate student, the remedy seems to lie in pointing out that what is being tested is, after all, only a hypothesis. The ultimate truth, it is important to recognize, lies far beyond the immediate experiment. It is when the student realizes this that he begins to feel more comfortable investing his efforts in something less than a magnum opus and can get some satisfaction out of making progress rather than coming up with a major achievement. The same is true of the client. What he is, or what he is to be, does not stand or fall by what he does today or tomorrow; he needs only to make some kind of progress, not transform his life into some final state of perfection all at once.

Probably there is nothing more exciting in the whole field of clinical psychology than the notion that persons in distress can couch their problems in the language of hypothesis, and that one can think with verbs in the invitational mood, even though our language has no structural form for designating such verbs. A client who regards himself as a victim of his unfortunate youth may, of course, mobilize all sorts of evidence in support of his conclusion. He may talk of himself objectively, marshalling evidence in interview after interview to support the indicative mood of the verbs he uses in describing himself.

As long as this goes on he himself is likely to be *immobilized*. We can call it intellectualization on his part, if we like, but, whatever it is, the outlook he expresses seems to him to be realistic. Sometimes we try to break up the rigid pattern of his self-perception by inviting him to be incoherent, as in the loosening efforts psychoanalysts often employ. Out of the confusion that ensues there may come some new construction of himself and his circumstances—particularly of his future. But confusion is anxiety and he *may* simply regress. Indeed certain patients are quite likely to regress to more primitive constructions when loosened psychoanalytically.

Sometimes the psychotherapist meets his greatest resistance just when his client is on the threshold of some important new insight. This, of course, is the moment of threat that I have been mentioning. And, of course, there are many other obstacles to be overcome in psychotherapy that have their parallels in other forms of human endeavor, as in art and in science.

CLINICAL PSYCHOLOGY AS PURE SCIENCE

I suppose this is as good a time as any for me to say that I have very little interest in applied psychology, and that is why I think clinical psychology is so important! An applied scientist puts his verbs in the indicative mood, while the pure scientists uses the invitational mood. The psychologist is at his best when he speaks the language of hypothesis rather than imposes psychological certainties on his clients. There are, unfortunately, a large number of psychologists—the majority of them perhaps—who think they dare not use the language of hypothesis when talking directly to persons; it is, they think, a language to be employed only when dealing with more remote matters. Most of them regard themselves as experimental psychologists, or perhaps more accurately as *the* experimental psychologists. But for me the most exciting experimental situation is the therapy room, and the most stimulating colleague in the research enterprise is my client.

This is not to say I find psychotherapy always a comforting and rewarding experience. It is sometimes, but mostly it is anything but that. I said only that it was exciting and stimulating. My clients and I go through some difficult times together. Both of us find ourselves trapped by the subject-predicate error of so-called objective speech. Both of us experience confusion, or *anxiety* if you prefer a clinical term, in which we become a little frightened at our own incoherence. Sometimes out of this confusion comes something new; sometimes we only regress.

I can, of course, insist that only my client, and not I myself, shall be permitted to risk confusion; and sometimes I do just that. Neither of us can put up with too much chaos at any one moment. But if I insist on risking no confusion in myself whatsoever I don't learn anything. I am only an applied psychologist. Without risking confusion, without venturing preposterous thoughts occasionally, I do not come to understand my client, I only diagnose him and I substitute my "interpretations" for the genuine experience of knowing him.

Of course I can make life easier if I entrench myself in some orthodoxy and, through repeated and patient interpretations, drill my client in my way of looking at things. When he agrees with me I tell him he has "insight" and when he doesn't I tell him he is "resisting"—both of these being terms that grow out of objective speech and the prestigeful use of the indicative mood in talking about psychological matters.

But clinical psychology does not have to be an applied discipline. It can, in the very best sense, be truly scientific. And when I say this I do not mean that the clinical psychologist uses his clients as unwitting guinea pigs in an experiment for which they have no responsibility. I mean that clinical psychology *can* be scientific in the therapy room, that the client *can* be—and indeed properly *is*—a colleague, and that the client and his therapist may come to talk to each other in the language of hypothesis.

THE THREAT OF PROFOUND CHANGE

But there is more than anxiety to be encouraged and used productively in the psychotherapeutic situation. There is threat, the experience that occurs at the moment when we stand on the brink of a profound change in ourselves and can see just enough of what lies

ahead to know that so much of what we are now will be left behind
forever, once we take that next step. It is here that the language of
hypothesis can be of particular help, both to the psychotherapist who
senses the warning that his own experience with the client will not
leave him unchanged, and to the client who can see that he is about
to invalidate much of what he has deeply believed over many years
of his life. It is at this point that it becomes particularly useful to
say, "Suppose—just suppose—we regard the floor as if it were hard."
Except we shall probably be saying something like, "Suppose we regard
your boss as if he were frightened," or "Suppose we regard your feelings as if they were a shield against the hazards of loving someone."

As I said before, the language of hypothesis invites one to get on
with the task of understanding life, to test, to calculate new experiences,
and to profit from mistakes, rather than to be overwhelmed with guilt
on realizing that he has made them. There is something in stating
a new outlook in the form of a hypothesis that leaves the person himself
intact and whole. It implies that being has an integrity of its own
and that we approach it, whether it is a truth about the external world
or about ourselves, by successive approximations, each of which is
subject to further examination. Truth, then, is regarded as something
to be adventured and tested, not something that is revealed to us whole
by God or nature—not even by one's psychotherapist.

This moment of threat, in which so many human enterprises are
abandoned, is not found exclusively in psychotherapy. The scientist
experiences it in his own life, and so does the novelist and the artist.
It is, no doubt, what the existentialists have in mind when they talk
about "the leap," although I would not want to pretend that I have
a very clear idea of all the things existentialists talk about.

On the night of November 10th, or shortly thereafter—the records
are not altogether clear—in the year of 1619, René Descartes had
three dreams. In the first dream he was a cripple seeking shelter in
a church; in the second he heard thunder and saw fire; and in the
third he was reading the words, "What way of life shall I follow,"
a quotation from a poem that was currently popular. What is perhaps
more important than his dream thoughts is the notion which he claimed
preceded them. That notion was that the methods of analytic geometry
might be broadly applied to other disciplines—hardly enough to scare
one into church, we might suppose, but then Descartes was a very
well-educated man whose intellectual ventures penetrated far deeper
than the superficial mimicry that ordinarily passes for cognition, and,
besides, the year was 1619. So upset was Descartes at the notion of
applying analytic geometrical solutions to a wide variety of man's

problems that he discontinued his inquiries and went on a long trip, lasting several months, in order to escape the threat that confronted him.

Descartes was a man greatly concerned with the reality of existence—"*Cogito ergo sum.*" He sought, moreover, to proceed in his intellectual endeavors by the exclusive use of objective language. The times did not provide him with a language of hypothesis, though he was clearly aware of alternative explanations for what he observed and he did experiment actively. For him, however, experimentation was a way of discovering which of several explanations was the true one. Thus he had not quite reached the point where he could use the language of hypothesis to its full advantage. If he had been able to use it, he might have saved himself a lot of discomfort and perhaps have accomplished some things that even his great mind fell short of achieving. Even a Descartes can experience his moment of threat and be disconcerted by it.

BEING ONESELF IS NOT ENOUGH

A good deal is said these days about being onself. It is supposed to be healthy to be oneself. While it is a little hard for me to understand how one could be anything else, I suppose what is meant is that one should not strive to become anything other than what he is. This strikes me as a very dull way of living; in fact, I would be inclined to argue that all of us would be better off if we set out to be something other than what we are. Well, I'm not so sure we would all be *better* off— perhaps it would be more accurate to say life would be a lot more *interesting.*

There is another meaning that might be attached to this admonition to be oneself; that one should not try to disguise himself. I suspect this comes nearer to what *psychologists* mean when they urge people to be themselves. It is presumed that the person who faces the world barefaced is more spontaneous, that he expresses himself more fully, and that he has a better chance of developing all his resources if he assumes no disguises.

But this doctrine of psychological nakedness in human affairs, so much talked about today and which allows the self neither make-up nor costume, leaves very little to the imagination. Nor does it invite one to be venturesome. I suspect, for example, that in the Garden of Eden it might have occurred to Adam to take a chance much sooner than he did if Eve had been paying a little more attention to her wardrobe. As it was I hear she had to bribe him with an apple. Later on they say she contrived a saucy little something out of fig leaves.

What I am saying is that it is not so much what man is that counts as it is what he ventures to make of himself. To make the leap he must do more than disclose himself; he must risk a certain amount of confusion. Then, as soon as he does catch a glimpse of a different kind of life, he needs to find some way of overcoming the paralyzing moment of threat, for this is the instant when he wonders what he really is—whether he is what he just was or is what he is about to be. Adam must have experienced such a moment. With him perhaps, as with modern Anglo-Saxon man, the indicative mood of his verbs might have put him in a quandary, forced him upon the horns of his own dilemma, rendered him ambivalent, perhaps even impotent.

It may be helpful at this point to ask ourselves a question about children at Halloween. Is the little youngster who comes to your door on the night of October 30th, all dressed up in his costume and behind a mask, piping "trick or treat, trick or treat"—is that youngster *disguising* himself or is he *revealing* himself? Is he failing to be spontaneous? Is he *not* being himself? Which is the *real* child—the child behind the mask or the barefaced child who must stand up in front of adults and say "please" and "thank you"? I suspect costumes and masks worn at Halloween time, as well as uniforms worn by officers on duty, doctoral degrees, and the other devices we employ to avoid being seen as we are, are all ways we have of extricating ourselves from predicaments into which we have been cast by the language of objectivity. They represent devices for coping with the world in the language of hypothesis.

But masks have a way of sticking to our faces when worn too long. Verbs cease to express the invitational mood after the invitation has been accepted and experience has left its mark. To suggest to a person that he be what he has already become is not much of an invitation. Thus it is that the man who has worn a uniform long enough to explore all its possibilities begins to think that he really is an officer. Once this happens he may have to go through a lot of chaos before he can make anything more of himself. A student who is awarded a Ph.D. degree can find a lot of adventure in being called "doctor" and the academic mask may enable him to experiment with his life in ways that would have seemed much too preposterous before his dissertation was accepted. But trouble sets in when he begins to think that he really is a doctor, or a professor, or a scholar. When that happens he will have to spend most of his time making noises like doctors, professors, or scholars, with the resultant failure from that time on to undertake anything interesting. He becomes trapped by verbs that have lapsed into the indicative mood when he wasn't looking.

AFTER CONFIRMATION, WHAT?

It may seem that I am advocating the use of a language in which nothing is ever confirmed. In a sense this is true—I am! The moment we find it practicable to regard the floor as if it were hard we don't walk away from it leaving it hard, but we always tack a little note on it that says, "But maybe it's something else too"—or instead, "I'll be back later to see."

One of the most amusing yet baffling experiences in psychotherapy is the way today's "insight" can become tomorrow's "resistance." Psychotherapists often stand on their heads to retain what they once hailed as a remarkable insight in their patient's step-by-step analysis. A few weeks later they may find themselves saying, "But that isn't exactly what I thought you meant." The therapist ends up trying to dress up his client's insight to fit the current circumstances and the new stage to which they—he and his client—have progressed in their mutual enterprise. And before he knows it his own dilemma has tricked him into lecturing his colleague in ways no respectable therapist is supposed to do. If he had regarded the client's new construction as a hypothesis rather than an insight in the first place, he could have saved himself a lot of anxiety once it became clear to both of them that the therapy must move on to other levels of construction. Moreover, it is precisely at this point in the psychotherapeutic progression that the language of hypothesis must be reemployed.

There is more to this than tactics in psychotherapy. It is very commonly believed by people who should know better that one is obligated to disconfirm one explanation before he dares entertain seriously the possibilities of any other. Scholars waste a great deal of time trying to disprove what others have claimed in order to make room for their own alternative explanations. If the floor is hard—really is—I am not going to get to first base with any notion of its being soft. Therefore, it seems that I must first prove that those who say it is hard are dead wrong. This is all a terrible waste of time, in my opinion.

Suppose, instead, we employ the language of hypothesis. We say, in effect, "To be sure the floor may be regarded as hard, and we know something of what ensues when we cope with it in the light of such an assumption. Not bad! But now let us see what happens when we regard it as soft." Out of this further exploration may come, not so much confirmation that it really is hard or that it really is soft—as Descartes would have reasoned—but a sequence of fresh experiences that invite the formulation of new hypotheses. For example, one may come up with a notion of relativism, that is to say, the floor is harder than some things and softer than others. Or he may come up with a notion of properties, the hardness aspect of the floor and its softness aspect. Or he may come to regard hardness not as anything that inheres in the floor, but as a dimension of appraisal useful in understanding floors. From this position he may launch out and contrive the notions of resilience and plasticity to account for what happened when he treated the floor as if it were soft.

THE INVITATIONAL MOOD
IN INTERNATIONAL AFFAIRS

Here then we have a language which can be employed in many situations, not the least of which are in the realm of international affairs. Suppose we regard the Soviet Union as "a democracy." Sounds heretical, doesn't it! But why not see what comes out of such a hypothesis? Now we are going to have a problem on our hands if we ask our John Bircher friends to explore this issue. To most of them, I suspect, such a proposal sounds like an invitation to jump off the edge of the world. As long as it sounds this way to them I doubt that they will be much tempted, and I doubt that it would do much good to point out such facts as that before a vote is taken at any echelon of Soviet government, from individual citizens on up, every effort is made to have it discussed in a face-to-face situation, and that such town meeting discussions involve about eighty percent of the voters. Nor would it do much good to point out to a fellow who thinks he has been invited to walk the plank that the unanimity the Soviet system demands is a rather mild version of our jury system in which unanimity is demanded of all twelve jurymen—a requirement that brings the minority members of a jury under almost intolerable pressure to go along with the vocal faction, just as it does in a Soviet election.

If our Bircher friends did allow themselves to consider facts such as these they might be brought to the brink of concluding that some features, at least, of the Soviet system are more democratic that the corresponding features in our own system. This, I am sure, would bring them to that moment of threat to which their limited notions of democracy have left them so vulnerable. Will the language of hypothesis enable our friends to surmount this intellectual barrier and examine matters further? Well, I don't know. Perhaps I have chosen too difficult an illustration; it may be asking too much of a sworn chauvinist to suggest that he employ the language of hypothesis in order to reach a better understanding of international issues.

One thing, of course, we shall not ask the Bircher to concede; we shall not ask him to deny that the Soviet system is based on dictatorship. And here is my point. It is not necessary for that hypothesis to be disconfirmed before another is entertained. Nor do we ask him, or ourselves, to agree that the Soviet system *is essentially* democratic. That would not be using the language of hypothesis. All we ask is that we apply the criteria of democracy to what goes on in that society and examine the outcomes of such an honest inquiry on our own part.

It does not follow that we must eventually choose between the hypothesis of dictatorship and the hypothesis of democracy. As in the case of our propositions about the floor, the explorations that ensue from the two hypothetical propositions may lead us to formulate some much better ones—ones that may throw as much light upon directions our own society may take as upon our proper posture toward the Soviet Union. Unlike Descartes, we shall look forward to a better statement of issues rather than to some knock-down-drag-out decision on issues that may be badly posed. It seems much more likely in Soviet-American relations that, if the conflict can be settled at all by means other than war, it will turn out that history will regard neither side as the perfect embodiment of democracy, and more thoughtful generations will find better ways to pose the issues than we, in our dread of political confusion, have yet found. Still, the chauvinists on one side or the other may finally have their way, and men, here or elsewhere, who oppose them will have to die in defense of their right to pursue their own propositions and to seek enlightenment for all.

CONCLUSION

There is a good deal more to the language of hypothesis than what I have tried to cover thus far in this discussion. I might have pointed

out that it is a dimensional language rather than a language of at-
tributes. By that I mean that when I say, "Suppose we regard the
floor as if it were hard," I am inviting my listener to envision a dimension or parameter that is not a part of the floor, but exists supposedly
independently of the floor. Having constructed such a dimension, or
personal construct, the listener is invited to plot the position of the
floor with respect to such a hypothetical dimension. This to say that
the language has its particular way of using nouns and adjectives as
well as its verbs. In the case of the floor, about which I talk in this
language, the basic noun has to do with a dimension or guideline
erected by myself, one which I hope will enable me to plot the position
of "floor" in my own psychological space. My adjectives are not so
much relativistic adjectives as they are statements of where a given
event is to be plotted with respect to the dimension symbolized by
my noun.

But enough of this; the object of this discourse is only to suggest
how a certain kind of language form can enable us to extricate ourselves from the kind of realism to which our so-called objective language system has bound us. Nowhere is this semantic enslavement
clearer than in the psychotherapy room. It is there one can see most
clearly how man can be trapped by his indicative verbs and how,
in turn, he has been led to believe that he must choose between mu-
tually exclusive versions of reality. Not only does he find that he must
risk the chaos of anxiety in order to come up with something new,
but also he discovers that once he has managed a new version of the
important issues in his life he must face a moment of terrible estrange-
ment from all that he has been if he is to make the existential leap.
It is here—at the moment I have called the moment of threat—that
the language of hypothesis enables his therapist to say, "But only suppose the floor is to be regarded as if it were hard," or, "But only
suppose your posture is designed to protect you from ever again having
feelings like those you once had for your mother."

I hope that, as well as inviting you to consider the use of another
language for coping with man's problems both in the therapy room
and in international affairs, I have led you to explore the implications
of a particular proposition, the somewhat unorthodox one of, "Suppose
we regard clinical psychology as if it were the purest of sciences."

Part II

PSYCHOTHERAPY

8

Sin and Psychotherapy

EVERYMAN'S EDEN

Not so many years ago a man was recalling a childhood experience. His maternal grandfather, a clergyman, had died and his grandmother had recently come to live with the family. Her addition to the household required some readjustments all around. It was decided that his mother should undertake full-time employment to help bear the increased financial burden and the grandmother should assume the household duties, including supervision of the children. He recalled one evening in particular when he was nine years old. He and his grandmother were alone and he was preparing for his evening bath. She expressed shock at the exposure of his naked body, and in that instant there had come over him the most awful feeling of isolation he had ever experienced in his life.

At the time the man related this experience he had been in psychotherapy for more than a year. While he had mentioned the incident several times before, it was not until this particular session that he was able to express the force he attached to its impact and to reflect clearly the way he had come to construe the experience in subsequent years. I should add that, with him as with other persons who have underscored similar experiences in their autobiographies, it was his construction of many experiences that gave this incident its semiotic place in the chain of events that were to follow.

SOURCE. Prepared for the Temple University Symposium on Psychotherapy, Philadelphia, Pennsylvania, March 9, 1962. Published by permission of Professor J. Page.

165

At the age of thirty my client had accumulated a remarkable series of failures in his life. In the university he had failed in course after course, and outside the university he had failed in job after job. He had neither been able to establish himself away from home nor had he been able to work out a comfortable relationship within the household where he lived with his aging parents. Only in recent months had his sense of unworthiness eased enough to permit him to have his first dates with girls.

Nor had the psychotherapeutic relationship been all that one might hope for. While there had often been moments when he had spoken of the anguish he felt, of his sense of helplessness, and of his apprehension about the confrontations psychotherapy might thrust upon him, there had been only fleeting instants when his communication with me had been unguarded. I was not the person he had been looking for.

Notwithstanding the tenuous relationship between us there had been some few occasions when he had gone beyond mere expressions of distress and had spoken with depth of feeling and insight. The interview I have mentioned was one of them. After telling me of the incident with his grandmother and how things had never been quite the same afterward, he fell silent. Then quickly he said, "It has always seemed as if that night I was thrown out of my Garden of Eden and through all these barren years I have been wandering about trying to find my way back in."

Ordinarily, I presume, when a therapist hears a remark like this he wonders if his patient has been going in for existentialism. But in this case, strangely enough, there was no evidence, either before or after, that his man had been reading in the existential vein, unless, of course, you consider certain passages from the Book of Genesis to be existential writing. To turn the inference around, it might be more cogent to speculate as to whether that ancient author of the Book of Genesis had been listening to my patient—or to someone like him.

The Penalty for Knowing Too Much

What about this knowledge of good and evil, this fruit that Adam and Eve ate? And what does it have to do with psychotherapy? Was—is—the exile Adam and Eve—and my patient—experienced to be regarded as a petulant retaliation for their dabbling in matters reserved for a superhuman being? Or do we face here a basic principle of human life, as true for the individual now as it was for the most ancient progenitors of the human race; that with knowledge come responsibilities and with responsibilities comes trouble? Adam and Eve, in this remarkably insightful story, sought the knowledge of good and evil, and that is precisely what they got, for they lived to see one of their sons grow to be a good man, and the other his murderer.

Modern man, no less tragic in his plight, has also sought the knowledge of many things that have proved too much for him. Some have sought sexual knowledge—not too difficult an achievement. But they usually found out more than they wanted to know. Others, somewhat more intellectually inclined, no doubt, have searched for the secret of nuclear fission. That was harder, but they found it. And, like the sons of Adam, they found there was a lot more wrapped up in that tiny little affair than they had any intention of being responsible for.

While we all have Eves to titillate our curiosity, none of us, neither scholar, business man, labor unionist, nor clergyman, can claim that he himself has not had an active part in welding the chain of events that has led up to where we are. And now all of us face the terror of an impatient and ruthless enemy who is held in check only by his own fears and his tenuous hope of gaining a less costly victory over us.

The realities come even closer home than that. We see our sons impressed into the uniformed roles into which society ordains its killers and its martyrs. These youngsters of ours will try to hold off catastrophe a little longer by the only means we know. Is it worth it? Well, of course it is worth it! It is the alternative that is not worth it!

So, confronted with all the terrifying varieties of knowledge they have sought—little things, big things, childish things, adult things— men everywhere, just like my client, are scampering hither and thither, from couch to picket line, from picket line to couch, trying to find their way back into the Garden of Eden, and altogether willing—even eager—to abandon all the good mankind has gradually achieved over the centuries in order to escape the bad that threatens to engulf them. For so many men and women today, whether it is from the fear of nuclear fission or from the dread of personal exile, the only way back to the amoral contentment of Eden seems to be through psychotherapy. They foresee no way of coping with the problems they face, other than to lie down and be treated for them.

Eden as a Psychological Problem

I hope it is clear that I am talking about a psychological problem and I intend to deal with it as best I can in a psychological manner, even though this is not the kind of undertaking most psychologists have any stomach for. The rather lurid title I have chosen for this paper is as exact a statement of the topic of my remarks as I could render. I make no apology for that!

I suppose I could offer an apology for making such a serious thing out of that spicy little story from Genesis. Forgive me for *that*, if you like. But I have reasons for it, too. First of all, it was a story used by a person in deep distress to let a psychologist know what he was experiencing. If his troubles had seemed to him to be more superficial or localized I doubt that he would have invoked the Eden metaphor. The depth of his perplexity opened the way for him to say something profound, and to voice the cry, not of himself alone, but of all lonely mankind. And, rather than take down what he said and discount it in proportion to his psychological disturbance, which is what psychologists usually do with such remarks, I am inclined to take what was said all the more seriously because it came from a deeply troubled man.

I shall want to say more about this point presently, but first let me go on to my second reason for talking about Eden. I am well aware that there is little precedence in scientific discourse for talking about sin, and much less for talking about the Garden of Eden. Scientists are reluctant to talk about things they cannot put their fingers on, or are not sure really happened the way they have been reported. But when a story has been told and retold through the centuries and it challenges, as this story does, generation after generation of scholars, then only the scientist who is willfully blind to human nature can ignore what is currently going on. Certainly the psychologist, least of all scientists, can afford to ignore it altogether.

So I have two reasons for talking about Eden; one because it was a focal image in the experience of a troubled person whom I know rather intimately, the other because it is a story that men seem unable to forget. There it is, an experiential phenomenon, just the sort of thing psychologists are supposed to look into—or, if you insist, a behavioral phenomenon, if the word "behavioral" makes it any more legitimate. As a psychologist it is up to me to make something out of it if I can.

But how? Shall I approach the psychological phenomenon of Eden by the classical methods of scriptural exigesis? Shall I use the methods of protocol analysis—the verb-adjective ratio, the proportions of self-reference and notself-reference, the balance between feelings of strength and threat, some kind of confabulation index, or an abstract-concrete typology? While all these are analytic devices that might throw some psychological light on the problems of man, permit me to explore with a somewhat different method, one that grows out of the philosophical and psychological assumptions underlying personal construct theory.

Personal Construct Analysis

Personal construct theory assumes, among other things, that any construct used by man is, psychologically speaking, a bi-polar affair. One does not understand a personal construct simply by apprehending some basis of *similarity* between objects; he must understand the basis of *distinction* as well. Both similarity and contrast are involved. So we look for the grounds upon which certain matters can be judged as similar to each other, and, by the same token, stand in meaningful contrast to certain other objects within the construct's range of convenience. Stated in Hegelian terms this is to say no thesis is complete without its antithesis. Perhaps I should add that I am aware that this dialectical form goes back a good deal further than Hegel, perhaps as far as the pre-Socratic philospher Anaximander. Be that as it may, I am not so much concerned with the classical logic of the dialectic as I am with its psychological appropriateness in describing how man characteristically functions.

So let us approach the age-old story of Eden, and the up-to-the-minute version blurted out by my patient, as psychologists. Moreover, let us approach it from the standpoint of this particular theory. Specifically, this is to say we will *not* look for motives to explain the preoccupation of Adam, Eve, and my patient, for personal construct theory completely abandons the notion of motivation. We shall, instead, attempt to understand how the writer of Genesis, and all those who through the centuries have followed the same channels of thought, came to grips with that perplexing something that makes man human. What were the personal constructs in terms of which he, my patient, and all the millions in between erected to cope with an existence they could no longer take for granted?

There appear to be at least three essential constructs in the Eden story, each, in succession, offering man a pair of alternatives. The first is the distinction between loneliness and companionship. Against this axis man made a choice; he chose companionship. Having made this choice it was not long before he was confronted with a second, this one based on the construct of innocence versus knowledge. We all know how that one turned out; with a little gentle nudging he chose knowledge. No sooner had he done so than he was faced with the third dimension of choice, the construct of good versus evil. He is sitll hung up on that issue. Good and evil have proved to be extremely elusive values, so elusive, in fact, that man now spends a good deal of his time trying to renege on one or the other of his previous choices in the hopes that he can return to Eden and not have to face the issue any longer.

Three Ways to Escape

Personal construct theory has something else to say about psychological processes. Not only do men erect constructs to guide their way through what otherwise would be undifferentiated confusion, and not only do they often find it necessary to make personal choices in terms of these constructs, they also select from their personal repertories the constructs they intend to apply to the situation at hand. So it is with the three constructs of the Eden story. Finding themselves confronted with the perplexing construct of good and evil, men have attempted to back up a step and reconsider their choice between the preceding pair of alternatives—innocence versus knowledge. This time they will choose innocence. Will it work? Can man make his mind run in reverse?

No, it turns out to be well nigh impossible to find one's way back into Eden and live with one's companions in the way he might once have lived—in sheer innocence. Not that many haven't tried—psychopaths, for example! Nor is it easy to go back to man's lonely beginning and live without companionship altogether, though many, including my patient, have tried that too. So, if both the front and the back gates to Eden are boarded up, then what devices remain for avoiding the awful responsibility for distinguishing good from evil amidst shifting circumstances, and then making a firm choice between them? One way would be to reduce the construct to obsolescence by devising some transcendent principle that goes beyond good and evil. Philosophers, patients, and a lot of the rest of us have had an occasional go at this one. Scientists are always trying it, I've noticed. They seem to think that if they just keep their minds occupied with research, they will hit on something and the problem of good and evil will go away and stop bothering them. But as far as I can tell, none of these dodges has ever worked, and man is just as much plagued as ever with the imminent necessity for distinguishing one from the other and for making up his mind daily which to choose.

I hope it is clear that what I am saying does not have to do with formal philosophy only or with distinguished philosophers only, such as Thoreau, who tried getting in the back door to Eden, and Nietzsche, who tried to outrun the issue by reaching for a transcendent principle. The writings of such people we treat well enough with awe. But the efforts to get unsnagged are much more common than that. Just about everyone tries it. And when ordinary folks seem to try too hard we are likely to treat their efforts, not with awe, but with—psychotherapy.

Psychologists Too!

This is where psychologists themselves come into the picture. Even the people who treat people are likely to try to wriggle out of the dilemma. Some attempt it by pretending to avoid moral judgments where their patients are concerned. They end up making medical judgments instead! They don't feel so guilty about making medical judgments, for all they have to do is conform to the latest medical dogma and keep up their dues to the local medical society. There are a lot of psychologists who are clamoring for an invitation to that kind of club.

There are some who go further in their efforts to avoid the issue of good and evil. They talk about absolute permissiveness in their relations with others, and this, they would like to assume, is, in turn, the foundation of a democratic society, that is to say, Eden reentered by the front door. Thus, they seek both to enjoy the warmth of human companionship and the safety of a regulated society, without once venturing to do anything for which they might later feel guilty.

And, of course, some psychologists try to run around to the back door. They advocate complete self-acceptance as the primary principle of life. Presumably they think they don't even need companionship, and, if they don't need it, their patients don't either. There is no Eve in their Eden, or, if there is, she stays over on her side of the Garden and minds her own business. The self-sufficient Adam doesn't need her, he never gets hungry for apples, and he is never caught weeping parental tears of guilt and remorse over his beloved sons, Cain and Abel.

Thus far I have mentioned three types of escape from the issues of good and evil. I have called them, respectively, the front and the back door attempts to return to Eden, and the attempt to outrun the issue. I may be mistaken, but I am going to assume that it is not necessary to cite illustrations of these attitudes from the case records of our clients or from the writings of our colleagues in psychology and psychiatry. In a group of clinicians, such as yourselves, a sufficient number of illustrations will surely spring to mind.

FOUR STRATEGIES

Let me go on, therefore, and describe some of the strategies mankind has employed for coping with the construct of good and evil on those occasions when he actually does try to face up to it. These, too, are as much the strategies of lowly persons, such as ourselves, as they are the formalized solutions of philosophers or societies.

Here personal construct theory has something else to say. Personal constructs are not abstractions that float around in thin air. They represent the ways we deal with things. If there were no elements to which the constructs were ever applied, there would be no constructs. The constructs of the individual man have to be understood both by his intentions and by his extensions. This applies to understanding one's own constructs as well as to understanding the constructs of the other fellow.

If a man has trouble distinguishing between good and evil he may try to straighten himself out by looking at cases. Look here; is this particular thing good? Is that particular thing to be called bad? How can I get the things here in front of me sorted out? Let us see how this works.

Law

First, I think we had better talk about the experience of the man who has done something he believes is wrong. This is not as simple a confrontation as many would have us believe. It might be simple if good and evil could be contained, once and for all, in a set of rules. A lot of people have thought of that strategy. But if you lay down a set of legalisms for governing future thought and action there can be only one outcome, and that is this: Tomorrow's vast challenges will be met with nothing more astute than yesterday's petty restraints. And the day after that, when you look back at what you have done, you discover, much too late, the evil you have allowed to infiltrate the world that has been entrusted to your care.

It is not so much the wrong that they have wanted to do that sends men to their psychotherapists, guilt-ridden and confused, as it is the wrong that has crept up on their blind side. I think most psychotherapists are aware of this now. Rules are useful enough as handrails for the morally nearsighted, and that, of course, includes most of us. But what we need to remember is that the man who willingly relies upon rules and laws to distinguish good from evil in his behalf is only seeking to avoid the foresight of what, in the end, good and evil will turn out to be. It is not going to be much comfort to him in the future, when he finds he has made a mess of things, to recall that he had closed his eyes and conformed to the rules.

What is this unctuous phrase that men so often quote once they have safely ensconced themselves in positions of legal power—"No man is above the law"? It sounds like the epitaph of an unsuccessful gangster. Indeed, for those who deign to accept this as the guiding principle of their lives, I suspect it is—even more appropriately so—an incriminating epitaph; it is their own! And for how many more of us, those of us who are certainly not the *visible* Eichmans of this world and who have only tacitly accepted legalized power as the sufficient embodiment of good and evil, might not this well be the concluding statement: "Here lies a man, long since deceased, whose spirit, in its quest to separate the evil from the good, never thought to rise above the law!"

Authority

A second way to deal with good and evil is by subordination to authority. If I cannot distinguish between good and evil myself, I will hang on to the coattails of someone who can. In turning myself over for safekeeping, I may take account of the man's credentials— whether he has been educated in such matters, whether he has been a devout follower of certain long-standing principles or an institution, or whether he has been properly ordained in some kind of apostolic succession. I may, if I wish, use other criteria. If he seems strong, I can assume that he will not involve me with failure. If he seems to have an untroubled conscience, I can assume that he must be free from sin and hence a pretty good sort of fellow to take after. If he asserts that he has no doubts, it must be because he has a clear perception of where the whole business is going to end up. If he seems protective, he may bail me out of trouble.

By making these less complex judgments we simplify the crucial issue into one of obedience and disobedience. If it is obedience, it is good; if it is disobedience, it has got to be evil! Now it is not so hard to tell when you have been disobedient. In fact, the fellow who has your dossier will often, for no more than a nominal fee, agree to remind you of your obligations whenever you step out of line.

Conscience

Without stopping to comment on the effectiveness of this method of meeting mankind's crucial issue, other than to say that it probably provides the greatest freedom from guilt feelings, let me go on to a third strategy. This is to rely upon conscience. Some say this is the same as running back to mother, and one psychoanalyst—I've forgotten who it was—Fenichel perhaps—has said that the voice of conscience sounds suspiciously like the voice of mother. Knowing the current bad feeling between analysts and mothers, you can probably guess what *he* had to say about conscience as a guide to human conduct.

Reliance upon conscience places the responsibility for distinguishing good from evil squarely on the shoulders of the individual man. The other two strategies I have mentioned burden him only with the responsibility for obedience to law or authority, leaving the more difficult task of distinguishing essential good from evil to the law-making process or to persons entrusted with authority. The law-making process is inclined to lag behind the times, as we have already pointed out, while persons entrusted with authority are always inclined to exploit their powers arbitrarily.

But what about conscience? How up to date is it in meeting tomorrow's challenges, and how selfless is it in addressing itself to the searching task of distinguishing good from evil? Certainly our psychotherapeutic experience with conscience—or the superego, if you prefer—leads us to suspect that it too can be both out of date and biased. In fact, it may serve only to make the kinds of distinctions between good and evil that parents make for their children. The outcome may be that one who tries to be guided by his conscience may still be dependent upon antiquated rules and arbitrary authority via the vaguely remembered admonishments of his parents. Certainly if one is looking for the ultimate distinction between good and evil he will fail to find it in the present conscience of individual men, just as he has failed to find it in laws or embroidered in the robes of ecclesiastical potentates.

Purpose

There is a fourth strategy I suppose I should mention. If we decide what kind of world is scheduled to appear in the future, we can say that anything we can do to hasten it is good, and anything we do to delay it is evil. Everything hinges on making progress toward Utopia. It is fatal to change one's mind about the nature of that Utopia or to admit that one's efforts have been extended in the wrong direction.

Psychologists do not often have experience with this kind of morality on this side of the Iron Curtain, though I have occasionally seen something like it here. When one is confronted with this point of view in a patient undergoing psychotherapy, he may expect a great tenacity, right up to the breaking point, then possibly a sudden collapse of the moral system.

Thus far I have not said anything especially helpful to the troubled mind. I have tried to show that Eden is a valid metaphor and that it expresses something in personal construct form that the psychologists who deal with distressed individuals ought to take seriously. I have mentioned the bi-polar nature of psychological construing, and I have made a very simple analysis of the Eden story in terms of three such constructs—solitude versus companionship, innocence versus knowledge, and good versus evil. I have said that man selects his constructs from those he has at hand, as well as makes choices between the alternatives they offer. Some men, perhaps all of us at one time or another, try to renege on the choices we have made and attempt to reinstate a previous issue. That is to say, we try to reenter Eden by the back or the front door. Some try to replace the good-versus-evil construct with one that transcends it. Finally, I have spoken of four strategies— I suppose I could just as well have made it a dozen—by which men see the meaning of the good and evil dimension of life through the method of extension.

I hesitate to mention it, but complete candor would require me to point out the fact that the four strategies I have discussed—*law, authority, conscience*, and *purpose*—correspond to four of the great ethical systems now of concern to the Western World—*Judaism, Catholicism, Protestantism*, and *Communism*. But I must hasten to add to such a volatile statement, that the methods employed by one group are often used by others.

The strategies change somewhat with the years. I doubt, for example, that nowadays the Jesuits would very much mind relinquishing their historical claim to the notion that the end justifies the means, although I do doubt that the Communists, in turn, would be so gracious as to acknowledge the contribution. I have another thought. Since the Communists take such delight in reading the history of things that haven't happened yet, it might be that the Calvinists could be persuaded to put predestination into the missionary barrel. They have always felt a little ridiculous about it anyway, so I am sure they would find it highly amusing to see men running around inside the Kremlin trying to reach their predestinations. I suppose, too, the Jews might have something to offer, something they would be glad to get rid of, but at the moment I don't know what it would be.

As for making additions to their ethical systems, I suspect, as a whole, the Protestants, splintered into goodness knows how many sects by their emphasis upon the democracy of the individual conscience, would now just as soon lay claim to some of Judaism's traditionalism. Not because it necessarily makes sense to them, but for the sake of moral unity! Judaism, in turn, recently confronted as never before by the issue of exclusive nationalism versus exclusive nationalism, certainly is calling the attention of all of us in this country at least, to the far-reaching possibilities of a brotherhood of man.

So much for cross-fertilization! I brought the matter up only because I was afraid my earlier attempt to clarify the prototypical ways man has distinguished good from evil appeared to oversimplify the issues to the point of stereotypy.

What I have said so far may suggest that man simply cannot distinguish good from evil. In the sense of making an ultimate distinction in time to enjoy the weekend, that is true; he cannot. But man does distinguish the two after a fashion. He may not do it well enough, but nonetheless, he does it. Through the ages he has undoubtedly improved his perceptiveness and, while circumstances seem to keep increasing in complexity faster than he can keep up, it would be a mistake to argue that he should give up the quest. His laws have improved, on the whole, and his ecclesiastical authorities are a good deal more decent lot than they were a few generations back. So I don't see any reason for believing the state of affairs is absolutely hopeless.

THE PSYCHOLOGY OF SIN

Let us examine sin still more intimately, and from a psychological point of view. I am aware of the fact that up to now I have not even attempted to define the term, as would be mandatory if this were a discussion of formal ethics or theology. Yet, it will be sufficient for my purposes this afternoon merely to discuss sin as a personal experience.

A man is walking across a busy street holding the hand of his little girl and keeping a sharp lookout from the speeding traffic. Half way across he inadvertently steps into an open manhole, fractures his leg, cracks several ribs, and loses the sight in his left eye. This is what you might call a traumatic experience. He is likely to have a psychological reaction to it, as well as a physiological one. Or to state it more accurately in personal construct terms, it is an experience he will be inclined to make something out of, psychologically. He may feel foolish. He may thereafter jump two feet into the air every time he hears an automobile horn. He may berate himself for paying so much attention to the cars that he overlooked the hazard beneath his feet. He may wonder if he is losing his faculties and attempt rigid countermeasures against that eventuality. He may even cast about in his mind to recall if he has done something for which Providence would be disposed to punish him. But however he may construe the incident, whether at a cortical level or a reflex level, it would not be like him to dismiss it as something inconsequential.

Be that as it may, and distressed and anxious as he may be over the inferences he may draw from his mistake, I think one thing is clear; his feelings are quite different from what they would be if he had allowed his child to step into that open manhole, fracture her little leg, crack several ribs, and lose the sight of her left eye. I am sure that one does not need to have the empirical evidence that comes from experience as a psychotherapist to verify the probable psychological difference between the two experiences. Moreover, the difference cannot be attributed merely to the fact that it is against the law of Moses to drop your children into open manholes, or that the clergy generally take a dim view of that sort of mistake. or that it tends to be counterrevolutionary. The difference is pretty much a matter of the fact that the man's mistake has seriously involved someone other than himself. And more than that, it has involved someone to whom he, in his role as a parent, is deeply committed.

Guilt

Here we have what I believe are sufficient grounds for reaching a psychological understanding of sin. They may not be sufficient for an ethical understanding; as a matter of fact, I am sure they are not, but that is another matter. It is precisely at this point that personal construct theory comes into the psychological analysis of the problem.

Now you may be surprised to hear me say at this juncture that I do not regard personal construct theory as a phenomenological system. Phenomenology is an ontology and a psychology of private and noninterdependent worlds. I do not see one's personal construct system as wholly private, nor do I see it as free to regenerate itself into some monstrosity completely oblivious to external reality.

But I would say that the feelings of the man who had dropped his child into the open manhole are typically the feelings that go with the realization of sin. We call this experience *guilt*, and personal construct theory would want to make it clear that guilt is distinguishable from the other forms of anxiety and from the mere realization that one has made a mistake.

To experience guilt one must have a construction of himself in a role. In my illustration it was a parental role, one I calculated to be important enough to make my illustration vivid. But when I talk about role in this connection, I must insist upon a special definition. The definition of role as a set of expected behaviors anticipated by one's self or others will not serve to systematize our clinical observations. Nor is it enough to say that role is merely the performance of some function in an articulated social system. These definitions, and the several others like them that are in current use among social scientists, do not provide us with the kind of scientific construct we can use for coming to grips with the problems of persons in deep distress. The definitions are largely couched in terms of extrapersonal operants, and it makes little sense to talk to a psychotherapy patient in such terms or their derivatives.

Let us say that a person copes with the world by erecting constructs or guidelines—verbal ones or reflexive ones—in terms of which he can fathom it and gain some sense of where he and it are going. Some of the constructs are erected for coping with the interpersonal aspects of his world. As long as these take no account of the outlooks of other persons, but only of their manifest behavior, we make no distinction between such constructs and others. But when his constructs provide the person with some notion of how matters appear to the other person, then we give them a special name, *role constructs*. This is to say, whatever one does in the light of his understanding of others' outlooks may be regarded as his role.[1]

Now for guilt in terms of personal construct theory. I am obviously talking about the personal experience of guilt, not about moral culpability. Culpability is something else, and may or may not be involved, as most every psychotherapist's observations would probably attest. Nevertheless, if you should disagree with this observation, I would not be inclined to press the issue, for reasons that will be more clear when I come to talk about the psychotherapeutic task of helping patients come to grips with the problem of sin.

---

[1] In my original definition of *role* I included the specification that there must be a conjoint enterprise involved. I now suspect that I was stepping outside the necessary implications of personal construct theory when I wrote that definition, though it seemed defensible enough at the time.

Guilt, in the personal construct theoretical system, then, becomes the sense of loss of role. The father in my illustration experienced guilt because he found himself a failure in the parental role. He suffered to the extent he was committed to that role, assuming he did not construe the incident as the culmination of a chain of other failures. And, to come back immediately to my other point, I see no reason to insist that a therapist would have to conclude that he was morally reprehensible for his mistake.

Loss of role can occur because of some sudden shift in one's construction of others' outlooks, leaving him the possessor of an invalidated life history. This is the sort of thing that happens when overeager young psychotherapists try to take on the problems of elderly clients. Fortunately, most elderly clients can stand up to them. One may feel guilty because of inconsistencies within his system. For example, it is a common experience to hear a client say, "I feel guilty because I don't feel guilty." One client a good many years ago, a Catholic girl, said she did not feel guilty for having extramarital sex relations, but she was overwhelmed with guilt feelings when she discovered the man was using a contraceptive. She was acutely aware of the speciousness of her judgment, and that, in turn, led her to wonder if she had any real moral sense at all, which led to another round of feelings of role loss, encompassing a good deal more than sex.

One may feel guilty because he remembers choosing to do something against his better judgment, or he may feel guilty simply because his judgment was faulty, as in my illustration of the unfortunate father. Moreover, since role constructs can just as well relate to one's interpretation of the outlook of a divine Being, one can feel as guilty for falling out of that role as for separation from a role based on an interpretation of more palpable personages.

Feeling Guilty for Being Good

One type of guilt manifestation that has proved most puzzling to those clinicians who are perceptive enough to observe it in their clients, is the feeling of the delinquent youngster who finds himself tricked into being "a good boy." In order to understand this well-documented phenomenon we need to make sure of our notion of role. I did not say that one plays a role only when he conforms to what he thinks others expect of him, nor did I say that he performs a role only to the extent that he correctly perceives the outlook of other persons. His role can just as well be designed to stand people on their heads and his interpretations of others may be wholly fallacious. Our unhappily good exdelinquent can put in hours of remorse and feel a great emptiness once he has found himself unfaithful to his role, antisocial and distorted as it may be. Indeed, it is not uncommon to find such a youngster attempting suicide, an act that makes both psychoanalysts and moralists turn themselves inside out to devise a coherent explanation. Sometimes it is said that such a person is upset because he has been disloyal to the delinquent society of which he is a member. But this is a crude oversimplification, based on the naive belief that morality is a simple matter of social identification.

There is a very interesting variant of this feeling-guilty-for-being-good. It turns up with increasing frequency in psychotherapy these days, and has become somewhat identifiable as a feature of our mid-century culture. The central idea seems to be that people should be themselves—an interesting kind of solipsism. Tell a young lady that she is a virtuous woman, and she is likely to start worrying right away. She will probably think you have accused her of being abnormal, bigoted, inhibited, intellectually dishonest, artificial, and not fit to associate with. It is pretty nearly as bad as telling a psychoanalyst he is neat and clean. Her construction undergirds a role when she takes the view that she must never appear to be anything other than what she has been at her worst. And her anxiety reaches the point of role loss and guilt when something happens to invalidate this position. Since psychotherapy is usually directed toward getting people to be something other than what they have thought themselves to be, it may become the occasion for acute guilt feelings in simple-minded men. The situation reminds me of the famous wood carving of the three monkeys in the Shinto Shrine at Nikko, Japan—"See no evil. Hear no evil. Speak no evil." The fourth monkey, "Do no evil," is conspicuously absent. After all, they are only monkeys, and there is no reason to expect monkeys to be anything but themselves!

After Sin, What?

Let us turn our attention away from the person who believes he has sinned, and who feels guilty, to the persons who point accusing fingers at each other. The most primitive way to deal with a person who has done something evil is to retaliate. He does something bad, therefore, something bad can be done to him. This makes nearly everybody happy, except, of course, the fellow who starts the trouble. This procedure has two psychological effects: it extends coveted privileges to those who haven't had the nerve to try the same thing, and it serves warning on others who might be similarly tempted to start something.

An incident in the life of Jesus is a case in point. You remember He came upon a group of men about to stone a girl to death. She had been caught in the local parking lot at a rather inconvenient moment in her emotional life. Jesus suggested to the gang that if they really wanted to do it in an orderly fashion the fellow who had never sinned should heave out the first stone. I have the feeling that being the kind of punks they were they all had a pretty specific idea of what he meant, and that none of them wanted to admit in front of the others that he was innocent of that sort of thing—though I suspect some of them might have been innocent in this respect. The upshot was that they decided to give up the project, perhaps to go off and get into some mischief on the other side of town. But up to that point none of the goings on really had much to do with the girl and the sin she had committed.

I suppose retaliation may have another function. After an orgy of reprisals it may be that folks are satisfied to go back home and behave themselves a little longer. But neither does this have much to do with the person who sinned in the first place. As a matter of fact everyone should feel rather grateful to him for giving so many people a good excuse for doing what they so much wanted to do anyway. A good deal of our social interaction, both formal and informal, is still pitched at this level of treatment, though I doubt if the sinner often receives all the gratitude he deserves.

A somewhat more socialized approach is to demand restitution. Assuming that when a person sins he injures someone, he ought to do what he can to restore matters to their original state. Often a prisoner is encouraged to regard the serving of his sentence as a "payment of his debt to society," though it is a little hard to see how his imprisonment, which rarely returns a profit to society, can be considered the payment of a debt. Sometimes the restitution is even more labored. A man does something regarded as a sin against God. He is told to take twenty laps around the track and repeat a prayer two hundred times. It is difficult to imagine how this could make God feel any better, unless you imagine a God who likes to sit and listen to the same prayer over and over. If restitution is the objective, it might be more to the point to suggest to the man that he stop praying for a week or two so as to make less of a nuisance of himself.

Punishment

By far the most common way of treating sinners is to punish them. In psychological circles this is known as negative reinforcement.

Throughout our culture it is pretty generally believed that behavior is controlled by red and green lights, known as punishment and rewards. There is the benign form of punishment that we use when we want to control the act of sin without bothering our heads about the personal constructs in terms of which the act made sense. This is the kind of thing we often do with children. From it they learn to keep a wary eye on parents, teachers, and policemen. Personal construct theory, which approaches behavior in terms of the constructions persons place upon their circumstances, would not consider this a very basic kind of psychological approach to the problems of human conduct.

And the same game is played under theological rules. Man makes a mistake. That upsets the Almighty. There is some disagreement on just how it upsets Him. Some say it makes Him furious and others say it depresses Him. Whichever it is, it is up to man to do something to restore the Almighty's peace of mind. So man punishes himself, or whoever it was who made the mistake. The Almighty wholeheartedly approves of this, and it makes Him feel so warm and permissive that He is disposed to forget the whole thing. He may even offer to pick up the tab for the damages caused by the sinful act. Under these theological rules man plays the classical role of a court fool in the Kingdom of Heaven.

A somewhat more mystical view, ably expressed by Elijah, is that punishment purifies the soul and enables the tortured individual to see the difference between good and evil with twenty-twenty vision. But lest you think that my simple way of stating this argument is intended to dismiss it, let me hasten to add that there is plenty of psychological evidence that some persons do make use of adversity to come to a deeper understanding of what is good and bad. I even suspect that the experience of sin is itself often just the thing to be woven into something constructive, though this is not the sort of remark one is supposed to make in front of the children.

As you can readily see, I don't think, taking all these methods into account, that we have yet found very good answers to the question of how to distinguish good from evil, nor to the question of how to get sinners straightened out. Some of the methods of treating sin turn out to be no more than methods of treating its guilt symptoms, and hence may work against their intended objectives. How often do we see the patient in psychotherapy who uses punishment to salve his guilty discomfort, yet scarcely gives a thought to how he got himself into trouble. Some patients even use punishment as a kind of prepayment for sins they think they might like to commit later on. This pay-as-you-go system may keep sinners from living beyond their means, but it contributes nothing to wisdom.

ASSISTANCE FOR THE TROUBLED MAN

Let us assume that, by and large, man was serious when he ate that apple; he really intended to gain the knowledge of good and evil. This is to say he has clearly embarked on an enterprise, and the task of those who wish to assist him is not to badger him into being good in spite of himself or to keep rapping his knuckles every time he reaches for something fragile. It is rather to accept his quest as legitimate and do what can be done to help him contrive a deeper understanding of how the distinctions between good and evil can be clarified. This is his task. He may not be up to it, but it is still his task, and it will be for generations to come.

We must concede, of course, that some men have lost interest in the quest. This is quite understandable when we consider the fact that most of the systems for dealing with good and evil are designed to circumvent the necessity for coming to grips with the problem. Why struggle with a perplexity for which you can never hope to devise more than a partial solution, when this culture, or that religion, will provide you with a thumb-indexed set of answers in tomorrow's mail, or, at the latest, during next Sunday's morning church service?

How to be Sick

But, as I have said, mankind, by and large, means to get this matter of good and evil straightened out to his satisfaction, even if it takes from now to eternity, as it likely will. In the meantime he can at least make progress. So let us turn now to the ways he has developed over the ages for assisting himself in his quest. There are a number of religious devices—prayer, penance possibly; certainly sharing the misfortunes of others is one device. These can be more than mere gimmicks for keeping your nose clean; they can be genuinely exploratory approaches to the much more challenging problem of understanding the real difference between right and wrong. There are also secular devices of a philosophical nature, and there are physical devices, one of which, in particular, I want to mention.

Man has always wondered if there isn't a relationship between

evil and illness. At first he wondered if illness wasn't a symptom of
evil. You remember Job decided that it wasn't, but was out-voted by
his neighbors. More recently men have turned this hypothesis end-for-
end and explored the possibility that evil is a symptom of illness. Understand and treat the illness, and the evil that tortures men's minds
will evaporate. The only trouble with that apple that Adam ate was
that it had worms in it. Treat his stomachache and he will be as
good as new.

There is some scientific evidence for this conclusion that I think
we will have to accept as conclusive. Alcohol, tranquilizers, prefrontal
lobotomy, will undoubtedly cause evil as experienced by the tortured
mind to fade. As a matter of fact, there is nothing like a thorough-going
topectomy to reduce the whole issue to inconsequentiality. Most of
us use sleep more or less for this same purpose, though some find
that sleep doesn't work and insist they can treat the ailment better
if they stay awake and keep very, very busy. Move up in your job,
keep up the payments, give the kids a little spending money while
they're young enough to enjoy it, keep up the payments—or did I say
that before? Above all, keep up the payments! You will find that is
quite enough good and evil to worry about.

But I would like to talk about illness. Illness is a conceptual model
of thought that has proved to have wide utility. The use of this conceptual model has enabled mankind to accomplish many things that
had long been believed impossible. Now I don't think this fact, important
though it may be, obviates the possibility that many of these same
benefits might better have been accomplished by other means. Even
a few medical men have thought of this, and are genuinely concerned
about it, though the drug manufacturers, whose advertising finances
the most important "scientific" medical journals, have found effective
ways to make it abundantly clear that reputable doctors should keep
such thoughts to themselves.

Which Is It: Illness or Crime?

Illness is one thing; crime is another. Yet both of these are, in
essence, conceptual models for dealing with man's failings. How man
has come to apply one model to some things and the other model
to others is a fascinating story of the history of thought. A woman
screams at her husband from ten o'clock to midnight, and raises goose
pimples on her neighbors' necks; that is sinful; apply the crime model
and punish her. But if she has read anything at all in the women's
magazines about psychiatry lately, she will realize that midnight is

no time to stop. She should keep it up until six A.M., if her lungs will hold out. No one will punish her for that. They will take her to a place where there is a bed with crisp clean sheets, the same neighbors will send flowers, and the nicest man will come and talk to her! And the really ecstatic thing about it is that her husband—*her husband*, mind you—will have to pay that man fifty dollars an hour! All this, and heaven too!

So we have developed a culture where two distinct conceptual models are concurrently employed, one that says sin should be punished, the other that it should be treated. Our courts have the casuistic responsibility for determining which model to apply to whom. This can be a bit sticky when you are dealing with women whose husbands can't pay fifty dollars an hour, though the issue is less complex if you take into account the fact that if a woman had been the right kind of person in the first place, she would have married a man who could afford to pay fifty dollars an hour.

Well, the upshot is that the people who can afford it, as well as a lot of folks who can't, have decided that a problem is not something you solve, but is something you lie down and are treated for. The idea is catching on fast.

Stifling Man's Quest

I don't think that either punishment or treatment has much to do with man's basic undertaking, and it is unfortunate that these should be the only apparent alternatives for dealing with the more urgent matters of personal conduct. It is unfortunate that our psychological approaches to such matters were ever identified with medicine or illness, just as unfortunate, in the long run, as it would have been if they had remained identified with a punitive social system or a stimulus-response psychology. I even think it is unfortunate that we must use the term "therapy" for psychological assistance.

There is a further misfortune—perhaps even more far-reaching in its deleterious effects. Men who want to take this matter into their own hands and conclude the question in their own terms of morality or insight, have learned how to produce and alleviate guilt feelings. The device of excommunication, whether employed by a church, a political party, a sorority, a household, or a psychotherapist who unnecessarily invokes a dependency transference, is the most powerful device man has ever invented for bringing about individual conformity and cutting short man's personal quest for distinguishing good from evil. When this is combined with the devices men have contrived to alleviate the pangs of guilt—man's natural clue to sin—through religious confession, Communist self-criticism, sorority pledging, family reinstatement, or psychotherapeutic replacement of the superego, the suppression of man's enterprise can become very nearly absolute.

When the Psychotherapist Shares the Enterprise

The important thing to remember is, despite all the blatant claims that are made on every hand, no one has yet constructed the final answer to the question of what is good and what is evil, and that the moment man gives up the enterprise he is lost. The psychologist who attempts to assist his fellow man should keep this truth central to his system of practice. The task is to assist the individual man in what is singularly the most important undertaking in his life, the fullest possible understanding of the nature of good and evil. This is not to say that man must always steer clear of sin; it is to say, rather, that he should learn from it, and not blindly allow himself to repeat it.

It will occur to you that some of this might have been inferred from the teachings of Jesus and his concept of realistic confession followed by repentance, a concept that is quite different from penance, and quite different from the current interpretations of confession and repentance. Jesus suggested that if you do something bad you should not run from the scene of the crime screaming, "I've sinned, I've sinned. I'll make up for it! I'll never do it again!" he suggests instead that you stop, turn around and look at what you have done, acknowledge that it was you rather than the Devil, society, or your ulcers, examine the mistake, and reconstrue the situation so that the possibilities of making a similar mistake in the future are minimized.

What, then, are the steps in the psychotherapeutic process of a person who finds himself overwhelmed by a sense of sin—the sense of the loss of a great and important role? Logic, I suppose, would dictate that you should find out whether he had actually sinned or not. But here personal construct theory, being the psychology of the human enterprise rather than a substitute for it, takes issue with logic, which claims to be the foolproof process by which valid conclusions are always reached. Let the person tell you exactly what he thinks he did; yes. Speculate with him on whether it will be judged in the end as something evil; to do less would be hypocritical and evasive. But most of all, open the matter to inquiry—yours and his. This inquiry is the chosen quest of all mankind, and that includes both you and your client. Don't abandon it under any conditions—whether guilt, fear, or laziness. Don't abandon it for any set of prefabricated conclusions. Above all, don't let your client abandon it!

Therapy is not likely to get off to a good start with the therapist saying, "Yes, you did," or "No, you didn't." He may, in some cases, say, however, "I agree, that does sound like it was the wrong thing to do, but simply to call it wrong does not really tell us much unless we go back over the experience much more carefully than you have apparently been able to do so far. Besides, we need to have a much better sense of how matters seemed to you at the time the incident occurred."

Here we have illustrated in a very simplified form two of the essential psychotherapeutic steps in a case where the client's sense of guilt is a presenting symptom. We can call them *confession* and *repentance*, if we prefer the religious terms, or we can call them *observing incidents* and *formulating constructions*, if personal construct terms are preferred. To be sure, these are not standardized remarks to be used in all cases; indeed, in this particular form they might be quite inappropriate in some cases.

There is more to psychotherapy than the exploration of salient incidents. The client will have to reconstrue his role, experiment with it, and keep it open to continuing revision. Keeping in mind the special meaning of *role* in personal construct theory, the task is to press forward to develop and test role constructs experimentally. For role constructs are more than constructions of impersonal objects; they are efforts to understand the outlooks of others. One must find a way to put these man-made hypotheses into a comprehensive framework that will transcend the little strategems of everyday social manipulation.

Throughout all this the psychotherapist has another kind of objective. Not only does he want to restore the resources of his clients and help him make his own determinations of the difference between good and evil in ways that are both valid and comprehensive, he wants also to restore the client as an on-going person. It is not enough for the client to be set back on his feet and given firm ground to stand on; he needs to prepare himself to advance into further explorations that we hope will not turn out so badly. But if he sins again, as he most certainly will if he is earnest in his quest, he should be able to profit from the next experience rather than be overwhelmed by it.

But this is enough to say about psychotherapeutic technique. After all, I promised you this would not be a how-to-do-it handbook for counselors who want to make people behave themselves without having to go into the grubby business of understanding them.

To come back to Jesus; do you remember what He said to the girl who had been so rudely exposed? He asked her where her accusers were and she said they were gone. Neither was He one of her accusers. She was on her own. Then He gently suggested that she might make something out of the experience so as not to repeat it. He didn't even forgive her; that sort of unction didn't seem to be called for. Notwithstanding all the words I have put into this paper, this that Jesus briefly said, or implied, is the substance of what I have to say about sin and psychotherapy. But, at that, I think it is quite a bit to say!

9

In Whom Confide: On Whom
Depend for What?

LET ME EXPRESS my appreciation of the opportunity to address this Society and to share with you, on this occasion, the memory of a distinguished and dedicated member of our profession.

"In whom confide? On whom depend for what?" Probably no experienced clinician can listen to these questions without being reminded of something he has heard many times before. Often it has been expressed in furtive undertones, as in the case of a frightened person who dares not ask the question out loud lest he receive the dreaded answer. Sometimes the question is explicit, but purely rhetorical, as in the case of one who is in the act of raising a barrier between himself and an intruding world.

It is of no matter, for the purposes of this discussion, that we customarily say of the one person that he is "neurotic" and of the other that he is "paranoid." I shall not try to classify symptoms nor to trace the pattern of learning that makes people say such things. You are invited, instead, to join me in an attempt to understand what each person *means* by such questions and the nature of the *experience* which, by asking them, he has offered to share.

Our point of departure is the place where we find man caught in the midst of a socially complex world for which he is psychologically

SOURCE. The Fourth Annual Samuel H. Flowerman Memorial Lecture presented to the New York Society of Clinical Psychologists on December 7, 1962. Reproduced here by kind permission of the Society.

unprepared—a world in which so few are able to face life at the one cocktail level of confidence. There are two popular explanations of how man has gotten in over his head. One is the "Frankenstein" thesis. It holds that material developments have outrun social progress. The other is the "babes in the wood" theory. It is that the complexities of society are beyond the psychological capacities of an animal who has only recently evolved from a lower form.

We should look at these two themes for a moment before proceeding along the alternative line I wish to develop with you. First, is it the imbalance between social and material progress that has gotten us into trouble? I think not. Indeed, our particular materialistic advance is itself as much a social development as it is the accumulation of wealth and hardware. It is the particular social form of this highly developed materialistic society whose viability is being urgently brought into question. Without the social structure and psychological outlook that takes them as its premises rather than its implements, neither wealth nor hardware would need be much of a threat to us. Granted, of course, societies have been built on other assumptions that turned out to be equally questionable.

As for the second popular theme, the one that man is still too much of a monkey to cope with civilization, I think this also is artifactual. The naiveté is not so much a vestigial trait, carried over from man's simian ancestry, as it is a tenet of the psychology he has devised for his everyday use. This version of psychology, which is the version in which you and I were trained, holds that our neighbors are precocious beasts to be enticed by food and sex or roused out of their naturally inert state to be propelled one way or another by motives and dynamics. The approach to such behaving organisms—I hesitate to say "persons" lest I be accused of being unscientific—is in terms of a psychology derived from the Nineteenth Century physiological model. The social upshot of this scientism is a particular kind of manipulative approach to interpersonal relations which has come to characterize and dehumanize our culture.

Now our theme, which stands in contrast to these two popular clichés, does not argue that the world is simpler than we think. If it were so simple, I might have to concede that man could as well remain simple too, and that it is possible for him to survive with no more psychological understanding than he had in primitive times.

But it is clear the world is not simple anymore. And it is equally clear that man is not coping with it as he ought. Moreover, the difficulty is something for us to pitch in and solve, not something we should lie down and be treated for. In other words, I regard the problem as one that can profitably be cast in *psychological* terms, though not in the sort of psychologisms I challenged at the beginning of this discussion.[1]

THE DEPENDENT SOCIETY

It is true that Twentieth Century society is so complicated it is hard to understand, and that this causes difficulties. But what is more important is that it is a society in which each person finds himself dependent upon many fragmentary sources of supply. To put it another way, we may say that civilized man has an intricate social system of dependencies. He must continually analyze and fractionate his personal wants so as to allocate them appropriately within this complex. The person upon whom he depends for one kind of support is not the one who is likely to help him in other ways. Moreover, a person must be sensitively aware of what he has to offer others in return if he is to make his own personal matrix of reciprocal supplies and demands actually function. Otherwise his associates will soon come to regard him as an overly "dependent" nuisance, and he will eventually become a very lonely man.

Yet so complex is the typical dependency matrix that rarely do two partners match themselves so well that each supplies all the wants of the other. What more often happens is that the reciprocal dependency breaks down, leaving one person clinging and wistful where the other is restless and impatient. Where one seeks, the other tries to escape, and where one tries to disengage, the other finds himself clutching desperately at every passing coatsleeve to satisfy his unfulfilled dependency.

It is in this sense that we can say that civilized man is a very dependent man. What others can give him and what he can give others are so narrrowly specialized that he is hard put to it to make the two match up in any comprehensive set of interpersonal relationships.

There is also a complementary sense in which civilized man is a particularly dependent creature. Not only are his sources of supply complex, and his services to others specialized, but his own shopping list is bulky and often illegible. The simple pleasures and obvious necessities of an older generation are no longer enough. Thus not only does he have to differentiate and allocate his dependencies within a

[1] The main body of this paper was preceded by a brief, informal summary of Professor Kelly's abandonment of motivational concepts, such as "affect," "needs," "psychodynamics," etc.

complicated system involving mutual relationships, but he vaguely craves a lot of things his hard-pressed grandparents were too busy to think of.

The point I have tried to make so far is that civilized man, as we know him, is a particularly dependent man, that it is difficult for him to allocate his dependencies on a reciprocal basis, and that he is often lonely—not with the loneliness of a person who has no companions at all, but with the loneliness of one who cannot reach the companions he has.

Adults Are More Dependent than Children

Let me press a little further this translation of civilization into terms of dependency. It is customary to characterize a child as "dependent" and an adult as "independent." But this is misleading. To be sure, a child cannot take care of himself, but then, when you come right down to it, neither can an adult. An adult appears to be self-reliant merely because he is often better able to distribute his dependencies in proper relation to his potential resources.

But how many adults can survive on what is sufficient for a child? Indeed, in some cases, children are more adept in placing their dependencies than are their parents. A child's ability to love and the utter simplicity of his demands often places him in a more secure position. There is a sense, also, in which he is freer to express himself, to think independently, and to rely upon his own imaginative devices for exploring his world. He may not have the power his parents have, but he often has more independence.

Of course, this state of affairs in the child's world is changing. Children are more and more being caught up in the complex dependency matrix of global wants and fragmentary supplies that characterizes modern adult life. The worlds of work and play are separated by a gulf that grows wider and wider. Many children never see their fathers at work, much less join them in it. Young people are excluded from society's productive functions and reciprocal dependencies, both by law and union regulations.

What, then, are the kids supposed to do? Why, they are supposed to enjoy themselves, just like any clean-cut, normal, healthy, young American psychopath! Enjoy themselves—play it smart! Play it cool—enjoy themselves! If, in the midst of all this emphasis on the self for the sake of the psyche, they turn out to be delinquent, then what they need is—you guessed it—*recreational facilities!* That will bring them "the joy of self-fulfillment!"

Playgrounds are supervised by specialists. Even joy has to come in pieces. Schools, in turn, assume an increasing authority over the child's life, and then divide it up into departmentalized instruction—a further fragmentation of the child's sources of supply. In certain sectors of our culture—often called the privileged ones—even the functional relationships and reciprocal dependencies of home life are replaced by a boarding school regimen.

Yet in spite of this growing complication in the matrices of children's dependencies, and the well-publicized "overdependencies" of youth, I still believe it is clear that they remain somewhat more independent than their parents. While it is true that they are somewhat restrained by an adult society—a somewhat incoherent adult society, nowadays— and they are often disciplined legalistically rather than humanistically, still it is the young child, not the overadaptive adult, who dares try what others tacitly regard as preposterous, who is able to fulfill his wants by spontaneous play rather than by conforming to the arbitrary demands of an employer, and who would rather be guided by the best he knows than acquiesce to the shenanigans of local racketeers.

And it is the adult, not the child, who yields his independence, bit by bit, in exchange for power, until at last, when he gets the power he no longer has either the vision or the initiative to direct it. He even forgets why he wanted it in the first place. Worst of all, when the adult is confronted by leisure and its long-awaited gift of independence, he is ill at ease because it provides no obvious demands with which he can comply.

Now I am not saying that adult dependencies have to be auctioned off and distributed in this particular way; I am saying only that this is the way things have been working out. What I have described is not the elemental nature of man; it is a particular psychological invention he has cooked up for himself—no more—and, for the time being, the poor fellow is trying to survive on it. Nor am I saying that a lot of dependency is a bad thing. I am trying to show that we have a society that handles it badly, so badly, in fact, that power without imagination has become the accepted criterion of the "mature" citizen. In many sectors of our society the man who is regarded as mature is the one who is placed in influential positions because he knows just enough not to experiment with untried formulas. He may be regarded as even more mature if he prefers facts to ideas, is concretistic in his thinking, and suppresses anything that appears to be a figment of eggheaded imagination. Even among psychologists the term "mature" has come to have an honorific meaning, though it is not very clear what it means to them, other than being something characteristic of older persons.

I can go further. We do not even need to take for granted, as most people do, that maturity, in the sense of adulthood, is a good thing. Perhaps it is childhood that is the good thing. In other words, I am simply trying to analyze a cultural state of affairs from a psychological viewpoint, keeping in mind that social leadership and personal initiative are not synonymous, and that we have a society in which independence characterizes neither its adults nor its most civilized members.

What I have been saying about the enbloc exchange of independence for power, so often observed in the modern adult, can be criticized by your pointing out to me that without the implements of power, such as money, credit, professional status, control of the channels of mass communication, or mastery of the devices by which pressure can be brought to bear on people who want to get ahead and are therefore vulnerable to such things—without such implements an imaginative person is not likely to have much impact on society. That is true. Imagination without any power at all may fail to produce a thing, except, possibly, on paper, or in the minds of a few impressionable bystanders. But the contrasting alternative—power without imagination—is worse. That is simple tyranny!

Dependency as a Problem in Psychotherapy

As experienced psychotherapists, I scarcely need remind you that there is no point in the course of treatment where the psychologist gets into more trouble than when he tries to get his client to act independently and responsibly. If you are accustomed to think about this problem in psychoanalytic terms, you probably recognize it as that stage of psychotherapy where the analysis of transference begins. Those who think in other terms will define the stage differently, though generally there will be little disagreement as to the nature of the behavioral phenomena we all observe.

Often what we see is a client who wants to live his new life in the therapy room and solely with his therapist, while continuing on the outside in the same old ways. Sometimes the impatient therapist will attempt to build a fire under his clinging client to make him jump, as when fees are assessed for "therapeutic reasons." In the analytic therapies the client is confronted, in one way or another, with his childlike dependency—a dependency that was readily accepted by the therapist during the early stages of the transference relationship, but now starkly reveals itself to the therapist as evidence of his client's helplessness. It is at this point in the confrontation that the client—now driven to a state of exasperation—most often expresses aggressive hostility toward his therapist. This is also the point where the *acting-out* behavior, which most therapists unnecessarily dread, is most likely to assume abortive proportions, and where panic is most likely to appear.

To put it simply, the client is often threatened by a stark exposure of his dependency, a dependency that is not only unworthy of the adult he pretends to be, but one which threatens to render him permanently impotent. Even the classical cases of so-called homosexual panic are, I believe, essentially derived from sensing this kind of hopeless dependency. To be sure, where there is homosexuality there is likely to be some guilt involved, too. But nothing is quite so likely to panic a client as the prospect of utter dependence, regardless of whether or not there is any homosexuality involved. It can happen even when the dependency is identified with someone other than the therapist. But it is particularly likely to happen when it is the therapist on whom he feels dependent, and when it is the therapist himself who calls attention to it. Moreover, it is amplified when the client realizes that his relationship with that nourishing person is temporary, that there is no reciprocal dependency that might bind the therapist to him permanently, and that he has exposed himself not to a companion, but to a practitioner who has nothing but a professional commitment to the relationship. It is then that he becomes frantic.

A client of mine once put it this way. "There is no one I can talk to; not really. Of course, there are lots of people who want to talk, but all they give you is crap! Nobody really cares, not a single person in this whole world. Not one single person!"

"What about me?" I asked.

"Oh, yes, *you* care," she answered immediately. "But you don't count. You are *supposed* to care. It's your job."

What a tragedy it must be to realize that your best friend is a psychologist!

But why? Why should the realization of one's dependency on a therapist be so much more disturbing than the host of other dependencies that encompass one's life? Or why should this particular matter of dependency be singled out from among all the other things in the client's life that have obviously been going wrong? To answer these questions I would like to turn to theory again for a few moments.

NO COGNITION, NO AFFECT, NO HOSTAGES TO CLASSICISM

I have said enough already to suggest that the problem of dependency boils down to the issue of how human wants and resources are differentiated, not *how much* dependency we have. The client who becomes alarmed over the *amount* of dependency he has transferred to his therapist is overwhelmed by the fact that he cannot move to make any decisions without running back to his couch, and by the fact, also, that his relation with his therapist is artificial and temporary. But if this massive dependency were properly distributed and many sources of supply identified he would not feel so trapped. Of course he does not see this. The reason he cannot see it is simply because he cannot, at this point, differentiate between aspects of his own dependency. He experiences the objective of his striving as a massive yearning, not as something that can be divided up, achieved by stages, or supplied from a variety of sources.

This brings us into an area of psychology that is still held hostage to classical notions of logic. How does one identify something—either an object accessible to the senses, or the objective of his own strivings? I think we know by now that our senses do not automatically tell us what an object is, nor do they, by themselves, even tell us that it is there. Certainly senses do not discriminate one object from another; that remains a much more complicated task involving the surveying of boundaries between events and the abstraction of some similarity of one event to others.

Classical logic is based on the assumption that events present themselves to us already separated from each other and distinguishable as entities. All we have to do is take these obviously distinct events and put them together in various ways. This process is called *conceptualization*, and the ways the events end up being put together are called *concepts*.

It is commonly supposed, even by some psychologists, that these concepts—or ways of putting things together—do not really emerge until they have been symbolized in some way, usually by words. Thus, conceptualization has become known characteristically as a verbal process and theories of psychology that concern themselves with the ways things are lumped together are likely to be called cognitive theories.

But the events of this world do not march up to us single file, differentiate themselves by announcing their names, and wait to be assigned to classes, or organized into working teams charged with the responsibility of making something happen. William James said that for the child it was more like a blooming, buzzing confusion. And Herbert Spencer, viewing the matter more macroscopically, once spoke of evolution as a change from an indefinite incoherent homogeneity to a definite coherent heterogeneity. The task of man, emerging psychologically in this Twentieth Century, as never before, is to pull his innermost experience apart and then to put it together again, a task requiring both analysis and synthesis!

Now I don't think that either cognition or conceptualization provides an adequate basis for understanding how persons may best order their lives. The inadequacy of this kind of thinking is particularly apparent when we try to help a client differentiate and allocate his dependencies.

CONSTRUING: A NEW LOOK AT THE
PSYCHOLOGICAL RECONSTRUCTION OF EVENTS

When a person makes a distinction between two objects, he does not assign one of them to a restricted class and relegate the other to a wastepaper basket containing everything else in the universe. Instead, he deals significantly and somewhat locally with both objects. Another way of saying this is to point out that one does not classify one object at a time; he distinguishes *between* that object and certain others that are relevant to the distinction, not between that object and *all* other objects. Objects not relevant to the distinction *are not psychologically* part of the context.

One thing more! When one makes a distinction, it make no sense for him to say to himself that the two objects *differ* from each other unless, by doing so, he identifies one or the other of the objects as having some property that *links* it to additional objects that enter into the construction. Otherwise, he is saying only that "A is A and B is B," whatever that means.

So in making distinctions, whether between external objects or internal experiences, two functions are served simultaneously. Objects within one's field of attention *are separated and linked to other objects*. Now let me emphasize that this is accomplished by the same psychological act, not by two separate or successive acts. The very same process that sets one's experiences apart also puts them together in different ways. It is impossible to do one without accomplishing the other. This is a key to understanding basic psychological processes in man.

Now what I am describing is not *conceptualization*, as psychologists and logicians commonly understand that notion. It may not even be very good *logic*. But it is descriptive of the way man starts to make sense out of his blooming buzzing confusion. Instead of trying to classify this particular process loosely as one of "conception" or "cognition," let us abandon these formalistic notions altogether and designate it as the psychological process of *construing*, or of forming *personal constructs*. And I must insist that the elemental *construct* I am postulating bears little resemblance to a *concept* and that *construing* is a far cry from *cognition*.

It would be quite understandable, linguistic traditions being what they are, if you were to visualize construing as a verbalized or conscious act. But that need not be so. Constructs can be *preverbally symbolized* and, as far as *consciousness*—whatever that may be—is concerned, a person may have a hard time representing constructs to himself, except as raw experience. There is not necessarily anything either cognitive or affective about this kind of construing. In fact, as I have already said, I do not think that these terms are very useful to the psychologist.

To come back from theory to clinical observation again, I believe there is no better place to observe this psychological process of *construing*—particularly *preverbal construing*—than in the client who, in the midst of psychotherapy, is struggling to make new sense out of some experience that lies just beyond the reach of his semantic language. But it can be observed in some degree at even less accessible levels, levels that lie even beyond the reach of his primitive semiotic speech. This can be done if one is careful to note the transitions and repetitions of his unsignified acts. The details of just how the clinician does this lie somewhat beyond the scope of this discourse. If you are skeptical about there being such a possibility, as at this point you have every right to be, I shall have to ask you to accept the claim on faith, for the time being. The point is not absolutely essential to the further development of my argument, though it would make subsequent matters clearer if we could first agree on it. Perhaps the particular issue can be handled more satisfactorily in some other context.

THE PERSONAL CONSTRUCT AS A DIMENSION OF FREEDOM IN HUMAN INTERACTION

Now we are ready to come back to dependency and the personal emancipation implied in its proper differentiation and distribution. Perhaps now it will make more sense to say that dependency is something to be handled by *construing*, not by *conceptualization*. Let us see how this works.

When I first mentioned the discriminating assignment of dependencies, I am sure that it seemed as though I were talking about some formalized sorting process involving the decision to do *this* with *that* and *something else* with *the other*. And I am sure, as clinicians, you knew that the surging experience of dependency could rarely, if ever, be handled quite so simply. The person who senses his own dependency often experiences it as a nameless craving only, a massive loneliness, or a desparate urgency to find something or be with someone. But no matter how oceanic the experience appears to be, it is, nevertheless, something that is construed—often with preverbal constructs. For every experience, to the extent that it stands out at all, stands out in terms of its similarities and distinctions. Thus the wistful person always senses that what he craves is something like . . . but not . . . He may even try to tell you what he wants in terms of words, though often he confesses later that his effort was scarcely more than an overwrought verbal gesture.

A construct is like a reference axis, a basic dimension of appraisal, often unverbalized, frequently unsymbolized, and occasionally unsignified in any manner except by the elemental processes it governs. Behaviorally, it can be regarded as an open channel of movement, and a *system of constructs* provides each man with his own personal network of action pathways, serving both to limit his movements and to open up to him passages of freedom which otherwise would be psychologically nonexistent.

The process of psychotherapy can be viewed as one of dealing with such basic psychological units of human life. Psychotherapy in its simplest form—though some would prefer not to dignify this kind of thing with the label "psychotherapy"—can be nothing more than getting a client to rattle back and forth in one of his construct slots. It has its place. Beyond it, however, there are many therapeutic possibilities, on up to the rather ambitious undertaking of replacing *core constructs*.

"SLOT-RATTLING" BETWEEN DEPENDENCE AND INDEPENDENCE

Without trying to spell out all the personal subtleties in how dependency is construed, let me say simply that the construct of *dependence versus independence* is, in one form or another, a major reference axis in the lives of most people. I think we shall have no trouble agreeing on that. Because it is a major axis in most personal construct systems, it is one of those likely to be invoked when one finds himself in an untenable position and must find his way out. I trust it is clear by now that I am not saying that it has to be invoked semantically, or even semiotically. I am saying simply that it is likely to be used as an avenue of movement when things get hot. The person who has his fill of what he diagnoses as "independence" will, if he uses the dependence-independence construct, be likely to consider "dependence" as an alternative. And the person who senses that he is about to be overwhelmed by "dependence" will, if he has no time to figure out a more subtle way, be likely to dash to the other end of the first slot he sees open to him and start acting in ways that he considers to be "independent."

The worst of it is that many therapists see the problem the same way as their clients. They see dependency as a consequence of transference—which to some extent it is—and believe, therefore, that if the client's transference goes, so will his dependency. Moreover, they are keenly aware of the fact that his dependency *on them* is unproductive and cannot go on forever, and because they, too, are trapped by the syntactical proposition that independence is the alternative to dependency, urge the client to get busy and start acting "independently." Or perhaps, the therapist, now that his own psychodiagnostic curiosity has been satiated wants to talk to someone more interesting. Or, possibly, the therapist is getting tired having such a big baby to take care of.

In any case, this is one of the stages in the psychotherapeutic relationship when the client is likely to do a good deal of impulsive slot-rattling. And the reason for it may be his own construction of the alternatives to dependency—and sometimes the therapist's construction, too.

But the issue, as I tried to make clear in the earlier part of this discussion, can be drawn in a different way. Both civilization and adulthood are characterized by a great deal of dependency. The problem is to construe dependencies differentially, and also to identify and distinguish a wide range of resources which functionally match those dependencies. While it is admittedly difficult to match up complex dependencies and resources, even after they have been identified, this is still one of the essential tasks of psychotherapy.

THE ECONOMICS OF DEPENDENCY

It might simplify matters if we could set up a system of monetary exchange under which each of us could translate his dependencies into terms of money. Then with our pockets full of loose change we could put a coin into the slot whenever we saw something we wanted. We wouldn't have to worry about our own psychological skills in eliciting the responses we wanted.

Some people, I am sure, think this is about what civilization amounts to, or what maturity means. Why barter for anything; just buy it! To get what you want you first exchange your services for money. You may have to sacrifice some of your independence, but you will acquire power, and power is what it takes to get anything in this world. Any kind of perceptive giving—giving affection, offering sensitive support to someone in trouble at a timely moment, or personifying the fulfillment of another's hopes—if these acts do not fit into the economic scheme, they are old-fashioned and waste of time.

If people don't like you, subsidize them! If the waiter doesn't think you are important enough, tip him! If you want to have a lot of friends, don't waste time getting acquainted with individuals, throw a cocktail party! If you want some tender affection, buy a mink coat. No! No! *Not for yourself!* And if you don't know for sure what you want, but, whatever it is, you want it awful bad, look in the yellow pages—for a psychologist! He already has a pretty good idea of what it is you want, and he has the professional "know-how" to get it for you "wholesale."

Perhaps I should be generous enough to include psychiatrists in this image of the commeralized erogenator, since I seem to be implying the usurpation of the long-established prerogatives of an older profession—the oldest. But this lecture is about clinical psychology—which has quite enough perplexities of its own—not about psychiatry, so I shall not presume to inflict my remarks on our brethren of the medical persuasion. Anyhow, quite apart from the prior claims of the ancient ego-healing arts, medical or otherwise, the idea of an economy based on the universal convertibility of psychological wants and supplies into a pocketable medium of exchange is not altogether new.

Well, as you probably suspect, I don't think this is a very good way to run a railroad. And as responsible psychotherapists, you don't either! It is just as important to differentiate the dependencies of those upon whom you, in turn, depend, as it is to purchase what you yourself have found essential. The differential understanding of others' dependencies also is a *construing* task—in the sense I have developed the notion of *construing* in the earlier parts of this discussion.

But there are some differences between the two tasks. One's own preverbal construing plays a much less obvious part in differentiating the dependencies of another person, although it still is involved in some degree, as any sensitive therapist knows. On the other hand, the task of construing others is made more difficult by the particular kind of psychological training most of us have had. So let me talk about that very important matter for awhile.

DETERMINISTIC THINKING AS AN OBSTACLE TO UNDERSTANDING

The science of the last century has gone in for determinism in a big way, as everybody knows. What may not be quite so apparent to us is the extent to which this kind of thinking has affected our culture and biased the way we try to get along with each other. Now I don't want to become embroiled in a criticism of scientific determinism to the extent that we will all forget about our topic. and especially it would be unwise to stir up the scientific dogmatists so near the end of the lecture. So let us avoid the issue of whether or not determinism actually exists or whether it is a good thing and concentrate simply on what has happened to us in the course of our thinking about each other in terms of present-day scientific determinism.

Simply stated, scientific determinism is the belief that one event is bound to lead to another. Put your finger on that event and you are well on your way to the prediction and control of what ensues. Applied to human affairs this means that you look to see what antecedents are necessary and sufficient to make such matters predictable. Applied to psychology this means that you look for the stimulus that accounts for man's response. Punch him here and he jumps there. Tickle her here and she—well! And all that sort of thing!

I scarcely need to point out that this is a strictly manipulative approach to human relations. There is no particular point in trying to understand a child if every time you give him candy he does what he is supposed to do. And if, whenever you buy something for your wife, she caresses you and fixes an extra nice supper, what else could you conceivably want to know about her? If each time you make a loan to a Latin American country, it votes with you in the United Nations, who can possibly say that you don't understand Latin Americans? It's all very scientific and it's psychological, too. And this is the way it generally works out.

But *how well* does it work out? How often it is we hear a man, who appears to be successful in handling his employees, complain that he is not really wanted at home. All his family expects of him is "financial support." His children expect candy and agree among themselves that all they need to do to satisfy the old geezer is avoid crossing him. His wife expects gifts from him rather than understanding, and she has found that all she needs to do to make him perform is prepare his favorite meal and rub the back of his neck with the tips of her fingers—while she occupies her own mind with a romantic story in the *Ladies Home Journal*. While all this scientifically valid psychology is being practiced in the home, probably both of them have been seeing psychotherapists for some time now, and the children have likely been placed in some good school, chosen because of its staff of well-trained counselors.

But now suppose—just suppose—the prevailing psychology of our times was not a stimulus-response psychology or even a psychology of biographical determinants. Suppose it was instead a psychology that concerned itself with how men construe the world around them, and particularly with how they construe each other. Suppose this was not only the psychology employed by psychologists, but the psychology employed by all of us. That is to say, it would represent the psychological outlook of our culture and times. What difference would it make?

First of all, it would be a good idea to identify to levels of construing. The first would be concerned with events and with men treated as events. By that I mean we would construe men's behaviors rather than their outlooks. Another person would be simply another moving object on our horizon. This is one level of construing.

But then suppose there were a second level of construing. This would be concerned with construing the constructs of other men. Instead of making our own sense out of what others did we would try to understand what sense they made out of what they did. Instead of putting together the events in their lives in the most scientifically parsimonious way, we would ask how they put things together, regardless of whether their schemes were parsimonious or not.

CONSTRUING AS A BASIS
FOR INTERDEPENDENCY

It is this second level of construing that opens the door to the reciprocal handling of dependency. We have already seen that dependency in our society is not so much a matter of the failure of independence as it is the failure to discriminate wants and resources and to allocate the one in proper relation to the other. We have seen, moreover, that where human interdependence is involved, the breakdown often comes when each person employs a psychology that tries to get what he wants from the other without being concerned with the other's outlook. If there is any reciprocity it is likely to be a simple transaction in which each person tries to give the other explicitly what he *says* he wants without trying *to understand what it is like to have such a want.*

But now let us apply this second level of construing to interpersonal relationships. This would not put the interdependent relationship between two persons on the basis of a simple transactional exchange of services. It would not be enough for each to give the other what he asked or appeared to need. Far more important than the transaction, or the exchange, would be the framework of understanding within which it took place. Even if one person did not get what he wanted from the other, the fact that his outlook was understood by the other, that the other could see what it was like to have such wants, and that the other can agree that, from the same point of view, he, too would experience a similar yearning—all this is likely to provide greater security in the dependency relationship than getting literally what was asked for.

It is because the psychotherapist often seems to be the one person in the world who has this kind of understanding that so many members of our society think they would rather associate with psychologists than people. And when one confides, whether to a psychologist or to a stranger, it is often with the momentary hope that here at last is a person who is more interested in outlooks than in payoffs. It is in the moment of disillusionment, when it becomes clear that, like everyone else, the stranger and the psychologist both regard human relationships as simple matters of put and take, the confiding person comes to regret the stupid mistake he has made, and he continues on his wistful way. After further encounters of this sort he may continue to confide, not because he has any real hope, but because he knows no other way to pursue his quest for a human relationship.

Fortunately, not all clients experience disillusionment with their therapists, for often psychologists are better than their psychological upbringing would lead you to expect. Moreover, as the therapeutic encounter comes to be recognized as a fertile soil in which basic psychological ideas can germinate, rather than as a field of applied science with a little status attached, the more we may hope that the psychological theories of the future will have significance for all human beings, their longings, and the way they trust and depend upon each other. A profession that does not deal intimately with man's dependencies, as one does deal intimately with them in psychotherapy, cannot ever hope to understand the undertow of psychological distress that flows beneath a troubled society.

IS IT ONLY THAT SOCIETY
HAS BECOME SPECIALIZED?

Is what I have said merely that society has become intricately specialized and this is bad? If so, then you have heard this lecture before—many times! But there is a good deal more to my thesis than this familiar sociological cliché.

It is true that our *society* has become a vast complex of specialized *services*. But let us look at it from the standpoint of the *individual*—just as I have been urging throughout my remarks. Looking at the supply of services only, it is clear enough that each individual plays his part by serving in only one or a few of the many specialties that must be articulated in an organized social economy.

But when we turn from the *services* a person renders to the *wants* he has, we find a contrasting state of affairs. Instead of each individual coming to specialize in what he wants, he is likely to do the reverse and extend his dependency over an ever wider range of demands. Thus we have *a psychological condition* which is much more problematical than the well-known *sociological condition*. What the individual wants from others is broad, complex, and undifferentiated, but what he has to offer them in return is narrow, concrete, and specific. The outcome is a society in which a lot of miscellany is available, but few people are able to find in all the clutter what they most earnestly crave.

Part of the solution lies in a reconsideration of the problem of dependency as experienced by the individual man. If, instead of trying to be "independent," he can differentiate his wants by construing them, so that what now looms up as a vague longing can be partly replaced by specific objectives, he will have a better chance of allocating his dependencies appropriately among the complex resources of a specialized society. This is a worthwhile psychological undertaking. It is one in which the clinical psychologist can help on a case-to-case basis.

But such an undertaking, I am sure, will not be enough. The man of the future, just as men of the past, is likely to find himself beset by mysterious yearnings, no matter how many of his previous wishes have been shaped into specific demands. He will continue always, in some degree, to depend in massive undifferentiated ways upon particular persons who share his most intimate life. This is to say he will still seek someone in whom to confide and the desires he cannot comprehend. But how can he hope to find anyone who will listen to him for long if he cannot listen in return? For this kind of mutual understanding both he and his confidant must be prepared to employ a psychology of personal constructs through which each may direct his attention broadly and sensitively to how the other construes his world, and not limit himself merely to the motives and stimuli that account for miscellaneous acts.

CONCLUSION OF AN UNPSYCHOLOGISTIC DISCOURSE

Now we come to the conclusion of what was intended to be an *unpsychologistic* discourse. In whom confide? On whom depend for what? I have tried to answer these questions in terms of a current society which unrealistically regards simple independence as the solution to all personal dependency problems, and which fails to recognize the need for an everyman's psychology that will accept a great amount of dependency and look for ways of allocating it. Such a new psychology is one based on the process of *construing*—which has practically nothing to do with conceptualization or cognition. Moreover, in a society where this kind of psychology directs attention primarily to the understanding of outlooks rather than the manipulation of behaviors, and to human striving rather than transactional exchanges of services, it should be possible to find suitable persons in whom to confide and on whom to depend.

Now, may I point out that, with the exception of the notion of *construing*—which I warned you would be my only technicality in tonight's discussion—I have spent the evening talking about psychology without resorting to psychological conventions. I have not invoked either stimuli or psychodynamics to explain human experience. And if, during the course of this discussion, you found yourself occasionally mumbling such words to yourself, I can only say that I did my best to stop you. My, it certainly is hard to give up bad habits! But—I understand! I even had the same outlook myself—once!

10

Psychotherapy and the Nature
of Man

A LONG TIME ago, so the story goes, Man made a fateful decision. He chose to live his life by understanding, rather than obedience. This was doing it the hard way. The outcome, as most of you know from the story—if not from making such a decision yourselves—was not a particularly happy one. Because the story didn't have a happy ending, a good many people, including the theologians who regard him as better off before the so-called fall from grace, think Adam bungled things. I presume they must be joined in this appraisal by the economists and other people who are impressed by the abundance of essentials with which he is supposed to have been supplied. Certainly the stimulus-response psychologists—at least those who worry about such things—must concur, since it seems clear that our ancestor did not act very realistically in terms of all his surrounding reinforcements. In any case, Man, the poor fellow, chose the toil and confusion of knowledge instead of the pleasant and obvious rewards of unquestioning obedience.

It should be said, I suppose, that Man probably would not have had the initiative to take this fateful step if he hadn't had some encouragement from his girlfriend. Without her he would probably have been content to do what he was told, as men are inclined to be when they are part of an all-male society, such as a football team, a monas-

SOURCE. Delivered at the annual meeting of the American Psychological Association, 1963.

207

tery, or The United States Marine Corps. But when women are around, or you can't get your mind off them, material security and inner contentment don't always add up to the same thing. No matter how much happiness is available at hand, you are likely to become restless and itchy to test the limits of your instructions. We wonder just what would happen if . . . ? All the luminous possibilities of the future become so fascinating that we are soon blinded to the obvious rewards of the present.

In any event, there was a woman around in the place called Eden. Apparently, if we can believe the story, she was not part of the initial experimental design. She had been introduced as a last minute concession without much thought to the problems of experimental control she might pose. The result was that things did not work out the way the Principal Investigator had specified in his original project proposal. In any event, while this may have been the first instance of a principal investigator adopting a punitive attitude toward his subjects for not confirming his hypotheses, it certainly was not the last.

Now, about this woman! She was not altogether a disobedient young thing herself, but she had had her feelings stirred up by something or other she had interpreted as rather suggestive—something symbolic, no doubt. And while, as frequently seems to be true of the opposite sex, she was disinclined to take any improper action herself—a fact that must be held to her credit—she was, nonetheless, disposed to drop the intriguing issue into the midst of Adam's idyllic contentment, just to see if he might not want to do something about it. This bit of domestic strategy is known as "sharing your problems." The upshot was that Adam did do something about it, and, as a dutiful mate, she went along with the deal. And, I am sure, something like this is what still makes man's world go round and round instead of standing still in obedient contentment, and what, more and more, turns it into the fascinating and fearsome puzzle it has come to be.

So notwithstanding all the psychology books whose authors hypothesize one kind of human nature and stay up nights with their typewriters demonstrating another—when they could just as well be in bed dreaming or otherwise occupied with drive reduction—the nature of man seems to be that he would rather coach the game than collect its winnings. This is to say that, in spite of all the solicitous admonishments and dire threats of the theologians and in spite of all the psychological reprints showing the conformity of rats and college freshmen to their reinforcements, man is pretty much inclined to end up choosing his own tenuous knowledge in preference to externally guaranteed happiness. At least he does this when women are around posing fuzzy issues in that irresponsible way of theirs—which is a good deal of the time. To be sure, he may start out acting like a rat or a college freshman, if that is what is expected of him, but before he gets through he is likely to be found usurping the role of The Creator Himself by hurling spheres into outer space, or, what may be worse, disengaging himself from the psychology of human behavior in order to act like a psychologist.

Sometimes it seems as if man is bent on doing everything he can to disrupt the regular operation of this lawful universe of ours. His persistent meddling with the future, rather than perpetuating the past or enjoying the present luxuries of The American Way of Life, reveals him as a perennial Adam who doesn't know that he is supposed to be himself, what his real motivations are, or when he is well off. There are, indeed, moments when I deeply suspect that man's only purpose in discovering the laws of human behavior is to contrive some way to escape them. This is certainly not the sort of thing psychologists are likely to talk about in public—at least not the scientific psychologists.

None of this is very sensible, particularly if you are supposed to "be yourself," always staying in your natural orbit, and revolving on your own unique axis. As in the case of Adam, who didn't perform according to his Designer's specifications, it is just this sort of nonconformity that drives the moralists to invoke the notion of "sin" and the psychologists the notion of a "neurotic paradox"—both notions representing essentially the same expression of frustration on the part of those who think man's behavior should follow the laws formulated to explain it, rather than vice versa. Worse than that, this tendency of man to cut loose from both his biography and his rewards, in order to reach out for the future and seize it in his own two fists, puts most of us scientists in an embarrassing position. It appears we must concede that human nature is disorganized, right after we have made a big case for science's supposedly most essential proposition: "All nature is organized."

What I have said so far about Adam frustrating his Creator to the point of exasperation and being called sinful for it, and the rest of mankind frustrating the psychologists to the point of being diagnosed as having come down with an attack of neurotic paradox, may make it appear that I am about to make a case for anarchy. But this is not my intention at all. If human nature does not work out the way it is supposed to, there is no reason to jump to the conclusion that it is either sinful or paradoxical. Nor need we conclude that it is unlawful—or lawful either, for that matter. But it does mean that our psychology is in difficulty. While I am not too sure, I think I can put my finger on what that difficulty is.

For my part, I am quite ready to assume—indeed it seems important to assume—that there is a reality out there, or, if you prefer, a truth deep inside all of us. If you are talking about psychology, I suppose it helps to think of its being inside. Just where it is probably does not matter much at this stage of the game. The point is that our grasp of it is approximate only. Moreover, it may be a little further out there, or a little deeper inside, than we have led ourselves to believe. This sort of thing has proved to be true before in science.

If this is so, then it may be that we have been taking the story of Genesis, or the findings of our psychological laboratories, a little too literally. To be sure, learning takes place under conditions of reinforcement. At least, it looks like a fact when we examine it with our Hullian spectacles. But how much of the truth is represented in this fact, or how close an approximation to the nature of man are we able to derive from this observation seen through the spectacles of current American Psychology? We don't really know. If we are making a mistake, it is not in assuming that there is a truth, or even in hoping that we can get closer to it than we are, but in claiming we have caught up with it, and especially in fostering the impression that we have nailed it at the one percent level of confidence.

For my own part, I would even go for the proposition that there is really such a thing as sin. But I am likely to recoil if someone knocks on my door, hands me a catalogue, and says, "Bless you brother; I hear you believe in sin, and here it is, with a glossary at the back." When this sort of thing happens, I am inclined to suggest that he inquire into the matter more deeply before publishing his findings, though I may not hand his catalogue back until I have thumbed through the pages and looked at the pictures. I might even say, after looking at it, "By golly, this is the most up-to-date compendium on sin I have ever seen, and, until I see a better one, I shall try to be guided by it." But, just as in the case of science, what we shall come to realize as sinful a thousand years from now may bear no more resemblance to the evils that preachers talk about today than does the morality of a thousand years ago—or even of a hundred years ago—resemble 1963's emerging sense of decency, especially as it applies to such matters as the equality of racial opportunity.

So the same goes for science in general and for psychology in particular. Let us hope we can keep getting a little closer to the truth. So, as a psychological experiment, Eden didn't work out as expected. Now whose fault was that? Adam's, for disobeying? Eve's, for posing a feminine question? The Serpent's, for his short-sighted version of the truth—"Relax, Honey, it won't *kill* you!" Or the Creator's, for moulding one kind of being and then demanding that he act like another? Or is there a fault in our own persistent failure to find a better interpretation of what goes on in the affairs of man? I am willing to assume that it is our fault, if for no other reason, because, pursuant to such an assumption, we may be led to reexamine the presumed nature of man—and of God, too, for that matter—and then take more realistic steps to get our affairs straightened out.

Well, let's see; I said the same approach to truth holds for the scientist as for the moralist, and then I went on to talk about the psychology of Eden, as if that had something to do with the psychology of man. Well, it does, but perhaps I should bring my illustrations up to date and talk about the psychology of the laboratory and the clinic, since you can't find much on Eden in the *Psychological Abstracts*. Nevertheless, I shall end up saying about the same thing as I said about the fellow who is rumored to be the original man.

So, just as in the Eden project, our experiments, also, fail to confirm predictions, our women get neurotic, our nations go berserk. Now whose fault is that? The subjects', for disobeying the laws of human nature? Is it the fault of those who go on posing questions when it would be a lot safer to remain ignorant? Is it the fault of the short-sighted politicians and advertisers who peddle glowing promises to gullible people—"Come on, Honey, it'll be good for you!" Is it the fault of those who create one kind of society and then lay down rules designed for another? Or is it ours, in taking it for granted that human nature resides not in man but in the psychological systems erected so ingeniously by Freud, or Hull, or Jefferson, or Marx, or in the statistically tempered conclusions of psychological experimentation? As before, I am willing to assume that wherever the fault lies, the responsibility continues to be ours, and that the nature of man, howsoever it may ultimately turn out, is to be sought in the lives of the men, women, and children who inhabit the earth—on both sides of the Iron Curtain, as well as on both sides of the tracks. From such an assumption, which is central to what I want to say here, we may launch our psychological efforts in directions most likely to bring us closer to the truth than we have so far been.

With all respect to the psychologists who erect systems between themselves and their fellow men, among whom I am as guilty as any, the next step in this discussion is to point out that the closer one gets to persons the closer he gets to the nature of man. Granted, of course, that getting close to a person does not guarantee that you will understand him! But, on the other hand, if you never get close to him it is doubtful that you can ever develop a very perceptive scheme for understanding him. This is precisely why I believe that clinical psychology is basic to a science of psychology.

To the extent that psychology fails to touch the intimate life of man it makes the same mistake that was made in Eden, a mistake compounded by the religionists who make all those legalistic and punitive interpretations of what happened there. The official rulebook said that Adam and Eve would be content as long as their bellies were full. But the point is Adam and Eve were not content! Somebody goofed! Oh, I am sure that if you had persuaded them to volunteer as subjects in a simple reward type of experiment they would have behaved according to specifications. They were probably polite and cooperative in such matters. But when it came to crucial matters, it would have taken a lot more perceptiveness than has so far been displayed, either by the narrator of the story or the theologians, to understand why indeed these two inquisitive persons on one crucial occasion chose to know what life was all about rather than to obey blindly and pick their daily supply of juicy reinforcements off the trees of the garden.

It is sometimes argued that a person in distress does not behave as he does when things are going well. This is true. When things are going well he tends to behave like other people, or according to the way the cultural anthropologist has written up the manners of his home town. But, for the psychologist who wants to understand the nature of man, which is better, to observe a person when he is conforming to the local rulebook, or to try to understand him when he has been thrown back on his own resources and no official rulebook seems to apply?

Of course, coming to the psychotherapist can be listed in the local rulebook. When it is, I fear that seeking psychotherapeutic aid turns out to be no more than a reflection of conformity and the clinical psychologist is as much misled by it as is the experimental psychologist who insists on having "normal" subjects for his research.

It may be inferred from what I have said so far that I do not have much enthusiasm for applied psychology. But, in case the point has been missed, let me emphasize it—I do have very little enthusiasm for applied psychology. And that is why I think clinical psychology, and especially psychotherapy, is so important. But perhaps the point is obvious.

In Eden, it seems to me, there was a mistaken effort to deal with the tenants in terms of applied psychology. The Creator, having had a lot of recent experience with making things, had a pretty clear idea of what the norm for created things was. In fact, He had the advantage of being able to use total population statistics, if we can believe the story. He didn't have to worry about probability theory, a fact that must have relieved Him considerably. In terms, therefore, of His well-established means, or even His working means for related subspecies, it was perfectly reasonable to expect His latest creative effort to conform to the norms. So, at this point He turned Himself into an applied psychologist and laid down the law, being careful to back it up with an optimal reinforcement schedule. At least this is what we are told.

Now the Serpent appears also to have approached the situation from the standpoint of an applied psychologist. He may have been trained as one from the very first—I don't really know. However that may be, he was at the disadvantage of having to fall back on small sample statistics, for up to that time he had had no successful experience with the "temptation technique," or "rational therapy," or anything of that sort. The story is explicit on this point. He had to base his predictions on a hypothetical construct. This, as every doctoral candidate knows, is not nearly as good as basing it on an intervening variable. Probably accounts for his short-sightedness! In any case, he used his small sample statistics, took a chance at ten percent level of confidence, and told Eve she would not die, as she had been led to believe she would if she ate of the Tree of Knowledge of Good and Evil.

Within their own theoretical frameworks both the Creator and the Serpent were right. Yet both were wrong. The Creator was right in believing that most of the time, in fact, *normally*, in a scientific statistical sense man does do what is expected of him. He conforms to the prevailing social norms and responds to his reinforcements. If he doesn't, we throw him out of the experiment, a procedure which you can see has an ancient and honorable precedent. Psychologists have been proving God right about the normal nature of man for some time now, and I must say the evidence is overwhelming. There appears to have been only one occasion in Eden when this doctrinal application of validated psychological research findings failed. And when you stack this up against what must have been the thousands of previous occasions when the prediction had held, you come up with a confidence level that must have reached the .0001 level—at least—and that should satisfy the most rigorous experimentalist.

But the one occasion when the prediction didn't hold appears to have been a crucial one, or else the Creator was an absolute determinist, for the confidence level did not seem to have satisfied Him at all.

If we are to believe the story, He went into a huff, punished His subjects most ingeniously, and threw them out of the experiment. According to one account, He didn't make any serious effort to put Himself into Man's shoes until 4004 years later—in the Year Four B.C., when he began to approach the problem from the standpoint of the psychology of personal constructs.

The Serpent's experiment checked out pretty well, too, at least there is no report of his being dissatisfied. In fact it was an outright triumph for small sample statistics. Eve ate the apple, and, just as the experimenter suspected, nothing happened. Certainly she did not die right away, as she was afraid she might, and when she did die a good many years later, the Serpent had already published his results and had been made Chairman of the Department. Besides it was too late by that time to get a verbal report on her reactions. So, for all practical intents and purposes, the temptation turned out a grand success and has been quoted in the reviews ever since.

But, from another point of view, the Serpent was dead wrong, for man has been knocking himself out over this matter of the knowledge of good versus evil ever since. Wars, persecutions, family discords, intolerance, suppression of his own creative efforts have followed continually, as man has tried to impose on himself and others his dogmatic notions of what is psychologically good and has tried to destroy everything and everyone he regarded as evil. Good has been defined in terms of conformity rather than sought out in terms of understanding. This, of course, is applied psychology, and, as I have indicated, I believe one of the ways we can correct the situation is to study the nature of man through psychotherapy and thus achieve a more perceptive science.

I am not saying that the nature of man is the nature of the extraordinary man. What I am saying is that the nature of man is revealed in his extraordinary moments, moments that may be illuminated in the course of his psychotherapy. And it is for this reason that I have no desire to be an applied psychologist or to agree that the mean of man's behavioral reactions in a conformity situation is an adequate measure of his basic nature. For to agree with this tenet is to agree that the psychology of man is a psychology of norms and static mediocrity. It is to concede that truth lies with the majority, and to join, I fear, in the clamor for a unified theory of psychology, as if truth were to be achieved by negotiations.

Psychotherapy, it must be conceded, may not provide us with the only opportunity to see man in the crucial moment when conventionalities have failed him and he is left with no resources other than his own nature. The nature of man may be exposed to observation on other occasions. Perhaps we can see his nature equally well when he faces death and looks back regretfully on a life of normal and conforming behavior. Perhaps we can see it as we look back over two or three thousand years of history in which the myriad of average, normal, conforming behaviors have been mercifully overshadowed by the signal achievements of men and peoples. Perhaps it can be seen in a kindergarten before discipline and socialization have set in. Perhaps it can be seen even in the laboratory, though the chances are that if it shows up there the subjects will be thrown out of the experiment, just as Adam and Eve were thrown out when they failed to confirm a certain experimental hypothesis having to do with the efficacy of reinforcements.

But wheresoever the nature of man may be observed in its nascent form, I am sure that the psychologist is nowhere more likely to run into its puzzling complexities and exasperating perversities than in his efforts to accomplish psychotherapy. It is there that one hopes to see the person struggling with changes in himself as he attempts to draw some compromise between the normalized psychological doctrines of the world around him and his own natural eagerness to reach out for what he is unable to attain. To cope with this problem is not always a very comfortable experience for a would-be scientist. Certainly it is not a very practical way for him to extend his bibliography, and this is perhaps the reason that clinical psychologists do not publish more than they do and why what they do publish seems so inconclusive. But dissatisfied as I am with the progress of clinical psychology, I am even more pessimistic about any science of psychology that cuts itself loose from the perplexing realities of psychotherapy. As Mark Twain once said, "Every dog should have some fleas, lest he forget that he's a dog."

11

The Psychotherapeutic Relationship

I HAVE BEEN so puzzled over the early labeling of personal construct theory as "cognitive" that several years ago I set out to write another short book to make it clear that I wanted no part of cognitive theory. The manuscript was about a third completed when I gave a lecture at Harvard University with the title, "Personal Construct Theory as a Line of Inference." Following the lecture, Professor Gordon Allport explained to the students that my theory was not a "cognitive" theory but an "emotional" theory. Later the same afternoon, Dr. Henry Murray called me aside and said, "You know, don't you, that you are really an existentialist."

Since that time I stepped into almost all the open manholes that psychological theorists can possibly fall into. For example, in Warsaw, where I thought my lecture on personal construct theory would be an open challenge to dialectical materialism, the Poles, who had been conducting some seminars on personal construct theory before my arrival, explained to me that "personal construct theory was just exactly what dialectical materialism stood for." Along the way also I have found myself classified in a volume on personality theories as one of the "learning theorists," a classification that seems to me so patently ridiculous that I have gotten no end of amusement out of it.

A few years ago an orthodox psychoanalyst insisted, after hearing me talk about psychotherapy, that, regardless of what I might say about Freud, and regardless even of my failure to fall in the apostolic

SOURCE. Presented at a symposium on "Cognitive and analytic conceptions of the therapeutic relationship," University of Houston, Texas, May 19, 1965.

succession to which a personal psychoanalysis entitled one, I was really "a psychoanalyst." This charge was repeated by a couple of psycho-analytically sophisticated psychiatrists in London last fall, and nothing I could say would shake their conviction.

I have, of course, been called a Zen Buddhist, and last fall one of our former students, now a distinguished psychologist, who was invited back to give a lecture, spent an hour and a half in a seminar corrupting my students with the idea that I was really a "behaviorist."

I think I should tell you all this at the outset, so that a little later on when you find that you are hopelessly confused by what I have to say, you will not be overly critical of yourselves or me.

While it seems perfectly clear to me that personal construct theory is not a cognitive theory, I am a little more puzzled about the question of whether or not it is a dynamic theory. Generally I have claimed that it is completely nondynamic. It is utterly innocent of any forces, motives, or incentives and, so far as I have been able to observe, all the other gremlins have been properly exterminated. But then, I may be quite mistaken about this, because I start with the assumption that something is going on, rather than the traditional assumption that the world is filled with a number of things that must be prodded into action by forces. And, since I assume that we start with a process, I am struck with the disturbing thought that personal construct theory may be the only truly dynamic theory available to psychology. So you can take your choice; this is either an all-out dynamic theory or an all-out nondynamic theory. I don't really much care which point of view you take, just so you take one or the other and not something in between.

Suppose we start out by making a distinction between what is man and what is his environment. There are some advantages in making such a distinction, although if you look at it too closely we will both have to admit that *man versus environment* is a somewhat fuzzy no-tion, especially when you realize that most of us have about as much trouble living with ourselves as we have living with other people—or, if you want to think of it that way, each of us represents a rather large chunk of his own environment.

Be that as it may, let us erect a construct of *man versus environment*, and then see what we can do with it. We must keep it clearly in mind that we invented this construct and must hold ourselves responsible for it. It would be improperly unctuous of us to claim that it was revealed to us—either on Mount Sinai or in a laboratory. It is my notion that if it doesn't turn out well there is nobody we can blame except ourselves.

Now, in seeking to understand man, we can, as most psychologists do, say that something is initiated within the environment which results in a response from the person who inhabits it. This is stimulus-response psychology. The cycle in which we are interested starts with a stimulus and ends with a response. The role of the person is to mediate between the two. In this model man's job is to process events in the environment into behaviors. The model serves very well the purposes of those people who want to see the world running on an orderly course with each event carrying full responsibility for its progeny. Some people are sure that science is nothing but this kind of construction of the world. Of course I don't agree.

Now you can go at it another way and say, from man's point of view, the world is known only through his perception of it. Since he has only his perceptions to go by, the world is, for any human practical purposes, what he construes it to be. What it really is, outside of his perceptions, is a purely academic question and, according to the logic of the logical positivists, it is unanswerable and therefore foolish. Well, this is the phenomenological point of view. I am not a phenomenologist, and therefore, of course, am not a logical positivist, although I read somewhere—in the Koch volumes, I believe it was—that personal construct theory was a phenomenological theory.

Or you can take another point of view toward man in his environment. You can say he is what he is because of his cultural context. This is to say that the environment assigns him his role, makes him good or bad by contrast, appropriates him to itself, and, indeed, his whole existence makes sense only in terms of his relationship to the times and the culture. This is not personal construct theory either, and as far as I know, no one has yet claimed that it is.

Now there are dynamic theories. I am afraid I am the fellow who has said that motivation—or psychodynamics—is the kind of explanation we resort to when we don't want to bother to understand a person. We simply say that man does what he does not as an expression of his construction of the world, but because he has been pushed into it by the agents which inhabit his psyche. This is a very ancient kind of theory, antedating by thousands of years the Greek mythology from which Freud drew his models of explanation. The fact that it is based upon notions of demoniacal possession does not necessarily discredit it. As a matter of fact, one might argue that psychodynamic theory, because it is so deeply primitive, must also be deeply humanistic. In terms of the model of man in his environment, psychodynamic theory sees man as driven by internal forces to strike out against and for his environment.

Now we come to personal construct theory. As in phenomenology, personal construct theory sees man looking out on his environment, but, unlike phenomenology, does not portray that environment as a figment of his imagination. It's a real world that he lives in. The trick is for him to make something out of it.

Personal construct theory envisions man as devising constructions to place upon the events of the environment—even constructions to place upon himself. These constructions are essentially dimensions of appraisal rather than categories or entities, but basically they are not scaler constructions; they are, rather dichotomous grounds for discriminating events and assigning similarity to them. Out of such basic constructs one may, in turn, build scales, even though the constructs themselves are not scaler in nature.

The difficulty in understanding personal construct theory as a noncognitive theory arises out of our assumption that all discrimination, as well as all of our sense of identity, is essentially cognitive. But human discrimination may take place also at levels which have been called "physiological" or "emotional." Nor is discrimination necessarily a verbalized process. Man discriminates even at a very primitive and behavioral level. For example, for him to be afraid on two different occasions suggests that he has somehow or other linked them or identified them as constructively the same object of danger.

There is another point—out of many—that should be mentioned in this connection before proceeding to the particular problem of the psychotherapeutic relationship. The languages of western Europe are constructed so as to imply that the logic of explaining behavior is based on the S-R unit. This is to say that the behavioral cycle with which we are concerned is one that starts with a stimulus and asks the question, "What response will ensue?" In effect this means that the stimulus is the question and the response is the answer. This model is implicit in Freudian theory and indeed it is implicit in most dynamic theories. Behavior is the answer; it is the thing we are seeking to produce. In psychotherapy the object is to get the patient to change his behavior. In learning, also, the object is to get the student to change his behavior. In industry the object is to get the employee to do his job. In politics the object is to get the citizen to support the leadership. Once you are able to produce the behavior you are seeking, you have your answer. Indeed, most psychologists like to say that they are primarily concerned with the production of behavior. I think this is very sad.

But, from the standpoint of personal construct theory, behavior is not the answer, it is the question. The personal construct theorist who serves in the psychotherapeutic capacity does not consider his objective the production of certain classes of behavior. He is concerned, rather, with the constructions that man, including himself and his patient, places upon the world and how these constructions are tested out. For him, behavior is not the answer, it is the principal way in which man may inquire into the validity of his constructions. Thus the time-linked unit in which the personal construct theorist is interested is not one that starts with a stimulus and ends with a response, but rather one that starts with a behavior—which is man's way of posing a question—and ends with an outcome which may or may not confirm the prediction which the behavior was designed to test.

And in this theory, then, the task of the therapist is to join with his client in exploring, by the only means available to man—by behavior—the implications of the constructions he has devised for understanding reality. From this point of view therapy becomes an experimental process in which constructions are devised or delineated and are then tested out. Psychotherapy is not an applied science, it is a basic science in which the scientists are the client and his therapist. Moreover, the answers at which they arrive during the course of formal therapy are never the final answers. What, hopefully, the therapy has demonstrated is a way of getting on with one's life, not an answer to the question of "how shall I behave?"

But now let me go further into the problem of the psychotherapeutic relationship. I often tell my students that a psychopath is a stimulus-response psychologist who takes it seriously. This is to say that our classic model of the psychopath (whether anyone actually conforms to that model altogether or not is another question) describes a man who thinks he can get along with his fellow man by producing the right stimuli in order to invoke accommodating behavior. In other words, he thinks of his fellow man only as an organism which mediates between stimulus and response, and he is continually looking for the stimulus which will produce the response he wants.

But personal construct theory, as well as clinical experience, suggests that there are other ways of relating ourselves to our fellow men. If we see a fellow man simply as a behaving mechanism, our treatment of him will differ very little from our treatment of an infra-human animal or even our treatment of an inanimate object. But if we understand our fellow man as a creature who himself has an outlook—who invents and tests and revises in terms of his outlook—our own interaction with him will be of a different order. In this case, our construction of him will be a construction of a creature who himself devises constructions. If we are to understand the person then we must seek out some interpretation of his construction rather than of his behavior merely.

Once we see man as a construing being, as personal construct theory does, of course, we have grounds for what I have chosen to call a "role relationship" with him. Our constructions of his outlook may not be accurate and, to the extent that they are not accurate, our role relationship may not be either predictive or effectual, but, accurate or not, our psychological construction of him will be quite different from what it would be if we regarded only his behavior as a matter of psychological concern.

Let me add further that our psychological construction of another person's outlook, while it does provide the basis for our having a role relationship with him, does not mean necessarily that we must conform to his expectations. Indeed, we may continually upset his expectations and may do so all the more effectively because we understand the outlook upon which they are based.

What I am saying, then, is that the development of that level of human relationship which I call a role relationship does not require mere accuracy or conformity and it may, indeed, lead to controversy and turmoil. But, nonetheless, it is what I would like to call a role relationship, in order to distinguish it from the psychopathic stimulus-response relationship advocated by most psychologists.

From the personal construct point of view, then, the task of the psychotherapist is to develop a role relationship with his client, and the task he poses for himself—to develop a reasonable number of role relationships with the people who constitute the client's most important surroundings. Often this task can be facilitated by encouraging the client to construe his therapist, not as a mediator of stimulus and response, but as a creature having an outlook.

I am suggesting that the psychotherapeutic relationship is not be-haviorally standardized any more than the object of therapy is to pro-duce a standardized behavior. The psychotherapeutic relationship is designed to get things done—the sort of things that all men have to do if they are to devise constructions of the world around them and are to check out those constructions by their use in prediction and by observation of the relation between predictions and outcomes.

Personal construct psychotherapy is a way of getting on with the human enterprise and it may embody and mobilize all of the tech-niques for doing this that man has yet devised. Certainly there is no one psychotherapeutic technique and certainly no one kind of inter-personal compatibility between psychotherapist and client. The tech-niques employed are the techniques for living and the task of the

skillful psychotherapist is the proper orchestration of all of these varieties of techniques. Hence one may find a personal construct psychotherapist employing a huge variety of procedures—not helter-skelter,
but always as part of a plan for helping himself and his client get
on with the job of human exploration and checking out the appropriateness of the constructions they have devised for placing upon the world
around them.

Now let me turn to one of the problems in psychotherapy of concern
to nearly all experienced psychotherapists—the problem of "transference." As you might suspect at this point in our discussion, the psychology of personal constructs, because it sees man devising constructions
to impose upon his fellow man, would be inclined to place a great
deal of emphasis upon transference. Indeed, from this theoretical point
of view, transference of one sort or another is the only device by
which one may approach a stranger. This is to say that constructs
must be employed which were originally devised for dealing with
others, and it is to be anticipated that they will, at best, be an imperfect
fit. But how else can we start?

A very young child meets a stranger. How shall he approach him?
Being human, and a child at that, he can probably do no better than
to construe the stranger as like one or the other of his parents. But
how right is he? This is a question which he can pose only through
his own behavior. Thus for the child his behavior at this point is the
posing of a question arising out of his construction of the stranger.
The behavioral question he poses may be badly put, and he may get
an ambiguous or a shocking answer.

But whatever answer the child gets, he will normally try some
reconstruction of the situation—transferring from his past experience
in somewhat different ways—and pose another behavioral question.

Transference becomes a problem in psychotherapy, however, when
a person keeps imposing the same transferred construction upon his
therapist and is unable to make anything of the disconfirming evidence
that is elicited by his behavioral questions. The problem of transference, as I see it then, is not that a person construes his therapist in
terms of transferred constructions, but that he is unable to complete
the experiential cycle and devise new constructions so as to get on
with his interpersonal relationships with the psychotherapist and
others.

There is another kind of transference, or perhaps I should say
transference may take place in a somewhat different way. Instead
of approaching the stranger as a total replica of some figure construed
in one's past, one may erect his construction of the stranger one dimen-

sion at a time. This, in fact, is what the more mature person is able to do, and one of the signs of transition from childhood construction to mature construction is this movement from "whole figure transferences" to "propositional construct transferences." Let me illustrate. I may approach my psychotherapist as another father. This is applying the whole figure construction of my father to my therapist. A disconfirmation of this kind of hypothesis is likely to imply a sweeping revision of my interpersonal outlook and hence may pose for me some threat to my total construction system.

But I can approach my therapist in another way. I may, for example, have seen my father as a strong figure. I may also have seen him as intellectual, as energetic, and in other ways. I can, however, transfer to my therapist only the construction of strength and reserve my construction of him in the other dimensions for later exploration. If now I find that he is not strong in the sense that I remember my father being strong, I experience disconfirmation in one dimension only. I may then revise my axis of reference, or my construct dimension, or I may turn to other constructs in order to get a more complete picture of my therapist in multidimensional psychological space, or "in depth."

What I have tried to do here is to suggest that personal construct theory, because of its particular way of viewing man's relationship to his environment, offers a distinctive approach to human relationships, and particularly to the psychotherapeutic relationship. I have tried to indicate that the task of psychotherapy is not to produce behavior, but rather to enable the client, as well as his therapist, to utilize behavior for asking important questions. In fact, the task of psychotherapy is to get the human process going again so that life may go on and on from where psychotherapy left off. There is no particular kind of psychotherapeutic relationship—no particular kind of feelings—no particular kind of interaction that is in itself a psychotherapeutic panacea, nor is there any particular set of techniques that are the techniques of choice for the personal construct theorist. The relationships between therapist and client and the techniques they employ may be as varied as the whole human repertory of relationships and techniques. It is the orchestration of techniques and the utilization of relationships in the on-going process of living and profiting from experience that makes psychotherapy a contribution to human life.

12

Personal Construct Theory and the
Psychotherapeutic Interview

BIOGRAPHY OF A THEORY

A GOOD MANY years ago when I first set for myself the task of writing a manual of clinical procedures it was with the idea that psychologists needed to get their feet on the ground, and I was out to help them do it. Other scientists had gotten their feet on the ground; why couldn't we? Elsewhere all about us there were those hardy breeds who had penetrated the frontiers of reality with boldness and forthrightness. Practical men they were who, with each bedrock discovery, discredited all those generations of anemic philosophers who never dared venture beyond the comforts of their own redundancies. And yet here was the gloomiest vista of all, the mind of man, only one step away—a deep cavern so close behind our very own eyes and still enshadowed in Delphian mystery. And here we were, psychologists, standing on one foot wanting very much to be scientists—and more than a little defensive about it, too—chattering away and so frightened of what we might see that we never dared take a close look.

Fancying myself thus as a practical man and seeing science as something which was, above all things, practical, it seemed that whatever I could do to bring psychologists into contact with human beings, novel as that might be, would help extricate psychology from the mishmash of its abstruse definitions. So I proposed to write as much as

I knew about how to come to terms with living persons. I took as my prototypes the ones who confided in me, particularly those who were in trouble, because, as I saw it, when a person is in trouble he acts more like what he is and less like something dangling from the strings of social convention. Out of such an undertaking, if enough psychologists were willing to join in, I could envision a gradual awakening of the ancient half-conscious mind of man and the ultimate fruition of its vast potentialities. It should be obvious that all this fantasy took place when I was very young.

That manual was never written, at least not that kind of manual. The business of being practical turned out to be not as simple as I thought. After more delay than should have been necessary, even for one short of wits, the notion finally struck me that, no matter how close I came to the man or woman who sought my help, I always saw him through my own peculiar spectacles, and never did he perceive what I was frantically signaling to him, except through his. From this moment I ceased, as I am now convinced every psychotherapist does whether he wants to admit it or not, being a realist. More important, I could now stop representing psychology to clients as packaged reality, warranted genuine and untouched by human minds.

Perhaps "realism" is not a good term for what I am talking about. It is obvious, of course, that I am not talking about Platonic realism. Nobody talks about that any more. The realism from which my clients and I are always trying to wriggle loose might possibly be called "materialistic realism." At least it is the hardheaded unimaginative variety nowadays so popular among scientists, businessmen, and neurotics.

REALISM AND DOGMATISM

What happened was this. Like most therapists with a background of liberal scholarship rather than strictly professional training, I soon became aware that dogmatic interpretations of clients' problems often did more harm than good. It was not only the client who suffered; therapists were affected in much the same way he was. Dogmatism produces a kind of mental rigidity that replaces thoughts with word, stifles the zest for free inquiry, and tries to seal the personality up tight at the conclusion of the last psychotherapeutic interview.

Understand, I am not yet ready to say that dogmatism has no place whatsoever in psychotherapy, especially when weighed against certain grimmer alternatives. It may even prove valuable to all of us as a firm point from which to rebel. But these are other matters.

What actually jarred me loose was the observation that clients who felt themselves confronted with down-to-earth realities during the course of psychotherapy became much like those who were confronted with downright dogmatic interpretations of either the religious or psychological variety. On the heels of this observation came the notion that dogmatism—the belief that one has the word of truth right from the horse's mouth—and modern realism—the belief that one has the word of truth right from nature's mouth—add up to the same thing. To go even further, I now suspect that neither of these assumptions about the revealed nature of truth is any more useful to scientists than it is to clients. But especially I am sure that both assumptions get square in the way of that supreme ontological venture we call psychotherapy and that they serve only to perpetuate its present unhappy captivity to fee-based medical materialism.

While my original views of ontology—and I am insisting that it is the same ontological process that runs its course whether the man is in the role of a client, a psychotherapist, a physicist, or an artist— have changed in some respects with the years, one of my original convictions remains with me. It still seems important for the psychologist to deal directly with persons on the most forthright terms possible. This is why I think of clinical psychology, not as an applied field of psychology, but as a focal and essential area and method of scientific inquiry. On the other hand, traditional psychology, it seems to me, is still much too self-consciously scientific and still much too peripheral to its subject matter. Instead of being so careful to do nothing that a scientist would not do, it would be more appropriate for the psychologist to get on with his job of understanding human nature. To the extent that he is successful, "Science" will eventually be only too glad to catch up and claim his methods as its own.

As for dogmatism, I certainly am not the first to say that it often works badly in therapy. Nor am I the first to recognize that the client has a point of view worth taking into account. But if one is to avoid dogmatism entirely he needs to alert himself against realism also, for realism, as I have already implied, is a special form of dogmatism and one which is quite as likely to stifle the client's creative efforts. A client who is confronted with what are conceded to be stark realities can be as badly immobilized as one confronted with a thickheaded therapist. Even the presumed realism of his own raw feelings can convince a client that he has reached a dead end.

ALTERNATIVISM

As my client's therapist I can temporarily avoid pushing him over the brink of reality by being passive or by accepting as nonjudgmentally as possible anything and everything he says or does. There is no doubt but that in this atmosphere of intimate ambiguity many clients will figure out sensible things to do in spite of a therapist's shortsightedness. This is good and, for a therapist who thinks he has to act like a realist, it is about as far as one can go without betraying the dogmatism implicit in his realism. But I am not a realist—not anymore—and I do not believe either the client or the therapist has to lie down and let facts crawl over him. Right here is where the theoretical viewpoint I call *the psychology of personal constructs* stakes out its basic philosophical claim.

There is nothing so obvious that its appearance is not altered when it is seen in a different light. This is the faith that sustains the troubled person when he undertakes psychotherapy seriously. It is the same as the faith expressed in the *Book of Job*—not so much in the overwritten poetic lines as in the development of the theme. To state this faith as a philosophical premise: *Whatever exists can be reconstrued.* This is to say that none of today's constructions—which are, of course, our only means of portraying reality—is perfect and, as the history of human thought repeatedly suggests, none is final.

Moreover, this is the premise upon which most psychotherapy has to be built, if not in the mind of the therapist, at least in the mind of the client. To be sure, one may go to a therapist with his facts clutched in his hand and asking only what he ought to do with them. But this is merely seeking technical advice, not therapy. Indeed, what else would one seek unless he suspected that the obstacles now shaping up in front of him are not yet cast in the ultimate form of reality? As a matter of fact, I have yet to see a realistic client who sought the help of a therapist in changing his outlook. To the realist, outlook and reality are made of the same inert stuff. On the other hand, a client who has found his therapeutic experience helpful often says, "In many ways things are the same as they were before, but how differently I see them!"

This abandonment of realism may alarm some readers. It may seem like opening the door to wishful thinking, and to most psychologists wishful thinking is a way of coming unhinged. Perhaps this is why so many of them will never admit to having any imagination, at least until after they suppose they have realistically demonstrated that what they secretly imagined was there all the time, waiting to be discovered. But for me to say that *whatever exists can be reconstrued* is by no manner or means to say that it makes no difference *how* it is construed. Quite the contrary. It often makes a world of difference. Some reconstructions may open fresh channels for a rich and productive life. Others may offer one no alternative save suicide.

A THEORETICAL POSTULATE

Here, then, is where one takes the next step, a step that leads him from a philosophical premise—called *constructive alternativism*— to a psychological postulate. Put it this way: *A person's processes are psychologically channelized by the ways in which he anticipates events.* Next, combining this statement with the gist of some of its ensuing corollaries, we can say simply: *A person lives his life by reaching out for what comes next and the only channels he has for reaching are the personal constructions he is able to place upon what may actually be happening.* If in this effort he fails, by whatever criterion, the prudence of his constructions is laid open to question and his grasp upon the future is shaken.

Let us make no mistake; here we come to the exact point where we all have trouble. If our misleading construction is based on dogmatic belief, that is to say it is held to be true because someone like God or the Supreme Soviet said so, we are not likely to have the audacity to try to revise it. Similarly, if it is believed to have had its origin in nature rather than in our own noggin—the position of "realism" I have been talking about—we are left with no choice except to adjust and make the best of matters as they stand. Or if realizing that it was altogether our own mistaken notions that led us afield, if it seems now that there is nothing left to do except to scrap our convictions, one and all, then utter chaos will start closing in on all sides. Any of these is bad. Fortunately, there are always other alternatives when predictions go awry. For the person who does not see any of them— psychotherapy!

VIEW OF PSYCHOTHERAPY

We have ruled out the notion of psychotherapy as the confrontation of the client with stark reality, whether it is put to him in the form of dogma, natural science, or the surges of his own feelings. Instead, we see him approaching reality in the same ways that all of us have to approach it if we are to get anywhere. The methods range all the way from those of the artist to those of the scientist. Like them both and all the people in between, the client needs to assume that something can be created that is not already known or is not already there.

In this undertaking the fortunate client has a partner, the psychotherapist. But the psychotherapist does not know the final answer either—so they face the problem together. Under the circumstances there is nothing for them to do except for both to inquire and both to risk occasional mistakes. So that it can be a genuinely cooperative effort, each must try to understand what the other is proposing and each must do what he can to help the other understand what he himself is ready to try next. They formulate their hypotheses jointly. They even experiment jointly and upon each other. Together they take stock of outcomes and revise their common hunches. Neither is the boss, nor are they merely well-bred neighbors who keep their distance from unpleasant affairs. It is, as far as they are able to make it so, a partnership.

The psychotherapy room is a protected laboratory where hypotheses can be formulated, test-tube sized experiments can be performed, field trials planned, and outcomes evaluated. Among other things, the interview can be regarded as itself an experiment in behavior. The client says things to see what will happen. So does the therapist. Then they ask themselves and each other if the outcomes confirmed their expectations.

Often a beginning therapist finds it helpful to close his cerebral dictionary and listen primarily to the subcortical sounds and themes that run through his client's talk. Stop wondering what the words literally mean. Try to recall, instead, what it is they sound like. Disregard content for the moment; attend to theme. Remember that a client can abruptly change content—thus throwing a literal-minded therapist completely off the scent—but he rarely changes the theme so easily. Or think of these vocal sounds, not as words, but as preverbal outcries, impulsive sound gestures, stylized oral grimaces, or hopelessly mumbled questions.

But at other times the therapist will bend every effort to help the client find a word, the precise word, for a newly emerged idea. Such an exact labeling of elusive thoughts is, at the proper time, crucial to making further inquiries and to the experimental testing of hypotheses. Particularly is this true when the team—client and therapist—is elaborating personal constructs. But before we can discuss this matter further we need to say something about the nature of personal constructs from the point of view of the theory.

PERSONAL CONSTRUCTS

We have said that a person lives his life by reaching out for what comes next and the only channels through which he can reach are the personal constructions he is able to place upon what appears to be going on. One deals with the events of life, not as entirely strange and unique occurrences but as recurrences. There is a property, a human quality of our own manufacture, that makes today seem like yesterday and leads us to expect that tomorrow may be another such day. To see this is to construe similarity among one's days. Without this view the future would seem chaotic indeed.

But to say that one's days are all alike, and nothing more, is to lose them amidst the hours and the years. What makes days seem alike is also precisely what sets them apart. We construe, then, by ascribing some property that serves both to link an event with certain other events and to set it in contrast to those with which it might most likely become confused. This construed dimension, embodying both likeness and difference, this reference axis, is what we call a construct. And constructs are personal affairs; regardless of the words he uses, each person does his own construing.

In this world—past, present, and future—ordered by each of us in his own way, constructs and events are interwoven so that events give definition to constructs and constructs give meaning to events. Take the client. The events, for example, that he recalls from childhood during the course of a psychotherapeutic interview serve to define the constructs that often he can otherwise express only through "intellectualization" or by "acting out." But constructs, on the other hand, give current meaning both to his memories and to his future plans and, particularly when they are precisely verbalized, they lay the ground for profitable experimentation.

The constructs one applies to himself and his interpersonal relationships have particular importance. Psychotherapy finds itself mainly concerned with them. While always fewer in number than one might wish, they nevertheless set the pattern of human resources available to the client and, when they are applied to his own changes of mood or behavior, they become wide-open pathways for shifting his position and altering the course of his life. Knowledge of them helps the therapist predict and control the client's possible reactions to threat, including the implicit threat that, to some extent, is always implied by psychotherapy itself.

THE VARYING TECHNIQUES
OF PSYCHOTHERAPY

The team of client and therapist can go about their task in a variety of ways. Essentially these are the same ways that, on one kind of occasion or another, man has always employed for dealing with perplexities. (1) The two of them can decide that the client should reverse his position with respect to one of the more obvious reference axes. Call this slot rattling, if you please. It has its place. (2) Or they can select another construct from the client's ready repertory and apply it to matters at hand. This, also, is a rather straightforward approach. Usually the client has already tried it. (3) They can make more explicit those preverbal constructs by which all of us order our lives in considerable degree. Some think of this as dredging the unconscious. The figure is one that a few have found useful; but I would prefer not to use it. (4) They can elaborate the construct system to test it for internal consistency. (5) They can test constructs for their predictive validity. (6) They can increase the range of convenience of certain constructs, that is, apply them more generally. They can also decrease the range of convenience and thus reduce a construct to a kind of obsolescence. (7) They can alter the meaning of certain constructs; rotate the reference axes. (8) They can erect new reference axes. This is the most ambitious undertaking of all.

Alteration or replacement of constructs—the last two methods mentioned—is essentially a creative kind of effort. Both involve first a loosening of the client's constructions, either by the use of fantasy, dreams, free association, or the introduction of varied and illusive content into the therapeutic interview. But creativity is not a single mode of thought; it follows a cycle. The second phase of the cycle involves tightening and validation of the newly placed or newly formed constructs.

I have summarized what goes on in therapy under eight headings. More might have been used. It is necessary only that I offer some sketch of how psychotherapy can be envisioned in terms of personal construct theory, that I try to make clear that what I am talking about is not restricted to the process tradition calls "cognition" (a term for which I find little practical use lately), that psychotherapy runs the gamut of man's devices for coming to grips with reality, and that the client and his therapist embark together as shipmates on the very same adventure.

ILLUSTRATIVE INTERVIEW

On the following pages is a verbatim transcript of an interview between one of my clients and myself. The client was kind enough to give his permission to have this interview published and discussed. All names of persons and places have been altered and even a few of the descriptions have been deleted or changed to protect the client's identity as well as that of others who are peripherally involved.

No one interview can illustrate all the facets of a theoretical point of view. The reader is, of course, already aware of that. Unless one takes the position that psychotherapy is wholly a matter of technique and couchside manner, the most that he can hope to see in one interview is how a particular client-therapist team has dealt with their problem at a particular stage of their venture. It is like dropping in on a research conference; what goes on depends on the make-up of the research team and the phase of their investigation at which one has caught them at work. Indeed, from the standpoint of personal construct theory, psychotherapy is a form of joint research effort.

This client was, at the time, a twenty-eight year old unmarried veteran who was attending a university. A man of superior intellectual ability, he was well-read and he exhibited spontaneous scholarly interests. Yet he was unable to make a go of it in either employment or classes. Before going into service, he had been able to finish a year or more of university study; but that was all. His most recent efforts had ended up in a succession of dismal failures. He completed none of the courses in which he had successively enrolled at the beginning of several recent sessions. This general failure pattern was the manifest complaint and the primary grounds upon which he applied for help.

He soon made it clear that he envisioned his current enrollment as a last ditch try. In fact, he told his father that he "could have his insurance money" if this effort did not pay off. While this suicidal comment represented certain situational features, it was not something to be ignored, especially in view of the client's exhaustion of the alternatives available to him under his current construct system. The following interview is of particular interest because of its bearing on this feature of the case.

A diagnostic appraisal of the case was made in order to set up the initial plan for the therapeutic program. While there is no necessity for describing that appraisal in detail, one feature of it is of particular interest. On the REP Test, a concept formation type of procedure in which persons associated with the client are sorted rather than blocks or objects, he showed an inability to deal with people except in concretistic ways. That is to say, his constructs showed limited ranges of convenience; they could be applied readily to certain figures only, whether as grounds for seeing persons as alike or for distinguishing between them. This is not to say that he lacked a general capacity for thinking abstractly, but rather that his construct repertory for dealing with role relations between persons lacked adequate span.

In the early interviews the client showed an interesting combination of interpersonal distance and undefended vulnerability. On the one hand, his use of language was overprecise and literal and his manner of speech was somewhat stylized. In the vernacular of psychotherapists he was obviously "an intellectualizer." Let, on the other hand, he made it clear that he expected therapy to deal with the most difficult and painful matters. He dreaded it. But it would have to be done. He expected to be hurt—not right away, please, but we shall have to get down to business soon. In fact, he lost little time in bringing up matters he had not discussed with anyone before and about which he felt deeply disturbed and guilty. He expressed his outlook toward therapy by saying that, first of all, he expected it to be objective and that he thought client and therapist should not feel themselves close to each other lest the therapist would hold off hurting the client and the client would try too hard to stay in the favor of the therapist.

The Client's View of Psychotherapy

The following passages, taken from an interview that occurred after the language pattern had responded to efforts to free it from its literalisms, dramatically illustrate his perception of the role of the therapist. Out of context these passages may seem unduly fanciful. In context, however, and in the light of the kind of exploration he and the therapist were undertaking at this stage, they portray vividly what he thought he was letting himself in for. The passages are taken from the eleventh interview.

C: You build a wall so that as you think back and hit that wall, you don't go beyond it and you don't redo the uncomfortable experience, or painful experience. And you keep building these and eventually all you've got is scar tissue and no . . . no abilities, so, ahh, as we are discussing here, I'm trying, I'm trying to the, now, I may be wrong, I don't know, in doing this. I don't know, ahh, if that's the direction of your question. But ahh, I'm trying to keep it so that if we should come to one of those and you ask me questions which tend to probe into or beyond it, I will not have any desire on my part to tint the situation, dodge the situation. I'll what, be as objective and, what, to describe the villain of the piece, diabolically clever with the scalpel as he grins and has some nice macabre music in the background and so on, and digs away with what, to get the proper stage lighting and everything in there.

T: And who is the villain, I?

C: No, no I'm just describing a, a situation. I was saying, ahh, instead of coming to the situation, coming to the place where there is a block as a friendly surgeon who's scared to really injure the patient . . . to come as a, ahh, what, ahh, the, ahh, soap-opera villain with his long mustache and, ahh, the slight off-color lights in the background and some slightly jarring music and a fiendish grin and chuckle and a sharp scalpel, just go in and devil take the hindmost.

T: Ummhuh, yeah. This is preferable to have the, having the physician who is afraid to operate because it might hurt the patient.

C: Well, I don't know that it's preferable but I would say that ahh, it certainly should. That's from the point of view I'm taking right now. It should get through, or at least, ahh, get through some of the scar tissue. I'm saying that if, ahh, there was a relationship, a friendship in here or something like that, ahh, each time we approached one of those situations, I would be like the friendly surgeon. Ahhhh, ahhhh, ahhhh . . . instead of going ahead and going right on in.

T: Ummhuh. So you'd like to create a situation here where you or I or both of us together could be just as diabolical as necessary in order to get through the scar tisse. That may be a little rougher phraseology than would fit the case, but, it . . .

C: Sounded pretty rough, yes. (laughs)

T: Sounded pretty rough.

C: But the idea in comparsion, yes, rather than each time coming to a scar tissue, sort of backing off and, and, what, playing around, going around and so on, just going on in.

T: This version of therapy then makes it look pretty rough, doesn't it?

C: I wouldn't say it's particularly rough. I'd say it's necessary, or at least based upon the description I have had of the situ, of how the mind

would built this up . . . and I've read some factors which say that
the mind's total capability from the experiences we have early in life
that are unpleasant are slowly cut off more and more and more por-
tions of the mind to where we're only using 2 or 3 percent when we're
fully grown.

T: Yes. So it's going to take something pretty courageous . . .

C: (pause) Well, I would say it wouldn't take a chicken-hearted surgeon
to do it.

T: You don't want to be chicken-hearted and you don't want me to be
chicken-hearted in here, huh?

C: Ahhh, (pause) no. I would say, let's not be chicken-hearted, that is
be afraid to get into it.

* * *

C: Yeah. I don't want to go into this thing and then, what, be at a
complete loss as to what we've covered, to have to have you play back
the record or something so that I can understand ahhh, what's happened. I want to be able, as we go along, now it may take longer, it
may be the wrong approach, I don't know. I can just say what I feel.
I feel if the approach is made this way, ahhh, the result will fit
together like building blocks.

T: So you're saying essentially, as much as you feel you *can* say and
still be (pause) appropriate, "For God's sake, don't throw me into
chaos, all at once."

C: (laughs) Yeah, yeah, yeah, that's it! I hadn't thought of it from that
point of view, but ahh, it fits, it fits what I've said very clearly.

* * *

C: It's like I'm, I am one of the convicts in the Spanish prison when
Columbus comes along and says, let's go sail across the seas. He knows
where he's going, but I don't. I don't think he really did, but at least
he had a better idea than I would as the highly prejudiced—what we
would consider ignorant nowadays—individual blindly stepping off
into nowhere.

T: And in a sense, the prisoner might say, "Sure I want to be out of
prison. But this is very sudden!"

C: Well, I think the attitude of many of the prisoners that were released
probably was it's good to be out of prison. I don't think there's any
argument there. However, the idea of Columbus, at that time there
were two conflicting points of view, one the world was flat like a table
top, the other that it was round. Well, Columbus took off sailing west
on the assumption the world was round and he would run into the

Indies. The prisoner I imagine, unless there were some educated ones amongst them which could happen at that time; even so, they were sailing out and eventually they'd just disappear into a void of nothing or a void of which, not a void, it wouldn't be, but a space in which there were sea demons and terrible dragons and all kinds of ahhh, concoctions and ahhh . . .

T: And here they were in a tight little imprisoned world with solid walls around them. At least they knew where they were.

C: Yeah.

T: And they knew the dimensions of their cells.

C: And it probably was very unpleasant.

T: Yeah, it was very unpleasant.

C: And unpleasant as shipboard duty would be with Columbus at least it was something. It was better than where they were.

T: Yeah.

C: But as they sailed west they approached this mythical drop off . . .

T: Yes.

C: They got more and more scared and probably were thinking, gosh, that cell looks awful darn nice.

T: Almost they wished for the walls again.

C: Yeah, I'll bet they did.

T: And you can sympathize with that.

C: I can see that.

T: The ahh, the metaphor fits you a little, huh?

C: Yeah, I would say it would, in this instance.

T: And here you have been within walls—and you have described it sometimes as "walls" I'm not sure just exactly *when*, but you've used the metaphor . . .

C: Yeah.

T: This simile before. Within the walls; you weren't very happy within these walls that limited your freedom.

C: Yeah.

T: Some of the walls were the walls of your home, maybe, but limited your freedom. What other kinds of walls?

C: There were walls there.

T: There were walls there, but at least you feel the dimensions of them in part.

C: Yeah. And I kept running into them in the most unexpected places too.

The preceding excerpt from an earlier interview should provide a fairly clear picture of how this client was approaching his psychotherapeutic task. In one sense his approach made him vulnerable and denied to him the comforting support that many clients get by transferring their childlike dependencies to the therapy room. In another sense, however, his verbalized determination to keep track of where he was going provided him a structured control over the situation, a control that he could use for coping with the turbulence he was expecting at any moment.

OBJECTIVES OF THIS
PARTICULAR INTERVIEW

The following interview is the twentieth in the psychotherapeutic series. The client's earlier manner of speech had been considerably modified by this time. It was more spontaneous (in our theoretical terms it showed more *impulsivity*), he was more willing to employ imprecise terms in order to catch fleeting thoughts before they escaped him (grasping for *preverbal* constructs), and he was beginning to portray fluctuating ideas without overconcern for their apparent contradictions (*loosening*). Moreover, he had dealt frankly with a few incidents which had been a long-time source of embarrassment to him (documentation of *guilt* and *threat*).

While up to a point these developments were therapeutically valuable, it was the therapist's judgment that this was a trend not to be continued indefinitely. Certainly therapy is not the simple task of laying bare vast areas of confusion and trusting in the client's utter dependence upon his therapist to keep matters in hand. There are always practical limits. Especially in the case of this particular client it is hard to see how a responsible therapist would want to lead him any great distance away from firm structure or let him sink much further into passive dependency.

We have here, therefore, not only a point of decision in dealing with this particular client, but a fulcrum across which to balance the weight of what different psychological systems have to offer. What is therapy? Is it an uncovering ritual that strips the client of all psychological clothing and reveals him as a naked brute? Is it stark realism warmed to body temperature by the therapist's attitude of acceptance?

Are the forces that victimize us so irrational that they cannot be dealt with intellectually? Is psychology a science that throws light only on what is bestial, what is fatalistic, or what is senseless? Or can psychological science offer an ontological way for these two, client and therapist, to do together what neither of them can accomplish separately?

The following interview was chosen because it illustrates the kind of decision the personal construct theorist feels called upon to make. What was done in this interview may not have been wise. It may not be what personal construct theory would suggest to other therapists. But the issue envisioned is one that looms up in the light of this particular theory.

The moment-to-moment decisions facing the therapist during this interview hinge on two main considerations. First, this client is one who has built for himself a brittle verbalized structure to deal with peripheral matters but who has allowed more central matters to degenerate into a chaotic condition. The constructs with which these more central matters are bound remain loose and poorly symbolized. He has, therefore, no satisfactory way to bring them into his sensible world, and hence no way to experiment with them or to revise them. Before we plunge too deeply into this chaos we need to tighten up what he has been saying about his world of feeling, label it with symbols that he can use, and prepare to put his constructs to some cautious experimental tests.

But there is a second consideration that makes this a risky business. If he spells out this vaguely expressed dimension in definitive terms, it will lie there, wide open before him. Will he use such a broad pathway to destroy himself in some moment of impulse? The reader will readily see in the middle passages of the interview how the construct tightening process followed by the client and the therapist clarified the two ends of the continuum—rational hope *versus* irrational despair. The therapist decided that the time had come to put this pair of alternatives into clearer terms and the client seemed to agree with him. Were we wise? We can say only that it seemed so.

The tempo of the interview was speeded up somewhat above that of the preceding interviews. The therapist responded frequently in the passive supportive affirmative—indicated in the following protocol by the conventional typescript spelling, "yeah" to distinguish it from the active assertive affirmative, "yes." Digressions into situational or concrete illustrative material were not discouraged during the interview because, as the reader may be able to see, they represented the client's attempts to reduce vague feelings, for which there were no adequate symbols, to terms which were, at least, tangible. This was a part of the process of tightening construction, and tightening was what we were trying to accomplish.

The emphasis upon precise word-finding will particularly attract the attention of some readers with therapeutic experience. In the present session this emphasis is as intentional as the lack of such emphasis was in some of the preceding interviews. The object of this interview was not to exude feelings, but to bring the construct dimensions, through which feelings threatened to run riot, into clearer focus and to bind them with adequate symbols for future reference.

PROTOCOL AND COMMENTS

T1:   Come in. (long pause) How are your resolutions for the New Year?

C1:   Didn't make any.

T2:   Have you before, in other years?

C2:   Ohh, I think maybe once or twice I have

What may appear to be "small talk" at the beginning of this interview was undertaken deliberately. This client was one who had resolved many times to set his house in order but who had been unable to keep impulses from throwing his tightly drawn plans into disarray. It was important to know whether we would be dealing with another such attempt to manage with tight constructions.

T3:   (pause) Ummhuh. (pause) Now, where do we stand? Are we at a place where we ought to start digging in deeper?

C3:   Well, I think at the moment, perhaps, we've gone as far as we can on the surface.

T4:   Yes, I have that feeling too.

C4:   You mentioned last time that we'd probably ought to be digging in deeper.

T5:   Yeah.

C5:   And I don't suppose I could say I've been *thinking* it over, that is—what—setting aside time to think it over or anything like that. But whenever I happened to—the thought crosses my mind—I've been—what—mulling it over a little bit.

T6:   Ummhuh.

C6:   Ahh, it makes sense.

T7:   I don't believe our time has been wasted, doing it the way we have. As a matter of fact, there's some depth to the things that have—

that have transpired here. Yet I think that we have to—(pause) We have to communicate on another level too. (pause) I may not be easy. I don't know. Maybe easier than—ahh, than either of us would expect, when we try it.

The client introduces content in the following passage and immediately uses it to document a construction of his own behavior. He points out his own reaction to the breakthrough of impulsive behavior and then goes on quickly to anchor his construction in other events. Of course, at this stage he has neither the words nor the syntax to express his constructs effectively. He must therefore weave back and forth between efforts to say words that will delineate the constructions and the citation of selected events upon which the constructs are focused.

C7: Ahh, one thing came up this week. I don't know. I suppose it has some importance. I don't know. Ahhh. (pause) Yesterday, ahh, I was killing some time, ahh, down on the pool table in the basement.

T8: Umhuh.

C8: And Mom came down and began to iron and began to chat a little and, ahh, there developed in me (pause) a desire to get up and go—run—get out—a, ahh, (pause) a feeling that, at the time, I described as "hate"—"hatred" towards my mother.

T9: Ummhuh.

C9: Now, this does not, what, this presents a problem immediately in that, ahh, in my picture this is not the feeling I should have.

T10: No, of course not.

C10: But, just the same, it was there.

T11: Yeah.

C11: And, ahh, I thought I'd bring that up. (pause) Another thing I, ahh, that came to mind and I suppose I have indicated already in my discussion—discussions *with* you, but, ahh, for some reason it didn't come through *clear* to me until just recently. And that is, ahh, when I have these explosions or blowups, they are triggered by an outside force—some *event* happening other than involving myself, and they *may* involve myself.

T12: Yeah.

C12: But, sometimes they don't. So I'm just using an outside force and, ahh, at least the most recent one which I happened, I think, since our last discussion, ahhh, immediately or, frequently after the immediate—the first—explosion, the first feeling of anger—

T13: Yeah.

C13: —against some *external* being—person—, ahh, there was a, (pause) you know, like a rubber ball bouncing off a wall, the feeling came back at *myself*, a feeling of disgust, a feeling of anger at myself for having (laughs) the original *feeling*.

T14: Yeah.

C14: —for losing control, and it seemed to me, that of the two, this was the most severe.

T15: Ummhuh.

C15: And, ahh.

T16: (pause) The ball comes back harder even than you thought?

C16: Definitely! or, at least, this is the *impression* I get the most experience.

T17: Yeah.

C17: The one that's most clear in my mind. Now the others I, I don't remember seeing them in these two distinct categories.

T18: Ummhuh.

C18: But it, what, *seems*, it feels, like this is the way they've gone.

T19: Yeah, (pause) Did you feel this way after, after your recognition of your, of this impulse of this feeling toward your mother yesterday?

C19: Yes, and, ahhh, I got out of the house and drove off. Now that was at 4:10 and I got back to the house at about five, ten minutes to five, about forty minutes.

T20: Yeah.

C20: And I'd say at least a *half* an hour of that time was spent in *anger* of varying degrees—

T21: Yeah.

C21: Against myself, (pause) primarily, for, what, having this feeling and trying to piece it out. Ahh, there was no, ahh, any, no progressive thought pattern or no constant progression of thought. It was just, ahh, (pause) I suppose, like a little kid with a hammer and stone, trying to break it up. He pounds at it any ol' way it happens to be turned up.

T22: Yeah.

C22: So that's just the way I was going at it.

T23: No logical sequences.

C23: No logical sequence, no pattern or anything, just, ahhh,—oh, I'd drive for awhile and then I'd think of something and then I'd pound at that, and then I'd, ahh, get nowhere, I suppose, is the only way to say. I *got* nowhere trying to figure the thing out, except that some of this is, was developed at that time. Ahhh, developed I won't say, ahhh, the *ideas emerged* at that time, but they became more crystallized, more, they fitted in more during that time. But I'd say half an hour of the time was spent blowing off steam. I don't know, I drove down Avon and up and around, and came out north of Barton Road across from the Calumet coming down Sixty-one and Digby Road, and it wasn't until about the time, well, are you familiar with that territory out there at all?

T24: More or less—yes.

The client has just confronted himself with the lack of logical sequence in what has happened. He turns to a recitation of times and places. It would be easy to call this resistance. But from the point of view of personal construct theory, resistance is a poorly drawn psychologist's construct and might better be abandoned. The client is groping his way through the experience here in the therapy room, just as he groped his way through it on the day he is describing Like anyone who gropes he reaches out for tangible objects. And he asks others to verify their presence.

C24: There's a road that goes up parallel to Calumet. It's got quite a few houses, new development out there, relatively new, four or five years old.

T25: West side of the Calumet, isn't it?

C25: It's on the west side of Calumet, parallel to it and relatively close to it.

T26: Yes, I know that road.

C26: Well, I went up that road and crossed over, ahh, north of Barton Road, I don't know what road I was on, but it goes out to Eton on one—. If I'd turned left going west, going to Eton, and I turned right, came over to Sixty-one, and down Sixty-one, Ahhh, it comes out. You know that antique shop on Digby Road?

T27: I know there is something—.

C27: There is one. There's a filling station that's next to it. Or something. There's two right there, and there's an antique shop on one side. Got some, oh, wagon wheels laying up against a fence there.

T28: That is a beautiful drive up on the west side there.

C28: Yeah, well, just as, I'd say about halfway up that drive this feeling of anger and so on completely left, well, completely—essentially—

completely left me. There was some still little stirring of it but I began to notice (pause) my surroundings. That is, it wasn't a case of knowing that they were there and not being able to, ahh, think about them or anything, because of the break-ins of this anger or whatever.

T29:   Yeah.

C29:   And then I drove around, watched the skaters on the Calumet and drove home. (long pause) Now, that's one thing. There's something else that has come up in my mind and I don't know how you intended it . . . (pause) Ahh, last time I was in here, you began to ask me the why behind my idea of going into the ministry.

T30:   Yeah.

C30:   And there was a little question there, on one part, ahh, the decision, of this as a possibility has been coming more and more crystalized.

T31:   Ummhuh.

C31:   And there's a little possibility—little question there of whether or not you were questioning whether or not that's where I fitted. I didn't know whether you were or not.

T32:   Pretty hard to, ahh, *not* to wonder, isn't it?

C32:   Well, it is. Well, what, there are *two halves* of me.

T33:   Yes.

The client now turns to an attempt to spell out a principal construct dimension. The therapist now has to decide how tightly this dimension ought to be drawn. If the client sees his alternatives in these terms only and if the implications gather up his whole life's pattern, will he not be endangered the next time he is caught up in impulsivity? This is a point of therapeutic risk. The decision is to go ahead and make the construct as explicit as possible.

There are, of course, many different kinds of comments that could be made about each passage—the kind of externalized control the client uses, his returns to anger and guilt, the fact that the full picture of hostility is not yet sketched in the interview series, the relation with the mother which is almost entirely construed preverbally at this time, the emphasis upon the notion of being "triggered" together with its gunlike or sexual implications and its association with his mother, and many other matters.

C33:   And when the black half is in command it makes absolutely no sense to even have this idea as—well, actually, there are two, *two* ways of looking at even *this* half. You can say, "no, this isn't it," and, on the other hand, you can say, "yes," because in the search for this perhaps I can help someone else. When I'm in my bright mood, like I feel like I am right now, it makes sense. (pause) Another thing, ahh, sometimes I have these dark moods: I get mad and then I get mad at myself in return, and I start mentally browbeating or whatever.

T34:   Yeah.

C34:   If there is something on the outside. But then, I can turn this off, like a radio. Now, ahh, and what, present an outside cheery appearance. Say, I'm down—usually, this is when I'm alone, I mean it's not when I'm in a group—but if I'm alone, something else will—becomes—more than, if one, unless it's my mother. I can still retain my anger when she's present—my father to some extent, but not so much—my brother, usually I turn it off.

T35:   Ummhuh.

C35:   But it's somewhat like a radio. *You, I turn it off*, and assume a different attitude! And this, I don't know, whether it just is turned off and suppressed or just dies out of its own accord.

T36:   There has to be something external or an occasion?

C36:   External, ahh, *to turn it off!*

T37:   Yes.

C37:   But, ahh, I can let it die out in, I suppose, anywheres from twenty minutes to half an hour or so, based on a rough estimate of time from previous occasions and on the time it took this last, ahh—

T38:   Yeah.

C38:   —situation to cool off.

T39:   (pause) What is the contrast between these two parts, the two main parts of yourself as you're describing them now?

C39:   Well, I doubt, I doubt if, ahh, they're this extreme, but they're sort of like black and white. One side is—

T40:   That's quite a contrast, isn't it?

C40:   Well, yeah, ahh, well, as I say, I don't think they're quite as extreme, but they *seem to be*, ahh, *pretty close*. On one hand I feel good, cheery, ahh, present myself, ahh, fairly well to the outside—

T41:   Yes.

C41:   Ahh, get along fine with friends. (long pause) On the other hand, when I'm by myself and ahh, what, kick myself when I'm down ahh, (pause) this black feeling kinda snowballs.

T42:   Yes.

C42: And down, and down, and *down* and DOWN! And it's, ahh, a steep curve going into and a gradual curve coming out.

T43: Yeah. Unless some event intervenes, where you just postpone it.

C43: Yeah, ahh, where, I don't know what you'd say. I do not desire the out—the other, the other people to see myself in this condition.

T44: Well, I can see where, in one case, you see *yourself* as seeing the world as bright. In the other case, it's—

C44: It's not so much the outside world, as its, ahhh—

T45: "Me," huh?

C45: Me! My own feelings!

T46: Yeah.

C46: Because, ahh, I take this assumption simply from the fact that I can *switch*.

T47: Yeah.

C47: So that when I'm what . . .

T48: (pause) There's no question as to whether, as to where the mood arises, *actually* arises. It arises within you then?

C48: Though it's usually *triggered* by something, some event.

T49: It's triggered. Something outside?

C49: Something outside!

T50: Yeah. And you turn it off some—

C50: Now I got *very, very* upset, ahh, last Wednesday, New Year's. Ahh, I was best man in a wedding Saturday.

T51: Yeah.

C51: And we had the wedding gifts that had to be delivered. And, ahhh, Mom was making the suggestion that Dad take them over and then when she suggested Dad take them over she said, "Do you want to take my present at the same time?" Then she said, "Maybe you'd better not." "Yes." "No." It went—four distinct different movements—yes, no, yes, no. Ahh, and I *exploded!* More violently than I had in a long time! And it took me, ahh, two to three hours to cool off enough so that I came back up. I went down to my room and stretched out and read some comic books and ahh— there was another book, I don't know what it was—but cooled off.

T52: This was between your father and your mother.

C52: No, between my mother and myself.

T53: Oh, between your mother and yourself.

C53: Though, I can be triggered, for instance, when my mother and my brother were discussing something.

T54: Ummhuh.

C54: I mentioned that either last time or sometime recently in the past, I was *triggered*. And I can be triggered when my father and my mother are discussing. It's not as likely.

T55: Anything that involves haggling *could* trigger you.

C55: Yeah.

T56: Particularly, if you get involved *directly*.

C56: Well, not necessarily. It's not necessary for myself to become involved directly.

T57: Just even to sit on the sidelines gets you triggered sometimes?

C57: Yeah. And yet, other times, it doesn't bother me at all.

T58: Yeah. You can remain detached at other times.

C58: I can remain detached at other times. I imagine it's, ahh, just how I'm feeling at that particular moment, whether I'm susceptible or not.

T59: Yeah. Now there are two men by the name of Zeons, you then would say.

C59: Yeah.

T60: Looking at these two men from the outside, not just superficially, but I mean judging them as objectively as you can, or judging them whatever way you can, what is the difference between these two men? . . . On what dimension does it lie?

C60: (very long pause) I'm not too sure exactly what you want. I, I'm a little puzzled here.

T61: Well, let's look at these two men. Can you tell me what the difference is between them? (pause) The two men aren't here now. I'm pulling you out from them—.

C61: Yeah, I'm trying to, trying to, ahh, what, find something to, ahh, to, to, first I'm trying to find out what they are like and then trying to see where they differ, ahh, because, ahh, I haven't, what, looked at them from the outside, I've only described to you how *I* feel.

T62: How *you* felt.

C62: When, ahh, when I'm in these moods.

T63: Yeah.

C63: Ahhh, how I don't know that this is an adequate description. These are estimates, stabs in the dark. The one seems too cheery, outward looking, that is, I'm using "outward" as opposed to, what, I was going to describe the other one as "inward looking."

T64: Yeah.

C64: Then of course, the other one is moody, dark, that's what I use the two black and white terms, ahh, light and dark. Ahh, (very long pause) the one—Now, ahh, I'm also ascribing, what, absolutes to these, to these charac, characters which may or may not fit. But, trends in this direction may fit.

T65: Yeah.

C65: Ahhh, the light one would be ahh, cheery, outward looking, enjoys life—.

T66: Rational?

C66: (pause) That does not necessarily fit, I don't believe.

T67: That's another dimension.

C67: Ahhh, the *other* one, I definitely add "irrational" to the dark one.

T68: Yeah.

C68: And, and if you—if you want to put opposite in there, I suppose you'd add "rational" to the light one, but it doesn't necessarily fit, it seems to me. Ahhh, "puzzled," "disturbed," "confused," "irrational," in that this, nothing seems to make sense.

T69: Which one of them wants to go to the seminary?

C69: The light, the cheery one. Well, I think they both do.

T70: They both do.

C70: But for different reasons.

T71: O.K.

C71: The cheery one because of the, ahh, because of the ahh, of what this is a step towards, in that it is a service to people, helping people.

T72: Yeah.

C72: The other one in helping self, trying to find some pattern. This can all be sifted out and made to fit into some sort of relative pattern, some sort of, some sort of an outline or at least *something* so it isn't a confused jumble of emotion and irrationalities.

T73: Looking for some way to extricate one's self from this jumble.

C73: Yeah. (pause) And, when I'm in a dark mood, it seems to me this idea, ahh, of the light mood, of going through seminary and so on, may be a rationalization, a reason which I build up for myself so that this one makes sense, but that is, so that it doesn't seem like I'm doing this strictly for a purpose of self. Which also seems to fit.

T74: When in a dark mood you're skeptical of the bright mood, huh?

C74: Yeah! In other words, what reasons I can give when I'm feeling cheery, feeling good, ahh, when I'm in a dark mood. I wonder if I don't *make* these reasons.

T75: Of Course.

C75: So that these don't *appear* as if I'm doing purely as a matter of self.

T76: So when you're in a dark mood you think *that* really is the real self; the other one is a superficial overlay, sometimes?

C76: Yeah. And, ahh, when I think about it, when I'm in a cheery mood, I can progress toward the darker mood because I'm thinking *towards myself*, which I do when I am in the dark mood. And, oh, I don't know, I just start edging over towards that way.

T77: So even when you're in a cheery mood, cheerful mood, and you wonder which of the two selves is real—

C77: Oh yeah.

T78: And you begin to wonder if it isn't the dark one.

C78: (pause) The dark one, in some ways, seems more real. It presents somewhat of a challenge to try and find out why I am the way I am. I think that's, ahh, I don't know. I don't know why the term "why" keeps coming up. But so many times, in fact, I think almost always—I could go so far as to say "always"—the term "why" comes into the question. Why am I the way I am? Why do I have these dark moods? Why? (sigh) Well, I suppose, by any approach to it, using the term "why" comes up.

T79: So "why" is always in this outcry.

C79: Yeah, What is behind it?

T80: (long pause) What do you think?

C80: (laughs) That's why I'm here. I don't know. (long pause) I suppose, somewhat it's background, the experiences I've had in life, both at home, school, work, play, what have you. And I imagine it's the fact that I have not allowed myself or forced myself, depending upon which viewpoint I take, to make very many friends. I am not particularly comfortable in a social atmosphere. (pause) But when I'm in my cheery mood I get along with people fine. When I'm in a dark mood I have to force myself.

T81: Ummhuh.

C81: Though I can force myself into a fairly acceptable cheery mood.

T82: That's this turning off that you mentioned awhile ago.

C82: Yeah. But it's, ahh, I tell you when I'm doing that, ahh, I'm tense. I definitely feel like I'm forcing myself.

T83: Ummhuh.

C83: Ahhh, I, I, I don't know how to say this. It's not—there are times when that's the case, and times when that's not the case. For instance, one time I was mad at myself, I was downstairs, my brother called that I had a phone call.

T84: Ummhuh.

C84: No problem. Just turn it off. Now, I think I was fairly well out of darkness. I was pretty well up towards, ahh, average between the two, or whatever you want to call it.

T85: Ummhuh.

C85: There are other times though, when I would be in a situation, where I'd be continually tense. I think this is becoming . . . less the pattern than it was in the past.

T86: Good.

C86: But it's still there! Particularly, it's there when I'm not prepared for class—or any other circumstances where I am *uncertain of the results*. I can build up a blacker picture than may be the case.

T87: So whenever you're confronted with something of any kind of importance, where you don't know what's going to happen—.

C87: Yeah. (pause) My imagination can get going, and, ahh, I don't know, the impossible makes it seem pretty rugged. Whereas—usually I'll say al—always—it's never *that* bad—as I paint it.

T88: But you do a good job of painting.

C88: Yeah.

T89: What *does* your imagination do at these moments of uncertainty? What are some of the worst of things that can happen?

C89: I don't know if I can describe any of them. When you ask for a description of something, ahh, there is—

T90: Just a whole lot of—

C90: Nothing comes to mind.

T91: Is that the worst than can happen to you? Sheer, utter confusion? (pause) Not knowing?

C91: (sigh) I don't know as I can say that. I was merely describing my feeling right now.

T92: Yeah. O.K., you might say it a little differently on other occasions.

C92: Ahhhh, (pause) Whenever I'm faced with a problem which I don't know, I'm uncertain about the (pause) event. (pause) Well, I'd say, ahh, I'm scared, which I assume to be normal. I assume that, ahh, when approaching an uncertainty or an unknown, most people are a little bit scared. But, I'd say I build upon this. I present the barriers as greater than they actually turn out to be. The problem is greater. I don't know whether I would say it's more serious, or more important than it was. Sometimes this happens.

T93: Ummhuh.

C93: But I'd say usually. It's just that the difficulty of *doing it* becomes greater in my mind. Although actually, when I arrive at the doing of it, it is not any more difficult than it would have been anyway. (pause) White-washed it instead of painting it black!

T94: Yeah. But the feeling—

C94: (pause) Fear that I'd fail, I think, is the simplest way of putting it.

T95: (pause) What would happen if you failed?

C95: I'd be in a black mood—kick myself.

T96: And then what?

C96: (pause) Well, after applying the club rather thoroughly, I imagine I'd (pause) get over with it—go on.

T97: But that isn't the way you feel at the moment. You're not thinking about getting over it. You're thinking of the worst that can happen, aren't you?

C97: Yeah.

T98: What is this worst that can happen?

C98: (pause) Be in a shameful position.

T99: Yeah.

C99: (silence).

We are now in a position where the black-white construct has a certain amount of tightness to it and it has been wrapped up in verbal terms to some extent. We now move back in the direction of documentation, choosing this time to get further away from local events. As we do this we may expect the construct to be tested out against other memories and, as a result of examination in other context, to be altered somewhat. The alteration is not something we can expect to happen in this interview, but perhaps in later ones.

T100: Lose face like when? What are some of the times when you've lost face in the worst possible ways? (very long pause) That's a hard question to ask, isn't it? But I think I should.

C100: (pause) Looking at it, from again the two viewpoints, there is one I can think of recently. Now, outside of home, I mean, whenever I get mad at myself I lose face with myself. But, other than lose face with myself, and, ahh, this again is strictly from the dark side viewpoint. (pause)

T101: Yeah.

C101: I blew up once in Freeport City, in the office. But, it was of a very short duration and it worked out exceptionally well, once I faced the problem—looked it—. It was a case I had to make a decision. I was the only person in the office that could make the decision. So, I think what actually I did, I rebelled against making the decision, at first. (pause) As near as I can remember, the secretary there placed faith in the decision and, and I said, "I can't do it!" She said, "You've got to. You're the only person here that can." In a minute or two I cooled and went ahead and made a decision and it worked out fine.

T102: That was loss of face, that is that you couldn't—

C102: That's from the black side of it.

T103: Yeah.

C103: I mean, from the other side of it I could see, ahh, that it's just a natural thing. But I mean, from the black side, I don't know if I'd say loss of face.

T104: What was the loss of face? That you were required to make the decision, or that *when* you were asked—?

C104: No, when I was asked, I blew up.

T105: Ummhuh.

C105: I rebelled against making the decision.

T106: And that was a face-losing thing to do.

C106: To blow up. Looking at it, I can see that it, I mean, looking at it rationally, I can see that it's, ahhh, natural to do it and so forth. But I, what, emotionally, was disgusted about—

T107: There's something shameful about losing your temper?

C107: (long pause) I don't know whether I'd use those words, but, yes, that meaning.

T108: Personally.

C108: I mean that *direction* of meaning.

T109:   Yeah. Say it better for me, can you?

C109:   Well, I was going to say, "disgusting," but I suppose, in, some ways, that's the same thing as "shameful"—"disturbing." Although I think that "disgusting," "disturbing," in that it is "disgusting," er, more than just "disturbing."

T110:   Yeah, yeah. "Disgusting." To say that it's disgusting—(pause) in some way, some ways, is to condemn it more. Isn't it?

C110:   You mean than shameful?

T111:   Yeah. (pause) Is it repulsive? (pause) Is a person who loses his temper the way you lose it, as you see it in a black mood . . ?

C111:   Yesss. (pause) I don't know that I'd say it. It, ahh, isn't something that clicks. But the idea fits, as I think about it. It does not seem to—it's just a little stronger—

T112:   Oh.

C112:   Than "disgusting"—"repulsive." I'd say it fits, but it's stronger.

T113:   Ummhuh. O.K.

C113:   I'd say "shameful" is less strong.

T114:   So the situation in Freeport City was an example of where you thought you'd lose face.

C114:   From the black side of it.

T115:   From the black side, yes. Looking at it from—

C115:   The white, light side—

T116:   What does it look like?

C116:   Well, rationally, I can picture it as a natural happening.

T117:   Yeah.

C117:   Or, if not natural, at least reasonable. I don't know if "reasonable" is a word to use there either. (pause) Actually, to find something in which I lost face with some group outside of myself, ahh, it's hard to do. It's very easy to picture myself losing face *to* myself, which seems to happen more often, which seems to have (pause) more *continual* bearing upon myself.

In continuing to explore the range of convenience of the construct we turn to the more remote past. It is important to understand how this is viewed in personal construct terms. The past is not seen as a simple determinant of present behavior. What he is about to describe is not "what made him that way." Instead, what he is about to bring up is a memory that serves to document, or make tangible, the preverbal construct with which he is currently approaching his world.

In fact he says as much; he is not sure it ever actually happened. But the "memory" still serves its purpose admirably.

T118:   O.K. When you were a child, how did you lose face?

C118:   (very long pause) Well, two events come to mind. And again, from the white side, they are perfectly natural events to have happened. And I cannot tell you, I know in one instance how I felt, that is, I know how I felt *as described by my parents.*

T119:   Yeah.

C119:   I know how I felt in the other instance because I can picture myself in the instance. The first instance would be about 1933. It would put me about two or three years old. I can picture, without even closing my eyes, the place. Now I've got—only got—I know there's a photo of the front of the house. Now that much has aided, I mean my picture of the place is aided by that. But in back of it, the only thing I have is a picture of it as aided by descriptions of it from my mother. But I can, I could see it before she started to enhance the description, and very clearly. Over a, what, a ravine or a creek. I mean it wasn't a ravine, it was, well, of course, I don't know. I can only picture it through, as I remember, as that occasion it was very deep, and I imagine it was, and I imagine it wasn't any deeper than this—

T120:   Yeah.

C120:   From the floor, but, at that age it looked deep. Ahhh, a hexagonal or octagonal porch timber, that is timber, unpeeled logs, so big, forming the railing, the floor, plank floor. And on this porch, out from behind the house, over this ravine, they stretched a net hammock.

T121:   Ummhuh.

C121:   I was in that hammock and got tangled up in it and I got (laugh) mad. Now, I don't, again this does not seem to be a natural event, and to my cheery side, my light side, it also seems to be a natural event.

T122:   Yeah. It could seem—

C122:   To my dark side, as I think about it, I get irritated by it. I won't say I get mad. Though, I'd say, using these two as points, irritated and mad, I'm about here, not *quite* as strong as "mad," but a good bit stronger than "irritated."

T123:   Well, you must have felt helpless at that time, *at the moment.*

C123:   Definitely. Well, there wasn't anything I could do! I was wrapped up like a, what, a fish does when it gets in a fish net. I suppose that's essentially, what, this was, I don't remember. It *seems* to be a net about this big in my mind. I don't know what size the net was. It could very well have been a fish net, made into a hammock.

T124:   And what was the other event there? I would like to come back to this if you don't mind. Before you forget—

C124:   Ahhhhhh, now, the year I cannot place, (pause) nor the location. It was either '37 or, I believe, '38: '36–'37 or '37–'38. Two years when my Dad came down here to Goodfield we rented homes, one in Hinton, one in Ilma. That is, there was one each year, whichever way it was, I don't know. Anyway, in the back there was a fish pond. I imagine this was in Ilma because it doesn't fit Hinton, cause Dad pointed out the street where the house was and it doesn't fit. Oh, I don't imagine the pond at the deepest wasn't any deeper than that.

T125:   Yeah.

C125:   And it was well, dumbbell shaped. Shaped like this.

T126:   Ummhuh.

C126:   Oh the center part was oh, yeah, wide, and the ends, that much wider on both sides, but it went out and then around. And the goldfish you saw in there. Anyway, I was along the side and a friend pushed me in and, ahh, I came out mad—what, madder than a wet hen, as the saying goes. Now this emotional reaction, I do not, did not remember until my folks told me how I felt coming out. Now, on the light side this seems perfectly natural and rational, and yet on the other side,—what bothers me I think is that *I had the feeling!* I had the feeling of *madness* over this, which does not fit from the, looking at it from the *rational* point of view. I mean, I can say I look at it rationally, that is, from the light side, and it appears perfectly natural to have been mad over it.

T127:   Ummhuh.

C127:   You, as I don't know, whether I was standing alongside, or bending over looking at the goldfish or what. I—Even, now, well, I don't know if you are tempted sometimes, when you see someone like that, to push them in just for the horseplay or heck of it.

T128:   Ummhuh.

C128:   And yet, from the other point of view, it seems, I don't know what to say—irrational to get mad, I don't know, it isn't, but that was the feeling I had about it, I *have* about it, not what

I *had* about it, I don't know *how* I felt. I can't picture myself in that situation, except *as I feel now.*

T129:   It still is attached (pause) to the memory, the feeling—?

C129:   Yes, Now, I don't know whether the feeling was one that developed *at the time* or whether it is one I have developed *in looking back on it*, through the description I have of it.

T130:   Good point.

C130:   When I thought of those two instances, I, in both instances, I don't know whether the feeling is one I have developed *from* the instance or whether it's one I developed *in reflecting upon* the instances.

T131:   But the instance seems to illustrate the feelings.

C131:   Yeah.

T132:   This is probably the more important thing, anyway.

C132:   Now, whether it is something I have assigned to this particular instance which has no bearing whatsoever to the instance, I don't know.

T133:   At least, as you think of it now, they are good examples of an old feeling.

C133:   To find something out of the air and grab hold of it, I'd say this is it. Ahhh, I, it's pretty foggy.

T134:   Yeah.

C134:   But these are two situations which I can reflect upon. Now, any, to picture anything, I can remember the pond, looking at it, as in the second instance. I can remember the porch, the first instance. Now whether I can, I can remember myself looking at it from another, from an outside viewpoint, of being tangled up in the net. In other words I can see it from an outside viewpoint. So how I felt, or what I saw *in the net*, I don't remember. That is, it is not clear. It is from an outside viewpoint. The same thing, ahh, from the pool instance. Now we have a picture of the pool, have a picture of me standing there, water pouring off and so on. And I can picture myself in that instance, looking at it from the outside, not from the inside.

T135:   You say you do have a real picture of yourself, or is it just a mental picture of yourself?

C135:   I think that we have a picture of me. I think we actually have a picture of me that was taken at the time. I don't know, but I think so.

T136: Would that have added to your humiliation—having your picture taken?

C136: From this side, no. It's perfectly natural to want to take a picture, I don't know! I don't know.

T137: But if this had been an instance in which you had been upset, had a great feeling of helplessness or something and had that—had that moment been crystallized in film—might have meant something?

C137: As a constant reminder of it. That is, here is something anytime you see it immediately you have these emotions, the emotions that you had at the time are brought to the surface again.

T138: As you look back on it, from the dark side?

C138: Now actually, seeing this picture the first time, I can't remember any emotions about it. But my folks. When I was told by my parents what happened here then I, what, I developed a story about it.

T139: You had a feeling about it.

C139: I had a feeling, well, I don't know if I had a feeling, I developed a story about it. I, what, what, whether what I have told you is one hundred percent true, I don't know. It was a emot . . . , an emotional—motion picture of what was happening at the time, *as I see it now*. What happened then, I couldn't tell you. For that reason, I think it was, ahh, thinking about it now, this is not something I have thought about in the past, but it makes sense, at least from this point of view, which is how I predict— happen to feel about it now. Ahhh, that this is a story which I built up from descriptions given.

T140: The fact that it is a story that seems to fit a mood is probably more important than whether the details actually happened in all the ways that you remember them this afternoon. (pause) So the story might be *emotionally* true without necessarily being altogether *historically* true.

The existentialist should have a heyday with the following passage.

C140: Yeah, I'll go along with that. (long pause) One thing puzzles me right here. In describing these situations, I have described them as an outsider looking at the situation. I have not felt, and cannot *see* myself as the individual in the situation. And, in reflecting upon other situations, not these, joyous, sad, or anything, now it's the same way. Now is this common, or is it?

T141: Partly a function of your being on your guard when you're in here.

C141: I mean this is, this is normal *all* the time. It's not—just when I, I mean, this is the way I think!

T142: But in the dark woods you have feelings.

C142: Yes. But they are all *strictly limited*, what, well, I suppose, if you were going to draw a picture of it, it'd be like this, looking down on it. That's a nose (laughs) believe it or not . . .

T143: Yeah.

C143: Ears, eyes. Looking down on the top, it seems to be limited right here. That's my emotional, in other words, it's all—

T144: Right on top of your head?

C144: Well, not entirely. I'm looking at a—

T145: It's in the plane view.

C145: Looking at a side view, I draw a square the same way.

T146: Yeah.

C146: Inside my head, or inside the being I am.

T147: Ummhuh.

C147: I don't have, ahh, ahh, ahh, a picture even of myself.

T148: Ummhuh.

C148: It's all inside.

T149: Ummhuh.

C149: And whereas, the other view, I cannot see myself in, I only see myself, what, looking at myself from the outside, as another person, or at least that seems to be the way it seems right now.

T150: Ummhuh. (pause) So there's a kind of, it's sort of undifferentiated, isn't it? (pause) It's ahhh—

Note how the client spontaneously comes back to the construct. Already he is ready to relocate one of its poles. There is progress in this interview, and it has been achieved by weaving between construction and documentation.

C150: Umh. Another thought just came to me. Ahhhh, (pause) (sigh) the description of the black is correct. The description of the white is only partially correct, because when I'm looking at myself and discussing my feelings, I look at myself as an outsider looking at myself. But, if I'm with another group, I was thinking of, I just spent the past two hours over in the Union in the coffee shop, drinking coffee.

T151:   Ummhuh.

C151:   Now, during this time, it was not a case of myself looking at myself as an outsider.

T152:   Ummhuh. (pause) Instead?

C152:   I don't know—it seems from the inside out. It's like right now—as I'm talking to you I'm looking from the inside out. As I'm talking to myself, I'm looking from the outside in.

C153:   Ummhuh.

T153:   Not outside *in* but outside at.

T154:   O.K.

C154:   I'm looking at myself, what, from the *surface* in.

T155:   Ummhuh.

C155:   From the outside to the surface, I'm looking at myself from the cheery side.

T156:   Ummhuh.

C156:   From the black side, from the surface *in*.

T157:   Ummhuh.

C157:   (sigh) If that makes sense. Kinda to try to—

T158:   So that it may have made sense—

C158:   To summarize my feelings, my ideas.

T159:   So then, in a situation such as that of the last two hours, you're not particularly introspective.

T159:   No, no. Although what we were doing ended up with just the four veterans talking things over.

T160:   Ummhuh.

C160:   And we were, what, reminiscing.

T161:   Ummhum.

C161:   And it was entirely, well, I was drawing upon experiences which I had (pause) enjoyable ones, and I suppose they were doing the same thing—told tall tales, rather around the table.

T162:   Ummhuh. (pause) Well, there are two phases to the mood, I take it then. One is whatever it seems to be at the moment it's set off and the other, whatever it is, when you realize you've *got it*, as in the incident yesterday. There was the anger you felt towards your mother.

C162:   Yeah.

T163:   When she sought to engage you in conversation.

C163:   Ummhuh.

T164:   And then the even blacker part of it came when you realized you were angry at your own mother.

C164:   Yeah.

T165:   (pause) And this snowballs. If I am a person that gets angry at his own mother, (pause) what kind of a person am I?

C165:   Yeah.

T166:   And how hopeless my life is.

C166:   Yeah. There seems to be nothing upon which—well, just a black morass of, well, I suppose a situation which would fit the tar-pit description given of the dinosaur age.

T167:   Ummhuh. Oh.

C167:   Bottomless pit of nothing, errr, not nothing but something there, I mean—(sigh)

T168:   Almost like the dinosaur struggling out of the tar pit, huh, trying to struggle?

C168:   Yeah. Quicksand, going down. A feeling of, well, I don't know. One term I've used recently, I notice, is "corruption."

T169:   Oh?

C169:   Ahhh, ahhh, I think in the, the, ahhh, medical sense, that is, a stinking mess—*plus!* And this in itself some—

T170:   Ummhuh.

C170:   As an apt word appears, it, ahhh, builds upon itself.

T171:   Ummhuh.

C171:   You might say, a perfect example of making a mountain out of a molehill or something. (sigh) That's looking at it from this side. Looking at it from this side (laughs) it's a mountain.

T172:   In both instances you recall, or formulate, or use to illustrate from childhood the hammock incident, the fish pond incident. What did they have in common? Feeling-wise, yes, they had this—they are examples of this black feeling.

C172:   A feeling, what, well, the word came to me, "to strike out"— "retaliate."

T173:   Ummhuh.

C173:   And yet, in absolute helplessness! In the first incident, I was tangled in a hammock. Not a darn thing I could do, I'd *had* it (laughs)!

T174:   Ummhuh.

C174:   Until Mom came with her—whether or—Mom, I think it was my mother, extricated me.

T175: Suppose she laughed at you?

C175: Well, I suppose so, it's a—

T176: Probably would—

C176: Something which you, ahhh, I mean, if I saw someone, *I'd* probably laugh too if I was helping them out. It's a logical thing.

T177: So even if she didn't, the very fact that you could see that it was laughable—

C177: Yeah.

T178: Was just enough?

C178: Its justification enough for the feeling.

T179: Yeah. Because you felt that you were *in* a laughable position.

C179: I would say it's perfectly logical. In *both* instances—it was a laughable condition.

T180: Ummhuh.

C180: I seem to picture myself coming out of the fish, outside of the fish pond, and I wouldn't say I'm anything, ahhh, (sigh) *not laughable at.*

T181: So the outside self would say this, "This, whether anybody laughs at it or not, it is laughable."

C181: Oh, yes, looking at it from this point of view, it's a perfectly enjoyable, laughable condition.

T182: Yeah.

C182: That is, from looking at it from the outside. Looking at it from the inside it's a (sigh) made me just *mad*, thinking about being laughed at for the situation. Two viewpoints, the same situation, both perfectly natural.

T183: Yeah.

C183: And when I'm in a good mood, I look at it one way, and when I'm in a black mood, I look at it another way. If I'm in a black mood, I usually do not recognize the good mood, until I begin to shade out.

T184: Ummhuh. Yeah.

C184: When I'm in the good mood I can recognize the black mood exists.

T185: Ummhuh.

C185: Or was, or did exist, or what. The viewpoint is existent, and yet it does not seem to bother me.

T186: Ummhuh.

C186:   I mean, it bothers, yes, but it does not seem to be of major impor-
        tance, only of minor importance.

T187:   Well, then when you are in the black mood you must almost
        hate yourself as you are.

C187:   *Definitely! Definitely!*

T188:   Particularly as you are in the good mood. You don't like that—

C188:   Ahhh . . .

T189:   Bright person, huh?

C189:   Ummh, I don't know. I never thought of it that way. When I'm
        in a *black mood*, I just plain hate myself.

T190:   At least you're suspicious of the good mood—suspicious if its
        motivations.

C190:   Well, I didn't, I don't even think of the good mood.

T191:   I see.

C191:   It's, it's *completely* cut off.

T192:   Ummhuh.

C192:   Until I begin to shake out if it, ahhh . . .

T193:   Yeah.

C193:   That is, I'm using the term "shake out"—I suppose it's as good
        as any.

T194:   Yeah, I think I follow that.

C194:   Climb out of the pit, or whatever.

T195:   Climb out of the pit like you climbed out of the fish pond.

C195:   Well, I was thinking, ahhh, combining, ahhh, color quality and
        this sinking feeling of a well. I mean, this is not how I feel
        like I'm climbing out of a well.

T196:   Yeah.

C196:   But, as say, a description of the situation, absolute blackness in
        the well, climbing out as you get clearer, closer to the light it
        becomes a lighter shade—

T197:   Ummhuh.

C197:   Therefore, combining the two feelings.

T198:   Yeah.

C198:   (pause) Now, I don't know. This just brought up something in
        my mind (sighs). I get this black feeling as, I can't say this
        is how it feels 'cause I don't think anybody *knows*. It feels like
        I'm in quicksand. The harder I struggle, down I go.

T199:   Ummhuh.

C199: Or a tar—a tar pool.

T200: Ummhuh.

C200: Pool of tar—it's the same thing. Down you go! Black and blacker!

T201: Ummhuh.

C201: And now I don't know. This thought pattern just came to me. The harder I struggle, the harder I try to find the reason, the blacker it gets and yet, when I relax, that is, when I give up, it planes off. The emotion planes off.

T202: Ummhuh.

C202: The intenser the emotion, the darker it is, the relaxing of the emotion, the well, the term came "boredom" of the emotion, I don't know—

T203: Ummhuh.

C203: Ahhh, if that word even fits, but the word came to mind.

T204: Ummhuh.

C204: Ahhh, it fades out.

T205: So it's almost as if while you're trying to fight it, you only lose.

C205: I don't know as that fits. It does. It doesn't. I'd say as long as I fight it *intensely* . . .

T206: Ummhuh.

C206: And what do I say, get *mad* at it . . .

T207: Yeah.

C207: I lose. But as I relax, ahhh, I cannot say this is how it happens— this seems to fit in the description. As I relax . . . the feeling disappears.

T208: Ummhuh.

C208: It doesn't disappear; it fades.

T209: Fades.

C209: But there continues a recollection of the feeling—I suppose, even a hatred of the feeling, a distinct dislike that the feeling even existed.

T210: Umh. (pause) So that's the next phase.

C210: I say it's a constant fade.

T211: Oh.

C211: I mean, it isn't fade, it is, what (sign) . . . well, back to my diagrams. (pause) If I were to draw it, this, just arbitrary, normal.

T212: Ummhuh.

C212: The black would be down here, and it planes off, and this would be normal, maybe even below normal, I don't know.

T213: Ummhuh.

C213: And this is my cheery self. Now this line, I don't know what—

T214: Ummhuh.

C214: Steepness it would be, or—

T215: Ummhuh.

C215: But, there seems to be, when the anger becomes, vertical or very steep.

T216: Ummhuh.

C216: And then it planes off slowly, even more slowly than I've shown it here.

T217: So when you go into it, it's a real plunge.

C217: It seems to, ahh, thinking back on it, it seems to be.

T218: Yeah.

C218: And then it shades off and then this feeling of recollection, I don't know if it'd be at the norm I've drawn here or below it or above it or where, but then as I, what, feel better, more cheery, more joyful, ahh, it gets above it and this, ahh, this part here is forgotten. Unless something brings my mind back to it.

T219: Ummhuh.

C219: And then I can go back down towards that—dark feeling.

T220: So it's hard even to think about it without being drawn back into it.

C220: Well, I wouldn't want to make an answer that couldn't be changed, but I'd say, "yes."

T221: Ummhuh, O.K.

C221: (pause) I wouldn't want to make *any* answer that couldn't be changed.

T222: Yes, of course.

C222: Each time you ask a question, there's, ahh, I wouldn't say *each* time but most, most, often, there is a complete blank, a lack of an immediate answer popping up and I have to sort of, what, battle around to try to find something that describes it and the terminology used, I make no guarantee of its accuracy.

T223: O.K., now Friday at four?

C223: Friday at four, Monday at four, Friday at four, and that is all we have scheduled at present.

T224:   That carries us up for quite awhile.

C224:   Goodbye.

T225:   Goodbye.

In a later interview the client described his fishpond experience not so much as one of anger as one of chaotic confusion. He had had little experience in playing with other children and to have a playmate behave in such an unpredictable way was simply incomprehensible. He had experienced a massive invalidation of the limited construct system on which he depended for dealing with interpersonal relations. In terms of personal construct theory he experienced *anxiety*—loss of structure.

Later interviews returned, of course, to the mother topic. But in this case as well as from the standpoint of personal construct theory, the objective was not catharsis or venting of feelings. Instead the objective of such further exploration was to dispel the long-standing anxiety by finding adequate structure for dealing with her, as well as with companions who behaved in unexpected ways.

Eventually the task was to carry forward the reformulation of constructs into a series of planned experimental experiences outside the therapy room. These were the "field trials," planned in the laboratory and later analyzed there to provide bases for reformulations and further trials. Thus the model of scientific enterprise is utilized in psychotherapy. And why not? Should not a client be allowed to become his own psychologist?

Part III

PROBLEMS

13

Hostility

It is a common experience among those who, in the headlong pursuit of their occupation, pause occasionally to sketch some guidelines for their patterns of thought to discover that the principles they have so carefully defined were once artfully portrayed in Greek legend. I have had this particular experience in connection with this afternoon's topic. It is a disconcerting experience for not only does it lead one to question his personal capacity for original thinking but it also casts doubt upon the wisdom of all those explicit verbal definitions upon which modern science so largely depends. Of the two, it is perhaps less upsetting to give up one's claim to originality. But definition—if one cannot define, how can he ever hope to progress? Yet it seems to be the irony of explicit thinking that such great emphasis is placed on the outer boundaries that it never touches the heart of the idea.

Not so the Greeks. They, while they might be accused of being perfectionists, were certainly never literalists, and even now it seems as if they were freer then to say what they meant than we are. So, before I start rounding up the precise scientific meaning of this *hostility* construct by modern-day methods of circumlocution, let me just tell you very briefly how the Greeks got to the heart of the matter and said it all much more simply than I would ever dare to.

There was a young man by the name of Theseus who had been reared under the domination of his mother. One day, out in the garage or some place, he ran onto an old sword and a pair of shoes that

SOURCE. Presidential Address, 1957, Clinical Division, American Psychological Association.

267

had belonged to his father. Right then and there he decided to make a break for it and go look up his father, who, it appears, had gone away to a national convention a number of years before and somehow had managed to stay away on urgent business ever since. Just how his father managed this is part of the story that has never been quite clear to me. I did hear, once, that some scandal was involved, but since it seemed to be none of my business I never looked into the matter. I am sure that it is not an important part of the story.

Now this young victim of "momism," as it existed in the classic Greek era, became quite a hero by the time he caught up with his old man—a combination of fact which, it seems to me, some alert publicity-minded psychiatrist ought to be able to capitalize on. For one thing, along the road, Theseus ran into a character by the name of Procrustes.

This fellow had bought a small place way out in the country where the road wound through a deserted canyon. Some people say his real name was Damastes, while others insist it was Polypamon. The mixup was probably because people going by were always in such a hurry that they didn't take time to read the Greek letters on his mailbox. In any case, people thereabouts all called him by his nickname, "Stretch," which is what the word "procrustes" means in English.

Stretch Damastes was hostile. That, of course, is the whole point of telling this story. I don't think he ever meant to be hostile. His feelings would probably have been hurt if anyone had even suggested the idea. As a matter of fact, it is quite possible that no one ever did mention it to him. In those times not many people went in for psychoanalysis and you could easily go for weeks without so much as once having someone interpret your unconscious motivation to you.

I am sure that Stretch was not really out to hurt people. The fact that his guests always seemed to have such a bad time of it was just one of those unfortunate things that so often seem to happen in spite of everything you do to make people comfortable.

Because he happened to be hostile, Stretch was one of those unlucky souls in this world whose fate it is to be grossly misunderstood. Why? In the first place he was genuinely interested in people. I mean *genuinely!* He had bought this little chicken ranch, or whatever it was, with the express purpose of setting up a kind of wayside motel where travelers who found themselves in this lonely spot at nightfall could be assured of some old-fashioned hospitality. Moreover, he had in mind that he would give them their supper and their lodging free. Breakfast, too, if they happened to want it! He was as thoughtful as that.

Stretch, like most hostile people, had a pretty clear idea of how guests should be treated. He really fancied himself as a host and along about sundown he used to stand out by the front gate, lean against the mailbox, and wait to see if he could persuade some traveler to stop in for supper. At the table he always proved to be an excellent conversationalist and, before his guest realized how late it had gotten to be, it would be time to go to bed.

There was a bed, as those of you who know the story probably remember. Some say there were two beds, but most everyone now agrees that there was only this one. Stretch was especially concerned that his guest would find the bed just right. He would fluff up the pillows, press down on the mattress to show how soft it was, and keep murmuring something about how much he hoped that the bed would be neither too long nor too short. In fact, he would fuss around long after the guest was yawning and ready to turn in. Showing all this solicitude was what really got him into trouble.

In fact, the poor man would get himself so worked up over his social role as a host that later, back in his own room and long after his guest was comfortably asleep, he would be tossing and turning, worrying himself sick over the possibility that there might be some flaw in his hospitality. Was his guest comfortable or not? Had he used the dainty guest towels in the bathroom? And the guest bed—that was what worried him most. Did it fit? Maybe he was a little too tall for it; maybe a little too short—which was it? Throughout the restless night the thoughts nagged and mounted until they were unbearable.

You can guess what happened, if you do not already know. In the wee hours of the morning Stretch would tiptoe to the door of the guest room, open it ever so softly, and peek in, just to make sure. You can also guess what he saw and what utter consternation seized him at finding his guest either too short or too long—never a perfect fit. And now, knowing how it was that Stretch was trying so hard to be a perfect host, it is quite easy to see that next he simply had to do what he did.

There are some folks—not very practical folks, I'm afraid—who think that what he should have done was cut off the bed to fit the guest; or stretch it, as the case might be. But if such people would only stop to think for a moment, they would readily perceive that this would not be socially adaptive behavior. It would be bound to make the bed the wrong size for the next guest, not to mention the damage to an expensive piece of furniture. Of course, Stretch could have gone back to bed, pulled the covers over his head and said, "To heck with it!" as some folks who do not have a sincere interest in people, no doubt, would do.

The rest of the story is not very important, now that we all appreciate Stretch's predicament and have feelings of genuine acceptance for him as a person. You know, of course, that Theseus, who was not a particularly sensitive person, did Procrustes in—not because of any deep sense of hostile regard, I'm afraid, but only because Procrustes happened to get in his way. Theseus was young and ambitious and had his heart set on being a hero. To his immature mind, life was simply an aggressive adventure and he still lacked that subtle capacity for exactitude in the interpretation of human nature that genuinely hostile people have.

Let me turn now from this classical mode of expression to the form of semantic discourse with which we are more familiar. It will take longer to say the same thing, and much of the meaning will be lost in literalism, but it will sound more scientific and much more like what a psychologist is expected to say on an occasion like this.

Over a period of a good many years—many of them not very productive of publications, I fear—I have attempted to come to grips with the psychology of man as if I had only recently come across the species. It was like pretending to be someone from Mars who had just dropped in to meet these earth-creatures for the first time and was trying to understand them. More and more, it seemed to me that what I wanted, in my role as a stranger on earth, was man's own account of things as he saw them, as he experienced them, and not merely what outsiders said about him.

Early in my clinical experience I found myself repeating over and over to my students, "If you don't know what is troubling a child, ask him, maybe he'll tell you." And often he did; although it never proved easy for a clinician to quiet down and hear what the child was saying. To do so he had to brush away his literalistic biases about what words naturally meant and pay more attention to what the child meant. He had to set aside also many of his diagnostic presentiments about what kinds of packages children come wrapped up in. And as for listening to adults; that is even harder. So often the adult has long since lost track himself of what it was he started out to say, many years ago. By the time he meets the clinician he can repeat only words and words, wearily making the kinds of vocal sounds that quickly reverberate themselves away into lexical emptiness.

If we were to develop a psychology of man from his own point of view—a psychology of man himself—it could obviously be neither a prejudiced kind of psychology, nor an objecive one. I repeat—*neither prejudiced nor objective!* Under no condition could it be the kind of psychology that merely points objectively to a man and says, "That thing out there; let me prod it. I want to see which way it will hop."

Instead, it would have to be an experiential kind of psychology that would enable one to look all about him and say, "So this is how it is to be a man. So this is the way the world looks through his eyes. So this is the sense of his behavior. So this is his framework of cause and effect. So this, at last, is the mind of man."

At first we—my students and I—started calling this new psychological point of view, "role theory." The term seemed a likely name for what we were thinking. Not only was our route to the understanding of clients via an appreciation of the part they were attempting to enact, but psychotherapy, we soon discovered, could often be developed in terms of a way of life—a role—rather than in terms of so-called insights which reduced behavior to motivation, and motivation, in turn, to atavism.

Soon, however, the term "role" began to appear widely in psychological literature in quite a different sense. So we temporarily abandoned use of the term and began talking about a psychology of personal constructs. By this we did not mean merely a kind of perceptual theory, nor did we mean merely the realm of objects that fall within a given man's purview. Rather, we had in mind a psychology that dealt with the manner in which man comes to grips with his world of reality. The task was not so much to choose a theory of psychology for ourselves but, first of all, to establish a frame of reference in terms of which we might appreciate any man's personal theory of psychology. For, it seemed to us, it would have to be at the level of the personal construction of events, without which construction no man has any psychological footing, that the task of the psychologist must begin. Indeed, only at this level of the man's personal construction, can it ever be said that an event becomes a stimulus for him, or that an action becomes an expression of motives within him, or that his behavior is learned. To overlook this crucial point at which events start to be interpreted as psychological variables is to become enmeshed in what Bertrand Russell and others have called the subject-predicate error of the Indo-European mode of thought.

So we turned to a psychology of personal constructs. The venture, so far, has been exciting. There have been hidden surprises waiting for us along the way. Some of them have been occasions for dismay. I have already mentioned one surprise when I said that we would have to abandon prejudice and *objectivity* both! The very thought of abandoning objectivity sounds just as wicked to the narrowly indoctrinated psychologist of today as the idea of abandoning other forms of revealed truth sounded to the fundamentalists of another generation. Yet the doctrine of objectivity, as currently practiced in our world of psychology, looks to events as if they somehow abstracted themselves and spoke out in their own direct revelations of profound truth.

As we pursue further our line of thinking the concept of *stimulus* drops out also. There is simply no way to keep it in. *Reinforcement* becomes a question-begging term, at least in the sense in which it is commonly used. The whole conceptual area of *motivation*, as we know it in psychology today, vanished. Even *learning* is washed up; when the theory gets through with it it sounds like a synonym for the verb *to become*. In brief, this is not a theory for anyone who likes to display his Ph.D. diploma on the wall of his office, for several times a day he will find it glowering down on him in silent disapproval.

Now, having stirred up this hornets' nest of scientific convictions, let us deal with a limited part of the confusion we have attempted to create. (This is known as establishing an initial atmosphere of unacceptance, in the hope that in what follows the listener will grasp more eagerly for a little of something he can make sense out of.) We have chosen the topic of hostility. Hostility is one of the clinician's most crucial concerns. Let us see what happens when we apply this kind of thinking to it. What will it help him to notice? What will it lead him to look for? What new openings to psychotherapeutic movement will it provide for his client?

In the psychological realm of discourse, as contrasted with some of our better developed realms of discourse such as physics, most of our concepts are projections of two principle axes of reference— pleasure versus pain and good versus evil. Since it is assumed that each of us automatically heads for pleasure and away from pain while trying to get other people to head for good and away from evil, our psychological dimensions all begin to look like one-way streets, every one of them leading in the same general direction. One is reminded of the fellow who offered to solve any city's traffic problem, simply by marking a system of one-way streets, all leading out of town. The hitch in such a traffic system is that it does not provide the citizens with any true mobility. So it is with much of our psychological thinking; our conceptual network is so aligned that it does not permit us much mobility in dealing with our personal problems.

The concept of hostility, as commonly understood, is just such a notion. If you have got it, it may be fun but it's bad. If the fellow next door has got it, you may get hurt. The only thing to do with hostility is get rid of it or get away from it. Nice people try to keep it bottled up and psychoanalyzed people try to dump it out somewhere where it won't do any harm.

The usual understanding of hostility is that it is an impulse to hurt someone, to cause pain. This definition, it must be noticed, puts the limiting condition in the experience of the other person, not in the experience of the hostile person himself. Yet if we are to have a psychology of man's own experiences we must anchor our basic concepts in that personal experience, not in the experiences he causes others to have or which he appears to seek to cause others to have. Thus, if we wish to use a concept of hostility at all, we have to ask, what is the experiential nature of hostility from the standpoint of the person who has it. Only by answering this question in some sensible way will we arrive at a concept which makes pure psychological sense, rather than sociological or moral sense merely.

What is it like to be hostile? How does it feel? How does hostility creep into the human enterprise? In order to get the answers to these questions we have to talk to people like Procrusets, rather than Theseus. It is in this respect that psychoanalysis has made two priceless contributions to the symptomatic understanding of hostility, although I fear the analyses have done little to develop hostility as a psychological concept.

One of these contributions has to do with the recognition of what is symptomatically called, "passive hostility." This is seen as a way of inflicting injury by letting people stew in their own juice. It involves keeping someone's juice as hot as possible in eager anticipation of his falling in and, when he does fall in, piously pointing out to him how hot it is.

The other psychoanalytic contribution to our understanding of hostility symptoms is the description of incorporative hostility that robs others of their individuality and brings them helplessly into the orbit of the hostile person's world. This is what is sometimes called, in the poetic idiom of psychoanalysis, *oral hostility*. One of its manifestations has been coined into the currently popular phrase, "smother love."

But while the clinical experience of psychoanalysts, as well as that of psychotherapists of other persuasions, has led us all to a greater sensitivity to the variety of symptoms through which hostility is expressed, it has not so far resulted in better conceptualization, nor has it contributed much to the improvement of psychological theory dealing with the essential nature of hostility. Hostility is still seen as the urge to hurt someone, sometimes as the urge to hurt one's self. Even guilt is seen as the urge to hurt turned against the self as substitute—preparing one's own juice to be stewed in. Oral hostility, still viewed as the urge to hurt, is described as the impulse to destroy as one destroys food by eating it.

But I think the Greeks, at least the early Greeks who mostly understood the impulses of man in terms of his adventures, probably sensed something about hostility that is easily missed by those who feel they must deal with man in terms of his pathological symptoms. In this early story of Procrustes they appear to have embodied part of what they knew about the nature of the hostile man. There is something humanly plausible about Procrustes. He did what people do. He could not bear the thought of being wrong in his estimate of the stature of his guests. Rather than change his estimate he corrected his guests. And so this part of the Thesean story has lived and the poetic imagery of the Procrustean bed has survived to this day.

It is at the point of Procrustes' failure to anticipate correctly the stature of his guests that the legend places the fulcrum of his hostility. But this point of frustration is still only the fulcrum. It takes a massive weight of personal meaning to tip the scales. In my paraphrasing I have underscored one original feature of the tale by describing Procrustes as an ardent host who was genuinely interested in people. It was only because so much of his world was centered in his claim to knowing the true dimensions of man that the invalidating evidence assumed such overwhelming proportions. When he peeked through the bedroom door that world of his threatened to collapse.

How to save it! If his bed—his only bed—did not fit his guest, his guest must be made to fit the bed. Regardless of the cost, the validity of his bed and the integrity of his world—which were one and the same thing—must be sustained. That piece of psychological furniture was for him, not just a bed, but a vital institution—more important by far than the physical well-being of just one guest. It was a key to his way of life. Under the circumstances he did the only thing as far as he could see, that made sense. And, as I said before, it is really too bad that Theseus did not sense the situation and do something constructive about it. Ambitious people are so often dull-witted about such matters.

From the standpoint of a psychology of personal constructs, each person, like Procrustes, devises as best he can a structure for making sense out of a world of humanity in which he finds himself. Some of this personal structure is cast in terms of words and he can name the parts for us. But most of it is expressed only in terms of talk—which is something quite different from semantic communication—and some of it stands way back in the shadows of human expression as a background pattern that is never traced with the fine lines of verbal detail.

Without such patterned structure it would appear that no man can come to grips with his seething world of people, nor can he establish himself as a psychological entity. If one wishes, he can look upon this personal structure of man as a network of hypotheses about human nature. But if he does think of it in terms of hypotheses he should be prepared to envision hypotheses that are not verbally formulated as well as the kind of explicitly stated hypotheses that are familiar to research settings. In any case, like all psychological structure and all hypotheses, this personal construct system tempts man to make predictions. And predictions, in turn, have a way of either occurring or not occurring, and usually being rather obvious about it. It is in terms of his predictions, then, that the mind of man comes at last into firm contact with reality. I would go even further and say that *it is only in terms of his predictions* that man ever touches the real world about him.

Having gone this far with our theorizing it seems that we have involved ourselves in kind of a psychological theory in which the notion of validation will have to play a major part. This is quite all right with us. It fits our clinical experience. It fits the report experiences of others. It offers promise of a psychology that will turn its attention to man's plastic future rather than to his fateful past.

Man predicts what will happen. If it happens, his prediction is validated, the grounds he used in making it are strengthened, and he can venture further next time. If it does not happen, his prediction is invalidated, the structure he used in making the prediction is brought into question, and the road ahead becomes less clear.

If now we wish to understand the implications of an event in a person's life, we shall, in terms of his kind of psychology, look not only at the event but also at the kind of wager that was laid on it. Events come and go without necessarily having anything to do with a person's psychological processes. Of themselves, they are neither validating nor invalidating, nor is it meaningful to describe some of them as reinforcements. Validity is a matter of the relationship between the event as it happened and what the person expected to happen. More correctly stated, it is the relationship between the event as he construed it to happen and what he anticipated.

It is in this relationship between anticipation and realization that the real fate of man lies. It is a fate in which he himself is always a key participant, not simply the victim. To miss this point and to allow ourselves to become preoccupied with independent forces, sociodynamics, psychodynamics, leprechaun theory, demonology, or stimulus-response mechanics, is to lose sight of the essential feature of the whole human enterprise.

Now let us strip the Procrustean legend of its rich narrative structive and trace the central theme of hostility in the more barren terminology of personal construct theory. A person has a construct system. It gives him identity. Right or wrong, it serves to put him in touch with reality. It provides him with grounds for formulating his anticipations, including his anticipations about people. Then, one day, perhaps after a long wait, his expectations are not confirmed. He is staggered by the implications of his disconfirmation for he has wagered more of his construct system on the outcome of his venture than he can afford to lose. If he accepts the outcome and all its presumed implications he will be left in a state of deep and pervading confusion.

But wait! There is still something he can do to save the situation. If he acts quickly he may be able to force the outcome to conform to his original expectations and give him a last-minute confirmation of his major premises about human nature. This is the hostile choice. The key to understanding hostility from the standpoint of the person himself is in this instant of decision. Or is it an instant of impulse—it makes no difference; this is where it is!

In the language of research, we may say that the hostile person distorts his data to fit his hypotheses. In the language of the classroom, he puts people in their place. In the language of economics, he extorts tokens of subservience to his system of values. In the language of the child, he threatens to scream loud enough to prove to the neighbors that his parents have made a horrible mistake. In the language of the divorce court, since his spouse did not conform to his idealized image of what a wife should be, the husband sees to it that she is exhibited to the world as the other kind of woman, "the kind of person he has always known most women were." Ditto, hostile wives and "the kind of person they always knew men were!" In the language of nations—we all know how clearly everything the enemy does expresses "his cruel and vicious nature."

Instead of saying that such goings-on are the outcroppings of hostility—hostility being an extrapersonal force that is supposed to invest the organism—we are saying that they are the hostility. The essence of hostility is not in its motivational property—anyone who is alive is on the move—but in its characteristic way of following up one's mistakes. It is the substitution of extortion for problem solving. It is the attempt to collect a bet on a horse that has already lost. The hostile person turns from events as they are to payoffs that belie reality. "See," he says, "I got paid, didn't I? That means I was right all along."

Psychologists make frequent use of the frustration-aggression hypothesis—the notion that the greater one's disappointment the more violently he will react to it. What we have been saying may appear to be a restatement of that hypothesis. But there are important differences. Hostility is not aggression, although the two terms are frequently used synonymously. The simplest way to look at aggression is to view it as adventuresomeness. It means actively formulating one's expectations specifically about many things, about big things and, sometimes, about remote matters. It means taking steps to bring one's hunches to test. And if oten means betting large stakes on the outcome.

While an aggressive person sticks his neck out, he is not necessarily hostile. He does not necessarily extort confirmation of personal hypotheses that have already proved themselves to be invalid. An aggressive conversationalist may press a point to the place where his companions have to come out and say exactly what they think. That, of course, is what the aggressive but nonhostile person wants to know. His companions may be furious at finding themselves smoked out but, unless their aggressive friend has a streak of hostility in him, he will not try to compromise them into agreeing with him. He only wants to know.

If we take the traditional view that hostility is the impulse to hurt, it is easy to see how aggression can be interpreted as hostility. The moment someone is hurt he cries "foul" or "ouch," and the aggressive person is immediately labeled as hostile, not so much because of any psychological property of his own make-up but because of the make-up of the person who is hurt. Of course, if we are rigorous about it, we can hold to the definition that hostility is present only when the actor *wants* to hurt someone. But this definition is hard to maintain in a world of social thought that describes persons in terms of how they are reacted to, rather than in terms of what they are up to. A psychology that is based on the outlook of man himself does not find it very helpful to define hostility in terms of its anticipated effect on others. It asks, instead, for an understanding of the hostile person in terms of what is at stake in his own life. If we want to understand Procrustes we talk to Procrustes, not Theseus. We talk to him about his bed. We talk to him about his role as a host. We find out what he expects guests to be like.

Now it is quite possible for an aggressive person to become hostile and, conversely, it is quite possible for a hostile person to pursue his extortionism by aggressive means. The aggressive conversationalist we mentioned may, for example, get himself so far out on a limb that when he discovers what his friends actually do think he may not be able to take it. He may then go to pieces in anxious confusion. Or he may pull in his horns. But he may—he just may—take the hostile course of action and try to put his friends in some kind of spot where they appear to confirm his point in spite of the realities of the social situation. On the other hand, take the person who is hostile to begin with. In his frantic efforts to make the data fit the hypothesis he may resort to vigorous measures. We can then say he is also aggressive. Not all hostile people do it this way; some express their hostility very effectively by the most passive of means. But they can. And when they do, it is correct to speak of aggressive hostility.

The frustration-aggression hypothesis, as any psychologist will tell you, is not a simple formula to apply. In order to use the formula one has to introduce a number of qualifications, both as to what is to be labeled frustration and what is to be construed as aggression. Nor can we, from the standpoint of the psychology of personal constructs, relabel the formula as a frustration-hostility hypothesis. The hostility is not proportional to the frustration—to say that would be to reduce the formula to the stimulus-response paradigm. The hostility is in the type of solution the person attempts—that is the personal construct theoretical view.

What about the person who is sadistic? Can we say that he is simply trying to make his experiment with social relations yield affirmative evidence? What if he feels like jumping up and down with glee and excitement every time he sees a person writhing in pain? Or what about the military flyers who slap each other on the back and show great delight at having scored a hit on a military target? Are they thinking of the agony they have left there on the ground? In either of these instances, our understanding of hostility would not place the psychological value primarily on the pain others experienced—even though we may reserve the right to judge such acts in terms of moral or social values—but on what is confirmed in the act. The sadist may (indeed, from our clinical experience we believe that he does) see in the other person's injury a long overdue confirmation of his own outlook, a confirmation that has been denied him in the natural state of affairs. The military aviator probably tries not to think of what is going on down on the ground in the target area in the wake of his bomb. In his case the suffering is less likely to be a relevant psychological variable. In both cases, what is happening to the other person is incidental, what is happening to the person himself is what is crucial.

It may be helpful to see hostility in the flesh. Before we illustrate in terms of case material, however, let us review the essential features of hostility from the standpoint of the psychology of personal constructs. A person construes human nature in his own way. He makes social predictions on the basis of this construction. To set the stage they must be crucial predictions; that is to say, he must have wagered more on them than he can afford to lose—more of his construct system, that is. He turns up invalidating evidence. It is clear that he was wrong about people. He can no longer ignore the fact. Moreover, he was overwhelmingly wrong—basically wrong. In the face of the harsh facts he can, of course, revise his outlook. But the revision would shake him so deeply that he is reluctant to undertake it. Alternatively, he could let matters ride—say to himself, "So I just don't understand people very well." But this too is an alternative he is reluctant to choose. Finally, he can close his eyes to reality and attempt to make people fit the construct bed his system provides. This is the hostile choice.

Consider a young woman, aged thirty. She grew up in a home where she was secure in her parents' love, where her father was a stable and constant figure and the neighborhood, with its beaches and sand dunes, was a safe and ever-interesting place to roam in search of childhood adventure. The only important male figure in her life, aside from her father, was a boy who was fenced out of that world with social taboos. At the turn of adolescence her girlfriends start to desert her and the forms of play they have enjoyed together and direct their attention to the female pursuit of catching boys with their newly found charms. What she had discovered, up to this time, to be true about both males and females now seems to be invalid. At first she is only puzzled. Later she is more than puzzled—she is confused and anxious. Her mother, too, seems perturbed that she seems so immature. What the child does not realize, of course, is that the mother knows that her own years are rapidly running out and she is unduly apprehensive lest her daughter still be a child when the time comes to go it alone. Soon the mother's death comes. The father is prostrated with grief and he is perceived by the child as letting her down. Her first efforts are to get herself another man. She will have a man, the kind of strong man her outlook insists men must be. Even cruelty is acceptable, if it is accompanied by strength. Yet, whatever male substitute she finds, the apparent failure of her father to live up to her expectations of him is still, to her, an inescapable fact. For a time she extorts from him the tokens of paternal support—clothes, luxuries, indulgences. This is hostility. But hostility is difficult to contain within reasonable bounds. She now has a disillusioned version of what men are—all men. To make a long story short, she fits all men, including her husband, into this Procrustean Bed. They are often surprised at how neatly she tricks them into confirming her hypotheses about the contemptible weak-kneed creatures. And so, to some extent, is she. Her gay and tantalizing manner is misleading. Like Procrustes, she is interested in people, she cannot live without their company. Like Procrustes, she is an excellent conversationalist. And, like Procrustes, she has a bed. Soon each man in her life wakes up to find that he has been chopped down to just the right size to fit it. This is hostility in the flesh.

Most psychotherapists understand, regardless of their theoretical persuasion, that the key to the alleviation of hostility lies in the proper use of aggression. The psychoanalysts and others look upon aggression as the dynamic feature of the hostile pattern and insist that it must be allowed to vent itself before it can be brought under self-control. The Rogerians provide an atmosphere of acceptance for their clients, in which we could say, in terms of the frustration-aggression hypothesis, that the frustration is minimized in order to keep the aggressive pressure down to a point where the person can gently come to terms with himself. (There is, of course, much more to both of these points of view.) Certainly both of these outlooks, I would insist, can be taken as grounds by clinicians for doing something effective about the hostility.

From the standpoint of the psychology of personal constructs, however, the emphasis is placed not on the conceptualization forces driving the individual in spite of himself but on what he himself does. Hostility is not a dynamism in the personality, it is part of the personality pattern. Unfortunate people are not acted upon by hostility, they themselves make the choices which are describable as hostile. The psychotherapist turns to aggressive experimentation under proper psychotherapeutic controls, not to drain it out, but in order to help the client find other ways of dealing with the invalidity that confronts him. He reinstates imaginative adventure, but with fresh ways of dealing with the outcomes. He helps the client to make use of negative evidence instead of displacing it with extorted and unrealistic positive evidence.

Probably all of us have daily bouts in some measure with hostility. Most of us are traditionally inclined to see this hostility as a force welling up within us. When seen in others, it is easy to interpret only as a desire to hurt, especially if we must bear the brunt. Yet whether we experience it in ourselves, or have to deal with it in our associates, the key to its understanding is an appreciation of the person himself. Behind the mask of his hostility, we find these key features: deep concern with social relations, his far-reaching convictions regarding human nature, the wager that he could not afford to lose, and his frantic effort to collect winnings long after the race was run and hopelessly lost.

14

The Threat of Aggression

THIS CONFERENCE has been convened to consider the topic of humanism in psychology. But I am not sure I have a very clear idea of what humanism is. Ostensibly it has something to do with man, though I have often doubted that it had to do with anyone I know. Nevertheless, I suppose that when psychologists get together and say that we ought to revive humanism it is because they are alarmed by the tendency of their disciplines to ignore man, except as an inexhaustible source of data, and to become preoccupied, instead, with their own bibliographies, expendable animals, and the rituals of laboratory science. A humanistic turn of events would, then, be one, I presume, in which the focal importance of living man would be reaffirmed, and psychology would no longer be pursued for its own sake.

Those who attempt to revive humanism are likely to point to the culture of classic Greece as an example of what they would like to restore. That culture, as I understand it, was characterized by man's audacity in the face of adversities imposed by the gods or by nature. Its heroes asserted themselves as men, as men they dared challenge what their history and their gods told them was inevitable, and as men they often suffered frustration and defeat. Yet while history, more often than not, continued to reaffirm its verdicts, the men we as humanists want to remember are those who refused to acquiesce to the facts of life.

SOURCE. Prepared for a conference on humanistic psychology, Old Saybrook, Connecticut, November 27–29, 1964, and also published in the *Journal of Humanistic Psychology*, 1965, **V**, 195–201. Acknowledgement is made of the kind permission of the Editor, *Journal of Humanistic Psychology* to include this paper.

HUMANISM AND CLASSICISM

But neohumanism, it seems to me, is often no more than a form of classicism; that is to say, a preoccupation with adventure as an historical fact, rather than a present enterprise, a preoccupation with a state of affairs to be revered and restored, phrase by phrase and stone by stone. And the modern classicist is related to the humanist's heroes of the Fourth Century B.C. or the Fifteenth Century A.D. in about the same way the Twentieth Century Daughters of the American Revolution are related to the Eighteenth Century signers of the Declaration of Independence.

There were, undoubtedly, classicists among the Greeks too, and it may be a little unfair to try to assess their role from this distance. Whatever it was they stood for, they were probably pretty skeptical of what was going on and I am sure they were always trying to revive something. I do not know what they managed to accomplish, but there is little reason to believe it was their influence that made Greek culture either humanistic or classic. Nor does our admiration for the humanism of other times and places make humanists of us now, any more than does tracing our ancestry to a hero who fought for civil rights in the American Revolution mean that we have any stomach for the civil rights battles of our own generation. Indeed, I must note that the most heroic figures in today's struggle for human values regard their ancestors more in pity than in pride.

Humanism is then, as I see it, not something we revive. Revivals are the work of classicists. Humanism, instead, has to do with the present, the novel, the defiant, the alive, and with what the classicists often argue cannot be done. Where the classicist documents historical certainties, the true humanist fumbles with present uncertainties. The classicist seeks to be historically right; the humanist continually risks being historically wrong in order to set something right. The humanist is aggressive, and hopes thus to achieve better things, but the classicist, threatened by the humanistic enterprise, equates aggression with hostility, and hostility, in turn, with destruction.

THE HUMANIST PARADOX

Now there is another theme in humanism. It is a secondary theme that derives from the first, and I think it makes sense only when expressed in the context of human audacity. This is the theme that whatever is truly characteristic of man is good and should therefore be preserved and protected against any distorting influence. Man, in the light of his audacious achievements, should be encouraged to go on being the kind of person he has so aptly proved himself to be; he should express himself; he should go right ahead and be audacious. But he should not be permitted to tamper with human nature; that is carrying audacity too far!

It is this secondary theme—a theme sometimes identified as permissiveness, sometimes as nonaggression, sometimes as respect for the dignity of man—that often colors the meaning of humanism. Thus, humanism appears to have created for itself a paradox. The audacity of man in general has proved to be so valuable a human asset that the audacity of any particular man must be restrained from impinging upon it. Man must express himself—that is very very important—but never, never must he express himself in such a way that anything human will be affected.

One way out of this paradox is to believe that the nature of man is such that if he does express himself—his true self—he will harmonize with all other men who truly express themselves. This is to say that the intrinsic nature of man is intrinsically compatible with its collective self, and that disharmonies arise only out of extrinsic distortions, or, possibly, out of temporary immaturities.

Another way out is to say that man cannot be manipulated except as his nature conspires. Whatever he does, it is he who does it. And the fact that he does it under certain imposed conditions in no way denies his dignity, but, instead, stands as a credit to his personal achievement ("under optimal psychological conditions," as we sometimes say). A child learns to play the piano well by being forced to practice four hours a day. That is not suppression; that is a human accomplishment. When he grows up he will probably be proud of it—and perhaps think of himself as a first class humanist. A depressed person is disciplined to a hospital routine of scrubbing floors and scouring toilets. As a result he finds himself too busy to worry. So, again, man prevails! See how the organism's ingenious adaptability has contrived to substitute reality for imagination? How fortunate! Not everyone is able to do that!

But it is difficult for me to see how either of these constructions can provide an escape from the humanist's paradox. The interpretation of man as a naturally harmonious being, who likes other people in proportion to his admiration of himself, seems to ignore the fact of human tyranny. Whether he can rise above this unpleasant fact is another question. But it appears to me to be as presumptuous to regard man as naturally good as it is to label him as inherently evil. Moreover, we are still much too busy sorting out good from evil to be altogether clear about which is which, or whether man is wholly one or the other.

The other construction of man—the construction of him as an ingenious conformist, a slave who is smart enough to know his place—is not very encouraging to the fellow who doesn't want to be a slave, or practice his music lessons, or live in Levittown, but on the banks of Walden Pond. He persists in thinking that under other circumstances he might accomplish a lot more. He may be right. And then, again, he may be wrong, for some men do accomplish more under a reinforcement schedule than when left to their own devices. And what is the humanist going to say about that?

THE MEANING OF THREAT

The human enterprise is, at best, a touch-and-go proposition. Any assumptions we make about what is good, or what is evil, or what will open the door to the future, are best regarded as only temporary, and any conclusions we draw from our experiences are best seen as approximations of what we may eventually understand. The human quest is not about to be concluded, nor is truth already partly packaged for distribution and consumption. Instead, it seems likely that whatever may now appear to be the most obvious fact will look quite different when regarded from the vantage point of tomorrow's fresh theoretical positions. Yet it is a misfortune that man should be so set on being right at the very outset that he dares not risk stupidities in an effort to devise something better than what he has.

This brings us back to the audacity of man, which, as you already know, I have come to regard as the primary humanistic theme. I like that theme. But let us not overlook the fact that this audacity is the very thing that men fear when they see it about to be expressed—and as often admire when it has run its course. In a world where vast experiments are being undertaken, where new psychological devices are being employed, and strange societies are being constituted, we dread the far-reaching implications of what is about to happen to us.

This is threat. To feel that one is on the threshold of deep changes in himself and his way of life is, I think, its essential feature. Threat is, from this point of view, an impending personal experience, not a set of ominous circumstances. Moreover, it is in the context of threat—or dread—that the two terms, aggression and hostility, become subjectively synonymous. This is to say that to encounter either in the actions of another person is to raise the specter of transformation in oneself. And may I point out also the curious fact that the two terms have become synonyms both in the language that diplomats use and in the language that psychologists use—as well, it seems, as in the language that humanists speak.

So how do we encourage human audacity without inviting one man's initiative to suppress another's? This is the humanist's dilemma. It is also the dilemma of democracy—how do you give political sovereignty to a people, or a state, bent on suppressing its minorities? So, also, it is the problem of the economist—how can you have a free enterprise system that produces the Bell Telephone Company, and still claim that you have anything that even remotely resembles free enterprise? And it is the problem of the liberal scholar—what happens when you are liberal with the board of trustees of a state university?

AGGRESSION

Before trying to find a humanistic answer to these questions, let me turn to a psychological matter. We call aggressive men hostile because what they do seems destructive, especially when it is pointed in our direction. We don't want them to meddle with our lives. Thus we judge them not so much by the character of their acts as by our own characteristic response to their initiative.

But what happens to us is not to be confounded with what is happening within them. What they undertake is not measured by what we experience. If one is to have an adequate psychology of man, it must be a psychology of the actor, not the victim. This is to say that behavior needs to be explained within the fact, not before or after the fact. Our own reaction to what another person attempts is scarcely enough to account for what he is trying to accomplish. Nor do our hurt feelings constitute a psychological analysis of his behavior.

Now may I go on to say that this equating of aggression with our projection of destructive intent is the outcome of Nineteenth Century notions about scientific determinism. To think scientifically about the psychology of man has seemed to mean that we must regard him as an intervening variable—called an "organism"—in a stimulus-response couplet. Our ventures collapse when challenged by an aggressive colleague. How shall we explain it? Simple! The collapse is the observed response; he is the obvious stimulus; and we are the organismic victim caught in the S-R squeeze. His aggression caused our downfall; and what more do you need to explain what the rascal was up to?

A stimulus-response psychology is, of course, one in which human responses are explained in terms of their external antecedents—their stimuli. And stimuli, in such a system, are reciprocally explained in terms of what they produce—their responses. That is the solipsism, or "equation," as we prefer to call it in mathematics. If I am threatened, then the person whom I see as the stimulus explains my experience. If I can cope with his aggression only by contemplating a profound change in myself, then the scoundrel must be hostile. Psychotherapists will recognize this as something that turns up rather frequently among their patients. But it is much more widespread than that; it is a conclusion commonly reached by all those who live out their lives according to the formula of stimulus-response.

But stimulus-response psychology is not the only possible kind of psychology. We can, if we wish, employ a psychology which casts its explanations in terms of what the person himself is doing, not what others do to him or what they think he has done to them. Aggression, in such a psychological system, is more akin to initiative. It is an expression of the audacity of man, even as he ventures into the realm of psychology. The aggressive man—like the humanist—may be one who risks being wrong in order to set something right—or in order to find out what rightly explains his fellow man.

HOSTILITY

Now hostility, in this way of thinking, may, or may not, involve aggression, and aggression may, or may not, involve hostility. The two constructs are propositionally independent of each other. If we are to employ a notion of hostility within this kind of psychological system we must understand the hostile person's enterprise in terms of his own outlook, not merely in terms of the threat that others experience when they seek to come to terms with him.

Since any system of psychology must provide some explanation of the means by which a person checks up on himself, it becomes important to understand how the implications of such a checkup are incorporated. In stimulus-response theory the checkup is cast in terms of reinforcement, that is to say, by ascribing some kind of stimulus quality to the response itself, or to its consequences, which will feed back into the system. But in personal construct theory the checkup is provided by confirmation of expectations. This is to say that if the expectations that follow from one's construction of events continually fail to materialize, a revision of the construction system is called for. This means that defeat must be recognized, failure identified, and even tragedy experienced if man is to survive, and all the more so if man is to achieve anything of epic proportions.

But a major revision of one's construct system can threaten him with immediate change, or chaos, or anxiety. Thus it often seems better to extort confirmation of one's anticipations—and therefore of the system that produced them—rather than to risk the utter confusion of those moments of transition. It is this extortion of confirmation that characterizes hostility.

A nation, before admitting that its long leap forward in the defense of human life has proved invalid, may destroy millions of lives when they disclose evidence of the failure of the system. A country may go to war to displace responsibility for its mistakes. A man may commit murder to discredit what has proved him wrong. And, since hostility may as easily employ passivity as aggression, we may resort either to spiteful "obedience" or "respect for law" to simulate the missing validity in a crumbling societal system. Or, in a family whose structure is no longer viable, we may offer indulgence to replace affection and to smother a child's unexpected independence.

Nevertheless, whether undertaken by aggressive or passive means, hostility is, in a personal construct theoretical system, an extortional undertaking designed by the person to protect a heavy investment in his own construction of life. And if, perchance, his hostility proves destructive of others, then that, unfortunately, is the way it must be. The economy must be preserved; the fact that the elderly starve in India or on the other side of town is incidental. Heresy must be controlled; too bad that intellectual curiosity on the campus must be denied. Bombs must be dropped; to be sure children will die, but who can say it was we who put them in the target area? From our point of view, it is a precious way of life that we defend—Cadillacs and all. But what the hostile man does not know is that it is he who is the eventual victim of his own extortion. With the adoption of hostility he surrenders his capacity to judge the outcome of his way of life, and without that capacity he must inevitably go astray.

The acknowledgment of defeat or tragedy is not a destructive step for man to take. It characterizes, instead, the negative outcome of any crucial test of our way of life, and it is, therefore, an essential feature of human progress toward more positive outcomes. Hostility does not, for this very reason, contribute to human achievement. Primarily because it denies failure it leads, instead, to the abatement of human enterprise, and substitutes for nobler undertakings a mask of complacency.

A STEP FOR THE HUMANIST

In this way of thinking, which I have proposed for the humanistically inclined psychologist, there are three key notions that must be lifted from the context of stimulus-response psychology and recast in the light of a psychology of the man himself. They are *threat, aggression,* and *hostility.* Threat, for the man himself, is the experience of being on the brink of a major shift in his core construct system. Aggression, for the man himself, is one's own initiative, not what that initiative may lead another to do or feel. And so with hostility, too; hostility is the extortion of confirming evidence to present to oneself when there seems too much at stake to undertake the personal changes that natural evidence requires.

The humanistic psychologist's dilemma—how to protect human audacity from human audacity without stifling human audacity—finds another kind of solution when we manage to step outside the stimulus-response solipsism. It is the hostile, and not necessarily the aggressive enterprise, that must be guarded against. The aggressive effort to understand man, or to experiment with ways of accomplishing psychological feats never before achieved, is not intrinsically destructive. It may, of course, be hazardous. It does become destructive, however, when one tries to make it appear that disconfirming events did not actually arise, or that what failed to occur actually happened. And this, in turn, is generated by the notion that we ought always to be right before we commit ourselves, a notion that later makes it very hard to concede our mistakes, or to revise our construction of the world when our heavily invested anticipations fail to materialize.

Humanism reflects audacity in man. But this audacity, when it substitutes extortion for disconfirmation, disengages itself from the world and abandons the future of mankind. Humanism, while it openly experiences defeat, does not succumb to it, for to do that would be to give up man's aggressive undertakings altogether, and, with them, all the aspirations that arise from being tragically human. Thus, the experience of tragedy, and not the sense of certainty, is the basis of all hope, and is indeed the most essential step in the bold pursuit of better things. And that, I submit, is a notion that lies close to the heart of the human enterprise.

15

The Role of Classification in Personality Theory

A THEORY IS a device to enable man to deal comprehensively with
what might otherwise be an overwhelming variety of events. Some
of the events may not even yet have occurred. Moreover, there are
myriads of them—some fascinating, some propitious, some perhaps
catastrophic—that may indeed never occur unless a theory prompts
someone to undertake them.

Strictly speaking, man invents his theory; he never discovers it.
What he discovers, often to his dismay, is how well the theory works.
But even that, as I suspect every venturesome theorist is painfully
aware, often turns out to be a matter of taste and momentary convenience. But whether or not it works to suit its users, the theoretician
must hold himself responsible for what he has contrived. Much as
he might like to shift the responsibility, he cannot ever claim that
his theory was dictated by the facts it seeks to explain. The facts tell
him only when he is wrong—and not always that. And besides, there
simply are too many ways of explaining the same facts—including
a lot of ways that haven't turned up yet—for any of us to claim
privileged communication with either God or Nature.

SOURCE. Prepared for a conference convened by the American Psychiatric Association on "The role and methodology of classification in psychiatry and psychopathology" in Washington, D.C., November 19–21, 1965. Published in M. Katz,
J. O. Cole & W. E. Barton (Eds.) *Classification in Psychiatry and Psychopathology*,
Chevy Chase, U.S. Public Health Service, 1968. Published here by permission of
the U.S. Public Health Service.

The process by which a theory is devised is known as abstraction, and the complementary process by which it is extended to events is known as generalization. Both may properly be regarded as psychological processes, or even as aspects of the same psychological process. That is to say, to understand them one may, instead of relying upon the principles of logic, employ some notion of man's style of life. Thus meaning is not extracted from nature, but projected by man upon it.

Neither abstraction nor generalization has ever been computerized, nor can either be realized by any unimaginative obedience to the canons of rationality, or by performing the symbolic transformations of mathematics, useful as these procedures may otherwise be. What can be computerized, for example, is the elimination of redundancy in a construction matrix. The resultant shrinkage in the matrix is sometimes mistaken for abstraction, for it appears to result in the expression of a great deal in relatively few terms. But the contribution the computer makes is to the economy of the language employed, not to conceptualization; albeit one must grant that linguistic parsimony may serve to clear away the clutter that stands in the way of fresh thinking. But housecleaning is not abstraction, and economizing does not constitute theoretical thinking. Occam's razor is a surgical instrument, not a creative tool.

A CONSTRUCTION MATRIX

By a *construction matrix* I mean a postulated grid in which events and abstractions are so interlaced that whatever appears to occur independently of one's intention is given meaning in depth by being plotted against whatever coordinate reference axes he has intentionally erected. And in this psychological hyperspace the humanly contrived axes of reference, in turn, acquire whatever objective significance they have through extension—or through "operationalizing," if one prefers a term that has more current usage.

This is to say that human constructions derive their objectivity wholly from the way they cast events into varying arrays—or simply from the lines of perspective they provide. Actually it is in terms of such arrays that consensual judgment becomes psychologically possible. Consensus itself, while often cited as the criterion of objectivity, does not properly define the psychological grounds on which objectivity rests. Only sociological grounds are implied.

But now, since we are talking about human experience, including our own particular experience as scientists, it may be more precise, instead of saying that the matrix is a schema in which events and abstractions are interlaced, to say it is man's observations and his constructs that are woven into the fabric of experience—the one ascribing meaning to the other and the other lending palpability to the one. And in this more phenomenological sense the grid might better be characterized as a "repertory grid," since it expresses one's own finite system of cross-references between the personal observations he has made and the personal constructs he has erected. I suppose it is apparent that all of us must have quite limited repertories, for the events we encounter are experienced only in such depth as our constructions will plumb, and our constructs have only that scope which is provided by the ranges of events to which we undertake to apply them.

A THEORY AS A PSYCHOLOGICAL VENTURE

In these few sentences I have tried to sketch the principles that are involved when one seeks to understand a theory as a psychological venture, rather than as a logical entity. Perhaps I have tried to say too much in altogether too little space. Obviously the far-flung implications of this psychological approach to human theorizing have not yet been mentioned. Nor do I have any intention of trying to spell them all out, except as they bear upon the problem addressed by this conference—"The role and methodology of classification in psychiatry and psychopathology."

What I have said is that a theory is a human contrivance, not something for which a man can escape personal responsibility by claiming he discovered it somewhere, that the abstraction process by which he fabricates his theory is a reflection of his own strategy for coping with events, and not a means of distilling truth out of the events themselves, that the condensation of a construction matrix—or *information net*, if you prefer a more limited and mechanistic notion—through the elimination of superfluous data and redundant terms is not to be confounded with abstraction, that man comes to grips with his existence by plotting his observations against his constructs and by testing his constructs against his observations, that meaning in the human role each man plays is limited by the variety of constructs he is able to devise, and that our constructions have no more substance to them than the extent of the events to which they are applied.

THE SCIENTIST AS A MAN,
OR MAN AS A SCIENTIST

There is something interesting that happens when one examines theorizing as a psychological process. He finds himself describing his own psychological efforts in the same terms he uses to account for those persons about whom he is psychologizing. This can be disconcerting, and, depending on the amount of cynicism built into his favorite personality theory, can lead to his having some very grave doubts about the validity of his efforts.

Most psychologists get around this by using different theoretical frameworks to explain the behavior of the scientist and the behavior of the ordinary man. For example, the scientist, they will say, systematically formulates his outlook, generates hypotheses from it, boldly ventures to make predictions, undertakes audacious experiments, courageously pits speculations against outcomes, candidly observes what happens, and completes the experiential cycle by humbly revising his outlook from the fresh vantage point to which his earlier naive commitments have led him. But ordinary men are held accountable in quite different terms. They are believed to be conditioned by the events that impinge upon them, sucked into the vacuums created by their needs, propelled by drives that invade their otherwise placid lives, caught up in the wake of their cultures, locked into the orbits of their biographies—lacking the imagination to attempt anything they have not rehearsed—or kept alive and kicking only by yielding to the persistent nagging of external stimuli.

But whatever we say about the behavior of the scientist is itself a personality theory, even though we may seek to limit its application to licensed scientists, or to other classes of "white folks." On the other hand, whatever we choose to say about human behavior in general is a personality theory that must deal not only with man's indiscretions, but hold itself accountable also for the structure of the scientific edifice that man, and man only, is known to have produced.

CATEGORIES AS OBSTACLES
TO THEORETICAL DEVELOPMENT

What happens when we undertake either to view the scientists as a man or man as a scientist? We get into categorical difficulties. And it is to just such difficulties imposed by categorization on theoretical thinking that a conference on classification, such as this one, should address itself.

If we view the scientist as a man we must regard his science with the same incredulity we apply to human behavior in general. This is to say that most of us would then have to claim that one's science is a symptom of his psychodynamics, or perhaps a product of his operant conditioning, though modulated, to be sure, by the psychodynamics—or the conditioning—of those with whom he is dynamically identified, or to whom he is conditioned. Thus, if we were to persist in accounting for scientists in terms of current psychological theories about men, I think we would soon be led to the conclusion that science is more a human predicament than a vital undertaking. On the other hand, if we apply the scientist paradigm to man, we someday are going to catch ourselves saying, in the midst of a heated family discussion, that our child's temper tantrum is best understood as a form of scientific inquiry.

In the one case—in the case of understanding science psychologically—we are limited by current personality theories that have never had to bridge the categorical boundaries customarily set up between natural logic and human behavior. Thus, by holding to the stubborn belief that science is human only when it is in error, we perpetuate some preposterous myths about the pure scientific enterprise. In the other case we are blocked by the ancient barriers that in Western culture seal off the classical categories of cognition, affect, and action. So we argue that since a temper tantrum has been categorized as an eruption of affect, one need accept no obligation to explain it in terms consistent with cognition. In each case, therefore, instead of using our constructs as reference axes in terms of which events can be seen in multidimensional depth, we continue to use them to construct pigeonholes in which events are tucked away and rendered inaccessible to other dimensions of appraisal.

But why not go all out and suggest that science, as we know it today, may be a reasonably apt—perhaps a tragically apt—statement of this century's human predicament? Or, if we may be permitted to take science itself as the model of a personality theory, why not then regard the child's temper tantrum as a frantic experimental effort to articulate some urgent question about human relationships for which no one so far has been willing to give him a candid answer? Why not? Why, in the first place, we say, because science "obviously" is a logical statement about nature itself, and therefore could not possibly be a Twentieth Century illusion created by man! Why not? Why,

in the second place, we say, "a temper tantrum is an emotional out-
burst," and therefore clearly could not be a cognitive inquiry! Thus
we see examples of the categorical barriers that block the free use
of theory in the extension of human inquiry.

A THEORY AS AN AID TO
CREATIVE THINKING

One of the unique functions of a theory is to enable man to reach
beyond what he already knows. Having devised a system of constructs,
and given it anchorage in his observations, one may state the parameters of some event he has never seen, but which might reasonably
be expected to occur under certain conditions. Thus a good theory
is fertile soil for producing something new, whether a new way of
coping with mental disorder or a fresh approach to the education of
the child. For my own part, I would place fertility at the top in any
list of criteria for a good theory, particularly for a good personality
theory. This, however, is not to overlook the importance of coherence,
relevance, comprehensiveness, parsimony, verifiability, rigor, and predictive efficiency in theory construction.

From this point of view, categorization, helpful as it may be for
certain practical purposes, proves itself to be almost completely sterile
in suggesting something new to be looked for. It rarely leads to experimentation, and while at times it may challenge one's legalistic ingenuity in reaching a "diagnosis," it fails to set one's imagination
on fire. It does, of course, tend to narrow down a scientist's field of
inquiry, and on some occasions that may be just what he needs in
order to develop a new construct more precisely within some limited
range of convenience. Yet "hardening of the categories," a common
affliction among scientists, usually marks the end of the creative phase
of a distinguished career.

EFFORTS TO ESCAPE
CATEGORICAL RESTRAINTS

From time to time in the history of human thought men have
been acutely aware of the barriers that categorization has raised against

their efforts to do creative thinking. It is no accident that dogmatism, the moat that surrounds all bastions of classical ignorance, is characteristically categorical in its logical form.

Among the obstacles produced by categorical thinking probably none has been more frequently assailed than that imposed by the dualism of mind versus body—or the spiritual versus the material. Typically the efforts to transcend this duality have taken the form of placing everything into one category or the other, as, for example, in idealism and materialism, or by envisioning some sort of interaction between mental things and physical things, as when we speak of psychosomatic disorders. But rarely in science have we given thoughtful considerations to the implications of categorization itself, and to the occasions when it would be better to structure our scientific efforts in other ways.

But now this conference has been called, and I am sure there is more afoot here than merely another updating of the approved system of psychiatric nomenclature. The notion of mental illness has itself been seriously challenged for the first time since the days of the Nancy School. Even the continued use of the so-called medical model in psychiatry is being thoughtfully questioned. Social psychiatry has brought fresh attention to the nature of psychological processes and has given relatively little play to pathological categories. Almost every new contribution to personality theory or to methods of treatment—from psychoanalysis to tranquilizers—has downgraded the importance of categorization of disorders and substituted some abstracted notions about how man copes with his circumstances. The new emphasis is upon what man does, rather than upon what happens to him—upon what he undertakes, rather than the state he is in.

CONSTRUCTS AS REFERENCE AXES RATHER THAN AS DENOMINATIONS OF EVENTS

Up to this point I have been comparing and contrasting the aims of theorizing with the effects of categorization. I have pointed out that they usually serve different ends and that they too often get in the way of each other. But categorization, with its preemptive claim to the events it structures, is only one of the forms of classification, and since this conference has to do with the role of classification in general rather than categorization in particular, we may ask ourselves if there is not some other way to engage in classification without obstructing the development of better personality theories.

The key to our problem lies, I believe, in distinguishing clearly between the events we wish to control and the constructs we devise for understanding them. In terms of the repertory grid I have invited you to envision, this means differentiating sharply between what is warp and what is woof. This is to say that any clinical observation we make has meaning only in terms of the constructs with reference to which we choose to plot it. And our constructs, in turn, are not homologous with the events they enable us to understand, even though our language is grammatically constructed to make them appear that way.

We observe a patient's behavior. But it makes no sense until we plot it with reference to some such notion as, say, *anxiety*. This does not mean that what we have observed is of itself an anxiety. It means, instead, that if we construe it in terms of anxiety it begins to make sense. Similarly anxiety is not to be regarded as a particular collection of behaviors, but rather as a notion we have invented in terms of which the events observed in a patient's life appear to fall into some orderly array. Anxiety, then, is not a category of patients, nor is it even a category of symptoms, but it is a contrived reference axis against which any behavioral observation may be plotted, even including observations that may stand out much more clearly in the light of other constructs.

PROPOSITIONAL RATHER THAN CONSTELLATORY RELATIONSHIPS

In this kind of epistemology constructs are propositionally related to each other rather than bearing constellatory obligations to each other, or preemptively excluding each other. Let me explain what I mean. I observe a bit of behavior. It makes sense, it seems to me, to regard it as an expression of anxiety. That is to say I have made a proposition about its position in relation to my notion of anxiety. But does this mean that I must also regard it as neurotic? Not necessarily, for I may, if I wish, devise a construct of neuroticism which does not embrace all forms of anxiety. The two constructs thus need not be constellatorily related in my chain of inference. And certainly I do not need to insist that my diagnosis of anxiety precludes all other considerations. This would be preemptive construction, and it represents the worst of what can happen in a system of diagnostic categories—the worst, that is, from the point of view of a theoretician who is always hoping to see things in a new and better light.

Theory building relies heavily upon the propositional use of constructs. Thus the theoretician, no less than the dedicated psychotherapist, keeps himself alert to potentialities not yet realized in a patient's life. But the more practical and decision-oriented a clinician becomes the more he hastens to group his constructs into constellations, making inferences from his placement of an event on one reference axis to its probable placement on another. He might, for example, say that because his patient's behavior looms up so clearly in the light of his anxiety axis he had better go ahead and regard it as neurotic too. And in hospital management, where so frequently the most urgent decision made during the first week is to which of the overcrowded wards the patient should be sent, the clinical director is only too happy to have the fellow tentatively, but preemptively, consigned to a diagnostic category before the intake staff takes off for the day.

So far I have described the theoretician's constructs as reference axes for appraising objects, rather than as names for objects or groups of objects. And I have pointed to the theoretical advantage of using them propositionally, so that the full range of implications of each construct dimension can be explored separately without being encumbered by the implications of other constructs previously assumed to be related to it. For example, we can examine empirically all the implications arising out of the construct of anxiety, without necessarily having to concern ourselves with neuroticism.

THE NONCATEGORICAL USE OF CLASSIFICATION: CLUSTER REFERENTS

Now it is possible to employ classification in science without resorting to categorization. Biologists, who are oldtimers in the categorization game, are just beginning to catch on to this notion, but librarians and efficient secretaries have known about it for a long time. Used in this way classification becomes a system of cross-referencing or indexing. Of course the books are physically located on some shelf and the papers have been put in some particular folder, and that much of it is categorical. But you don't keep track of the books and papers by running from shelf to shelf and from file to file. In this sense the classes not only overlap, but cut across each other, as the terms of classification are rotated into alignment with other axes of reference.

When we use classification in this noncategorical way the classes are retained as abstractions and are not walled off concretistically to encapsulate events. Though they have the logical form of classes, they are actually used as nonparametric reference axes. A particular set of behavior observations, for example, can then be described all at once as "anxious," "fragmented," "flattened," and "hallucinatory"— assuming that these classes can be clinically distinguished. Nor does this require that any of these be regarded as a subset of another.

In describing the observations in this way we have plotted them according to their proximity to certain criterion events whose projections have been clustered along four parametric reference axes—anxiety, fragmentation, flattening, and hallucination. But the behavior observations we are to classify are not, in this usage, related to the reference axes directly; instead, they are understood in terms of their proximity to clusters of other observations which have been so rated. This is what we do, for example, when we use a ward behavior rating scale and come up with a "diagnostic" profile of each patient's behavior. This procedure permits some retention of the abstractness of the classification system, although it sacrifices a certain amount of conceptual precision and flexibility. Moreover, one need not find himself hopelessly confronted with the barriers that are erected by disease entity thinking or by other forms of categorization that raise dogmatic obstacles to creative or analytic inquiry.

FACILITATING THE CLINICIAN-THEORETICIAN EXCHANGE

Ideally, from the point of view of a personality theorist, it is most important for any system we use to maintain a clear distinction between events and reference axes—or between observations and constructs—keeping in mind particularly the postulated nature of the latter, and keeping in mind also the interplay between the two in producing meaning for events, and tangibility for constructs. If, for example, a clinician speaks of anxiety, the theoretician will shudder at any implication that anxiety was what was observed, instead of being the postulated dimension of reference for the clinician's observations—or the cluster of behavioral criterion referents he judged to be similar.

The theoretician is always concerned with envisioning fresh ways of looking at man, and if what is brought to his attention comes all sealed up in some clinician's favorite conceptual wrappers with a note that it must be taken or left in the state in which it was delivered, he is likely to feel that there is nothing he can now contribute except, possibly, to bundle up the packages into gross cartons without breaking their seals. This is precisely what happens to the research psychologist when he is asked to "come in and do research" on a twenty-year accumulation of clinical records. All he can find in the files are the wrappings within which the original observations were once classified. The observations themselves, which might have provided some grounds for reconstruing patients and their behaviors, have long since been lost—probably never got beyond the interviewing rooms where they originally occurred. "Doing research" on case files has, in my experience, always proved to be a waste of time as far as personality theory is concerned. In fact I am inclined to argue that the nosological system in current use does more to impede the development of improved personality theories than to accelerate it. If we cannot replace it, we ought, at least, to abandon it.

UNIVERSAL REFERENCE AXES— NOW, IF POSSIBLE

But if the convocation of this conference means we have now reached that stage of scientific and philosophical enlightenment where we can stop erecting categorical barriers in dealing with patients, and can regard the patient as the entity rather than the disease as the entity, and, furthermore, if we are at a point where we can use our constructs as multiple reference axes—plotting each set of observations against a set of key constructs, as physicists do with their notions of *mass, time,* and *energy,* then this conference may prove to be most timely.

Perhaps I should have attempted to suggest what such a key set of constructs for psychiatrists might be. I don't know whether *anxiety,* for example, could be made a universal reference axis against which psychiatric records would project all diagnosed cases. Certainly it is a notion widely employed in diagnosis, and in spite of the variety of notions about its derivation, seems to lend itself to considerable consensus in clinical observation. The construct of *projection* also suggests itself, though it may have picked up too much of a constellation of other constructs. It therefore might better be replaced by a more propositional reference axis, such as the I-E axis—internal versus external perception of the locus of control. Certainly *schizophrenia* is much too constellated in current usage to serve as a reference axis but *loosened construction,* often used in one form or another as a term in putting together a diagnosis of thought-disordered schizophrenia, might have possibilities.

There are many others that might be candidates for a universal system of reference axes, but I have here limited myself rather strictly to the topic assigned me in' this conference—the role and function of classification in personality theory. Besides, the proposal of a complete set of significant constructs is a rather large undertaking. I doubt that I am up to it.

Even if it does not prove practicable for the participants in this conference to go all the way and recognize the appropriateness of postulated reference axes that give the best theoretical structure to clinical observations, and if we must, instead, temporize by endorsing the notion of a noncategorical classification system based on relating our observations to two or more clusterings of events, we shall have made some worthwhile progress. Simply to look at a bit of behavior, first in terms of its gross similarity to one type of criterion cluster—or set, if you prefer to relate this to mathematical set theory—and then to view it in terms of its similarity to other sets, is at least to put it in a concrete perspective. Certainly a concrete perspective is better than none at all. Each concrete referent set can be used as a vantage point from which to view the behavior of the man, and while we may be pretty fuzzy about what abstract constructs are being invoked, perhaps at long last we can break out of our categories and come to see the man from the perspective provided by simultaneously having more than one viewing angle.

16

Nonparametric Factor Analysis
of Personality Theories

N. I. FARBEROW and E. S. Shneidman (1961) have recently published a book in which eight different personality theorists deal with the clinical problem of suicide. In order to focalize the points of theoretical similarity and difference the authors presented to each theorist-clinician the summary of a protocol prepared by N. D. Tabachnick, psychiatrist. The protocol was a summarized report of a series of anamnestic interviews with Mr. A. S., a 23-year-old man who had made a serious attempt at suicide. The contributors were asked to expound their systematic positions with respect to suicide in general and then to make a blind analysis of the protocol summary. In addition, the participants were given a set of 76 cards on each of which appeared a different statement that might or might not be judged as applicable to the patient. They were then asked to Q-sort the statements into a format normally distributed into nine categories. Six participants replied to this request. A few illustrative items are reproduced in Table 1.

One of the theorists, H. L. Ansbacher, has raised the question of what a factor analysis may reveal about the relationships between the clinical judgments. Do Q-sorts applied to a particular case throw light on the differences between the clinical implications of various theories? This information of itself would be of considerable psychologi-

SOURCE. Reprinted from *Journal of Individual Psychology*, **19**, 115–147, November, 1963, by permission.

TABLE 1

Illustrative Items from the Q-Sort Deck and Their
Ratings by Six Theoreticians[a]

No.	Theoreticians' Ratings					
	Fut.	Klo.	Ans.	Gre.	Kel.	Dia.[b]
1. He likes and seeks the companionship of others	4	2	3	3	2	3
2. He usually withdraws in social situations	2	6	5	4	6	4
3. He is obviously uncomfortable in his contacts with authority.	4	3	6	5	5	1
4. He gives in immediately when attacked	6	4	5	4	6	7
5 He seems to adapt to his environment quite well.	6	5	6	5	7	8
6. Nearly all his interpersonal relationships are superficial.	2	7	4	3	1	4
7. He meets aggression from others with counter-aggression.	9	5	5	8	3	5
8. He has very few friends.	4	4	2	3	3	3
9. He blames himself when criticized.	1	3	4	3	5	5
10. He has difficulty in relating to people.	4	5	5	4	3	1
16. He is rather cold and impersonal in his interactions with women.	5	8	7	5	5	2
17. He goes out of his way to please people.	6	1	6	2	5	3
20. He tends to retreat from the stress and strain of everyday living.	7	5	1	3	1	3
31. He retreats when other people become aggressive toward him.	3	4	3	4	6	5
39. He faces unpleasant situations in a direct manner.	5	7	9	7	9	7
46. His relations with mother figures are fairly happy.	9	4	3	7	2	5
72. He adapts fairly easily to authority demands.	7	3	2	4	4	9
74. He is rather neutral toward others.	4	6	4	5	5	6

[a] From *The cry for help*, by N. L. Farberow & E. S. Shneidman (eds.), pp. 307–310. Copyright 1961. McGraw-Hill Book Company, Inc. Used by permission.

[b] Samuel Futterman, Bruno Klopfer, Heinz L. Ansbacher, Maurice R. Green, George A. Kelly, Solomon Diamond.

TABLE 2

Interrelations Between Theoreticians on Q-Sorts for Mr. A. S.[a]

	Futterman	Klopfer	Ansbacher	Green	Kelly	Diamond
Futterman		.21	.21	.38	.06	.23
Klopfer			.48	.33	.16	.13
Ansbacher				.53	.56	.28
Green					.38	.33
Kelly						.50
Diamond						

[a] From *The cry for help*, by N. L. Farberow & E. S. Shneidman (Eds.), P. 312. Copyright 1961. McGraw-Hill Book Company, Inc. Used by permission.

cal interest, since recent studies have raised doubt as to whether the theoretical orientations of experienced clinicians actually make any difference in the way they go about handling their cases.

But there is also another intriguing possibility. If we put our minds to it, we may be able to contrive some new and discriminating device for bringing to light the essential likenesses and differences among any given set of theories. That also seems worth trying.

Now let us see what we can do with these two possibilities. Suppose we start with Farberow and Shneidman's intercorrelations between the Q-sort data they obtained. These are shown in Table 2. Upon a suggestion by Ansbacher, Harold Gulliksen in discussion with Sam

TABLE 3

Conventional Factor Analysis of Theoretical Differences[a]

Clinician	Theory	Factor Loadings			h^2
		1	2	3	3f
Futterman	Freudian	.38	− .37	.38	.43
Klopfer	Jungian	.48	− .33	− .23	.39
Ansbacher	Adlerian	.79	− .06	− .32	.74
Green	Sullivanian	.68	− .19	.11	.51
Kelly	Personal construct	.69	.47	− .04	.71
Diamond	Nondirective	.54	.27	.32	.46

[a] From personal communication by Harold Gulliksen to H. L. Ansbacher.

Messick and Henrietta Gallagher computed a parametric factor analysis of the data. His factor loadings and communalities are shown in Table 3.

INFORMATION PROVIDED
BY FACTOR ANALYSIS

It is to be noted that Gulliksen's factorial composition of three factors is anchored in terms of theoreticians. If we are sure we know what the theoreticians stand for, we can make an educated guess as to what the factors represent. But suppose whatever the theoreticians stand for is precisely what we want to find out. In this case our guess will not be so educated, though we can make some secondary inferences from the net of interrelationships represented by the factors.

An alternative approach would have been to anchor the factorial construction in terms of items. But in this case we tend to lose track of the theories. Whether, in the final analysis, such an alternative approach would yield any meaning not produced by the standard approach is a matter of some difference of opinion among factor analysts, though it seems to me that in a problem of this sort the two methods do permit one to make inferences which supplement each other.

Questions One Is Bound to Ask

In either case certain basic questions arise to plague the person who wants to know something about the practical implications of theories. If the factors are expressed in terms of theoreticians only, how can that tell us anything about the substance of the agreements and disagreements? On the other hand, if the factors are expressed in terms of items only, how will we know what the analysis has to do with theories?

While we are at it, let us ask some other questions, too. Can one ascribe meaningful names to the three factors produced by Gulliksen, and are there ways, other than name calling, to ascribe meaning to them? Are there alternative methods of mathematical treatment which might provide us with a better understanding of Mr. A. S., or of the clinical differences between the six theoreticians? To what extent can we generalize about the operational differences between clinicians or about the differences between theories when only one target case is involved? Are Farberow and Shneidman's items of such a nature as to explicate the full range of theoretical differences?

Then there are those cases in which the clinician has difficulty applying a categorical statement to the patient in the face of a history of contrasting or gradually shifting behaviors. For example, in the case of Mr. A. S. there is a report of numerous childhood fights, yet he describes his avoidance, as an adult, of interpersonal conflicts he felt he could not win. In the light of such a report how does one come out with a flat statement that he either was or was not inclined to give in immediately when attacked (Item 4)? Obviously this kind of difficulty is inherent in the application of any kind of trait theory, as well as in outright typology.

There are also some basic issues, such as those that always puzzle one when he attempts to understand persons from the way in which they cope with prefabricated propositions. For example, some clinicians use the terms "hostility" and "aggression" practically synonymously, while others see a vast difference in what is implied by the two terms. This is more than a matter of mere semantics; it has to do with dispositional patterns in the ways human behavior is perceived—quite apart from differences in the technical usage of terms. Is there any way to surmount this discrepancy, or must one retreat into pure phenomenology?

A glance at some of the differences in theoreticians' judgments serves to indicate how complex a matter it is to use the Q-sort items to spell out the substance of theoretical distinctions. For example, Ansbacher and Kelly assign the highest rating to the statement, "He tends to retreat from the stress and strain of everyday living" (Item 20), yet Futterman rates this statement at 7, indicating that he believes it is significantly untrue of the patient. But on Item 31 Futterman and Ansbacher agree that "He retreats when people become aggressive toward him," while Kelly is inclined to disagree. Here is an instance in which theoreticians not only disagree with each other, but two of them may appear to be disagreeing with themselves.

We could, of course, say that there is an "error factor" operating here. But there is also the likelihood that the three men have different notions about the nature of retreat, of stress and strain, and of aggressiveness. Can we then say that the pattern of differences in judgment reflect theory-based differences in the way the patient is seen, or do they reflect theory-based differences in the way the terms are seen?

There is another intriguing point. The factorial pattern produced by Gulliksen's analysis would likely have been substantially different if Herbert Hendin, who commented on the protocol from a modified Freudian point of view, and Louis E. De Rosis, who takes the Horney point of view, also had done the Q-sorts. Now what shall we say has happened to meaning? Isn't it a little silly to argue that what is basic to Futterman and Klopfer changes when data from Hendin and De Rosis snuggle up alongside it? To draw such a conclusion would be to let gnosiological relativism run wild. It must be obvious, therefore, that factor analysis does not produce what is commonly understood to be substantive meaning. At least, it fails to do in this kind of matrix.

What Dependable Meanings Emerge?

What kind of meaning referents, then, does this factor analysis erect? First of all, it tells us something holistically about the particular pool of judgments coming from the six theoreticians. But it tells us nothing absolute about the men— only how their judgments are related to the pool. Following the logic of Thurstone (1935), it is simply an economical way of representing the complex array of data provided by the six sets of Q-sorts.

It is always a little disappointing to be frustrated in our search for the absolute. Yet as long as we live in a world where we are dependent on partial or transient systems of knowledge, we must understand things in terms of their similarities and contrasts with other things, and with constellations of other things.

Still, it is worth something to know that the factorial description of the pool of information does throw some light on the interindividual differences of opinion. Consider Gulliksen's third factor, for example. Evidently it would be economical to say that there is a constellation of issues at stake in the Q-sorted data which pits Futterman and Diamond against Ansbacher and Klopfer and leaves Green and Kelly in the middle. Since this is a parametric factor analysis it does not say that this set of issues is one in which Futterman and Diamond say something is true and important in the case of Mr. A. S. while Ansbacher and Klopfer merely say it is unimportant or only half true and half untrue. As far as the factorial information is concerned, it might be that it is a case of Futterman and Diamond taking the ho-hum stand, with Ansbacher and Klopfer making a federal case out of it. Yet, it is interesting to know there is some scalar alignment to be envisioned among the clinicians, and it may help one guess what one theory involves from his prior knowledge of what some of the others involve. But it remains for him to guess just what that may be.

Some additional meaning is provided by the communality values (h^2) in Table 3. With the factorial composition developed along these particular lines, it occurs that varying amounts of individual communality are "explained." Again, this gives us no particular insight into the unique meanings of the six theoretical systems, but rather indicates only the comparative extent to which the three-factor system has drawn upon each of the six sets of Q-sort information.

The Minimax Problem Posed by Human Limitations

There is a more general way in which the function of factor analysis can be stated. Factor analysis provides one kind of answer to a minimax problem—how to encompass the maximum amount of information within the minimum number of parameters. The problem can also be stated as one of minimizing the differences between small units, such as test items, while maximizing the differences between large units, such as factorial constellations. How small and multiplex the items must be before it becomes desirable to minimize their differences, and how large and sweeping the factors can become before they become top-heavy with overgeneralizations, is basically dependent on something else—the limitations and capacities of the human mind, or of particular human minds.

If one could think in terms of 76 dimensions at once, there would be no point in factor analyzing the Q-sort data in Farberow and Shneidman's book. On the other hand, if one's thinking about personality matters is limited to one dimension, the three factors produced by the analysis will still leave him confused by the complexity of the information at hand: Points such as these were ably made by T. L. Kelley in his volume on factor analysis, published in 1935, incidentally within a few weeks of L. L. Thurstone's classic work, dealing with the same subject. T. L. Kelley had mentioned the point, though less lucidly, in 1928 (Kelley, 1928).

Conforming to Precast Structure

Beyond the minimax problem of producing a manageable compromise between the simplification and proliferation of information, there is the problem of bringing the information into alignment with the construct systems of those who are expected to understand it. Suppose a theoretician could think in 76 directions at once—or even three directions, for that matter—it does not follow that he can think clearly in line with the particular 76 constructs involved in the deck of Q-sort items, or the three constellated constructs represented by Gulliksen's factor pattern.

Nevertheless, the factor analysis may enable him to bring the information into alignment with the dimensions of his own personal system in two ways. First, an examination of the items comprised by one of the factors in an "inverted" factor analysis and the pattern of a factor's loadings on the six clinicians in a "conventional" factor analysis may give him some faint clues as to which constructs selected out of his own repertory may be appropriately invoked. Second, a successive reading of the items and a continued examination of the pattern of factor loadings may enable him to do some fresh abstracting on his own. If so, he can be expected to add suitable constructs to his own personal repertory, constructs that he may, with a little practice, be able to generalize beyond the fragments of data at hand.

It is in these respects that factor analysis has conceptual utility as an instrument for bringing information within man's reach, even though it does not uncover natural meanings or of itself create ideas.

THEORETICAL RESTRICTIONS
OF THE DATA

Before proceeding to the description of our nonparametric approach to this problem, it is appropriate to take account of other kinds of limitation in the data. If one examines the items of the Q-sort deck, he will note a certain similarity running through most of them. Nearly all the items have to do with interpersonal relations. Such items tend to have the advantage of being more directly related to observable behavior than are more abstract or "psychodynamic" items. But they do limit the diversity of the clinicians' responses. Furthermore, it may occur that a particular type of item may be in closer alignment with the terms of reference of some personality theories than with the terminology of others. The Adlerian and Sullivanian systems, for example, tend to place considerable emphasis upon interpersonal relations, while the Freudian system reduces its observations to a considerably different set of terms. This may mean that Ansbacher and Green, who represented the Adlerian and Sullivanian systems, might have been able to make more complete statements of their positions in terms of the Q-sorts than was Futterman, who represented the Freudian system.

Adding Other Types of Items

It would be possible, of course, to add other types of items to the Q-sort deck, and thus provide for a more complete explication of some of the theoretical viewpoints. One would have to do his best to keep the new items within a common clinical language. For example, suppose he introduces an item having to do with the patient's use of the "conversion mechanism." While the item might make sense to a Freudian and provide him with a terminological framework in which he could express his appraisal of the case more fully, it might, at the same time, introduce a meaningless complication to the nondirectivist, in whose system such a term is likely to be peripheral, if not ambiguous.

There are down-to-earth practical items, however, that represent issues likely to be faced by any clinician, regardless of his conceptual network. An examination of what the different clinicians have said about Mr. A. S.'s treatment suggests a number of such common issues. For example, one item might be, "He will respond best if some form of psychotherapy is started immediately rather than being delayed," or another might be, "He is subject to wide and unpredictable mood swings."

Theoretical Restrictions of the Protocol

There is another respect—unavoidable—in which instrumentation of this study bears unequally on the different theoretical positions. The protocol itself, upon which the different theoreticians had to base their assessments, cannot be considered as theoretically sterile. While Tabachnick, who elicited the protocol, is to be congratulated for his consistent efforts to avoid theoretical bias, it is clear that one's outlook determines what kind of relationship he will establish with the patient, what questions he will ask, what observations he will be alert enough to make, which ones he will consider important enough to report, and how he will paraphrase what the patient has said. For example, this writer, in reading the protocol summary preliminary to making his appraisal, was struck with the congruency between what was reported and what an Adlerian theoretician would probably consider to be important. This was what led to his comments on the style-of-life paradigm (Farberow & Shneidman, 1961, p. 259). This is not to say that the interviewing clinician was careless or that he was an Adlerian; it is to say, rather, that he had to be *something* and evidently he sensed this particular perspective as closest to the unvarnished facts. What neither he nor any other clinician can escape is the tendency for facts to come into focus only in the light of prior personal assumptions—assumptions that are theoretically either explicit or implicit in the practical way one looks at things.

The Patient's Theoretical Orientation

But we must recognize that there were other theoretical impulses at work here. As we have already suggested, there is a theoretical commitment underlying the Q-sort items, and there is the commitment of the clinician who elicited the protocol—one without which he would have been unable to make any clinical contact with the patient. Beyond these there is the commitment of the patient. His outlook had something to do with the kind of relationship he was prepared to establish with the interviewer, the questions he must have asked or avoided asking, those he chose to answer and how he chose to interpret them, what he remembered, what he considered important enough to report, and how he put his observations into the formal language of words. No matter how clever the rest of us may be, it was this fellow's deeply engrained theory that structured the field, not merely as to what was produced in the protocol, but as to the very course of the events in his own turbulent life.

Limitations in Format

This brings us to the last of the possible built-in biases which might have made some theoreticians more comfortable with the protocol than were others. Tabachnick, in his effort to make his report as theoretically sterile as possible, on occasion quite properly fell back upon direct quotations from Mr. A. S. This produced the kind of protocol to which personal construct theory, with its emphasis on the personal constructions of the patient, and nondirectivism, with its empathic emphasis upon acceptance of expressed feelings, both tend to give considerable credence. Freudians, however, are not so likely to take such initial statements at face value. During the early stages of therapy they depend, instead, on what they consider to be more subtle cues to underlying mechanisms, many of which are not communicated by a literal transcription of what the patient has said. The Jungian also is inclined to discount such literal transcriptions.

These relationships between direct quotations in the anamnesis and the different theoretical positions of the clinicians do not suggest that the personal construct theorist and the nondirectivist could do a better job of interpreting the quotations. It suggests only that they may have been more comfortable with such information and hence possibly better able to use it to stabilize their conclusions, such as they were. On the other hand, Tabachnick's choice of statements worth quoting appears to be more in line with the sort of thing that would make a psychoanalyst prick up his ears, and somewhat less in line with what would alert the personal construct theorist and nondirectivist.

There are, therefore, many interesting technical and adventitious relations between the patient and the theoreticians, the items of the Q-sort, and the protocol, as well as theoretical divergencies among them. It would be difficult, indeed, to determine from the data whether one of the systematic points of view is more comprehensive in its general logical form or more precise in its particular application to this case than are the others. What the data may reveal, however—and this is of importance—is something about the issues at stake between the different theories. But to bring these issues into focus we shall need to employ a different mathematical approach.

NONPARAMETRIC APPROACH

Consider an item in the Q-sort series such as No. 72, "He adapts fairly easily to authority demands," on which there is considerable difference of opinion among the six clinicians. (See Table 1.) Ansbacher and Klopfer agree that this statement significantly describes Mr. A. S., the former rating it 2, that is, one of the eight most applicable statements, and the latter rating it a 3, one of the 18 most applicable statements. But Diamond rates this item a 9, one of the three most inapplicable statements, and Futterman tends to agree with him, rating it a 7, one of the 18 most inapplicable statements. Green and Kelly give it an intermediate rating of 4, only one of the 30 applicable statements.

Interpretation of Data in the Intermediate Range

Perhaps Green and Kelly saw Mr. A. S. as being near normal in this matter, or so mixed in his responses to authority demands that no clear-cut statement could be made. Or perhaps the statement seemed so ambiguous to them that they could do no better than assign it an intermediate position, hoping thus to avoid committing themselves. There is the further possibility that one or both of them considered the statement true enough, but not of sufficient clinical importance to place it among the items they were required to select as best describing the psychological structure of the case. Finally, they may simply have considered the item irrelevant. So what shall we say their intermediate ratings mean?

This problem of interpreting intermediate range data is always perplexing. Looking at the problem psychologically, this writer is inclined toward the use of dichotomous constructions, with all items omitted, rather than assigning an intermediate scalar value, when they cannot be clearly identified with one construct pole or the other. If, for some reason, Q-sorts in more than two categories do have to be made, then at least it might be better to specify that they conform to a U-shaped distribution rather than to a Gaussian curve. This matter has been discussed by the writer elsewhere (Kelly, 1955, p. 144) and Cromwell and Caldwell (1962) have produced experimental evidence indicating the relationship between a U-shaped distribution and personally relevant meaning. But all of this has to do with a set of issues which cannot be treated at length here.

Equivalent Patterns

To come back to our present data, we have, with respect to the ratings on Item 72, a pattern of differences between the theoreticians, with Ansbacher and Klopfer pitted against Diamond and Futterman, while Green and Kelly straddle the fence.

Now if we examine the ratings on Item 16, "He is rather cold and impersonal in his interactions with women," we will note a somewhat similar pattern. Ansbacher, who rates it a 7, and Klopfer, who rates it an 8, are still pitted against Diamond, who gives it a 2, though Futterman, the Freudian, has deserted his erstwhile nondirectivist colleague and joined Green and Kelly on the fence, all 5's. Still, except for the reversal of ratings, the two items reflect about the same pattern of disagreement between the theoreticians. Can we say, therefore, there is a common factor underlying the two patterns?

This is a tricky question. If we say the items share a common denominator, we must be careful to imply only that they provide grounds for a similar pattern of practical disagreement between theoreticians, and not that the substance of the two items is necessarily similar. But this pattern of disagreement—and agreement—narrows down our search for the substance of theoretical differences. We may, therefore, profitably delineate the pattern further by searching for other items where it is manifested.

Parametric versus Nonparametric Factors

But suppose, instead of inquiring specifically about the pattern we have observed in Items 16 and 72, we ask a more general question.

Suppose we ask ourselves if there is a pattern—any pattern—of agreement and disagreement between the theoreticians that is commonly reflected in a considerable number of items. That is to say, let us look for big things first, whatever they may be.

We can ask this question in two ways; we can ask if there is such a pattern that occurs regardless of the absolute ratings given by the theoreticians, or we can consider certain absolute ratings and ask which items conform closely to them. The first procedure involves a parametric factor analysis. Thus, if one item yielded a pattern of ratings of 1, 2, 3, 4, 5, and 6, respectively, for the six theoreticians, it would be parametrically the same as another item which yielded a pattern of 4, 5, 6, 7, 8, and 9, respectively, for the same theoreticians. The ordinal sequences being the same, the factorial composition would be considered parametrically identical.

The second approach involves a nonparametric analysis, and the two item patterns would be considered identical only if they disclosed exactly the same cardinal ratings by the respective theoreticians.

Most factor analytic methods are based on the parametric approach, but when it is desirable to find relationships which will permit the prediction of the absolute ratings of one particular item from the ratings assigned to another, a nonparametric approach is preferable. The writer has elsewhere proposed a nonparametric approach to the factor analysis of dichotomous personal constructions of events (Kelly, 1955). While there are certain inherent difficulties in such an analysis, some of which have been pointed out, the more common criticisms of the method have been based on the mistaken assumption that a factor must always be conceived parametrically.

Successive Approximations: First Trial

Let us see how a nonparametric method of analysis may be applied to the nine-step ratings in the present problem. Suppose we approach each factor by successive approximations. To start with, we shall be looking for a rating pattern that will match as closely as possible the largest possible number of items, but not one that is so general that it foils our efforts to discriminate theoretical differences. This is to say we must keep our minimax criterion in mind.

Perhaps the most obvious first step would be to determine the mean of each theoretician's ratings. The pattern of means would obviously be the best fit for the total of the items. But each clinician was instructed precisely as to how many ratings of each value he could make and, if he followed his instructions, he would come out with a mean rating of five. A pattern of fives for all six clinicians would then be the best fit for the 76 items and the items which fitted the pattern best would be those given intermediate or neutral values—hardly a very exciting basis for understanding theoretical differences.

In order to locate those items which elicited more extreme judgments, and thus possibly make meaning stand out in greater relief, we can go through all the items with a pattern of fives—a process called "scanning"—to cast out the ones that match such a drab pattern. Item 74, "He is rather neutral towards others," for example, has a pattern of 4, 6, 4, 5, 5, and 6. Obviously no one crawled very far out on either limb of this statement. Our scanning pattern of all-fives comes within four points of matching it. This is pretty close, so we may tentatively eliminate the item from the pool as not being likely to shed much light on theoretical issues.

Suppose we arbitrarily eliminate from the pool all items whose match with the scanning pattern of all-fives is less than ten points. This leaves us with the items marked with an asterisk (*) in the

TABLE 4

Nonparametric Analysis of Q-Sort Items, Items 21–75 Omitted[a]

Item No.	Theoreticians' Ratings							First Factor Trials				Matching Scores Second Factor Trials		Third Factor Trials		
	Fut.	Klo.	Ans.	Gre.	Kel.	Dia.	$\Sigma(X-5)$	1	2	3	4	1	2	1	2	3
1.	4	2	3	3	2	3	13*	5*	4*	5*	4*		11			12
2.	2	6	5	4	6	4	7	±17	±12	±11	10	8	5*			−6*
3.	4	3	6	5	5	1	8	14	11	12	11	13	8*			−9
4.	6	4	5	4	6	7	6	−14	±11	±10	−9		6			7
5.	6	5	6	5	7	8	7	−11	−8	−7	−6*		±11			10
6.	2	7	4	3	1	4	13*	13	10	9	8		±13			−12
7.	9	5	5	8	3	5	9	−17	±14	±13	−12	−6*	−7*			12
8.	4	4	2	3	3	3	11*	5*	4*	3*	2**		11			12
9.	1	3	4	3	5	5	9	13	8	9	8		5			12
10.	4	5	5	4	3	1	7	12	9	8	7		10			−11
11.	4	5	5	8	7	4	7	−11	−8	−7	−8		9			−10
12.	5	4	6	2	5	3	7	9*	8	7	8		9			−10
13.	4	4	7	7	9	6	11*	−9*	−6*	−5*	−6*		11			−12
14.	3	8	5	5	5	5	5	−15	−10	−11	±12	−10*	−7*			−6
15.	4	7	7	7	6	6	9	−8*	−2*	−3*	−4*		−9			
16.	5	8	7	5	5	2	8	−14	−9	−10	−11	−13	−10	−9	−7*	−5
17.	6	1	6	2	5	3	11*	11	10	11	12	10*	11	8	12	±14
18.	2	3	5	5	4	6	7	15	10	11	10	8*	5*			8
19.	7	5	6	5	8	8	9	−11	−10	−9	−8		−11			10
20.	7	5	1	3	1	3	14*	6*	9	8	9		−14			13
76.	3	5	4	5	2	2	9	11	10	9	8		11			−10

[a] From Farberow and Shneidman (pp. 307–310).

TABLE 5

Successive Approximations of First Factor

Successive Trials		Theoreticians' Ratings						Criteria
		Fut.	Klo	Ans.	Gre.	Kel.	Dia.	
f_{1t1}	Totals	137	115	87	97	101	113	$\Sigma(X-5) > 9$
$(N = 31)$	Means	4.4	3.7	2.8	3.1	3.3	3.6	
	Pattern	5	3	1	2	2	3	
f_{1t2}	Totals	128	91	69	78	82	98	
$(N = 27)$	Means	4.7	3.4	2.6	2.9	3.0	3.6	$f_{1t1} < 10$
	Pattern	5	3	3	3	3	3	
f_{1t3}	Totals	102	74	54	71	68	80	
$(N = 21)$	Means	4.9	3.5	2.6	3.4	3.2	3.8	$f_{1t2} < 7$
	Pattern	5	4	3	3	3	4	
f_{1t4}	Totals	97	77	59	72	73	83	
$(N = 22)$	Means	4.4	3.5	2.7	3.3	3.3	3.8	$f_{1t3} < 7$
	Pattern	4	4	3	3	3	4	
f_{1t5}	Totals	98	93	68	77	79	88	
$(N = 23)$	Means	4.3	4.0	3.0	3.3	3.4	3.7	$f_{1t4} < 7$
	Pattern	4	4	3	3	3	4	
F_1	Gulliksen's F_1 loadings	.38	.48	.79	.68	.69	.54	

column head "$\Sigma(X-5)$" in Table 4. We may now total the ratings for each clinician among these remaining items only. In adding these totals we shall, in effect, reverse some of the items, just as if they had been stated in the opposite way. Take Item 39, "He faces unpleasant situations in a direct manner," with a pattern of 5, 7, 9, 7, 9, and 7, for example. If we consider this item reversed, e.g., "He does *not* face unpleasant situations in a direct manner," the ratings would presumably be 5, 3, 1, 3, 1, and 3. We shall therefore balance the table by aligning all items so that extreme ratings will tend to be represented by low numbers only, rather than by low and high numbers both. This reversal of items, corresponding to "reflection" in conventional factor analysis, is accomplished simply enough if one turns end-for-end all items in which the average rating of the six clinicians is greater than five. The columnar totals are shown in the first row of Table 5 and the average (mean) of each clinician's ratings is shown in the next row beneath.

We may now set up our first trial scanning pattern for Factor One (f_{1t1}). It is derived from the 31 items selected by our casting out the "flat" ones. (See left-hand column, Table 5.) We would, of course, tend to get, though not always, the best total matching score for all the selected items if we scanned with the means in Table 5. But we shall not do this for two reasons. First, such a scanning pattern would require us to tote up fractional amounts, and it seems preferable to keep our task simple by sticking to whole numbers. Second, the pattern is still rather "flat" and we are looking for sharper differences between the clinicians, even if we have to sacrifice some generality our first factor.

In order to increase the possibility of getting sharper differences among the clinicians into our first factor pattern, we shall expand the range of ratings in the pattern. We do this by assigning arbitrarily a rating of 1 to the lowest average (2.8)—appearing in Ansbacher's column—and a rating of 5 to the highest average (4.4)—appearing in Futterman's column. The other expanded values are determined by interpolation, and are rounded to the nearest whole number. The first trial scanning pattern in our search for a first factor (f_{1t1}) produced by this method is shown in the third row of the first panel in Table 5. We shall use this pattern as a first approximation to the first factor, although it is obvious that in subsequent trials we shall have to let the regression effect pull some of the extreme scores (e.g., Ansbacher's artificial 1) down to more moderate values.

The matching value for each item is shown in Table 4, in the first column under "First factor trials," e.g., Item 1 matching this pattern with a value of 5. In this column where the match is better—lower matching score—for the item when it is reflected, the score is shown as a negative number, e.g., Item 4). In some cases the match is the same for the item when it is reflected as when it is not. In such a case, e.g., Item 2, the score is preceded by $\pm$.

We shall apply this first trial scanning pattern to all items, including those we temporarily eliminated from the pool. The lower the matching score shown in the column, the closer the item matches the trial scanning pattern. From these lower matching scores we may determine which items show promise of fitting together to shape up our first factor. Suppose we say, somewhat arbitrarily to be sure, that any item shows promise when its ratings average one and a half points or less from the ratings in the scanning pattern. These would be the items with a value of less than ten in the column. They are marked with an asterisk (*) in Table 4. There are 27 of them, and that fact is noted at the left of the second panel in Table 5. Our new criterion for selecting the items from which to derive the second scanning pattern—a matching score of less than 10 when scanned with the preceding pattern—is noted in the right-hand column of Table 5 $(f_{1t1} < 10)$. Our "criterion" column in this table also indicates that we have dropped our initial requirement, applied only in the derivation of the first trial pattern, that items not match the all-fives pattern too closely.

Scanning with the Second Trial Pattern

Now suppose we add each theoretician's ratings of the starred items only, taking care to use reflected values for items whose matching scores for f_{1t1} were negative. The totals and means are shown in the second panel of Table 5. These new values, when rounded, constitute the second trial scanning pattern, f_{1t2}. The item-by-item matching values obtained with this trial pattern are shown in the second column under "First factor trials," in Table 4.

Now suppose we tighten up our criterion of what we shall consider a promising item. Suppose we limit ourselves to those items with matching scores of six or less in the f_{1t2} column. The theoretician totals and averages are shown in the next panel of Table 5, as before. From the rounded averages the third trial pattern emerges, f_{1t3}. It is slightly different from the preceding trial pattern, so we shall run it through in a similar fashion, with matching scores shown in the next column in Table 4.

Using the same criterion for a "promising item," $f_{1t3} < 7$, we may proceed to develop additional scanning patterns until the successive approximations come to a standstill. This actually occurs when it turns out that the f_{1t5} rounded scanning pattern turns out to be the same as the preceding f_{1t4} scanning pattern. No column 5, therefore, is shown in Table 4.

We now have our "first factor." It is shown in the fractional scanning pattern ("Means") in the next to the bottom panel of Table 5, or in the rounded values ("Pattern") in the row beneath. It is also shown in terms of the closely matching items whose matching scores are shown in the fourth column of first factor trials in Table 4. The items which match the scanning pattern best (3 or less) are marked ** and those matching fairly well (6 or less) are marked *. A list of the first factor items, together with their patching scores, appears in Table 6.

What is the nature of this factor? Obviously it is one in which Ansbacher (average rating of 3.0) is at one end of the continuum and Futterman (average rating of 4.3) is at the other (Table 5). Green and Kelly tend to agree with Ansbacher, Diamond agrees slightly, and Klopfer tends to concur in Futterman's judgment that the type of item is not particularly applicable to the case, one way or the other.

How shall we "name" it? If we return to Table 6 we find the best matching scores are found opposite Items 8, "He has very few friends"; 45, "His friendships seem rather stable and have relatively few conflicts"—reflected; and 53, "Friendly gestures from others

TABLE 6

Some Items in the Q-Sorts and Their Factorial Assignments.[a]

Item No.	Principal Items in Order of Conformity to Factorial Scanning Pattern	Matching Score	Other Factor
	Composition of first nonparametric factor		
	Fut. 4, Klo. 4, Ans. 3, Gre. 3, Kel. 3, Dia. 4 (last pattern, Table 5)		
8.	He has very few friends.	2	
45.	His friendships seem rather stable and have relatively few conflicts.	−2	
53.	Friendly gestures from others arouse his suspicion and hostility.	−3	
1.	He likes and seeks the companionship of others.	4	
15.	He is constantly fighting his environment.	−4	
25.	He becomes quite aggressive in most social situations.	−4	
32.	He competes very strongly with father figures.	−4	
41.	He gets along well with most people.	−4	
51.	He runs away from hostility in others.	4	
22.	He escapes in fantasy when threatened.	5	
24.	He is uneasy and uncomfortable around other men.	5	
29.	He reacts in a hostile and aggressive fashion in his interpersonal contacts.	−5	$(F_2 - 6)$
55.	He rarely responds to positive gestures from others.	−5	
62.	He responds in a realistic fashion to hostility in others.	−5	
65.	Even the mere presence of other people produces immediate withdrawal in him.	−5	
5.	He seems to adapt to his environment quite well.	−6	
13.	He has quite a few relatively warm interpersonal relationships.	−6	
21.	He meets the demands of his environment in a rather reasonable fashion.	−6	
23.	He tries to manipulate those around him to serve his own ends.	6	
26.	He generally feels accepted by others.	−6	
	Composition of second nonparametric factor		
	Fut. 3, Klo. 3, Ans. 5, Gre. 4, Kel. 6, Dia. 5 (last pattern, Table 7)		
31	He retreats when people become aggressive toward him.	6	$(F_2 3)$
43.	He is quite passive in most of his interpersonal contacts.	6	
73.	He becomes negativistic when people show a friendly interest in him.	−6	$(F_3 - 6)$

TABLE 6 (Continued)

Item No.	Principal Items in Order of Conformity to Factorial Scanning Pattern	Matching Score	Other Factor
	Composition of second nonparametric factor		
	Fut. 3, Klo. 3, Ans. 5, Gre. 4, Kel. 6, Dia. 5 (last pattern, Table 7)		
31.	He retreats when people become aggressive toward him.	3	(F_16)
57.	When others show an interest in him, he immediately becomes aggressive and demanding.	−3	
35.	He becomes actively hostile when he is criticized.	−4	
47.	He yields meekly to the demands of others.	4	
2.	He usually Withdraws in social situations.	5	
9.	He blames himself when criticized.	5	
18.	He accepts rather passively any impositions made upon him.	5	
30.	He is unable to recognize affection when it is offered to him.	5	
49.	Rejection from others only makes him more aggressive.	−5	
50.	He is tactful and considerate with other people.	5	
4.	He gives in immediately when attacked.	6	
29.	He reacts in a hostile and aggressive fashion in his interpersonal contacts.	−6	$(F_1 - 5)$
59.	He is responsive to the needs and wishes of others.	6	
	Composition of third nonparametric factor		
	Fut. 7, Klo. 3, Ans. 3, Gre. 5, Kel. 4, Dia. 7 (last pattern, Table 8)		
72.	He adapts fairly easily to authority demands.	4	
16.	He is rather cold and impersonal in his interactions with women.	−5	
14.	He does not invest affect in his interpersonal relationships.	−6	
38.	He is quite responsive when people show an interest in his welfare.	6	
64.	He actively seeks social contacts.	6	
73.	He becomes negativistic when people show a friendly interest in him.	−6	$(F_1 - 6)$

[a] From Farberow and Shneidman (pp. 307–310).

arouses his suspicion and hostility"—reflected. Some of the other items that match the scanning pattern closely are 1, "He likes and seeks the companionship of others"; 15, "He is constantly fighting his environment"—reflected; 25, "He becomes quite aggressive in most social situations"—reflected; 32, "He competes very strongly with father figures"—reflected; 41, "He gets along well with most people"—reflected; and 51, "He runs away from hostility in others."

It should be kept in mind that this first nonparametric factor is not to be taken as a statement of the main or outstanding feature of Mr. A. S.'s case. That is something revealed simply by extreme ratings. It is, rather, a cluster of issues in which there is consistent agreement and disagreement among the clinicians. It is, therefore more descriptive of the clinicians as a heterogeneous group, than of the group's consensus of opinion or the "real" dynamics of the case.

It is possible to compare the first factor obtained by this nonparametric method with the first factor in Gulliksen's conventional analysis. Figure 1 shows a plot of the loading of Gulliksen's first factor against the mean rating totals taken from the next to the last panel of our Table 5. The alignment is remarkably regular, probably more so than one could ordinarily expect, since the two factors, the one parametric and the other nonparametric, are only remotely comparable.

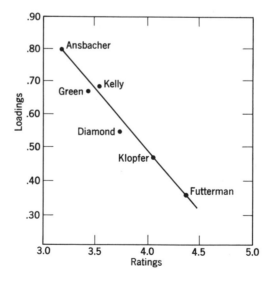

FIGURE 1. Mean ratings of items in first nonparametric factor versus loadings of first parametric factor.

Second Factor

Now we can examine the items not generalized by the first factor and see if there is another scanning pattern which will economically represent a considerable group of them. Suppose we say that any item which does not match our first factor scanning pattern with a score of less than 10 has not yet been adequately represented. This is to say that the scanning pattern is acceptable for an item if it averages no more than one and a half points of matching the item ratings. This is an arbitrary decision, but then, so are all decisions regarding acceptable fiducial limits. This criterion is stated in the right-hand column of Table 7, with the notation $\Sigma(X - X_1) > 9$.

According to our criterion there are 17 items that fall outside the constellation of the first factor. In developing our scanning patterns for the second factor we shall confine our attention to these items. Our first trial scanning pattern for these 17 items is developed as it was for the first factor—by averaging each clinician's ratings, taking account of reflections, and then by expanding the scanning pattern. In this case, however, the expansion is from one (Futterman and Klopfer) to six (Kelly), since Kelly's average rating for these items is greater than five. The average and expanded values are shown in the first panel of Table 7. The matching scores are shown, as before, in the first column under "Second factor trials" in Table 4.

We now proceed to the second trial scanning pattern for the second factor, f_{2t2}. There are two criteria now to be met in selecting the

TABLE 7
Successive Approximations of Second Factor

Successive Trials		Theoreticians' Ratings						Criteria
		Fut.	Klo.	Ans.	Gre.	Kel.	Dia.	
f_{2t1}	Totals	59	57	81	72	88	82	(a) $\Sigma(X - X_1) > 9$
(N = 17)	Means	3.5	3.3	4.8	4.2	5.2	4.8	
	Pattern	1	1	5	3	6	5	
f_{2t2}	Totals	28	35	58	41	64	55	(a) $\Sigma(X - X_1) > 9$
(N = 11)	Means	2.5	3.2	5.3	3.7	5.8	5.0	(b) $\qquad f_{2t1} < 11$
	Pattern	3	3	5	$\prime$	6	5	
f_{2t3}	Totals	38	43	67	50	72	65	(a) $\Sigma(X - X_1) > 9$
(N = 13)	Means	2.9	3.3	5.2	3.9	5.5	5.0	(b) $\qquad f_{2t2} < 10$
F_2	Pattern	3	3	5	4	6	5	
	Gulliksen's F_2 loadings	−.37	−.33	−.06	−.19	.48	.27	

items, a minimum matching score with the scanning pattern of the
first factor—to keep the two factors at arms length from each other—
and a maximum matching score with the scanning pattern of f_{2t_1}.
If we hold to the same criterion in the first instance, a matching score
of greater than nine with the first factor scanning pattern, and then
impose the additional requirement of a low matching score on the
trial scanning pattern we have just used, there will be scarcely any
of our 17 items left. In order, therefore, to keep our pool of items
from shrinking unreasonably we shall apply a more liberal second
criterion and accept any item that matched the first trial scanning
pattern, f_{2t_1}, with a score of ten or less. There are 11 items which
now meet both criteria. Each is marked with an asterisk in column
1 under "Second factor trials" in Table 4. The averages are shown
in Table 7.

In developing our third trial scanning pattern for the second factor
we can, at last, afford to tighten up our second criterion very slightly,
just as we did in developing the first factor. For f_{2t_3} items we shall
require that the f_{2t_2} scanning pattern have matched the item ratings
with an average score of nine or less. Thirteen items meet the tightened
criteria; their average ratings, still taking reflections into account, are

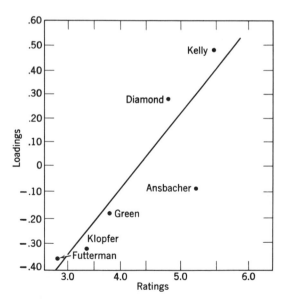

FIGURE 2. Mean ratings of items in second nonparametric factor versus loadings of
second parametric factor.

shown in the next panel of Table 7 and are marked with asterisks. The rounded values of these averages show no change from those of the preceding trial scanning pattern, so we may consider that we had already reached a satisfactory statement of the second factor in the second trial. No third trial column is shown in Table 4.

Figure 2 is a plot of our second factor average ratings against Gulliksen's second factor loadings. Again, there appears to be a closer relationship than one might normally expect.

There are 13 items which match our second factor scanning pattern with a score of six or less, and 40 which match it with a score of nine or less. (See Table 6.) Some of the items, of course, match both factors rather closely, e.g., Item 31, "He retreats when people become aggressive toward him." The two scanning patterns match each other with a score of nine, indicating that they are by no means orthogonal to each other.

Third Factor

There is some question about the value of proceeding to the development of a third factor. If we apply the same criterion as we did before in selecting our remaining "unexplained" items (matching scores of greater than nine with both preceding factors) we shall have only four surviving holdouts—Nos. 16, 17, 46, and 72. This hardly seems enough to make a fuss over. Nevertheless, we shall persist in our enterprise to see what comes out.

The procedure is the same as before, except that we have two criteria to meet in selecting our initial pool of items—matching scores of more than nine on *both* factors one and two. In developing the scanning pattern f_{3t2} we shall impose a third criterion—a matching score of less than 12 with the preceding pattern f_{3t1}. We can tighten up this requirement in developing f_{3t3} and require that items match f_{3t2} with a score of nine or less. This calls for the sacrifice of one of our precious four items, No. 17, but we are carrying out our ground rules literally. When we start to construct f_{3t4} we find that we shall be dealing with the same three items. There is no point in continuing further, so we shall let f_{3t3} stand as our final F_3 scanning pattern. The successive trial scanning patterns for this factor are all shown in Table 8.

Figure 3 is a plot of our third nonparametric factor against Gulliksen's third parametric factor. The correlation is genuinely surprising in this case, since our factor was based on only four leftover items, hardly a very stable basis for approximating the mathematically more elegant conventional factor analysis.

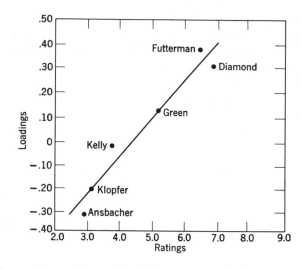

FIGURE 3. Mean ratings of items in third nonparametric factor versus loadings of third parametric factor.

TABLE 8

Successive Approximations of Third Factor

Successive Trials		Theoreticians' Ratings						Criteria
		Fut.	Klo.	Ans.	Gre.	Kel.	Dia.	
f_{3t1}	Totals	23	14	20	20	18	17	(a) $\Sigma(X - X_1) > 9$
$(N = 4)$	Means	5.7	3.5	5.0	5.0	4.5	4.2	(b) $\Sigma(X - X_2) > 9$
	Pattern	7	2	5	5	4	4	
f_{3t2}	Totals	27	10	14	18	16	25	(a) $\Sigma(X - X_1) > 9$
$(N = 4)$	Means	6.7	2.5	3.5	4.5	4.0	6.2	(b) $\Sigma(X - X_2) > 9$
	Pattern	7	3	4	5	4	6	(c) $\Sigma \quad f_{3t1} < 12$
f_{3t3}	Totals	21	9	8	16	11	22	(a) $\Sigma(X - X_1) > 9$
$(N = 3)$	Means	7.0	3.0	2.7	5.3	3.7	7.3	(b) $\Sigma(X - X_2) > 9$
F_3	Pattern	7	3	3	5	4	7	(c) $\quad f_{3t2} < 10$
	Gulliksen's							
	F_3 loadings	.38	−.23	−.32	.11	−.04	.32	

Relations Between the Factors

The method of counting the matches between patterns gives us a measure of the relationship between them, but since they are not construed as scales, i.e., are nonparametrically construed, it is not immediately apparent what degree of mismatching would correspond to orthogonality, or complete independence between factors. To compute such a measure would require our making some assumptions about the probability of two patterns matching each other by chance. As far as this study goes, this does not seem particularly worthwhile. It is of interest, however, to report how closely the three factor patterns match each other. The pattern of the first factor, F_1, matches that of F_2 with a score of nine, and F_3 with a score of 10. The pattern F_2 matches that of F_3 with a score of 11. The factors are thus spaced about as far apart as one would expect, considering the criteria we applied.

INFERENCES

At the beginning of this paper we posed a number of questions. Some proved to be unanswerable and therefore remain with us as warnings against the temptation to nail down our conclusions too tightly. Others could be answered on logical grounds. Still others were deferred until after we had developed a method of analysis. Now that the mathematics has been completed, we are ready to return to the dangling issues.

Items and Theoreticians

In a problem of this sort the conventional method of factor analysis would base its factors either on items or theoreticians. Yet it would not do both at the same time. That is to say, it would not refer to theoreticians and items in the same factorial terms. The method we propose does do both at the same time. It discloses plausible patterns of agreements and disagreements between theoreticians, and it points out the specific items in which each pattern is consistently manifest. Thus the method pinpoints theoretical alignments in terms of who says what.

Since the factors emerging from this computation are expressed nonparametrically, they invite attention to those items which certain theoreticians believe to be both true and important in the clinical case under observation. If the factors were regarded parametrically they might have greater abstractive transitivity, but they would not point up the issues in this manner.

The Grasp of Meaning

Factor analysis can be regarded as a way of displaying information in an economical way. As we have suggested before, this is the answer to a minimax problem—how to reduce a maximum of information to a minimum of terms. It is the baffling complexity of psychological processes that makes psychologists seek to encompass a maximum of information, and it is the limited ability of the human mind to orient itself in hyperspace that makes them try to keep the number of factors at a minimum.

But there is another problem, too. Man has difficulty construing along unfamiliar lines, even when they are drawn with mathematical simplicity. His notions are held fast in a network of personal constructs and any ideas or feelings that have not yet found their place in that network are likely to remain exasperatingly elusive. Science, therefore, not only has the task of coming to simple terms with events, but it also has the psychological task of achieving some accommodation between what man believes and what, indeed, confronts him.

Following this line of reasoning, it is possible, and often desirable, to compute nonparametric factors in such a way that they tend to be aligned with those items which seem to make the most sense (Kelly, 1955). But thus far we have not done so in this case. We shall, therefore, first try to make sense out of our factors by verbal inference only.

Name Calling

Table 6 displays items arranged according to their alignment with the nonparametric factors we have computed. Items are arranged in each factorial group in order of the closeness with which they match the factor's scanning pattern. From these arrays of items one can formulate some kind of modal statements to represent the factors.

In some instances an item matches the scanning pattern of more than one factor. This is shown in the right-hand column. Item 73, for example, matches the scanning patterns of F_1 and F_3 equally well. We shall have to exercise some caution, therefore, in making inferences from such items.

Each factor's scanning pattern is shown also. The rounded scanning pattern of the first factor, F_1, is seen to be one in which Ansbacher, Green, and Kelly are pitted against Futterman, Klopfer, and Diamond. Moreover, it is a pattern in which one group judges an item to be somewhat true and significant, while the other sees it to be possibly true, but not significantly so. With this pattern spread before us and with out knowledge of what the theoreticians have said about their theories we can make some educated guesses about what the factor refers to.

Where a matching score is shown to be negative in either of the last two columns of Table 6, it indicates that the meaning of the item must be reflected in order to be aligned with the factorial scanning pattern. In the first factor, F_1, for example, Item 15, "He is constantly fighting environment," must be considered in a reverse sense, while Item 8, "He has very few friends," can be taken as it stands.

FIRST FACTOR: EMPHASIS ON INTERPERSONAL RELATIONSHIPS. As we examine the items listed under the first factor in Table 6 we find the closest matching scores in Nos. 8, 45, and 53—all concerned with friendships. But as we go further down the list to the less closely related items, we unveil a picture of a person who seeks friendships but who fails because he cannot muster the aggression, in the sense of initiative, necessary to hold his own.

It is this kind of item that Ansbacher, the Adlerian, thinks is both true and important in Mr. A. S. while Futterman, the Freudian, is inclined to pass it up. Green, the Sullivanian, and Kelly, the personal construct theorist, also make more of this "social" type of item, while Klopfer, the Jungian, and Diamond, the nondirectivist, regard it more as Futterman does (Figure 1 and Table 5). This alignment of theoreticians suggests that the issue at stake may be the comparative emphasis on interpersonal relationships, on the one hand, and interpersonal dynamics on the other.

SECOND FACTOR: DISTINGUISHING BETWEEN AGGRESSION AND HOSTILITY. The second factor is one which pits Futterman and Klopfer, average ratings of 2.9 and 3.3, respectively, against Kelly, whose average rating of 5.5 puts him slightly on the opposite side of the fence. Diamond is strictly neutral, if we may interpret a rating of 5.0 to mean neutrality. Ansbacher leans ever so slightly toward Kelly's somewhat negative position (Figure 2 and Table 7).

As we run down the list of items in order of their matching scores, we see the kind of aggressiveness—or lack of it—that the Freudian and Jungian think is important in this case. To this writer, who makes a point of distinguishing between hostility and aggression and regards the latter as a dimension ranging from initiative to inertia, these items seem more to imply hostility, and Mr. A. S. appears to him to have some of it.

The editors, Farberow and Shneidman, point out—quite correctly—that the terms are commonly used synonymously and therefore—questionably perhaps—draw their generalized conclusions in the case without distinguishing between them (pp. 299–300). But the factor analysis suggests that here is a possible major issue between the theoretical approaches.

THIRD FACTOR: EMPHASIS ON AUTHORITY RELATIONSHIPS. The third factor is one in which the Freudian and the Rogerian team up against the Adlerian and the Jungian (Figure 3 and Table 8). This is enough to raise anyone's curiosity. The most distinctive item in this constellation appears to be No. 72, "He adapts fairly easily to authority demands." Diamond and Futterman make a point of saying that he does not; Ansbacher and Klopfer insist that he does. Is this alertness to difficulties with authority the predisposition that makes bedfellows of the Freudians and the nondirectivists, and distinguishes them from the Adlerians and Jungians?

After examining the factorial structure, Ansbacher gives the following interpretation which seems to sum it up quite well.

Factor three would be the bias to assume hostility toward all authority figures. According to the various items pertinent here, assumption of a negative attitude to mother, women, authority figures, men—a general hostility, is involved. This would be in accordance with Freudian theory of suicide as an act of aggression primarily. That this bias should also be present in the Rogerian, could be made plausible by remembering that Rogers, maybe more than others, believes permissiveness to be curative. The Jungian and the Adlerian, possibly the most optimistic, do not show this bias of assuming a generalized negativism and hostility (personal communication).

Our three-factor analysis leaves one orphan item, No. 17, "He goes out of his way to please people." Klopfer selects this as one of his three most descriptive statements.

TESTING HYPOTHESES

What has been accomplished so far is a mathematical display of information that may provide grounds for making inferences about the theoretical issues at stake among the six clinicians who judged the Mr. A. S. protocol. But we need not stop here. On the basis of our inferences we can set up hypotheses and, using the same computational scheme, test them out. Mathematics and clinical judgment may be used in an interlocking fashion, notwithstanding the prejudices of mathematicians and clinicians against each other.

The Aggression-Hostility Hypothesis

In discussing the second factor the writer said he suspected the theoreticians differed from each other in the way they clinically construed aggression and hostility. Suppose we test this hunch.

When the writer uses the term, "aggression," he thinks of an axis of reference running from initiative to inertia on which a person may be described as well up toward the initiative end. He regards "hostility," on the other hand, as a dimension of appraisal at one end of which are represented efforts to immobilize persons or to extort their conformity to one's outmoded predictions of them. The opposite pole would be, not inactivity, but a liberalism of curiosity directed toward providing the greatest freedom of movement for others at the expense of one's preconceptions of them. Whether or not others are hurt is irrelevant, but any effort to incapacitate them would be regarded as hostile. Similarly, the aggressive person, who keeps upsetting apple carts, may be regarded as hurtful by those who do not like to be disturbed or have their circumstances altered. But that does not mean that the actor is hostile. This distinction between aggression and hostility is anchored in personal construct theory—but that is a long story and there is no need to go into that here.

In originally making the Q-sorts, the writer had to do the best he could with items obviously written by someone who did not use the terms in the same way he did and who probably also did not consider it important to distinguish between behavior along such reference lines.

Now suppose we impose this hypothesis about the distinction between hostility and aggression upon the data, such as they are. First the writer selected eight items that seemed to him to suggest the aggression axis, ranging from initiative to inertia. These items were used as an initial pool from which to derive an "aggression factor." Using the same method of nonparametric factor analysis, a scanning pattern was developed against the rather tight criterion of a matching score of no more than four. Only three of the items survived, but five additional items were picked up from elsewhere in the deck. The structure of this "aggression factor" is shown in Table 9.

Next the writer chose twelve other items that might suggest the hostility axis, ranging from extortion to curiosity. Six of these items survived and two additional items were picked up, as also shown in Table 9. It is to be noted that here, as in the "aggression factor" items, both the terms "aggression" and "hostility" are to be found.

There is another point of interest. All eight of the "aggression factor" items turn out to be critical items in Factor I and none is from Factor II. Of the eight "hostility factor" items seven turn out to have been critical items in Factor II and none was a critical item in either of the other factors. Not only does our hunch about the issue of aggression and hostility appear to be confirmed, but it also appears that

TABLE 9

Composition of Hypothesized Factors

Item No.	Principal Items in Order of Conformity to Factorial Scanning Pattern	Matching Score

Aggression factor

Fut. 5, Klo. 4, Ans. 2, Gre. 3, Kel. 4, Dia. 5

65.	Even the mere presence of other people produces immediate drawal in him.	1
73.	He becomes negativistic when people show a friendly interest in him.	−2
53.	Friendly gestures from others arouse his suspicion and hostility.	−3
8.	He has very few friends.	4
15.	He is constantly fighting his environment.	−4
25.	He becomes quite aggressive in most social situations.	−4
32.	He competes very strongly with father figures.	−4
43.	He is quite passive in most of his interpersonal contacts.	4

Hostility factor

Fut. 2, Klo. 4, Ans. 4, Gre. 4, Kel. 6, Dia. 5

47.	He yields meekly to the demands of others.	1
31.	He retreats when people become aggressive toward him.	2
49.	Rejection from others only makes him more aggressive.	−2
35.	He becomes actively hostile when he is criticized.	−3
2.	He usually withdraws in social situations.	4
9.	He blames himself when criticized.	4
40.	His immediate response when threatened is to fight back.	−4
57.	When others show an interest in him, he immediately becomes aggressive and demanding.	−4

aggression—as I understand it—is a principal component in our big general Factor I.

Differences Between Theoreticians

Now let us see what this means in terms of theoreticians. The two scanning patterns are shown in Table 9. If we compare the scanning patterns we can see that the antithesis of "hostility"—as I construe it—is something that Futterman reads into the case as important, but the antithesis of my kind of "aggression" is not. Ansbacher does not see my "hostility" as particularly important, but the opposite of my "aggression" he does. As for myself, I apparently saw Mr. A. S. as slightly hostile but also somewhat inert. The other theoreticians do not distinguish significantly between these two factors.

CONCLUSIONS

Our nonparametric method of factor analysis permits us to examine comparative clinical judgments in terms of items and clinicians, both at the same time. While the data at hand have certain limitations that limit the amount of analysis one might attempt in an ideal situation, it is possible to see within these clinical judgments certain systematic differences. This suggests that theoreticians do make clinical decisions related to their theoretical systems.

The Emerging Theoretical Issues

On the first time around, a broad general factor of difference between theoreticians seems to be the relative *emphasis placed upon interpersonal relationships.* The Adlerian placed greatest emphasis on this factor, with the Sullivanian, the personal construct theorist, the nondirectivist, the Jungian, and the Freudian, following in that order.

The second factor, a somewhat narrower one, I guess has something to do with *distinguishing between what I would call "aggression" and "hostility."* It puts the Freudian and the personal construct theorist at opposite ends, with the Jungian and the Sullivanian leaning toward the Freudian, and the nondirectivist and the Adlerian indifferent.

The third factor, a very narrow one, finds some of the theoreticians taking diametrically opposed views. It has to do with *emphasis on affect and authority relationships.* The Freudian and the nondirectivist regard it as important that Mr. A. S. cannot manage such matters. The Adlerian and the Jungian take the opposite view, while the others take an intermediate stand.

In testing the hypothesis that there is an issue at stake related to the distinction between hostility and aggression two clear-cut factors emerge. One of them, aggression, appears to account for a significant component of Factor I (interpersonal relations), but not the other. The Freudian sees the lack of hostility as important, but not the lack of aggression. The Adlerian does not see hostility or the lack of it as important, but the lack of aggression. The personal construct theorist sees Mr. A. S. as slightly hostile, but also exhibiting some lack of aggression. The others make no important distinction. I would take this as confirming my hypothesis about some theoretical confusion in the area of hostility and aggression.

Summary

Factor analysis, so often regarded as a means of forcing data to yield up neatly packaged meanings, leaves much to be desired. The use of Q-sort items also has many pitfalls. But for the purpose of clarifying the differences between theoretical positions, a nonparametric method of factor-analyzing Q-sorts, which embraces both items and theoreticians in the same factorial composition, may prove to be of assistance. In an illustrative case involving a suicidal attempt, where six theoreticians Q-sorted items after study of a blind protocol, certain interesting alignments between a Freudian, a Jungian, an Adlerian, a Sullivanian, a personal construct theorist, and a nondirectivist were suggested.

REFERENCES

Cromwell, R. L., and Caldwell, D. F. A comparison of ratings based on personal constructs of self and others. *J. Clin. Psychol.*, 1962, **18**, 43–46.

Farberow, N. L., and Shneidman, E. S. (Eds.) *The cry for help*. New York: McGraw-Hill 1961.

Kelley, T. L. *Crossroads in the mind of man*. Stanford, Calif.: Stanford Univer. Press, 1928.

Kelley, T. L. *Essential traits of mental life*. Cambridge, Mass.: Harvard Univer. Press, 1935.

Kelly, G. A. *The psychology of personal constructs*. Vol. 1. New York: Norton, 1955.

Thurstone, L. L. *The vectors of mind*. Chicago: Univer. Chicago Press, 1935.

17

Epilogue: Don Juan

IT HAPPENS that twice in the past year I have gone to see the same opera. This is not by any means a normal thing for me to do. But for several months after seeing this particular opera for the first time I had had the nagging feeling that I must have missed something that should have been quite obvious. So a few weeks ago, when I saw that Mozart's Don Giovanni was to be produced, I persuaded my wife that we should buy tickets.

I particularly wanted my wife to be with me this time. She notices many things that escape my attention and I rather hoped that, after seeing the production, she could explain to me in simple language just what was supposed to be going on.

So we sat through it, craning our necks to see around the high stalls that partition off the crannies of the Paris Opera House, and now and then catching rewarding glimpses of some magnificent staging. The building was apparently designed by a music lover who thought it might be just as well if the audience listened rather than looked, or else by an architect who had worked his way up from designing horse barns. I suspect the latter. I spent the evening with the sense that there must be a manager and feedbox somewhere in the shadows behind me. As a matter of fact there was nothing of the sort, only a little couch in a dark corner behind the half dozen or so chairs, presumably intended for those who might be overpowered by the emotional impact of great operatic moments.

When it was over my wife called my attention to the fact that the music was great—which it was, I must agree; that people appreciated the drama—which they did seem to; and that a lot of folks, including some close relatives of ours who are musicians, would have their feelings hurt if I described the way the opera had appeared to me the first time I saw it. This last, of course, remains to be seen. But she is probably right. She usually is about such things.

But I can see now that none of this makes sense unless I go back a few months and describe my impressions the first time I saw Don Giovanni. On that occasion the architecture had a very definite bearing on what happened; that, and the thing they give you to read before the performance, the paper that is supposed to tell you what to expect.

I was by myself on that occasion. After arriving fairly early for the performance and settling down in my seat behind a post, I discovered it was much too dark to read anything. When I looked around the slowly filling gallery I saw that most of the seats were behind posts and there was scarcely enough light for reading anywhere. This, too, was an opera house built either by a music lover or by an architect with an obsession. If he was a music lover he must have expected such thunderous applauses that only a forest of supporting columns would keep the balconies from tumbling down. But, then, perhaps he was only a farsighted architect who figured it would be a long, long time before the "Met" would replace the building and he had better draw up something that would stand. In any case, between the designer and his posts and the manager's conservation of electricity, I was effectively prevented from reading what the usherette had thrust into my hand when she showed or rather, led, me to my seat.

I suppose I could have gone back to the lobby to read my program. It was light enough there. But I had been standing outside in the winter rain for some time waiting to snag a ticket, my feet were tired and wet, I was cold, and the plush seat felt too good to leave. Besides, I was not sure I could find my way back.

So, not being informed in advance of precisely what I should see, I was on my own. What I actually did see was probably the faintly coherent patterns of my own particular kind of outlook, reflected off the rapidly shifting events of the play.

You should know, I suppose, that my outlook, while it embodies many things, incorporates something of what my fellow psychologists believe (although I find most of their beliefs highly questionable) a little of what psychiatrists are trying to propagate—which sounds to me pretty wild when it is pitched at any level of abstraction above that of straightforward clinical observation—and much of what I have picked up on my own during a good many years spent more or less trying to help people disentangle themselves and trying to figure out how they got that way. All of this I find very confusing. So when I describe what I saw, it is *my* Don Giovanni, not Mozart's. Or, better, it is the reflections of my personal world shimmering off the polished facets of Mozart's magnificent creation.

I am sure that I am not the first to see Don Giovanni with a nude mind. In every audience there must be many individuals who have not been told what they are supposed to see. What unique stories they might disclose if only they dared. For one it might be the everlasting antiphony of strength and weakness, of timidity and daring; for another, the story of one honest man, true to his passions, aware of his impulses, open in his thoughts, and caught up in a world of hypocrites; for another, an orgy of delicious indulgence, vicariously enjoyed and unmarred by any feelings of guilt, since in the end the full price of punishment is to be paid, and unmixed with fear, since it is Don Giovanni who is to do the paying. But people are usually ashamed of seeing what they are not supposed to see, so these are the stories that are never told.

I, too, might not be reporting what I saw if it were not for the vivid impression I got out of the experience. Nothing occurred to interfere with this impression until I read the printed story. That was after the performance was over, the impression was too deep to be easily erased, and I had returned to the hotel room where the light, while not particularly good, was still good enough to read by. By that time I was ready to be stubborn about the whole thing.

As I had watched and listened everything seemed to hang together and make pretty good sense. It was dramatic too. I had heard enough about operas to know they are all supposed to be dramatic. Knowing this much in advance, the dramatic features were perfectly obvious to me. But it turned out that there were other things I did not know in advance, so, naturally, those were the things that I missed altogether.

What I saw was that Squire John, to give him—more appropriately I think—an old-fashioned American name instead of Don Giovanni or the more familiar Don Juan, was obviously in trouble from the word "Go." Throughout the evening I had felt rather sorry for him. There he was, in scene after scene, keeping up such a brave front, while being slowly driven to exasperation by one frustration after another. Imagine, then, my surprise when after the performance I read that he was supposed to have been having himself a fine time, right up to the last when he was clump-clumped off to hell by the solid marble ghost of the man he had murdered. It was incredible. In spite of the official document there in my hands I could not believe that that was the way it had happened.

My own interpretation of his final scene, as I had listened to the story come to its soul-stirring climax, was that here at last someone was taking a personal interest in John. It seemed quite appropriate, dramatically, that it should be the spirit of the very man he had done in. Since it was so obvious that John had never gotten along well with his parents, the long-delayed fatherly advice and guidance were particularly touching, especially coming from a municipal statue out of the park.

Up to that moment there was precious little warmth and sympathy to be had from the live people whom John had picked up as companions. And how like life that was! Through moistened eyes I witnessed this final triumph of tenderness over a lifetime full of cruel misunderstandings. Moreover, the Paris production, although it treated this final scene quite differently, seemed to make even clearer the new-found feeling between John and his father-figure.

But now I find I am ahead of myself again. To tell this story properly one should start from the beginning.

The curtain rises. It is night. There on the stage is our maladroit hero for the evening, introducing himself to the audience by pretending to rape some woman, whom he obviously cannot see too clearly, and doing it there right in her own front yard. The venture would appear to have started out as an effort at seduction. But things had not gone well, and John, who must not have been able to measure up to expectations, was being chased out of the house. The whole audience, if not John, could see that he was embroiled with a very much aroused female who was half again his age and fully twice his size. Despite the fact that she was bundled up to the ears in a huge padded nightgown we could see that she was bent on making the situation look like a classic case of rape, if she could only keep him from getting away.

John had his hands full. Not being very perceptive, he was doing his best to go along with the act the way she wanted it, and at the same time protect himself from the frustrated and enraged prima donna. He clutched at her as best he could, but every time she shrugged her shoulders his feet would fly off the ground. The truth was that both of them were getting pretty well fed up with each other and there were moments when I was sure she was about to send him sprawling, like the time he got his head in the way when it came her turn to sing.

And, my, how she could sing! If only John had had the sense to sit on his hands during the evening and listen to her sing instead of making a pass at her. She would have liked that, I am sure, and it would have kept her mind off matters that were peculiarly troublesome to her.

Well, this is the way it went. One could not help but feel sorry for the fellow, right from the very start. His taste in women was as bad as his understanding of them. It must have been painful to discover that he had failed to meet the girl's standards of what a masculine lover should be, and he had allowed the whole thing to break down into a clumsy juvenile effort at bold conquest. Here was our hero, now fully introduced to the audience as a man who, like so many unfortunate people in the world, was totally unprepared to play his part in an adult relationship.

But let us go on with the scene and see how gross human tragedy is compounded out of persistent faults and petty virtues. It now happens that the girl's father, who has been watching from the wings, is unable to restrain himself any longer. So he comes barging in to try to straighten things out before they get any worse. But he is too late. By this time John, frustrated in his efforts to be manly, is furious at himself, the girl, and about everything in sight, and he is in no mood to listen to advice. He turns his rage on the father, as if somehow here was the fiend behind this maddening woman. In a moment the old man, who I am sure only wanted to be helpful, is dead, the victim of John's nimble sword and wildly diffused hostility.

That pretty much concludes the opening passage of the opera. Here in a brief and deftly contrived scene, presented on a partially darkened stage with a few beautifully composed operatic lines, the tragic plight of this young man and of so much of mankind was unerringly sketched. Now, human nature being what it is, there remained only the task of unfolding the inevitable consequences.

Anna, now an orphan and free to embellish her own mistakes, has a fiance—also a dope—by the name of Ottavio. It isn't quite clear what explanation she gives him for being out in the front yard in her nightgown with another man, especially when she can't even say who the fellow was or what he looked like. But anyway, instead of letting the matter drop at a point where it might eventually have been forgotten, she sets out to get Ottavio mixed up in the affair. Somebody must be punished. That is the way to untangle human affairs. Ottavio is quickly taken in, he agrees to take a conventional stand in the matter, and he swears he will run the fellow through if Anna can ever point him out. Anna, who knows perfectly well who it was, decides to hold off a little longer to see what she can stir up. Maybe she can make it into something really big.

Not long after this happened, dear old John, who seems incapable of learning from experience, swaggers into another trap. This time he is spotted at a distance by a cute little flirt named Zerlina. Here is a sharp-eyed earthy creature who has no difficulty reading her male. No doubt she has heard of John, suspects he might be amusing, and, attracted by the idea of having a fling on the eve of her nuptials, decides to unzip his ego. The moment she sees him up close she pinpoints his weakness and knows she will be perfectly safe as long as help is within screaming distance. She is.

Where Anna had made trouble for John because she failed utterly to understand him, Zerlina's unerring insight was her implement for mischief-making. Meanwhile, Zerlina's fiance, who, in turn, has seen through her for some time but doesn't have the courage to do anything about it, takes advantage of the opportunity to go off and "have a round with the boys." Let her tease someone else for a change. Besides, good-hearted John has offered to drop in later and pay for the drinks.

A pair of the most clever and amusing scenes in the whole opera come next. The first shows John being trussed up for his tryst with Zerlina. It is a two-man job. No casual slacks and smoking jacket for our John! With the help of his valet, who laces him up the back, he encases himself in layer after layer of upholstery material. Needless to say, the valet, who can readily imagine what is going to happen at the critical moment, finds this vastly amusing. In fact, he has been keeping a diary of such misadventures and is not above reciting from it whenever he meets someone who is inclined to take John seriously.

Now the next scene shows John escorting Zerlina off to look at the etchings she was so eager to see. After a few moments—scarcely enough time to formulate a critical appraisal of more than one or two of them—there is a scream, a pause, and they are back, John's inaccessible back-lacings still tied in hard knots, and Zerlina wide-eyed with surprise. The same old John! Quite obviously, if he had been intending to make a pass at the girl, he had failed, as before, to think the situation through.

John then tries to explain to everybody that it was his valet, Leporello, who had slipped up on Zerlina while he himself was up in the attic trying to remember where he had put those blasted etchings. Though this is the truth, no one believes it. I thought that Zerlina might have vouched for his story at this point, but she didn't. Perhaps she was too much upset over the fact that her carefully planned strategy had left her rear unprotected.

Anyway, John gets out of there just in time to save his skin from a jealous mob who would have unlaced him fast enough if they had ever got their hands on him. Now he is in more trouble than ever, and he has two strikes against him.

Not all of John's girlfriends were unsympathetic. There was Elvira, who had visions of making a man of him. But he would not listen. He wanted to do the job himself and in his own way. She was annoyed by that, as one is always annoyed when a friend refuses to be made over.

But still Elvira keeps hoping that John will end up making such a fool of himself he will be ready to listen to reason. Leporello, who likes nothing better than to see situations deteriorate, pulls out his notebook and does his best to convince Elvira that John is a hopeless fool already. But it is only when she falls in with the self-righteously indignant Anna and her stooge Ottavio that she is finally willing to abandon her project and take up the official line.

I suppose we should not be too critical of this institutionalized animosity. No man is above the law, as they always say. After all, John was now a murderer and, in his present disturbed state of mind, really quite dangerous. If this had not happened before the days of Organized Medicine someone could have complained, and in less time than it would have taken to tie his gussets he would have been quietly clamped into a "protective environment."

But now that we think of it, John was not the only dangerous person to have running around loose at night. Ottavio, too, was dangerous. He was pledged to kill the first man Anna pointed out to him. So, in turn, Anna, also, was dangerous. Then there was Leporello, the cynic who delighted in seeing people disillusioned; he was dangerous in an accessory-before-the-fact sort of way. And Zerlina, who was forever playing with matches, was likely to start fires that could not be put out.

In fact, we can see how each one, in his own way, was dangerous— Ottavio with the pledged loyalty of a soldier, Anna who could not distinguish between justice and punishment, Leporello who could not see beyond facts, Zerlina with her love of danger itself, and Elvira, who was ready to abandon what she could not mold; all of these—but it was our dim-witted John who got cracked at the end of the whip.

And now the stage goes dark again. John walks the empty streets in the chill of night, clanking his sword and trying to think brave thoughts. Dogging his footsteps is the gloating realist, Leporello. Before them, out of the shadows, looms the statue of Anna's father, the man John had murdered in blind rage. In his loneliness John reaches out to this wise old man and expresses aloud his wish that tonight of all nights they might be having supper together and talking about matters that so much filled his heart. Slowly, the massive head nods assent. Needless to say, at this point Leporello is flabbergasted; in his world things like this can't really happen!

But this is no hallucination. Supper is served, there is a knock at the door, and there stands the marble ghost. In open defiance of the facts of life he has dismounted from his horse in the park and come all the way on foot.

Yet, for all the wisdom of his years, the old man is still human. Like many a well-meaning father he opens the conversation by asking John to "repent." Repent? Of what should he repent? Can John repent his own stupidity—how can one repent what he cannot comprehend? Should he repent his misery—how does one renounce his own punishment? Repent his efforts to find love in the arms of a woman—where better to seek it? To us, who have developed repentence to a fine art, these may seem like stupid questions, but we must remember that John was not overly bright and these were the only ways he knew to pose the issues.

But soon wisdom and fatherly concern prevail. The two men clasp hands. For a moment John's knees weaken, but he is sustained by the firm hand that holds his. In the background someone has built a heart-warming fire against the dreadful cold of this long night, and, with a comforting arm around his shoulder, John strides confidently off to meet his destiny.

Left behind are the petty characters of the drama, their scapegoat no longer to bear the brunt of their half-ventures, talking among themselves about how quiet things are with John gone, and thinking that perhaps they ought to find some way of getting along with each other. None of them seems very happy about the prospects and one suspects that sooner or later they will find themselves another Don Juan.

There are some, no doubt those who read their programs in advance instead of letting the opera speak for itself, who insist that John was being ushered off to hell. To hell, indeed! And just what do they think they were looking at all evening! No, they are wrong. Surely Mozart's sense of dramatic integrity would never have led him to add mere fire and brimstone to the tortures already displayed.

Then there are some who say the music itself sounds the notes of doom and thus tells a story quite different from mine. But who has heard the notes of doom and lived to write them down? The music speaks of power, yes, and of massive forces rising in crescendo to bring the story to its conclusion. It speaks of destiny, too. But what destiny is worthy of the mighty chords with which Mozart has rendered these final scenes—a trash fire at the city dump (Jerusalem's gahanna), or is it compassion's recovery of man's soul from torments he can neither understand nor endure?

* * *

Now that I have told my story, it is only fair to say what the classical yarn is. I suppose that in the end I shall be forced to concede that it was the classical story that Mozart had in mind. But—still—let me stand firm on my personal experience a little longer. Think of this: may there not be two levels of wisdom—the protective screen of words behind which we think thoughts that have no words of their own, and the torrent of words with which those feelings sometimes burst through? May not the classical story of Don Juan, then, have been the screen behind which Mozart dared conjure with the forbidden feelings of a troubled man, and the opera itself—the one I thought I saw—have been the torrent bursting through to express what he could not say?

The classical Don Juan is written down as a man of courage, fearing neither man, fate, nor conscience. Surrounded by lesser beings who crave adventure but fear to seize it on their own, he stirs the envy of men and the hearts of women. Openly he does, or seduces them into doing, what they secretly wish they might do on their own. But by this he stirs their animosity too, for what woman wants to wake up in the morning and find both her lover and her virtue gone, or what man will stand idly by and see his own just rewards embraced by another. So Don Juan leaps from bed to bed and fight to fight, no less successful in one than in the other. What are we to do with him? Surely the eventual triumph of such wickedness must be forestalled at all costs. So nothing less than hell itself must be invoked at the end of the story to insure the justice that man himself cannot contrive.

But is this the happy end of evil? Look! There Don Juan strides through the very gates of hell. He has refused to cringe. Behind, we, the timidly innocent, are left gaping. So what has been proved? A question: Is virtue only another name for fear? Having struck this unresolved chord, the classic story ends. Now poets and philosophers—and perhaps all of us—continually find ourselves drawn back to this libertine and the question he poses.

For my own part, as you already know, I think the composer, or the production staff, or the artists, had spontaneously found an answer and portrayed it well. But could they bring themselves to say they had found it, or even let themselves think they had found it? Probably not! Such naivete would have brought ridicule down upon their heads, and people who study their programs in advance, as I am sure they must, are not ones to invite ridicule.

* * *

There is another version of Don Juan, a psychiatric version. Perhaps we might say there are two such versions, the one narrowly medical and the other Freudian. The latter makes more interesting reading. And, besides, it was by using the broader logic of medicine that Freud attempted to construct his particular humanistic model of man. That makes it somewhat medical and a reasonable representation of how psychiatry thinks about John.

Freud's Don Juan dangles helplessly from the end of his biography, and the sooner he comes to realize it the sooner he can squirm himself into a comfortable position. The amorphous forces that awaken infant life are quickly shaped by experience. It is only after it is too late to reshape them that John, or anyone else, can step in and take a hand. By then he is outnumbered by the grotesque gremlins who have moved in on him. Now, as with any member of a minority group, his task is to gain insight into his master's foibles and get busy practicing the subtle art of compromise. The Don Juan we see barging around is little more than an imperceptive and impulse-ridden baby for whom the necessary compromises have been too long delayed.

To understand Don Juan, then, we must first understand the amoral impulses of an infant. As he seeks his place in the family he first competes for, and then loses, the enveloping affection of the one woman in his life—his mother. Yet he often finds himself allied with her against the man who has defeated him—his father. So what does that make of him?

Who is he? What is he? Whatever his infantile answer to those questions might be, he cannot accept it. So he spends the rest of his life frantically trying to prove what he cannot believe. He seduces women, some of them young and beautiful—the kind of prize for which strong men compete—or maternal women, who will play mother to his appealing wistfulness. But none is the embodiment of the prize he once sought and lost. He allies himself with restless women against their kind of men, but that is not a man's game. He destroys men in combat, but does not thereby himself become a man. Still, in its way, each of these conquests results in a momentary victory. But it is momentary only, so soon he must try again. How is such a child to know that the conclusive achievements of adulthood are quite another order of experience?

Our psychiatric Don Juan, then, is a desperate man, precariously balanced between infancy and maturity, between masculinity and feminity, between cuddling softness and brutal assault. He acts out the parts he cannot think through. For all his gay boyish appeal he is as dangerous to himself as he is to others. He is as quick to plunge into the fires of hell as he is to thrust others into them. His conscience, having no firm anchorage in early loyalties, fails to serve him in the moments of his infantile crises. Not a very pretty picture, this psychiatric Don Juan, nor very heroic, either.

The psychiatric version of Don Juan does not attempt to cope with the issues posed by the classical story. The question of good and evil, and how one may be made to triumph over the other, is ignored. Fear and innocence remain as much confounded as ever. There is nothing toward which man fumbles his way except to be comfortably at peace with himself. Nothing out yonder! The horizon is the end of the world.

John is a patient, a very sick one, who needs professional care. And if he is sick we are all sick and we had better turn ourselves in for treatment. If we are not too resistant to our psychoanalysts we may eventually be able to hobble around on our own, but every day we must remember who our masters are and make the necessary concessions to keep peace with them.

Where the classic story sets forth the question of man's destiny, the psychiatric diagnosis fetches up John's case history. The Don Juan of literature challenges our ontology: He tempts us, frightens us, enrages us, sets us wondering what we have become. The sickly John simply turns us over in bed to have a look at our psychodynamics.

* * *

Now that we have three versions of Don Juan, and one more to come, there will be those—there always are—who will want to be told which is the correct one. This presupposes that there really is, or was, such a person in the first place. At least, it seems to presuppose that! But, instead of accepting the presupposition, we had better put it in the form of a prior question: Was there ever really such a person?

We might hedge a little and say, "Well, I suppose there must have been, at some time or other, somewhere, a fellow they called, 'Don Juan'." As a matter of fact there may have been as many as fifty-six fellows who were called that, including forty-three who were christened with that name, eight who earned it on their own, and four who were falsely accused. Suppose there were; it seems reasonable enough. So we reply, "Yes; there really was a Don Juan." That, of course, is not what was asked, but, perhaps, the obliqueness of our reply will be overlooked.

But this does not help us much. We have to ask our question another way. Let's be specific: Was there ever such a person as Mozart thought he saw, or as Freud thought he saw, or as I thought I saw? That sounds a little better. But is it not the same question we started out with, stated in another way, and just as hard to answer? Take my "Don Juan," whom, as you would probably guess, I am rather fond of; if there was, indeed, such a person, then such was the person there was. That makes my version of him self-evidently the correct one. What does this do to Freud's version? Nothing at all; we have only to look for another fellow who fits it. So our whole line of discourse falls apart because we have not agreed on an object of reference. Perhaps we never can agree—really!

And if there never was anyone resembling any of the Don Juans described by Mozart, Freud, or me, then the question of which version is the correct version makes no sense at all. You can't go around asking what is the "correct version" of something that doesn't exist. And if it does exist, before I can answer your question, you will have to tell me about it or present it to me in some way before I can be expected to say what the "correct version" really is. When you get through I will have to think over very carefully what you have said or shown me and come up with an answer.

And what will I say? Limited, as I am, to your representation, I have no grounds for saying that you do not know what you are talking about. Unless I can claim some other access to what you describe, what is there for me to say, indeed, except, "Yes, that is absolutely the correct version," or, simply, "So that is that!" Who am I to say you are wrong or what you have shown me is wrong? So, as these things go, you are right, Mozart is right, Freud is right, I am right, and just about anybody can be right. Good Heavens! There must be something wrong with our question!

Perhaps the trouble is we can't make up our minds what we are talking about. Let's see if being "objective" will get us off the hook. You just point to the fellow we are to talk about—don't say anything, mind you—just point to him, and then we can get down to the question of whose version of him is the correct one.

Good! Now suppose he has his Sunday suit on, or the suit Don Giovanni wore to the party for Zerlina. You wait till he is all fixed up, then you point to him and grunt or make some nonverbal signal to indicate he/she/it is what you have in mind. Keep the words out of it; that will let the creature speak for itself!

But wait a minute; haven't you been a little prejudiced in his favor and have you not chosen to point him out under particularly favorable conditions?

You could ask him to take his suit off, I suppose. But that is hardly fair either, since normally he must wear some kind of clothes, if only the tops of his pajamas. If we have him stand there without anything on we can hardly say he looks himself. Moreover, if all this takes place in the dime store or in the First National Bank, won't we get a biased impression of some sort?

Now I see I've used up a whole page of manuscript and I'm still no closer to telling you what the correct version of Don Juan is. I haven't even mentioned yet the distortion that this renegade himself will put into the picture. Suppose when we ask him to take his clothes off, he calls the police and has us thrown into jail. Not only is this likely to damage our ability to judge him fairly, but it points up the fact that he will resort to all kinds of underhanded tricks to keep us from seeing him as he really is.

It is just because of things like this that the whole science of psychology is in such a bad fix. People insist on acting up, distorting themselves, misleading us, and otherwise refusing to let us make objective scientific observations that are free from all biases. If people would only be natural, and if we could only point them out to each other without having them show up in some particular biased way, we might develop a very fine system of psychology to explain what makes them tick. It might even be that psychology could become a precise science like physics, where everyone, except a few of the most brilliantly confused scientists—whom we rarely see anyway—knows what he is talking about, and where you can always ask such questions as, "What is the correct version of Don Juan?"

Let's try again. Our task has turned out to be to nail down an objective reference point against which we can determine who has the correct version of Don Juan. Let us concede, reluctantly, that whomsoever we point out as the authentic Don Juan will be a fellow who is bound to be acting so as to give a distorted picture of himself. That is to say, we shall admit that it is natural of a man to act unnaturally. Almost anybody you can think of is likely to be presenting his own biased version of himself in some way, either to his public, his wife, his children, his associates, the people he imagines are looking at him—but aren't—, even to himself. If "being yourself" is anything different from trying to be something other than yourself, then it is hopeless to try to put a finger on what it is.

We shall have to make another concession. Whomsoever we point to and say, "There, that is Don Juan, climbing in the window," will, by the very way we point him out, be cast into a particular version of him. Even if we felt that this was too suggestive of a particular kind of mission, it would do no good to hold off. We would only end up a few moments later exclaiming, "Oh look; there he is now, jumping out the window."

We could say, simply and in a level monotone, "There, that is Don Juan," pointing to the fellow sitting on the curb with his head in his hands, and being careful not to say one word more. But most people would see through this sort of camouflage and, just as sure as the world, some young lady is going to burst out, "You mean thing! Why did you have to go and point him out just now, right when he has that awful headache? You should have shown him to everybody last night, when he had his guitar. Yummy! You should have seen him then!"

So you see how difficult it is going to be with all the different versions that creep in: Don Juan's public relations version, our version in the way we point him out, and the version of the people we point him out to. But, as I say, we can't let this stop us. We shall just have to let Don Juan put on whatever kind of act he wants, we shall have to point him out regardless of what he happens to be doing at the moment, and people will just have to picture him through their own rose-colored impulses. There just is no such thing as being neutral in such matters.

This clears the way for us to point to something and to say, "There, that's it. Whose version of that is correct?" We may not be quite as hopeful of getting an ultimately satisfactory answer as we were before, but at least we now have some grounds for trying.

Since, at last, that difficult matter is decided, I would like to suggest that we point to the Don Giovanni I saw that first night at the opera. That rather pins down what we are talking about. The fact that the singer may have been a family man who shudders every time a frustrated female calls him "Darling," is quite beside the point. Moreover, none of us really has the faintest idea how, in real life, he reacts to women on the loose. No, we shall confine ourselves to what we saw of him on the stage.

To be sure this selection of a person, against whom to test our versions for their correctness, gives a slight edge in the controversy to Mozart and me and rather puts Freud at a disadvantage. Still, the fellow who played the part that night may have been psychoanalyzed. Like as not he had; a lot of artists are these days. If he had—and it had "taken"—he would be bound by the sacred code of *Insight* to portray a Freudianized version of the opera's hero.[1] That would put Freud back in the running along with Mozart and me.

Now that we know what we are talking about, how shall we decide whose version is correct? In making this decision we must not overlook the fact that a lot goes on that is never put into words. Everybody knows that, and some people are always making a big point of it. So let's not limit our considerations to what the actor sang, or what Mozart wrote down, or what I said. There must have been many times when the singer's version of Don Giovanni led him quite spontaneously to make subtle discriminations and, on the basis of them, turn this way or that inflect one way rather than another, or catch his breath here instead of there.

So with Mozart, too; he might despair of writing out a logical explanation containing the whole truth of why, at a particular place, he put one note in the score in place of another, even though he wrote under quite rigidly formal rules. He might only suggest that it was put there because it fitted some distinctive repetitive theme that was reflected from deep inside the character of the Don Giovanni he envisioned. Indeed, that must have been the very nature of Mozart's hero, a rich pattern of such likenesses and differences—subtle, interwoven, and action laden. But, more than that, Mozart must have sensed that his listeners for generations to come would discover their own lives shot through with these same unnamed constructs. So he wrote the notes and story of the legendary figure and wagered that they would stir men and women of another generation in strangely familiar ways.

So Mozart's version is the right one, after all, is it not? And why? Simply this: His fine distinctions delineate a theme which runs basically unchanged, from boudoir to hell, and straight through whatever lies between. Only a theme of immense power and compelling validity can ring true when struck against such widely varying circumstances.

This happened: Not only did Mozart erect a man out of the distinctions and similarities he personally envisioned, he tested that structure, and found its brutal integrity defied all the vicissitudes of human whims and circumstances. Gradually now the genius is possessed by what it has produced. The composer's hand is guided across the pages of the manuscript and he can scarcely bring the opera to its conclusion

---

[1] *"Insight"* is what you are left with after you have been stripped of your imagination.

in any way except that dictated by Don Giovanni. The image he constructed became the man about whom he wrote. Thus it happens that imagination put to test, becomes the key to realization. The world of reality has no other key. Nor does truth have any other access.

As we look further afield we find even broader grounds for believing that Mozart's image of Don Juan was a correct one. Here was an image that projected itself into the future, moment by moment, scene by scene, enabling Mozart to anticipate what he was about to write, or what it was that his Don Giovanni would do next. That much we have already guessed. But as we continue to look we see that others found it was, or could be, their image too. And in the structure of its basic lines they, also, found the story unfolding itself naturally and predictably. Once they grasped Mozart's basic constructs, they could no longer be utterly amazed by what was about to happen on the stage.

There is still more to attest the correctness of Mozart's Don Giovanni. At the end of the performance, as the audience rose to put on coats and go out to shout for taxicabs, they were to find the same story, first here, then there, among friends or in the depths of their own unspoken desires. Echoed again and again in the winter air were still to be heard the distinctive notes that had given continuity to what had happened on the stage, still valid, still foretelling what lies ahead along the dark paths we walk.

* * *

Now that we have done so handsomely by Mozart's Don Giovanni what are we to do with Freud's animated figure of Don Juan, whom we left a few pages back frantically chasing his tail. If Mozart is right then Freud must be wrong—so goes the logic of our times. Or take my lowly bungleheaded John, of whom I am no less fond than before: I must be terribly wrong about him.

If we follow the time-honored notion that what has proved to be correct displaces all versions that disagree with it, then the magnificent Giovanni takes over, and, sure enough, once more it has to be poor old John who is in the wrong. He is not even an honest-to-goodness version of himself!

We could say, I suppose that one was more or less right and the other more or less wrong. But isn't that only a polite way of avoiding the issue? The kind of logic which assumes that there can be only one correct version is only a little worse than the logic which says one only partially replaces the other. Both are the kind of grounds upon which dogmatism, absolute or partial, rests. And dogmatism, while often a great comfort to faltering minds and restless swords, is the implicit enemy of creative thought.

But certainly it is proper to pit alternatives against each other— Mozart's Giovanni against Freud's Juan and my John—and see what follows. What, then, is to happen to the ones who come out second or third best in the competition? Is my John valid only to the extent he is found to be in agreement with Giovanni? Is that the way to judge the truth, by testing its conformity to what is already believed to be correct? Not at all! The test for John must be the same as the test for Giovanni; how well does the construction of the figure antici- pate what happens or what can be made to happen—in the story, among the audience, in the world off stage, and in the hours and years that follow.

Giovanni has survived these tests well. John has been tested only in the world of my own experience. Undoubtedly there are such things as partial truths; I have not said there weren't. Some are more sweep- ing than others; they cover a wider range of human experience or they have spanned a greater period of time. And, in this case, there are truths that have been subjected to more thorough tests than others; over a broader range of events or over a greater span of time. But it is not the partialness or the weighty documentation of truth I am talking about; it is the tentativeness with which we may ever say that we have stated the correct version of something.

Nor am I saying that what exists in the light of our understanding today may cease to exist in the light of what we shall know tomorrow. I am saying only that it is the understanding that is likely to change. What is to be emphasized is the temporariness with which any man's version of the Don Juan story can be said to be the correct one. That, you will recognize, is quite a different thing from saying that correct- ness is partial, or that it is relative, or that it changes with the times, or that it is what people agree upon or that it is only what one chooses to believe.

John, then, stands in his own right as an alternative construction of the story. Through the impulses of how many of my readers he can live and breathe as a human being, I do not know. His bungling may seem odd and inconceivable. Nor do I know how long he can survive through changing times. But of this I am reasonably sure, his validity does not depend on how closely he conforms to Don Gio- vanni, nor does it require any proof that Don Giovanni is false. It is only in a world run by tradition-bound dogmatists that the bungling John must bow to the masterful Giovanni, and only in a world run

by envious ones that Giovanni would be forced to relinquish his claim
to greatness in favor of the proletarian John.

*　*　*

There is a fourth version of Don Juan that enjoys a unique access
to reality. It is his—Jack's—own intimate story. While Mozart constructed a figure and let the structure guide his hand until the opera
was done Jack conjured up an image and let it guide his life until
it was done. So he, too, built in his own image. Moreover, this kind
of building was for him, as it must be for everyone, his way of living.
Before he knew it he was what he made of himself, though, no doubt,
the project never seemed quite complete.

What Jack was was a puzzled man sketching and resketching plans
to be executed. What Jack was was a man following and discarding
blueprints he had given himself—some clear, some illegible, but nevertheless the only ones he had to go by. What Jack was was the outcome
of what he had done. He was architect, builder, and occupant of the
structure—all three. And these three aspects of his daily existence
were linked so that the occupant turned out to be a builder by trade
and an architect by disposition. This, just this, was what was going
on as we tried to follow the antics of this strange man.

Perhaps it is this triple redundancy that makes us so reluctant
to hear what Jack has to say about himself. Some say it is because
we cannot depend on him to tell the truth about himself. Others argue
that he cannot be expected to find words for feelings that are too
deep to fathom. Still others claim that he simply does not know what
he is up to. So each observer, sensing the redundancy of man—architect, builder, and occupant—finds a different reason for disregarding
the version of Don Juan to be found in Jack himself.

I am not sure what we can do about the redundancy business.
We have already talked about it when we examined the simpler redundancy that occurs when any observer looks at Don Juan through
his own spectacles. But I don't think that our own redundancies, as
observers, are any more tolerable than Jack's would be. Besides, before
we get through, we are going to be more or less stuck with both sets
of redundancies anyway, for what we can observe, albeit with whatever
objectivity we can muster, it sill going to be the act that Jack puts
on. And, in turn, whatever Jack's expurgated version of himself may
be, we will still have to twist and turn it into alignment with our
own terms before we can bring it into any kind of focus.

As for Jack's intellectual honesty, we ought to admit that if he were able to tell the whole truth about himself—or even if he wanted to—he would have to be quite a different kind of person from the fellow we are after. We would have to call him "Frank," "Earnest," or "Camile," or something like that. It just wouldn't be our Jack. And besides, what would a person who was perfectly honest about himself do about the conflicting truths of different levels of his personality, or the changing states of mind that make him different from moment to moment? Wouldn't he have to gloss over these in order to be "honest"? Or, if he didn't gloss them over, wouldn't he have first to bring himself to some uniform dead level of existence, and bring to a halt all those life processes that make what was true and poignant at one moment trite and obsolete when applied to the next? I think we had better take Jack in all the ways that he is, and as fast as he comes.

As for the inadequacy of words to denote what is going on, that is true. But not all expression is through the denotations of words. There are connotations too—a lot more of them. Besides, man has other ways of expressing himself than by making noises in the air or squiggles on a piece of paper. And, come to think of it, what is wrong with the words he is able to use? Is the fact that ours are better—if, indeed, they are—make his not worth listening to? I suspect this whole objection has something to do with the kind of logic we were talking about a page or two ago, the kind that assumes there is never room for more than one interpretation of what exists. And, to top it all off, we are going to be using our words to talk about his words, sooner or later anyway, so why not hear him out?

One more objection to be dealt with, the objection that he does not know what he is up to. Well, who of us does?

So let's listen to Jack's version.

Now, where on earth did he go? Has anybody seen him around in the past half hour?

Jack! JACK!!!

Jack, if you are reading this, won't you please speak up; we would like to hear your version of what it is like to be a Don Juan. Not that anybody is going to take you too seriously; we still prefer our own versions of what you are. Still, what you have to say might prove to be amusing. Naive, of course, but amusing!

Bibliography of Published Writings in Personal Construct Theory

1. *The psychology of personal constructs.* 2 vols., New York: Norton, 1955.

2. With Alvin R. Howard. A theoretical approach to psychological movement. *J. Abnorm. & Soc. Psychol.*, 1954, **49**, 399–404.

3. I itch too. *Amer. Psychol.*, 1955, **10**, 172–173.

4. Issues: Hidden or mislaid. *Amer. Psychologist*, 1956, **11**, 112–113.

5. Man's construction of his alternatives. *The assessment of human motives.* **G. Lindzey, (Ed.), New York: Rinehart, 1958.**

6. Suicide: The personal construct point of view. In *The cry for help*, **E. Shneideman and N. Farberow, (Eds.), New York: McGraw-Hill, 1961.**

7. Personal construct theory as a line of inference. *J. Psychol.* (Pakistan), 1964, **1**, 80–93.

8. Nonparametric factor analysis of personality theories. *J. Individ. Psychol.*, 1963, **19**, 115–147.

9. The abstraction of human processes. In *Proceedings of the XIV International Congress of Applied Psychology*, Vol. 2: *Personality Research*, G. S. Nielsen and S. Coopersmith, (Eds.), Copenhagen: Munksgaard, 1962.

10. Comments on Aldous, the personable computer. In *Computer simulation of personality: Report of the Princeton Conference*, S. Tomkins and S. Messick, (Eds.), New York: Wiley, 1963.

11. Europe's matrix of decision. In *Nebraska symposium on motivation*, M. R. Jones, (Ed.), Lincoln: Univ. Nebraska Press, 1962.

12. Sin and psychotherapy. In *Morality and mental health*, O. H. Mowrer, (Ed.), Chicago: Rand McNally, 1966.

13. *A theory of personality.* A paperback edition of The Psychology of Personal Constructs, comprising the first three chapters only. New York: Norton, 1963.

14. A psychology of the optimal man. In *Goals of psychotherapy*, A. R. Mahrer, (Ed.), New York: Appleton-Century-Crofts, 1966.

15. Look who's talking: A review of *Transactional analysis in psychotherapy: A systematic individual and social psychiatry* by Eric Berne. *Contemp. Psychol.*, 1963, **8**, 189–190.

16. The language of hypothesis. *J. Indiv. Psychol.*, 1964, **20**, 137–152.

17. The strategy of psychological research *Bull. British Psychol. Society*, 1965, **18**, 1–15.

18. The threat of aggression. *J. Humanistic Psychol.*, 1965, **5**, 195–201.

19. The role of classification in personality theory. In *Proceedings of the Conference on the Role and Methodology of Classification in Psychiatry and Psychopathology*, **M. Katz, J. O. Cole & W. E. Barton,** (Eds.), Chevy Chase: United States Public Health Service, 1968.

20. Fixed role therapy. In *Handbook of direct and behavior psychotherapies*, Jurjevich, R. M. (Ed.). In press.

Author Index

Subject Index